Silver Fox of the Rockies

Silver Fox of the Rockies

DELPHUS E. CARPENTER AND
WESTERN WATER COMPACTS

DANIEL TYLER

FOREWORD BY DONALD J. PISANI

UNIVERSITY OF OKLAHOMA PRESS : NORMAN
Also by Daniel Tyler

(ed.) *Western American History in the Seventies: Selected Papers* (Fort Collins, Colo., 1973)

(ed.) *Red Men and Hat-Wearers: Viewpoints in Indian History* (Boulder, Colo., 1976)

De Truman a Nixon: Uso y abuso del poder presidencial (Mexico City, 1981)

Sources for New Mexican History, 1821–1848 (Santa Fe, 1984)

Mythical Pueblo Rights Doctrine: Water Administration in Hispanic New Mexico (El Paso, 1990)

Last Water Hole in the West: The Colorado-Big Thompson Project and the Northern Colorado Water Conservancy District (Niwot, Colo., 1992)

This book is published with the generous assistance of The Kerr Foundation, Inc.

Library of Congress Cataloging-in-Publication Data

Tyler, Daniel
    Silver fox of the Rockies: Delphus E. Carpenter and western water compacts / Daniel Tyler; foreword by Donald J. Pisani.
      p.   cm.
    Includes bibliographical references and index.
    ISBN 0-8061-3515-8 (hc: alk. paper)
      1. Carpenter, Delphus E.   2. Lawyers—Colorado—Biography.
3. Water rights—United States—States—History.   I. Carpenter, Delphus E.   II. Title.

KF373.C37164 T95 2003
340'.092—dc21
[B]

2002029137

The paper in this book meets the guidelines for permanence and durability of the Committee on Production Guidelines for Book Longevity of the Council on Library Resources, Inc. ∞

1 2 3 4 5 6 7 8 9 10

For my grandchildren:
Philip, Cody, Jesse, and any others who may come along.

Contents

List of Illustrations   IX

List of Maps   XI

Foreword, by Donald J. Pisani   XIII

Acknowledgments   XVII

Introduction   3

1. Lineage and Love Letters   26

2. Education and the Beginnings of a Career   50

3. The Making of an Interstate Streams Commissioner   88

4. The Colorado River Compact: Phase I   123

5. The Colorado River Compact: Phase II   157

6. The Struggle for Compact Ratification   202

7. Last Years as Interstate Streams Commissioner   242

8. Vindication   268

9. Carpenter and the Compact Legacy   278

Notes   301

Bibliography   359

Index   375

Illustrations

Carpenter family genealogy   28

Daniel Carpenter   30

Nancy Scott Carpenter   31

Leroy Carpenter and Martha Bennett   34

House in which Delph Carpenter was born   41

Delph Carpenter and his older brother, Alfred   56

Delph Carpenter, age ten   58

Delph Carpenter irrigating family farm   61

Delph Carpenter as a law student   62

Dot Hogarty on her wedding day   65

Captain Michael J. Hogarty   67

Delph Carpenter as a young attorney   69

Delph Carpenter on his bronco   71

Delph Carpenter in his senate seat   81

Denver Daily News cartoon of Delph Carpenter   85

Re-argument brief, *Wyoming v. Colorado*   103

Colorado River Compact Commission   129

Delph Carpenter, 1922   145

Dot Hogarty Carpenter   161

Flag placed on unidentified peak in Rawah Wilderness Area   164
Delph Carpenter's plan   182
Bishop's Lodge, Santa Fe, 1920s   184
Colorado River Compact Commission at Bishop's Lodge   185
Signing of Colorado River Compact, 1922   199
Herbert Hoover   200
Hoover Dam   240
Judge Donald Carpenter   281

All photographs are from the Carpenter Papers, Loveland, Colorado, unless otherwise noted.

Maps

Interstate Water Allocation Compacts in force, 2000   7

Greeley and Weld County, showing location of principal   38
   irrigation ditches and Carpenter's Crow Creek Ranch

Colorado and its neighboring states   91

South Platte River Basin   92

Republican River Basin   106

Colorado River Basin, 1921   151

Arizona, showing planned location of Highline Canal   168

Colorado River Basin, showing 1956 Colorado River   262
   Storage Project

Foreword

Delph Carpenter is an imposing but neglected figure in the history of water rights in the American West. As a Coloradan, he attempted to protect his state's water rights—and the water rights of other western states—from what he took to be an overweening federal government that sought to limit or even extinguish those rights. Colorado's position at the headwaters of such western streams as the Rio Grande, Arkansas, and Colorado Rivers gave it an important strategic position in the West. Delph Carpenter played the leading role in creating the Colorado River Compact of 1922 and in devising the negotiating process followed in all but three of the sixteen water allocation compacts approved between 1922 and 1971.

During the first two decades of the twentieth century, two major threats to the security of western water rights emerged. One was the federal assertion of inchoate rights to the surplus water in western streams, particularly interstate streams. The federal irrigation projects launched by the national government after passage of the Reclamation Act of 1902 dramatically increased pressure on the West's limited supply of surface water. In particular, Carpenter worried about two federal projects: Pathfinder Dam, completed on the North Platte River in Wyoming in 1909, and Elephant Butte Dam, completed on the Rio Grande in southwestern New Mexico in

1916. The other danger was that the Supreme Court would rule eventually that the doctrine of prior appropriation—"first in time, first in right"—applied across state boundaries, preventing the states from "stockpiling" water for future needs. However, in *Kansas v. Colorado* (1907), the U.S. Supreme Court called for an "equitable apportionment of benefits" between states that shared interstate rivers, suggesting that they possessed what amounted to treaty-making powers. They could act almost as sovereign nations, therefore, in resolving water conflicts. This became the guiding principle of Delph Carpenter's career.

The greatest fear of such states as Colorado, Utah, and Wyoming was that the rapid population growth in southern California beginning in the second decade of the twentieth century meant that part of the West would capture a large share of the Colorado River almost by default. The historian Norris Hundley has explained this process in two excellent books, *Water and the West: The Colorado River Compact and the Politics of Water in the American West* (1975) and *The Great Thirst: Californians and Water: A History* (revised edition, 2001), but *The Silver Fox of the Rockies* is the first book to tell the story from the perspective of the upstream states in the Rocky Mountain West.

Tyler considers the interstate water compact a major accomplishment because such agreements reflect the interests of local water users, bind federal agencies to honor state water rights, frequently reduce litigation, and promote "cooperative federalism." The interstate compact built on the assumption that the western states had to settle their own differences, but it also implied a new partnership between federal and state authorities. In many ways the compact anticipated the Tennessee Valley Authority created in 1933 and the debate over extending the concept to western river basins after World War II. Tyler also recognizes the weaknesses of the compacts. They take a long time to draft, they are expensive to negotiate, and, as contracts, they are difficult to amend. Moreover, they depend heavily on data gathered at the time of negotiation—data that can prove false. For example, those who negotiated the original Colorado River Compact in 1922 estimated the river's volume at about one-third more water than the Colorado has carried in the eight decades since. Because that compact required the upper basin states to guarantee 8.5 million acre-feet of water to the lower basin states, frequently less water is available to the upper basin states than was expected in 1922.While compacts limit litigation within upper and lower basin states, and even within many individual states, they can also stimulate litigation. For example, California and Arizona—both lower basin states under the 1922 compact—have gone to court four times to litigate their rights to the river. Other critics of compacts argue that they do not reflect the goals of the larger society or operate in a democratic way; that they limit the rights of the less powerful water users within a basin, particularly Native Americans; and that they pay scant attention to environmental needs.

This is not just a book about water, it is a book about a fascinating man. Delph Carpenter was driven, and he could be rigid, opinionated, and irascible. He was not a "Progressive," but he had the Progressive tendency to see the world in stark black-and-white terms, as a world of heroes and villains. He was also a Progressive in assuming that if the right facts could be gathered—facts everyone agreed upon—then no water problem or conflict was insoluble. He exhibited deep faith in the power of human reason to improve society.

This book has many strengths, ranging from the importance of the subject, to the way Carpenter is allowed to speak for himself, to the careful research in sources at the Colorado and Wyoming state archives, the Hoover Library, and the Northern Colorado Water Conservancy District, where the bulk of the Delph Carpenter papers are located. Norris Hundley was the first historian to use the collection, in researching his book *Water and the West*, but Tyler is the first to use it for a full-scale biography. He also employs Colorado newspapers, published government documents, papers from state archives, and many other sources. The book's most valuable contribution is its point of view. Tyler takes the states' rights arguments of Carpenter and other Coloradans seriously.

Most of the existing literature on natural resource management in the West—particularly that published from 1900 to 1970—is sympathetic to national control. In those pages, westerners who supported the expansion of federal authority became heroes, and those who opposed federal control became villains. The implication is that the West had to be protected from itself, and in such a story states' rights arguments become a cover for predatory self-interest and corporate control over water. Easterners sought to preserve and protect the nation's natural resources, according to this view, and westerners sought to develop those resources as rapidly as possible. There is truth to this interpretation, but also distortion. Historians need to take seriously the frontier individualism that animated Carpenter—and such diverse westerners as Herbert Hoover and Ronald Reagan. That individualism often manifested itself in hostility toward federal conservation policies, including the expansion of national forests and national grazing preserves, as well as control over water. So this book treats one of the most important themes in the history of the twentieth-century West.

Daniel Tyler is an optimistic man, and this is an optimistic book. Unlike so much of the historical literature on western water, including much that I have written, this book avoids using the past as a whipping-post for the present. Over the last eight years that Tyler has studied Delph Carpenter, he has come to admire the man and his accomplishments. Others may see Carpenter in a different light, as a spokesman for states' rights and localism, but surely even they can admire the passion and dedication Carpenter brought to his job, as well as his conviction that his career as a water lawyer had made the West a better place to live. For all the cynicism of modern observers, life in the West would be much more perilous had Delph Carpenter never lived. I am delighted that Carpenter has finally found a biographer, and particularly one with the diligence, sensitivity, and grace of Dan Tyler.

DONALD J. PISANI

University of Oklahoma

Acknowledgments

The story of Delphus Emory Carpenter and interstate water compacts first came to mind when I was writing *The Last Water Hole in the West: The Colorado—Big Thompson Project and the Northern Colorado Water Conservancy District*. Arizona, California, and Nevada would have fought against the removal of Colorado River water from the Colorado River basin in the 1937 Colorado–Big Thompson Project had it not been for Carpenter's skill in persuading these states to accept a limit of 75 million acre-feet, averaged over a running ten-year period, as their fair share of the river in perpetuity. When I finished that book in 1992, W. D. Farr of Greeley suggested I write the Delph Carpenter story, but it was not until a year later that events at the home of his son, Judge Donald Carpenter, made this study possible.

Donald and his wife, Doris, were living in a remodeled schoolhouse surrounded by farmland on the west side of Greeley. In the summer of 1993, water spilled out of irrigation ditches and entered the basement of the Carpenter home where Donald had been preserving and organizing his father's books and papers. He called the Northern Colorado Water Conservancy District (NCWCD) for assistance and arranged to have the documents stored in the basement archives of the NCWCD. The flood had caused minor water damage, but most of the documents were rescued in time, dried, and sorted in eighty-seven boxes along with maps, pictures, books, and other family mementos. Under the supervision of James E. Hansen III, Colorado State University professor of history and supervisor of the archives and records management graduate program, the Carpenter Papers were sorted out, roughly organized, and recorded in an eighty-page inventory prepared under the direction of Anne A. Manzler in the late summer of 1993. Since the fall of 1993, after Judge Carpenter generously agreed to allow me use of this collection to write his father's biography, I have worked on this and other collections to extract the story of Delph Carpenter's contribution to the history of water development in the American West.

Delph Carpenter was a thorough and disciplined collector of all types of printed matter. He saved a great deal of correspondence, kept duplicate copies of his own letters, and filed away the legal cases, maps, diaries, government reports, newspaper articles, and other materials related to his work on interstate compacts. Judge Carpenter did an excellent job of sorting and arranging these items, but when the flood occurred, the collection was still pretty much in a state of disarray, desperately needing the skills of a trained archivist. Much work remains to be done to make the Carpenter Papers fully accessible to future scholars. Readers of this biography should be aware that references to folders and box numbers in the Carpenter Papers at the NCWCD will probably be invalid when this collection is eventually moved for professional care from the NCWCD to a university, historical society, museum, or public archive.

Although the principal resource for this biography was the Carpenter Papers at the NCWCD, research was also done in the records of the federal government and in states where Carpenter conducted compact negotiations. A grant from the Colorado Water Resources Research Institute made research possible in the archives of all Colorado River basin states. The Hoover Presidential Library, West Branch, Iowa, provided me with two grants to work in collections related to the Colorado River Compact and the personal relationships between Carpenter, Hoover, and other government figures. This library has its own Carpenter Papers, which should not be confused with the far more extensive collection of Carpenter Papers at the NCWCD.

This biography of Delph Carpenter does not consider the ramifications of interstate water compacts on all western rivers. Nor does it describe in detail the activities of the many men who participated with Carpenter in the formation of these compacts. Rather, it is an attempt to tell the story of Carpenter's original contribution to western water compacts through his own words, sometimes in letters and diaries, and at other times through interviews released in the press. Because he wrote well, for the most part, and expressed reasons for his actions in letters, I found it useful to quote him extensively. To me, this technique seemed to make him human, exposing his vulnerabilities as well as his strengths, frailties, frustrations, courage, consistencies, and inconsistencies. Hearing him speak through his own words made it possible for me to understand the burdens of his private and professional life, his response to success and failure, and the goals he set for himself at various stages of his life.

At the end of eight years of delving into the work of Delph Carpenter, I have great admiration for what he accomplished for the West. I wish I could have known him, although I might have been uncomfortable with his Type A personality, his occasional stubbornness, and his frequent self-analysis. But in dedicating this book to my grandchildren, I want to say that I admire his courage, and I think that those who knew him for the most part learned to respect his physical and intellectual strength, his genuine courtesy to others, and his willingness to go to great lengths to bring people to consensus. I have indicated in the last footnote of the last chapter that, in my opinion, the man whose leadership most closely parallels these attributes is Arizona's Bruce Babbitt. The same might be said about Colorado's Hank Brown. I'm sure there are many others whose vision of the West includes officials and private parties at all levels talking to each other in search of solutions to land and water problems. Their hope is that litigation might be avoided. When Carpenter spoke of all problems being essentially human problems, he was expressing confidence in humanity's ability to resolve conflict through open, honest, and fact-based negotiation. This humanistic equation is sorely needed in today's world, dominated as it is by globalization, technology, and litigation.

Although some critics will surely continue to fault Carpenter's system of interstate compacts, and the inflexibility some compacts present in the face of changing circumstances, I have not been able to find much negative commentary on Carpenter's accomplishment, or on his leadership, throughout thousands of pages of written material reviewed for this work. Before Donald Carpenter died, his son Bill expressed the hope that this biography would be titled, *Silver Fox of the Rockies*. I have respected his request, not only out of regard for the family but because I conclude this study convinced that Carpenter was as unique and rare in his own environment as the silver fox is in the Rocky Mountain West.

I am, of course, responsible for the errors, omissions, and misinterpretations readers will find in the following pages, but what might be deemed useful by readers would not have been possible without the patient confidence of the Carpenter family. To Doris, Ward, and Bill Carpenter, I am deeply indebted. Since beginning this project in 1992, I have felt like the professor in Russell Hill's novel *Lucy Boomer* (1992) who learned about a stash of heretofore unknown and historically significant documents. When the owner of those documents allowed him unrestricted access, he recognized the chance of a lifetime to tell an important story. The Carpenters took a similar chance on me, generously authorizing my use of a family collection with no strings attached. I am grateful, and I hope the wisdom of their trust will be evident in the following pages.

I am also beholden to the Northern Colorado Water Conservancy District. In addition to providing me with an elegant office with easy access to the Carpenter Papers, computer, phone, and copying privileges, manager Eric Wilkinson and chief engineer Darell Zimbelman made it possible for me to come and go and to get help from District employees on a number of problems associated with this biography. I wish to thank specifically Brian Werner for his unfailing encouragement, Julie Stoupa, Candys Sinden, Doris Farnham, Mike Carmon, Chanda Johnson, Brad Leach, Jean Maxwell, Candee Werth, and the late Sandy Rice. Additionally, graphics expert Jeff Dahlstrom expertly worked on maps and brought to life many old photographs used in the book. His interest in this project was unflagging. Stephanie Sibert, the computer guru's guru, saved me when my word processing skills proved inadequate. Lori Ozzello edited each chapter as it was finished. Sharpening her wit and pen, she provided valuable suggestions throughout the book. Greg Silkensen, historian in his own right and now a full-time employee of the NCWCD, spent a summer doing research on Carpenter in various state, federal, and private archives of Utah, Nevada, New Mexico, California, and Wyoming under a grant from the Colorado Water Resources Research Institute. His careful perusal of documents in these states resulted in the accumulation of materials that enabled me to broaden the perspective of Carpenter's relationship with and impact on all the Colorado River basin states. Silkensen graciously left "Arizona" for me to do in the winter.

On three separate occasions I spent time at the Hoover Presidential Library in West Branch, Iowa. Archivists Dwight Miller, Dale Mayer, and Pat Wildenberg were unfailingly supportive during my stays. Patricia Forsythe, executive director of the Hoover Presidential Library Association, and Patricia Hand, manager of academic programs there, enriched my experience through extensive courtesy and simplification of the grant process. I am proud to have been twice named a Hoover Scholar.

Others who assisted me in the past eight years are Martha Campbell, librarian extraordinaire at the Colorado Supreme Court Library; Andy Bistline for his genealogical assistance; archivist Eric Bittner at the National Archives and Records Administration—Rocky Mountain Region in Denver; Jason Brockman and Erin McDanal at the Colorado State Archives; Peggy Ford at the Greeley Museum; Doug Ernest at Morgan Library, Colorado State University; my colleagues at Colorado State University, especially Charles J. Bayard, Robert Ward, James Hansen, Mark Fiege, and the late Liston Leyendecker; and friends whose brains I picked to make this a better volume: Norris Hundley, Jr., Donald J. Pisani, David Robbins, Janet Fireman, Colorado Supreme Court Justice Greg Hobbs, Dr. Kim Nguyen, and my old and reliable anthropologist friend, Hermann K. Bleibtreu, who read the entire manuscript between travels to exotic places and concluded, after writing a very useful critique, that he just did not like Delphus E. Carpenter.

Jay Fultz edited the entire manuscript for the University of Oklahoma Press. He pushed me to be more objective, asked tough questions, and did his job with sensitivity and professionalism. For his attention to detail, I am profoundly grateful. I also want to acknowledge the encouragement and advice I received from Chuck Rankin and Alice Stanton at the University of Oklahoma Press. And for his fine work as professional indexer, I thank Galen Schroeder.

To Silvia Ruíz, son Alejandro, and daughter Cristina, who endured my obsession with this project, I say thank you. Writers are not easy to live with. I am grateful for your understanding.

And to Monica, cowboy poetess, here it is as promised.

Silver Fox of the Rockies

Introduction

Hoover Dam, known around the world as a marvel of engineering, a monument to construction enterprise during the Great Depression, could not have been built without the conclusion of an agreement on water allocation amongst the seven Colorado River basin states and the federal government. This agreement was primarily the work of Delphus Emory Carpenter, who articulated, refined, and promoted the Colorado River Compact, and other interstate compacts, that reduced conflict and facilitated growth in the American West.

In the spring of 1877 two events occurred whose serendipitous relationship would affect development of the modern West. On March 3, Congress approved the Desert Land Act, authorizing settlement on certain arid lands in the West. On May 13, Carpenter was born in Greeley, Colorado. He lived seventy-four years. During this time the West experienced bursts of exponential growth accompanied by a strident debate over who would control the unappropriated surface water. Carpenter's effort to preserve the autonomy of western states in the spirit of the Desert Land Act clashed with federal government plans to centralize control over the nation's natural resources. His innovative application of the Constitution's compact clause to interstate streams forged a compromise between states' rights advocates and government officials that enabled western development to occur with minimum litigation.

The Desert Land Act stated that buyers of 640 acres of the public domain would have to pay $1.25 an acre and commit to irrigate eighty acres within three years. Laws passed in 1866 and 1870 set a precedent for the 1877 legislation. They approved appropriation of non-navigable water by land-seeking pioneers for irrigation and reclamation, provided the settlers followed local customs and procedures. But what the Desert Land Act specifically mandated was "bona-fide prior appropriation" on the public lands, and "many legal scholars have assumed not only that Congress was, in effect, voting for appropriation" as the most applicable water system for the West,[1] but that state and local authorities should define the administrative rules. The Desert Land Act also addressed the geographical area that would be the focus of the government's reclamation policies after 1902. It connected land ownership with water projects and echoed guidelines in the earlier acts by emphasizing the need to preserve water supplies "free for the appropriation and use of the public for irrigation, mining and manufacturing purposes subject to existing rights." Taken together, these three statutes underscored the western conviction that congressional support for arid lands settlement would be at the disposition of state and local authorities, not the federal government.[2]

Carpenter dedicated his life to the preservation of state sovereignty over water. He was raised by Iowa parents who established a home in the Union Colony on the Cache la Poudre River in 1871.* In the tradition of other cooperative experiments in the West, the Union Colony, soon named Greeley after its sponsor, Horace Greeley, founder of the *New York Herald Tribune*, offered town lots and farming lands to settlers who were promised a community free from alcohol. Its principal leader, Nathan C. Meeker,

* The Union Colony was one of a half dozen cooperative and semi-cooperative agricultural ventures attempted in Colorado in the 1870s. Some failed, but the Union Colony's location on fertile lands at the junction of the Cache la Poudre and South Platte rivers, combined with the farmers' access to the Denver-Pacific Railroad, assured success. In 1869, the agricultural editor of the *New York Herald Tribune*, Nathan C. Meeker, announced his plans for establishing a utopian colony in Colorado. It was named for his boss, Horace Greeley. Settlers who were selected by Meeker for their farming skills and sobriety paid $155 for town and farming lots. They were required to aid in the construction of irrigation ditches. In return, they received free transportation to Colorado for family members and livestock. The first wave arrived in the spring of 1870. Although problems arose from faulty irrigation designs, settlers who objected to enforcement of temperance regulations, wild cattle trampling their fields, and an unexpected infestation of locusts, the colony persevered. Its charter expired in 1880, but the town of Greeley has continued as the center of Weld County, now the fourth most successful farming county in the United States.

honored the community's commitment to provide water through ditches and canals, the construction and maintenance of which proved problematic to flat-land farmers from the East and Midwest.

Carpenter took advantage of the many legal challenges presented by irrigation. He made a career for himself in water law, earning a law degree from the University of Denver while serving as an apprentice to Denver attorneys. After four years as state senator, he was appointed Colorado's interstate streams commissioner and became lead counsel in litigation involving Wyoming, New Mexico, and Nebraska. He was also the driving force in applying the compact clause of the Constitution to settlement of conflicts between two or more states sharing a common water supply. His most noteworthy accomplishment was to demonstrate how states could preserve better control of their water supply by negotiating compacts that would obviate costly litigation. If such agreements were consummated prior to construction of federal dams, reservoirs, and irrigation projects, economic development could take place with full disclosure of the amount of water available and at a pace appropriate to the state's unique economic circumstances.

Carpenter grew up believing passionately in the states' right to control and administer their own water. The Reclamation Service, created by the Newlands Act in 1902, fought to claim surplus western water for the federal government. Unfortunately, the act did not make clear what laws were to operate in the West when the Service began construction of dams, reservoirs and canals. Section 8 said nothing was to "interfere with the laws of any State or territory relating to the control, appropriation, use or distribution of water used in irrigation, or any vested right acquired thereunder," but it also stipulated that rights of the federal government should be protected.[3] As historian Donald J. Pisani has pointed out, only Colorado, Wyoming, and Nebraska,—states west of the Mississippi River—had established administrative procedures to regulate water rights, and only Wyoming and Nebraska had the mechanism to adjudicate conflicts. Because the Reclamation Service failed to insist on water law reform as a precondition to project construction, a very critical difference of opinion developed between the states, represented by Carpenter, and the federal government, represented by the Reclamation Service, regarding ownership and control of western water.[4] When this situation was exacerbated by perceived indecision from the Supreme Court in 1907 (*Kansas v. Colorado*), battle lines were drawn.[5]

Carpenter understood the visceral importance of western rivers to the future growth of the region. Along with John Wesley Powell, he believed that successful economic development would depend on the prosperity of irrigated agriculture. In his 1878 *Report on the Lands of the Arid Region*, Powell had urged Congress to pass laws establishing new rules for land ownership in the arid West. He did not want small farmers to lose control of their property to corporations that might monopolize water distribution systems. His proposed bills failed because his vision did not jibe with that of a majority in Congress. Powell, historian Donald Worster argues, "was too old-fashioned, agrarian, backward-looking, and nostalgic for a vanishing village America, which he wanted to see recreated in the arid region." By contrast, politicians of that period "were in the grip of a dream of their own. It promised that the West would become another Eden of easy, abundant wealth, and happy, innocent, people."[6]

Carpenter grew up believing in that same dream. He, too, wanted a Jeffersonian America in the West. Unlike Powell, however, Carpenter feared the power of the federal government and viewed the Reclamation Service as the real nemesis of agrarian independence. Two projects—Pathfinder Dam, constructed on the North Platte River in south-central Wyoming in 1909, and Elephant Butte Dam, completed on the Rio Grande in southwestern New Mexico in 1916—convinced him that the Reclamation Service was prepared to bully the western states into relinquishing local control of the water needed to justify the agency's existence. Both projects established federal presence on waters originating in the Colorado Rockies. As a result of these dams, Coloradans faced an embargo on development of lands along the Rio Grande and a servitude or obligation on the North Platte that required them to provide water for high plains farmers in Wyoming. In neither instance was Colorado adequately consulted. The two federal projects committed the water originating within Colorado's boundaries to two downstream states. The Reclamation Service had proceeded in defiance of the acts of 1866, 1870, and 1877—all three of which represented congressional expectations that western water would be under the control of state and local authorities. Carpenter saw the potential for future conflict when plans were announced to settle servicemen in the Colorado River basin at the end of World War I. If the pattern of conflict continued, Colorado's status as an equal and quasi-sovereign state of the Union would be challenged. Such was the importance of water to the growth and development of a semiarid state.

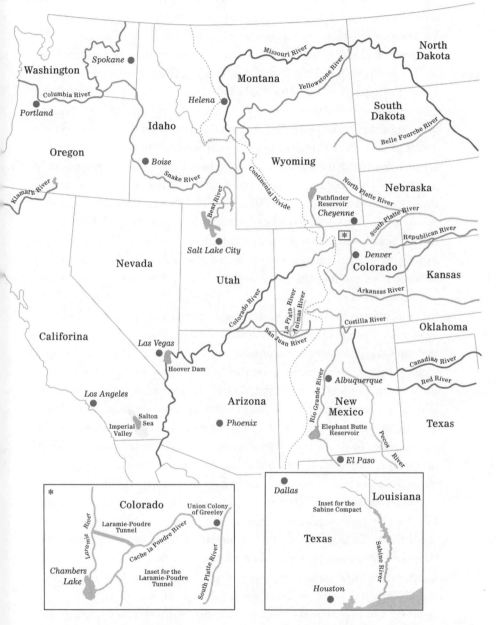

Interstate Water Allocation Compacts in force, 2000. (Drawn by Jeff Dahlstrom, Northern Colorado Water Conservancy District)

In principle, Carpenter found federal projects to control flooding, develop water storage, and expand irrigation quite acceptable. Like the Progressive reformers of his day, he endorsed the goals of efficiency and elimination of waste, but Colorado and its lofty mountains constituted the source of ten rivers whose flow was as important to neighboring states as it was to Colorado.[7] The potential for interstate conflict was enormous; Coloradans insisted they owned all water surfacing within their boundaries while the Reclamation Service based its construction mandate on the assumption that the federal government was legally entitled to surplus water, meaning water not already put to beneficial use and recognized as a vested property right under state law. Even Powell had seen that every significant stream in the West crossed state lines. "Will it not be an act of wisdom," he wrote, "to settle these disputes in their incipiency before the passions of the people are inflamed and before rights and interests are established?" His urgent plea for Congress to devise a plan "to divide the waters in some wise and just manner that will command the judgment of men" went unheeded.[8]

The culture of rivers and streams is dictated by geographical location. Upstream residents tend to manifest an attitude of superiority. Their connection to reliable water is guaranteed, especially during periods of drought. Their major concern comes from the fact that most western states accept the principle of first in time, first in right. Economic development downstream, where warmer temperatures encourage agriculture and population growth, results in a prior use of water and therefore a potential legal claim to that water in times of scarcity. Downstream residents worry excessively about upstream transfers of water out of the river basin and upstream consumption that diminishes downstream flows at critical times.

This river culture was clear to Carpenter during most of his professional life. Reclamation projects with federal water rights, such as Pathfinder and Elephant Butte, had the potential to limit growth and economic development in headwaters states by demanding delivery of water in years of drought. Carpenter wanted states to negotiate water distribution agreements *before* the government began building such projects. An interstate compact, he believed, would obviate the need for litigation and would become a permanent law of the river. If all parties, including the Reclamation Service, honored the principle of states' rights, compact agreements would free states to grow at their own pace. Competition with neighbors, who might be tempted to assert a priority right to common water by virtue of earlier appropriation, would be unnecessary.[9] The agreements reached would provide security and a sense of permanency that would encourage capital investment, an argument the West used to defend replacement of the common- law riparian system with the doctrine of prior appropriation.[10]

Carpenter struggled mightily with the priority issue. The doctrine of first in time, first in right was a two-edged sword. It had allowed pioneer settlers to have the best water rights and, as a young attorney, Carpenter was prepared to defend the prior appropriation doctrine at any cost. He believed in the principle not only because it was state law but because it recognized the economic and financial risk assumed by the early pioneers. Growing up on his father's farm near Greeley brought this lesson home. His family's private property, he believed, included both land and water that should be protected as a sacred right. On the other hand, Carpenter knew that if the doctrine of priority were extended across state lines, head-waters states would face the burden of having to supply water to earlier settled regions in California, Arizona, New Mexico, Wyoming, Kansas and Nebraska. To Carpenter this was a troubling scenario that required inno-vative thinking.

Carpenter found the legal framework for a solution in the United States Constitution. When it came to water, the only way western states could preserve an "equal footing" with other states in the federal union was to insist on local control.[11] The compact clause of the Constitution (Article I, section 10)[12] legitimized negotiation of interstate agreements, subject to the approval of Congress. The thirteen original colonies had used a simi-lar approach to resolve disputes among themselves, subject to approval of the Crown. In 1777 the tradition was continued through Article VI of the Articles of Confederation.[13] The compact clause of the Constitution, approved ten years later, represented an ongoing endorsement of a process through which semi-sovereign states might resolve some of their own problems before seeking approval from the central government. Framers of the Constitution recognized the imperfect relationship between states and the federal government. In all likelihood, they feared the possibility of combi-nations of states working together to increase their political power at the expense of the nation. In response they forged a compact clause that allowed states to make agreements among themselves but subject to a congressional veto.[14]

Until 1922, almost all interstate conflicts settled by compact involved clarification of boundaries and fishing rights. Carpenter was the first to apply the compact clause in defense of states' rights on interstate streams. He feared that Colorado and other headwaters states would lose control of their future if the doctrine of priority was applied by the Supreme Court across state lines. What made more sense was an interstate compact based on the principle of equity. Carpenter was convinced that the concept of equitable apportionment, which the United States first enunciated in *Kansas v. Colorado* (1907), could serve as a model for compact negotiations between states.[15] States' rights would then be guaranteed in the West, where water control was fundamental to economic growth and survival.

Equitable apportionment of interstate streams through compact agreements thus became Carpenter's guiding precept, and it was his principal contribution to the West of the twentieth century.[16] It was a way to counter both the Supreme Court's threat of jurisdiction over interstate squabbles and federal claims to unappropriated, or surplus, western water. It would allow preservation of states' rights and honor the frontier individualism of pioneer communities by protecting, at least in part, the priority of their claims. In addition, it would permit the West to accept federally funded reclamation programs under terms of the region's own choosing.

Equitable apportionment of water through interstate compact agreements also strengthened western state opposition to the centralization brought on by industrial growth, World War I, and the policies of the Progressive Era (1900–1920). Along with Populism and the New Deal, Progressivism was one of three major reform movements in the history of the United States. A middle-class urban response to the post–Civil War excesses of big business, Progressivism counted on the power of the federal government to effect change. Specifically, its reform leaders sought the power of the federal government to eliminate waste, maximize productivity, and renovate the democratic process. It also contained a conservation movement aimed at curtailing devastation of the public domain caused by avaricious timber, livestock, and mining interests.* The principal architect

---

* Examples of Progressive reform measures include the 1890 Sherman Act that regulated large corporate trusts, the Elkins and Hepburn acts of 1903 and 1906, respectively, that regulated railroads, and the Federal Reserve Act of 1913 that reformed the currency system. Following publication of *The Jungle* by Upton Sinclair, Congress passed the Pure Food and Drug Act in 1906. It was directed at curbing abuses in the food processing industry. In the area of natural resources, Progressives endorsed creation of national forests

of this movement was Gifford Pinchot, President Theodore Roosevelt's chief of the Department of Agriculture's Forestry Bureau.

Conservationists advocated a twofold course of action. They invited government control of the remaining public lands to prevent further destruction and monopolization, and they proposed a resource planning policy that would promote efficient development of the West's remaining natural wealth.[17] To Pinchot, conservation was a science, but it was also a utilitarian and evangelical faith strengthened by his commitment to better the life of the little people who had been co-opted by monopolies. Government, Progressives believed, would have to check monopoly in order to preserve political and economic democracy in America.[18]

Carpenter, along with most small stockmen and farmers in the West, was anticonservationist. His hostility was founded on the fear of an expanding centralized government. The Roosevelt-Pinchot plan to create additional forest reserves and to institute grazing and timber cutting restrictions on federal lands seemed to be aimed at the yeomen farmers and stockmen whose opportunities for economic advancement would almost certainly narrow when land from the public domain was withdrawn and placed under federal regulation. Pinchot and some of his closest cohorts were easterners. As Colorado historian Michael McCarthy has noted, from the vantage point of anticonservationist westerners, Pinchot was the "epitome of egotistical, theoretical Eastern bureaucracy." He was seen as a tyrant, according to McCarthy, and "was attacked in Colorado not so much for what he did as for what he—or whom—he represented."[19] By 1910, conservationists considered Colorado the heart of enemy territory.[20]

Thus, Carpenter's application of the compact clause to interstate streams during the Progressive Era represented a major challenge to national trends. Progressives favored multipurpose development of the nation's rivers through commissions with broad powers to authorize and construct projects. As government officials, they were eager to apply the "gospel of efficiency" to the nation's waterways.[21] They did not want to strengthen local control. Carpenter, on the other hand, was antagonistic

---

in 1891, a 1906 Antiquities Act that protected large areas of lands with historic and prehistoric significance, and the Inland Waterways Commission, established in 1907, that gave the United States power to control the nation's rivers and streams. The Newlands Act of 1902 is also seen as part of the Progressive movement, because it used government to help subsidize irrigation projects in sixteen western states.

to centralized planning. His small-farm upbringing, discomfort with "effete" eastern intellectuals, and distrust of urban populations, where Progressive support was consistently strong, led him to reject Progressive policies and the national figures who encouraged a greater federal presence in the West.[22] His formative views of government arose at a time when the federal government was evolving from that of a nineteenth-century pump-priming facilitator of frontiersmen to a twentieth-century planner and administrator of western property.[23] The withdrawal of millions of acres from the public domain and the National Forest Service's rapid growth as a model of what strong, expansive government would look like, combined with his distrust of the Reclamation Service to forge a determined defense of states' rights.[24]

Carpenter's defense of local control relied on his understanding of the nature of federalism. European transboundary water conflicts had been resolved satisfactorily by international treaties. If the proper constitutional relationship between states and the federal government was to be preserved, Carpenter believed, the doctrines of equitable apportionment and equitable utilization would need to be applied to interstate water conflicts in the West in the same manner they had been implemented in Europe.[25] Such an application would defend against a growing federal presence.

Like that of the Swiss Alps, Colorado's geographical position was unique. Because its high mountain peaks sheltered the headwaters of so many interstate streams, Carpenter's compact plan would inevitably produce a ripple effect throughout adjacent states. Before the *Kansas v. Colorado* decision of 1907, few Coloradans doubted their right to all water originating within the state's boundaries. Carpenter began his own career fiercely defending this view. After the Kansas decision, however, he recognized that the principle of equitable apportionment between states, formulated by the Supreme Court in that case, required Colorado's willingness to accept the idea of limited territorial sovereignty. A dispute between the United States and Mexico that ended in a 1906 treaty also guided Carpenter's thinking. After initially claiming "absolute territorial sovereignty," the United States conceded Mexico's right to an equitable share of water from the Rio Grande.[26] In other words, while a state or nation had the technical legal right to insist on absolute ownership and use of all water originating within its boundaries, the need for social harmony, what the law called comity, required sovereignties at the headwaters to seek an equitable division of water with their downstream neighbors.

This came to be Carpenter's view, a view driven by international examples of limited sovereignty. He believed that negotiations between states
should be conducted on the same level as diplomacy between nations.
Claims of absolute ownership of water by a headwaters state constituted
"an unreasonable exercise of sovereignty and thereby . . . a trespass on the
lower state."[27] Between states, he believed, negotiated compacts would work
far better than litigation. The potential for friction would be reduced and
ratified compacts would function as a more permanent response to conflicting water demands. He did not convince everyone, and the approximately twenty-five water allocation compacts that sprang from his thinking
and exist in the arid West today[28] have received mixed reviews.[29] But in
pioneering the application of the compact clause to interstate water conflicts, Carpenter preserved the principle of local control of water and made
possible the construction of major reclamation projects such as Hoover
Dam. For better or worse, the enactment of compacts on western rivers
forestalled the establishment of river basin authorities by the Department
of Interior.[30]

In the 1920s, Carpenter's heyday, the role of states in the federal system
was being squeezed by proponents of centralized government, and Carpenter responded to the threat with energy and conviction. In 1877, the year
of Carpenter's birth, Colorado had been a state for only a year, but much
of the land still had the appearance of a frontier community, although
urban areas showed signs of growing stability. With farming becoming more
diversified and dependent on irrigation, the state's constitution embraced
the concept of local control of water and stated a preference for domestic
and agricultural uses over the needs of manufacturing.[31] Only a few years
earlier, a dispute between Fort Collins and Greeley over water shortages on
the Cache la Poudre River had resulted in the state's adoption of prior
appropriation as the rule governing water adjudication.[32]

It was an important clarification at a time when Colorado was about to
become a state. Three major railroads connected Denver to markets in
the East, and speculators, hoping to raise the value of prairie real estate for
an expected wave of new immigrants, were beginning to construct canals
and reservoirs. Cattlemen still dominated the plains, but the Indians who
had been there first had been removed from eastern Colorado and sentiments were growing to push the Utes from their reservation on the West
Slope. To anyone cognizant of the transformation taking place, water was

the key to Colorado's economic development. By 1877, the state was in transition to a post-frontier phase of settlement, a phase increasingly dependent on intra- and interstate water disposition.

Thirty years later, the nation was in the midst of the Progressive Era and Carpenter was in his first year as a new member of the Colorado state senate. Carpenter's four years as a senator coincided with the two terms that Democrat John F. Shafroth served as governor, and Shafroth's commitment to reform dominated the years 1908 to 1912. In matters of natural resource conservation, both Shafroth and the majority of the state legislature maintained unswerving hostility, a feeling shared for the most part by Carpenter. Colorado legislators preferred to massage their notion of the West as an American Eden, a Garden of the World, where, as historian McCarthy has observed, "sturdy yeomen farmers settled, put in crops, built cities, and established republican civilization."[33] On other Progressive issues, however, Governor Shafroth succeeded in guiding the legislature toward reform. With his leadership, the state assembly legislated a primary election law, regulated child labor, enacted an eight-hour day for certain occupations, and hammered out a labor disputes act, a constitutional amendment providing for initiative and referendum rights.

Amid this reform, Carpenter was frequently in the opposition. In a Democratic state legislature, Carpenter, a conservative Republican, was outspokenly hostile toward conservation and any further meddling by Washington bureaucrats. He chafed at the regulatory paternalism inherent in the programs of Roosevelt and Pinchot, and he strongly resisted the initiative and referendum movement.* The hue and cry for such a reform concerned him, because it appeared to undermine the established legislative process. If special interests could buy the votes they needed to pass laws state legislatures had already rejected, or failed to consider, representative government would be replaced by contests among the rich and powerful for citizen support. Democracy would be sabotaged. "The guarantee of government stability and the protection of life, liberty and property of citizens," he noted would be "entrusted to the confusion and turbulence of elections and to the caprice and whims of the hour."[34]

---

* The initiative and referendum movement was an attempt to give voters more power by establishing rules for putting citizen-written laws on the ballot, and providing these same voters with the opportunity to overturn laws passed by the legislature.

As with his opposition to an expanding federal government, Carpenter spoke out against what he perceived to be a dangerous national trend. It would be difficult to argue that he was a political reactionary, but meddling with established political processes alarmed him. When the initiative and referendum became law in Colorado, its initial implementation by the people was a vote on a one-sentence amendment to a 1911 bill introduced by Senator Carpenter. Voters defeated the referred sentence, but the Carpenter Reservoir Bill became state law. It protected the senior (older) priority rights of reservoir owners against encroachment from ditch companies with junior (later-in-time) water rights. In 1911, the implementation of his Reservoir Bill was a more important result for Carpenter than a referendum victory. He was determined to defend the doctrine of prior appropriation so long as it benefited his own interests and those of the people of Colorado.[35]

The year 1911 was important for Carpenter and the West. In that year, Wyoming filed a lawsuit against Colorado when the Greeley-Poudre Irrigation Company completed a tunnel designed to divert 125,000 acre-feet of water from the Laramie River to the Cache la Poudre River. If allowed, the tunnel project would divert water from Wyoming for the benefit of people in Colorado. Wyoming was thus threatened by permanent loss of water to a river basin in Colorado. Carpenter, attorney for the Greeley-Poudre Irrigation Company, was appointed lead counsel to defend the state's interests in the case, *Wyoming v. Colorado*.[36] The U.S. Supreme Court accepted this case immediately and gave every indication that it would rule on the issue of interstate priority. In contrast to the *Kansas v. Colorado* (1907) case, in which two different water systems were in operation, Colorado and Wyoming based their respective water codes on the principle of first in time, first in right. The High Court was poised to provide a solution to interstate water conflict that would establish a precedent to be honored by all states in the future.

The case dragged on interminably. Following eleven years of testimony and Carpenter's herculean efforts to prepare witnesses, file briefs, and offer testimony in Washington—all of which were geared towards protecting Colorado's claim to all the water originating within its boundaries—the Court finally decided in 1922 that Wyoming was entitled to a prior appropriation right on the Laramie River. Colorado would be able to divert only a limited amount of water through the Laramie-Poudre Tunnel into the Cache la Poudre River. It was a watershed decision. What Carpenter feared most—Supreme Court endorsement of prior appropriation on interstate water courses—was seen as a more specific expression of the court's doctrine of equitable apportionment enunciated in *Kansas v. Colorado* (1907). Moreover, the decision implied endorsement of interstate litigation. As a result, the 1922 decision forced Carpenter to move with greater determination toward what he believed to be a less acrimonious and more permanent compact solution on interstate streams. One of the results of his efforts was the seven-state Colorado River Compact of 1922.[37]

Carpenter pulled out all the stops in the *Wyoming* case and lost his health in the process. In his four years with the state assembly he had demonstrated his familiarity with water issues, and no one could have done a more masterful job of presenting Colorado's position in the suit with Wyoming. As head of a special senate committee investigating the condition of Colorado's rivers, he had become aware that each river flowing across state boundaries represented a possible lawsuit. In his 1911 report to the legislature, therefore, he strongly urged the state to continue its endorsement of the priority doctrine. A few months later, when he began preparation for the suit with Wyoming, he embraced the priority doctrine for all it was worth, emphasizing Colorado's early and superior utilization of Laramie River water. He hoped that the Court would be sympathetic to these arguments and that Colorado could, in fact, prove its claim to the earliest use of these waters. In both the lawsuit and the legislative report, Carpenter warned against the possible encroachment of the federal government in matters pertaining to water control, and he specifically targeted the Reclamation Service as the agency to be watched most carefully.[38]

Carpenter was not an opponent of reclamation per se. Reclamation meant simply to place arid lands in production though irrigation. Founders of the Union Colony believed in reclamation as their guiding principle. The colony's organizers—Horace Greeley, Nathan C. Meeker, and Robert Cameron—were his heroes. Carpenter's father, Leroy Carpenter, had aided in construction of the colony's first ditches and son Delphus had endorsed the Reclamation Service's plans to store water and build canals to foster western settlement.[39]

During the Progressive Era, however, the Reclamation Service attached itself to the coattails of the conservation movement. Its multipurpose approach to western rivers—incorporating flood control, improving navigation, and creating water storage for irrigation—also included electrical power generation. The Newlands Act had not included hydroelectric power as a function of the Reclamation Service. Following a 1908 report of the Inland Waterways Commission and construction of Roosevelt Dam on the Salt River in Arizona, however, centralized development and federal control of power generation became a major objective of conservationists and the Reclamation Service.[40] Power sales were viewed as the key to financing irrigation projects, but the debate between proponents of public and private power grew so strident that the Service rarely advocated expanding this part of its multipurpose program.[41] Even so, Carpenter recognized the power issue as a potential extension of the federal government in state affairs and saw how it made more complex the many aspects of successful compact negotiation. With electrical consumption increasing more than three times faster in southern California than in other parts of the United States, it seemed clear that any proposed reclamation project on the Colorado River would, by necessity, include a discussion of power ownership and distribution.[42]

Progressives believed that electrical power, or even its anticipated arrival, would bring more settlers to the West. Surplus workers in urban centers could be lured to the semiarid lands if reclamation projects made both water and power available to sites for new homes. Unfortunately, for farmer settlers, the early projects were poorly planned and prohibitively expensive. By 1922, farmers had been able to repay only 9.5 percent of $135 million invested in reclamation.[43] The Reclamation Service had focused too much on engineering and competition with the Army Corps of Engineers and not enough on the social and economic ability of settlers to make a living from irrigated agriculture. About a dozen hydroelectric power plants were in operation by 1923, but too little effort went into preparing settlers for the difficulties they would face in a semiarid climate. The result was that farmers were soon at odds with the Reclamation Service over the high cost of repaying the government for constructing irrigation systems.[44]

Although most of the early projects were failures, Carpenter was more concerned that Reclamation Service solicitors, in conjunction with the Justice Department attorneys, would look for ways to obviate Justice David Brewer's ruling in *Kansas v. Colorado* (1907). The United States had entered that case in 1904, because Reclamation Service director Frederick Newell feared that the effectiveness of the Service under the Newlands Act would be undermined if either Colorado or Kansas won outright. Consequently, federal attorneys testified to the alleged constitutional right to regulate interstate streams in the West. Stating an interest in building reservoirs for storage, they challenged Colorado's argument that Arkansas River water was the property of Colorado, the state of origin.[45]

Justice Brewer, speaking for a unanimous Supreme Court, discarded the federal government's arguments. Their attorneys had not made a case, he said, arguing that he "strongly backed a state's sovereign right to devise its own water regulatory institutions."[46] This was not what Newell wanted to hear, but for Carpenter and others who believed the acts of 1866, 1870, and 1877 established the authority for a state to administer water within its boundaries, it was an important victory. What angered Carpenter was the Reclamation Service's decision after 1907 to defy the Court by employing other tactics in order to tie up water and land through purchases, withdrawals, and resort to friendly federal courts.[47]

Although a crippled institution with little congressional support, the Reclamation Service still seemed a threat to states' rights in the West in 1920. Most of its projects were unmitigated disasters, and the possibility of the government establishing control over western rivers was highly unlikely.[48] Nevertheless, growing evidence of an increasing federal presence, especially the establishment of national forests in the West, worried Carpenter. So did visible demographic and economic changes occurring before and after World War I, developments that contributed to Carpenter's anti-government paranoia.

Some of these changes were striking. Los Angeles in its downstream location, for example, was experiencing disproportionate growth. More than 90 percent of the eight million immigrants to the West between 1898 and World War I lived in towns and cities and Los Angeles was the poster child. By 1922, it had grown to a community of almost five hundred thousand and was still growing.[49] Moreover, California's agriculturally rich—and thirsty—Imperial Valley was exporting cotton, cantaloupes, lettuce, milk fat, watermelons, peas, asparagus, tomatoes, milo-maize, wheat, alfalfa, sheep, poultry, and eggs to all parts of the nation.[50] And, it was recruiting federal help to do more. The Imperial Irrigation District, formed in 1911, joined in a partnership with the Reclamation Service to build a new irrigation canal from the Colorado River and storage dams to steady the river's flow and prevent flooding.[51] Western roads and railroads had been expanded substantially by 1920, contributing to better markets and population growth. Consequently, several areas were outrunning their water supplies. Food demands during the war brought a boom to irrigated agriculture, but the good times were short-lived. Western farmers and stockmen, who fed half the nation before 1920, suddenly faced a severe economic depression that began in 1919 and continued for more than two decades.

The West was not an economically diverse region; it had become overly dependent on agriculture. It had only 5 percent of the nation's manufacturing.[52] Mining of copper, precious metals, and coal continued to be important, but capital and markets were in the East. A colonial relationship between East and West persisted, but it was more complex than that. Each western state had its own special interests, and all were vulnerable if government officials and well-heeled entrepreneurs took a divide- and-conquer approach to them.

If anything unified the West, it was a distrust of federal power. Western states rarely voted as a bloc, however, and they tended to compete for the internal improvements that Congress approved. Moreover, jealousy among them brought what historian Harry Scheiber has called "rivalistic state mercantilism," that is, each state's attempt to gain advantage through control of commerce.[53] This rivalry and the West's geographical distance from the nation's capital, Scheiber argues, dictated a "curious blend of dependence and independence, of collective action and individualism, that sprang from the peculiarities of the western experience at the opening of the twentieth century."[54] Regardless of how often or how vociferously westerners spoke of their cherished individualism, they "wanted federal investment to build the infrastructure of their economy."[55]

It was just as well that Carpenter's view of the West was in certain ways more attuned to the romantic dreamers than to the pragmatic economic and political realities of his time. It was better that he believe he could bring well-meaning westerners together to resolve complex interstate water problems. But he was a realist in matters of American federalism. It was the federal system that made interstate compacts possible, and Carpenter's comprehension of the historical relationship between states and the nation underlaid his innovative thinking. A literal, strict constructionist interpretation of the Tenth Amendment to the Constitution provided parameters for his recognition of limited state sovereignty and a guarantee of states' rights against illegal federal usurpation.

In his application of the compact clause to solve problems on interstate rivers, Carpenter frequently noted that by joining the Union, states gave up their right to wage war against each other. The equivalent of war, he believed, was the frequent and unfortunate resort to litigation in the U.S. Supreme Court. No case should be accepted by that judicial body, Carpenter argued, without the states first attempting to negotiate agreements through diplomacy. If a compact could be arranged, ratified, and approved by Congress, it would represent the successful exercise of the states' reserved powers according to the Tenth Amendment. Although an interstate compact would diminish state sovereignty to some extent, it would supersede state laws and assure signatory states the comity necessary to avoid conflict (war) in the Supreme Court.[56]

Carpenter applied his theory in successfully negotiated interstate compacts on the Rio Grande and the South Platte, Republican, La Plata, and Colorado rivers, and he participated in compact negotiations on the Upper Colorado, Arkansas, North Platte, and Little Snake rivers with varying results. A variety of entities across the country copied his compact model to apply it to conflicts over water rights, electrical power, and other interstate matters.

Carpenter never doubted the legality of applying the compact clause to interstate streams, but it was not until 1938 that the U.S. Supreme Court gave judicial confirmation to water allocation compacts. In *Hinderlider v. Cherry Creek Ditch Company* (1938), involving the La Plata River Compact, the Court recognized the superiority of an interstate compact over existing state laws.[57] For the West's future it was another watershed moment. The case involved Colorado and New Mexico's sharing water from the La Plata River. Carpenter had negotiated a compact between the two states in 1922 that required rotating use of available water between the states under conditions of reduced flow. It represented the equity hammered out by two states whose water doctrines recognized the principle of prior appropriation.

In 1928, however, during a period of low flow, Colorado state engineer M. C. Hinderlider shut down the diversion head gate of the Cherry Creek Ditch Company in Colorado in accordance with the compact. The company claimed that the state engineer's actions violated the ditch company's vested rights and that the act was unconstitutional and void. The trial court ruled against the company, but the Colorado Supreme Court reversed the lower court's decision, stating that the compact was nothing more than a compromise between conflicting claims and that the property of Colorado citizens had been taken with no regard to vested rights.[58] On the second of two appeals, the U.S. Supreme Court decided in favor of the Colorado state engineer. The compact was not only held to be valid but "binding upon the citizens of each State and all of its water claimants, even where the State had granted the water rights before it entered into the compact."[59]

When his friend and colleague Ralph I. Meeker informed him of the good news, Carpenter had been bedridden with symptoms of Parkinson's disease for four years. Nonetheless, both men were extremely pleased. "Sweet news from Washington," Meeker wrote. "Congratulations on your 'Compact Baby,' Mr. Silver Fox of the Rockies."[60]

It was a propitious moment and an appropriate nickname for Carpenter. Although Congress had approved the Colorado River Compact of 1922 in its passage of the Boulder Canyon Project Act in 1928, prior to the *Hinderlider* ruling, the High Court had not ruled that an interstate water compact took precedence over state law. The decision validated the constitutional underpinnings of Carpenter's compact theory and established a precedent that paved the way for the proliferation of interstate compacts during the next twenty years.[61]

In using the moniker "Silver Fox," Meeker meant to be complimentary. The animal to which he referred was, like Carpenter, quite unique. Silver foxes belong to the family of red foxes, but they are larger, seen less frequently, and are marked by a black body with some white coloration on the back and sides.[62] As with other red foxes, they are known to have great patience and strong survival instincts in the face of hostile predators. They are territorial, notably adaptable, and legendary in their determination and acute sensitivity to their surroundings, attributes that make possible their success and survival.

Whether or not Meeker had the stereotypical crafty fox of Aesop's fables in mind, he undoubtedly meant to convey the idea that, like foxes in general, his good friend Carpenter was a persistent and dogged pursuer of very specific goals. Carpenter had proved resilient under pressure and had shown marked sensitivity to the opinions of others during tense and prolonged negotiations. He could be stubborn, but if this was a defect it was less important when acquaintances became aware of the courage he needed to function in the public arena after 1922. From that year on, the Parkinsonian symptoms sapped his strength and left him in almost constant pain. Eventually, the humility that came from not being able to feed himself or to speak clearly forced him to stay home. He remained intellectually active, however, thanks to the extraordinary care and assistance of his wife, Dot.

Carpenter knew he could not pioneer in the same way his father's generation had broken new ground, created communities and established the infrastructure of an agricultural society based on irrigation. Still, he was determined to expand on that generation's progress. As a tool for promoting western growth and balanced economic development, the interstate compact was his contribution to the preservation of that pioneer spirit. Although he sometimes apologized for his rural, small-town upbringing, Carpenter was enormously proud of his Greeley roots. "To those of us who make up the second generation of the Union Colonists," he wrote in 1920, "another and different task is assigned. Our forebears promoted and constructed. We have been reared during the period of reckoning following the original construction. Ours has been the atmosphere of overcoming original mistakes or reconstructing financial blunders. We are, by environment, trouble shooters, as it were. Ours is the duty of correcting mistakes and defending what we have, as well as that of pioneering in fact and in law."[63]

Carpenter believed his farming and ranching experience qualified him to participate in regional and national affairs on the same level as Ivy League intellectuals. He frequently evaluated his own progress through life and generally gave himself good marks. In the course of a thirty-year career, he created few enemies, and the longer he lived, the more kudos he received from acquaintances, admirers, and former critics. They recognized not only the significance of interstate compacts but the lessons Carpenter taught about how to conduct successful negotiations among parties with disparate objectives.

Carpenter was skilled in leading diverse groups to consensus. Successful negotiation required an understanding of the human condition. Every problem, he believed, was essentially a human problem. In a litigious environment, the tendency exists to diminish the importance of courtesy, tolerance and compassion. Under pressure, most participants in negotiation too quickly become adversaries, claiming their rights under the law. Because Carpenter experienced personally the bone-numbing consequences of time-consuming and inconclusive litigation, he learned to become a forceful and outspoken proponent of negotiation. He was an attorney who rejected court-imposed solutions.

When newly elected Democratic Governor Edwin C. Johnson removed him from his position as Colorado interstate streams commissioner in 1933, Carpenter was justifiably depressed. He had never conceived of the job as being politically partisan. His loyalty to Colorado and to a better future for the West had been a complete emotional, physical, and intellectual investment. This is not to say he was above the self-promotion, self-interest, and self-justification common to any human being. At times, he was obsessively desirous of recognition, and his unwillingness to vacate his office in the Capitol Building after Johnson fired him illustrated all too clearly a tendency to personalize his job.[64]

Carpenter was not irreplaceable. The exigencies of a severe economic depression required the governor to slash expenses wherever he thought best. Carpenter offered to work for less. He believed the best interests of Colorado mandated completion of compacts on the Rio Grande and on the North Platte and Arkansas rivers. It was a task he knew best how to accomplish. By 1933, however, he had reached his physical limits, and Johnson knew it. It was time for Colorado's interstate streams commissioner to return home to Greeley. Although he continued to answer correspondence and to provide advice when it was requested, Carpenter became bedridden in 1934 and pretty much remained so until his death in 1951.

Carpenter learned from his parents that success in life required a great deal of personal sacrifice. In addition, they trained him to think about the effect his actions had on future public welfare. And Carpenter's efforts had long-range effects. His interstate river compacts bought time for western states to pursue their own pace of economic development without fear of competition from neighbors. Whether these same compacts will prove flexible enough to be modified in the twenty-first century remains to be seen. Recent popular, environmental, and municipal demands on the West's water supply suggest the very real possibility of increased compact litigation, just exactly what Carpenter hoped to avoid.[65] But at a time when its rivers were of critical importance to recovery from economic depression and the management of exponential growth following two world wars, Carpenter's compacts helped the West develop the energy and industrial bases and urban communities that have enabled it to keep pace with growth in other parts of the nation.

Also contributing to Carpenter's impact on the future of the West was
his insistence on accurate research. The Colorado–Big Thompson Project
(C-BT), for example, authorized in 1938, resulted from his 1922 projec-
tion that farmers on Colorado's Eastern Slope would eventually require a
limited amount of supplemental water from the Colorado River.[66] When
negotiations with Wyoming over the North Platte River failed, Coloradans
began drilling a thirteen-mile tunnel through the Continental Divide to
bring water from the Colorado River on the Western Slope to the South
Platte River for irrigation on the Eastern Slope. Carpenter had visualized
this development during the 1922 discussions with Colorado River basin
states. He allayed the fears of Arizona and California that Colorado might
divert large amounts of water from the river before it reached the lower
basin, convincing them that topographical considerations would prevent
the upper states from diverting more than 500,000 acre-feet of water out
of the Colorado River basin. Consequently, when the C-BT contract was
signed, lower basin objections were reduced to murmurs. Carpenter's
1922 estimate and today's diversion data are remarkably close.

It was this ability to visualize the future that set Carpenter apart. The
vision was flawed in certain aspects because he imagined a modern West
based on irrigated agriculture with water under control of the states and
government projects serving the needs of local interests. Government
centralization under the New Deal was anathema to him. When his friend
Herbert Hoover failed to win reelection in 1932, Carpenter was unprepared for and unsympathetic toward President Franklin D. Roosevelt's
expansion of federal power. His reaction suggests that he was intellectually
rooted in the past, a tragic figure, perhaps, who never quite caught up with
his era's changing demography and economics. If so, he was hardly alone.

Nonetheless, there is something refreshing in Carpenter's passionate
adherence to pioneer principles of self-direction and individual liberty.
The fight between states and the federal government for control over the
West's natural resources continues today. The proper relationship between
nature and man's endeavors remains an active debate. Carpenter was
more a disciple of John Muir than Gifford Pinchot. Although he believed
that rivers should be used to benefit western farmers, he spoke often of
nature's power and of the land as the final arbiter over how water could
be appropriated for beneficial use. In this sense, Carpenter may appear
to be a romantic visionary, profoundly affected by his pioneer past and

reluctant to accept the social, political and economic evolution through which the nation was moving. But such a judgment would be presentist. In seventy-four years, Carpenter lived as full and active a life as his body would permit. His legacy of river compacts, negotiation over litigation, local control of natural resources, modification of the prior appropriation doctrine, and defense of states' rights has helped shape the West of the twenty-first century. Whatever his faults, as a booster of the rural West the Silver Fox left ample evidence of a career that succeeded in implementing new strategies for resolving interstate conflict in the twentieth-century west.

CHAPTER 1

Lineage and Love Letters

This motto *I give to the young and the old;*
More precious by far than treasures of gold,
T'will prove to its owner a talisman rare
More potent than magic, it's never despair
—"NEVER DESPAIR," IN CARPENTER PAPERS

The life of Delphus (Delph) Emory Carpenter is best understood as a final chapter in the history of a pioneering family, moving west over three generations from Vermont to Colorado. The character traits that sustained him through difficult times were forged by the values of grandparents and parents seeking fortunes in undeveloped lands. An indomitable will, respect for hard work, strong religious faith, sense of fair play, patriotism, and temperance—these were some of the qualities deeply ingrained in the family lineage.

In his career as an attorney, Carpenter also pioneered, but his frontier was water. The way he dealt with the vicissitudes of his profession and the extent of his success as a constitutional lawyer, negotiator, peacemaker, and politician were reflections of a genealogical legacy he readily acknowledged. Displaying determination, energy, perseverance, and occasional despair,[1] Carpenter recognized the importance of struggling for life's rewards. "The most fortunate thing that can be granted a man in the battle of life," he stated, "is good parentage and moderately poor circumstances. A child so born has triple the chance of the child of wealth. He is forced to overcome obstacles when he meets them. Such triumphs breed leaders."[2] Carpenter was a leader.

Born in Greeley, Colorado, to Leroy S. and Martha B. Carpenter on May 13, 1877, he was the second of three boys. An older brother, Alfred B., arrived March 6, 1873, and a younger brother, Fred G., was born on August 15, 1881. Martha gave birth to each of her sons in the same five-room house that Leroy and his father built a mile north of Greeley in the summer and fall of 1871.[3]

Delph's grandfather, Daniel Carpenter, who began the family's westward migration, was a typical nineteenth-century pioneer. Born in Barre, Vermont on February 8, 1796, he moved to Canada with his parents at the age of eight. As rumors of war proliferated in 1812, the family found its way back to the United States where at age sixteen Daniel enlisted in the U. S. Army. He served first as teamster and later as a volunteer on the Niagara frontier, where he experienced minor skirmishes with British forces. When the war ended he settled in Genesee County in western New York.

About 1818, Daniel again moved west, this time to an area that became Newville, Ohio. Just before the move, he married Sally Northway. The journey to Ohio in a sleigh during the dead of winter was their wedding trip. Sally bore eight children in Newville before her death in 1838. Daniel remarried, this time to Nancy Scott. Nancy and Daniel had five children, one of whom, Cyrus, died in infancy. The second son was Leroy S. Carpenter, Delph's father, who was born on August 18, 1843.

While the children were growing, Daniel engaged in all kinds of merchandising. He built a tannery, a soap factory (ashery), and a cooper shop. He purchased farmlands and provided credit to retailers importing manufactured goods into the county. He even owned a distillery, closing it down when he realized the liquor he made was contributing to the decadence of neighbors. For the rest of his life he lectured against "demon rum" as a member of the Sons of Temperance. He joined the ranks of the Ohio militia, rising to the rank of colonel, and also served briefly in the Ohio legislature. By the late 1840s, Daniel was relatively prosperous and well established, but a financial panic extending from 1847 to 1848 made

Carpenter Family
(limited genealogy)

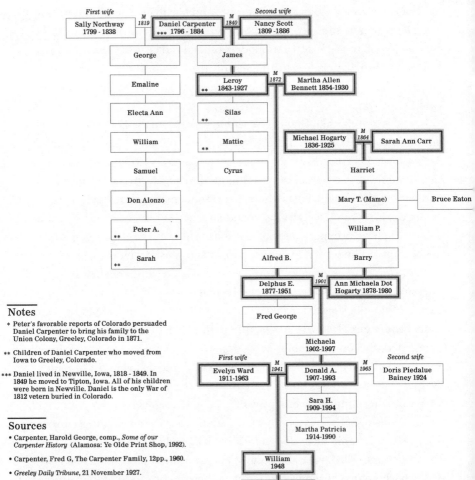

First wife	*Second wife*
Sally Northway 1799 - 1838	Nancy Scott 1809 -1886

Daniel Carpenter *** 1796 - 1884 (M 1819 / M 1840)

George

James

Emaline

Leroy ** 1843-1927 — M 1872 — Martha Allen Bennett 1854-1930

Electa Ann

Silas **

William

Mattie ** — Michael Hogarty 1836-1925 — M 1864 — Sarah Ann Carr

Samuel

Cyrus

Harriet

Don Alonzo

Mary T. (Mame) — Bruce Eaton

Peter A. ** *

William P.

Sarah **

Alfred B.

Barry

Delphus E. 1877-1951 — M 1901 — Ann Michaela Dot Hogarty 1878-1980

Fred George

Michaela 1902-1997

First wife
Evelyn Ward 1911-1963 — M 1941 — Donald A. 1907-1993 — M 1965 — Doris Piedalue Bainey 1924 *Second wife*

Sara H. 1909-1994

Martha Patricia 1914-1990

William 1948

Ward 1952

Notes

* Peter's favorable reports of Colorado persuaded Daniel Carpenter to bring his family to the Union Colony, Greeley, Colorado in 1871.

** Children of Daniel Carpenter who moved from Iowa to Greeley, Colorado.

*** Daniel lived in Newville, Iowa, 1818 - 1849. In 1849 he moved to Tipton, Iowa. All of his children were born in Newville. Daniel is the only War of 1812 vetern buried in Colorado.

Sources

* Carpenter, Harold George, comp., *Some of our Carpenter History* (Alamosa: Ye Olde Print Shop, 1992).

* Carpenter, Fred G, The Carpenter Family, 12pp., 1960.

* *Greeley Daily Tribune*, 21 November 1927.

* Carpenter, Amos B. In Re Daniel Carpenter, No 950, p.575 of the Genealogy History of the Rehobeth Branch of the Carpenter Family in America.

* Wallingsford, M., Carpenter and Hogarty Genealogy, handwritten, Washington, D.C., 1908.

it impossible to collect all the money he was owed. In 1849, the year of the California gold rush, he settled his affairs as best he was able and moved west again with his new wife and children in a covered wagon pulled by a yoke of oxen. This time he located north of Bethel, a few miles west of Tipton, Cedar County, Iowa.[4]

In Bethel, Daniel built a rude log cabin in which he settled his family. It was located on land he entered as a soldier's homestead. Daniel was bankrupt but confident that Iowa offered opportunity. Physical prowess and self-confidence helped him recoup losses incurred in Ohio. Family yarns passed down during the years recount his willingness to handle logging chains bare-handed in wintertime and his success as a long-distance swimmer, a skill utilized by bridge builders in the preliminary stages of developing river crossings. Daniel was nothing if not the rugged frontiersman of western lore. With Davy Crockett and Daniel Boone, he would have been right at home.

Little by little, he rebuilt his fortune in Iowa. As recalled later by grandson Delph, Daniel was the quintessential pioneer, able to "ride like a centaur and shoot like an Indian," generous to a fault and living in a humble cabin "where the latch string was ever out and the fires of hospitality were never allowed to sink into white ashes."[5] As he had done in Ohio, Daniel again acquired lands and businesses, succeeding well enough over the next twenty-two years to garner a small fortune of about $20,000. He was recognized in the community as a staunch Republican and founder of the Bethel Methodist Church. Security and comforts were his to enjoy in the waning years of life, but he preferred adventure. Disturbances caused by the Civil War, family health problems, and a visceral westering spirit (what his grandson referred to as empire building), nursed and cultivated since leaving Vermont, persuaded him that, at an age when most of his peers were long dead, it was time once again to spit in the fire and call the dogs.

Son Peter's enfeebled condition was a principal reason for moving. In 1861 Peter had enlisted in the war as an assistant surgeon in the Fifth Iowa Infantry. In the fall of 1864, in failing health, he was allowed to resign from the army. In her reminiscences, his wife, Mary P. Carpenter, recalled that Peter had caught a bad cold while waiting in the rain to cross the Tennessee River en route to an engagement near Chattanooga. Sickness settled in his lungs and soon turned into a form of consumption, probably

Daniel Carpenter, grandfather of Delph.

Nancy Scott Carpenter, Daniel Carpenter's second wife.

tuberculosis.[6] Detached from military service, he tried to resume a medical practice in Ohio near Newville, but his health continued to deteriorate. In 1869 he went to Colorado, hoping the dry air would heal his ailing lungs. The improvement was immediate. He filed on a homestead near the Cache la Poudre River, one mile north of Timnath and twenty miles from what would soon become the Union Colony of Greeley. Although his health suffered markedly on the return trip to Iowa, Peter gathered up his family and moved to Colorado, arriving in the winter of 1870. The first of Nathaniel Meeker's colonists began settling the town of Greeley a few months later.

Daniel was not far behind. He had read about the colony Meeker was planning near the junction of the Cache la Poudre and South Platte rivers. He knew that it would cost $155 per family for a membership in the colony and he was hopeful that the dry climate would be as healthful for his daughter Martha (Mattie) as it seemed to be for Peter. Pioneering at the age of seventy-five was most uncommon, but Daniel was lured by a cause he had embraced for many years. Meeker had declared that no liquor would be manufactured or sold in the Union Colony. Daniel was eager to spend his remaining days in a community free from demon rum. He also wanted his family to live where alcohol was forbidden and he liked what Meeker had to say about the Union Colony's salubrious climate.

In Horace Greeley's *New York Herald Tribune*, Meeker wrote that Colorado was "a decidedly healthy region; the air remarkably pure. Summer is pleasant. The winter is mild with little snow and agues are unknown. Already consumptives are going thither for their health."[7] This promotional language was also typical of editorials appearing in the early issues of the *Greeley Tribune*, most of which were written for the benefit of easterners contemplating a move to Colorado. Although much of what Meeker wrote was meant to attract paying colonists, his columns also revealed a personal struggle with his own health. He had spent about half his youth battling the ague in Illinois.[8] The new colony might benefit from a national perception that the West was a panacea for most illnesses, but he recognized the need for "invalids" to be realistic about their expectations. The dry air and altitude, he wrote, were especially beneficial to those with lung disease, even providing relief for asthmatics. But those whose infirmities were too far advanced would encounter no miracle cure in Colorado's sunny climate.[9] Tragically, Peter was among the health seekers who arrived too late. He died of pneumonia a little more than three months after Daniel arrived in Colorado with Leroy and four other children on April 12, 1871.[10]

Leroy, born in Newville, Ohio, on August 18, 1843, was already twenty-seven years old. He had attended Iowa State University for a year, attaining prominence as an orator. He also studied for a short period at Cornell College in Mt. Vernon, Iowa. Essentially, he was a farmer, his experience limited to the Cedar County area and the various enterprises of his father. One can imagine the family conversations in the fall of 1870 after Peter had returned to sing the praises of Colorado: Should Daniel and Nancy again risk their fortune and health in a new country? Would Mattie's marginal health also improve in Colorado's dry air? Was it right to leave loved ones behind in Iowa? Would the officers of the Union Colony be able to enforce restrictions against distilled spirits among the flotsam and jetsam arriving on a new frontier? The family's strong commitment to temperance and the Methodist Church must have carried a great deal of weight in their collective decision to leave home, but the attractiveness of virgin lands served by a railroad in a semiarid climate also functioned as motivation to go west. When Leroy wrote a first letter to his future wife, Martha Allen Bennett, in December of 1870, he seems to have been focusing mostly on Colorado's economic opportunities. "I have sometimes thought of taking a trip out west to look at the country," he said, "and if I could get sufficient means might get a piece of western land provided I liked the country and soil."[11] Four months later, with Daniel leading the way, the Carpenter family was westward bound on the Union Pacific Railroad.

Martha Allen Bennett was a teacher. She and Leroy had met while she was employed at Hatfield near DeWitt, Iowa. Introduced by one of Leroy's uncles from Oskaloosa, they were friends at the time Leroy moved to Colorado. In Leroy's mind, more than a casual acquaintance had developed. He signed his first letter to Martha, "Your affectionate friend." They already sensed a commonality of interests, values, and experiences.

Like the Daniel Carpenters, the Bennetts had come to Iowa from the east. Martha's father was a tanner from Virginia; her mother was the former Mary Ann Wood of Brownsville, Pennsylvania, where Martha was born April 19, 1854. She was in Iowa the following year, growing up with seven siblings on a large farm. She studied to be a teacher, receiving her

Leroy Carpenter and Martha Bennett, taken in Iowa within weeks of their 1872 wedding.

second- class certificate at the age of fifteen in February 1870 and her first-class certificate in April 1871.

With these licenses she was authorized to give instruction in the public schools of Clinton County. She could teach orthography, reading, writing, arithmetic, geography, grammar, United States history, and the theory of teaching. Intellectually gifted, Martha revealed diverse talents on a phrenological exam, popular at the time, which noted her strengths to be "conscientiousness," "mirthfulness," and "love of society." Not far behind in ranking were her "love of children," "sense of humor," "self-respect," "love of poetry and music," and "desire to travel."[12] Although totally unscientific, the analysis of Martha's character, based on the bumps on her head, proved in the long run to be amazingly accurate.

Within weeks of receiving Leroy's letter regarding his possible trip west, she replied that buying land in Colorado "would be quite a good purchase for I expect that the land that can be bought now for a small sum will be worth considerable in a few years."[13] No other statement could have revealed more clearly her far-sightedness, prudence, and entrepreneurial spirit. A sense of adventure would enable her to leave a good job and a large, loving family for the sagebrush plains of Colorado. The courtship by correspondence, more than seventy-five letters, which sustained Leroy and Martha over the next sixteen months, provides rare insight into the nineteenth-century values that eventually aided in shaping the character of their sons Delphus, Alfred, and Fred.

Leroy wrote his first letter from Greeley on April 15, 1871. He had been there for three days. The trip by train from Iowa to Colorado had taken exactly one week, much of that on the Union Pacific Railroad, which charged the Carpenters $59.70 per person for a one-way ticket. Leroy wrote that the air was clear and the nearby mountains had the "appearance of approaching rain in the summer" because of their dark color. The colony was growing, with newcomers arriving on every train. "We don't know what our opinion is yet," he wrote, "but [we] intend staying long enough to find out what it may be." A little homesickness crept into his last lines: "When I left you in DeWitt, I felt somewhat lonesome, but there are times when we may meet and times when we must part through the course of a lifetime. . . . Hoping to hear from your heretofore interesting pen, I would remain your friend, Roy Carpenter. P.S. These are the first lines I have written since our arrival here."[14]

Leroy judged that the population of Greeley was about twelve hundred. The *Greeley Tribune* stated that there were two thousand settlers in April of 1871, that "not less than 100 per week" were arriving, that town lots had increased 50 percent in value, and that there were six hundred houses in town.[15] Although the newspaper might have confused facts with promotion, no one could deny that the Carpenters had arrived at a good time to invest in land.

At first they lived in a rental house, but Leroy soon reported they had purchased and moved into a bigger home on a half-acre lot in town on May 16. They also bought eighty acres on the bench land above the river, one mile northwest of town. Daniel paid $1,350 for the town lot, house and farmland.[16] Additionally, he purchased a quarter-section of railroad land near Peter's place in Larimer County, six miles southeast of "Camp Collins," and five acres one mile west of Greeley for $250. This piece of land was served by Colony Ditch No. 3, the town's principal source of water from the Cache la Poudre River. [17] With two colony memberships at $155 each, Daniel's total outlay for land and colony rights was $2,470.[18]

Sometime in July, he paid an additional $400 for eighty acres adjoining his first eighty acres of bench land, thus controlling all of the southeast quarter of section 30-6-65. Because this land was above the Cache la Poudre River, it required irrigation water from a man-made canal. The Union Colony's Ditch No. 2 had been surveyed to pass a mile north of the Carpenter properties. It was still in the process of being built when the Carpenters were buying land.

Not surprisingly, the Carpenters, from rainy and humid Iowa, were destined to experience some difficulties before they learned about the exigencies of irrigated agriculture. And not surprisingly, Leroy's son, Delph, grew up knowing the value of perfected water rights in what is now Weld County, one of the most productive farming areas in the arid West. "Irrigation in America," Delph Carpenter reflected in 1910, "was born in Cooper Union Hall in New York, christened in Greeley June 10, 1870, and reared and rocked in the cradle of the Cache la Poudre Valley."[19]

Carpenter credited Meeker with being the West's pioneer in reclamation. However, as editor of the *Greeley Tribune*, Meeker frequently expressed his frustration with the first colonists. They were slow to take advantage of the water flowing in canals (ditches) constructed with colony funds. In his view, some settlers under Canal No. 2 were guilty of delaying construction of the proper laterals to their fields; others were wasting water, causing problems for their neighbors. Most simply expected rain. "Farming by irrigation," said Meeker, "requires such perfection in all the details that everything should be ready at every hour on any day, and this condition can be established and maintained, because there is no bad weather to cause delay. Farming here must be reduced to a system and it may become scientific." Meeker also noted that some of the farmers were losing crops because they failed to irrigate in time. "We should shape all our plans and actions," he warned, "upon the assumption that moisture from the clouds is never to be depended upon, except to germinate grain"[20]

Learning the principles of irrigated agriculture meant hard work. Meeker knew that there were areas on the north side of the Cache la Poudre River where men came on at midnight to work the water. In one place a group of men had been working for thirty-six hours straight without sleep, stopping only to eat. In other places, by contrast, Canal No. 2 was running full and nobody was using the water. Mistakes and delays were inevitable during the first year of irrigation, but Meeker firmly believed that "[the colonists] ought to study irrigation so thoroughly [as] to have every requirement so complete, that in a few years we can present to the whole world a model for others to imitate."[21] This was an admirable goal and it was ultimately achieved. But in the first year of the Union Colony, Canal No. 2 was so defective that even those who depended on it lost their crops in the summer of 1871.[22]

Leroy began work on Canal No. 2 early in May. To Martha he described the labor as strenuous. He correctly anticipated that five acres of Carpenter oats would dry up for lack of water. Ditch (canal) work, he wrote, "brings the sweat and tries the nerves sometimes too much for health." Possibly because of the strain he felt, Leroy expressed doubts about staying in Colorado, but, more optimistically, he wrote Martha that "we are in hopes to like it if possible."[23]

Like most people uninformed about irrigated agriculture, Martha could not really comprehend the significance of these ditches. How far apart were they dug, she queried? Doesn't it look odd to see them all over the country? Might she fall into them without a "carpenter" to rescue her? And would they not make an excellent place to put all the drunkards?[24] Patiently, Leroy answered her questions, recognizing that her curiosity and sense of humor revealed a growing affection for him. "When we come to

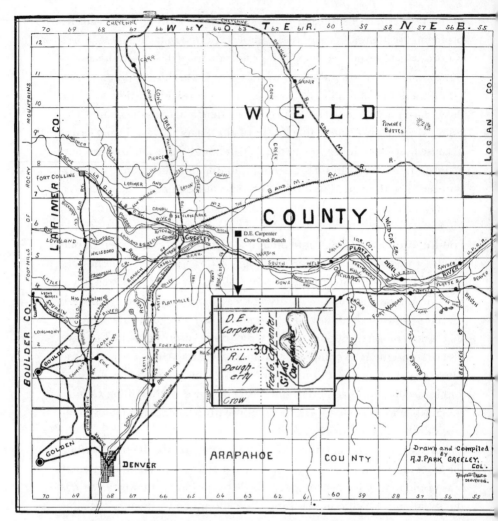

Greeley and Weld County, showing location of principal irrigation ditches and
Carpenter's Crow Creek Ranch. (From "Farming in Colorado," issued by the
Greeley Board of Trade, 1887)

these ditches," he assured her, "I may carry you over and then you may
carry me over. Will that suit you?"[25]

Leroy's teasing begged another question: How much did Martha weigh?
His interest had little to do with objectifying his future bride and much to
do with his growing understanding of what it would take for any woman

to survive in a fledgling western community. By early summer he had already declared to her an interest in marriage, expressing hope that a time would soon come when their conversations might be enjoyed without hindrances. Martha had replied that if it was God's will, such would be the case.[26] Assuming she had accepted his indirect proposal of marriage, Leroy considered himself engaged, leaving to Martha the responsibility of fixing the wedding date in the following spring when she would be of legal age (eighteen) for them to be "united in the sacred bonds of matrimony."[27]

"I have a girl in the east," he wrote, "[and] no one on earth could take her place in my affections. . . . [S]he not only has a part, but the *whole* of my heart. And having been blessed, I sometimes think providentially with my fullest ideal of having the heart and some day her hand. . . ."[28] With a commitment to marriage, he could speak to her about more personal things, such as her weight, certain that she would understand why he wanted her to be "fleshy."

"You may think it curious when I tell you that your weight is more than mine ever was," he wrote, "[b]ut a stout, hearty wife will be a good introduction to Colorado."[29] Leroy mistakenly, but hopefully, guessed Martha's weight to be in the range of 150 pounds (about ten pounds too high). When she pointed out his error, he confessed that he was more accustomed to judging the weight of men. He still believed, however, that one's healthiness was proportional to one's "fleshiness." Although Martha quite readily responded that she weighed more than when they first met, she expressed concern about being able to carry Leroy over the ditches.[30]

As Iowa newspapers reported increasing sickness, Leroy continued to worry about her well-being. He urged vaccination against smallpox (she replied that she had been vaccinated a few years previously) and quoted a stanza from the Methodist hymnal that might help her repulse the dreaded spotted fever.[31] He read with trepidation Martha's description of a new disease called "break neck" (spinal meningitis), which was being reported in Clinton County.[32] Fortunately, his worst fears were never realized. In a last letter to Martha before they were married, he expressed pleasure that she was so "fleshy," proving that she had been "well kept and that [she was indeed] ready for market. . . . I love you as I love no other female," he confessed, "and hope that my affections will retain their needed love. . . . I am glad to know that I am to have a wife of some flesh as we may be more comfortable together."[33] By that time, Leroy was convinced that

Colorado was a healthy climate. He had not been sick since his arrival and he expected Martha to be as fortunate.

Martha's comfort would require a decent residence, so Leroy began sharing house plans with her early in their correspondence. The first Carpenter house, he told her, would be built on the westernmost eighty-acre parcel, the one that Daniel bought first. "[I]t is near town," Leroy noted, "and a little nearer the railroad, being a few rods over $1/4$ of a mile from the tracks. [We] want to put a house on it instead of the other piece, as before spoken of, to make the homestead good. This is intended for us (you and I)."[34] Construction commenced in August on a five-room house, including a parlor, kitchen, two bedrooms, and a loft. It was completed in October. The entire family, including Leroy's sister Sarah, moved into the house in the fall of 1871. This is "our house," Leroy wrote Martha. His parents would leave "any time that you and I need the house." Of course, that would mean that the newlyweds would have to care for themselves, but Leroy looked forward to the challenge. "[T]o once have a home of our own," he told Martha, "with a feeling that each other is loved on the part of both, that certainly must be happiness."[35]

When a second residence could be built on the adjoining eighty-acre parcel for his parents, Leroy ventured, "We will make them hustle out of [our house] in a hurry, won't we, Martha?"[36] For the time being, Leroy could only boast of the location and convenience of the new home. Situated about $1\frac{1}{4}$ miles from the Methodist Church, with a view looking down on Greeley, the river flowing about half-way between house and town, their place occupied a prominent position on the reputedly "wild frontier."[37] "To tell the truth," Leroy told Martha, "you and I have the nicest farm to live in when we get it fixed that is to be found in Greeley Colony."[38] Sister Mattie sent Martha the house plans. "How conveniently it is arranged," Martha wrote Leroy, "and how pleasantly situated from your description. I think you have a very good idea of comfort in the laying out of houses."[39]

Martha was right. The house endures today as the Union Colony House in Centennial Village at Island Grove Park. It has been restored by the Greeley Questers in cooperation with the City of Greeley.* Leroy and Martha lived in this house for ten years with neither electricity nor plumb-

---

* The Wesley Sargent family, last legal owners of the house, may have suggested that it be moved to the city, but when Donald Carpenter sought permission for the move, the owner of record was Ken Monfort. In 1976 the Carpetner house went to its new location.

The house in which Delph Carpenter was born, presently located in Centennial Village, Greeley, Colo.

ing. They pumped their water for cooking and washing from an outside well and bathed on Saturday nights in a galvanized tub filled with water warmed by the stove.[40] It was home for them and their three children until they moved nearby to Daniel's old place in 1881.

Daniel's house, a two-story building, was first mentioned in the *Greeley Tribune* when it was in the planning stages during the winter of 1872. The newspaper reported that Daniel was importing forest and fruit trees of all kinds to plant around the house.[41] Daniel and Nancy moved in during August of 1872. They remained at this location until 1881, when Daniel sold the property to Leroy and moved into the town of Greeley. Daniel died in 1884 at the age of eighty-eight. He was recognized as one of two veterans of the War of 1812 to settle in Colorado and a man whose faith in the future of irrigated farming was inherited by his sons.[42] Leroy sold the other eighty acres and farmed his father's place until 1926 when he, too, moved into town.[43]

Leroy's and Martha's lengthy courtship correspondence provoked discussion of themes that prepared them well for the challenges of married life in Colorado. Good housing in an untested climate was important and Leroy did his best not to frighten Martha during the unexpectedly cold and snowy winter of 1871–72. However, Meeker's published views of Colorado's moderate weather soon appeared irresponsible. Early in December, heavy snows kept the trains from getting through from the east. Temperatures plunged below zero and range-dependent cattlemen began suffering considerable losses.

By January a foot of snow lay on the ground, trains were snowed in and Daniel had to purchase two bobsleds just to get around. Brother Silas remembered snow three feet deep, one hundred days of continuous sleighing, and range cattle that had to be forced out of the colony's enclosures.[44] By the end of January, Leroy reported to Martha a thermometer reading of forty degrees below zero, trains unable to move and a volunteer group of one hundred men from Greeley heading out to rescue snow-bound passengers. It was, indeed, a bad winter, requiring Leroy to heat the house with expensive coal (seven dollars per ton), because wood was so scarce. A new gristmill in Greeley was producing buckwheat, cornmeal, and snowflake flour, but meat was in short supply, unless one could hunt antelope and jack rabbits. Unfortunately, Leroy confessed to Martha, "I am not a hunter; you must wait until I learn (if I ever can)."[45] Her response triggered an exchange about women's rights.

"I guess we can find enough to eat in Colorado," she said, "and as I stoop to eat what pigs do, we can have some corn bread and you can teach me to use the gun . . . I can do the hunting and you do the work in the house. Women's rights, you know."[46] Leroy answered, "Yes, my dear, you may learn to shoot, for I want you to know how to defend yourself and shoot game if I am not at home. . . . I believe in giving the woman some chance."[47]

More than marksmanship was involved in this exchange. Both Susan B. Anthony and Elizabeth Cady Stanton had lectured in Greeley in June. Leroy may have attended. He frequently wrote about the intellectual stimulation provided by lecturers at the Lyceum. But whether or not he was present for the women's talk, the *Greeley Tribune*, which he read, praised them modestly for their speaking ability and commitment to a cause.[48] The newspaper also reported that ninety-eight women voted in the post office election in December, lauding them for being "well dressed and well behaved."[49] Obviously, the fear of suffragette radicals who might upset the status quo was as much an issue in Greeley as in other parts of the country. Nevertheless, Leroy professed an open mind. He reported attending discussions of women's rights and inquired of Martha her views on the subject. Her reply reflected both the delicacy of the subject and the importance it represented for two people contemplating marriage.

> You desire my opinion of women's rights. I have never exercised my thinking powers very much upon the subject but think that if women can retain their modesty and be esteemed as highly as true women are by their fellow mortals that they may vote. I do not think it will make much difference except in the liquor question. That, I think, would receive a severe blow from the increase in the number of voters. And I certainly think women ought to receive as good compensation for a certain amount of labor performed equally as good as a man. If every woman votes as her husband or parents, of course [it] will only double the number of votes on each side and that is all, but if every, or the majority, of women vote as their own minds dictate, I am not prepared to say what would be the results, *except* in [the] liquor question.[50]

More than suffrage, Martha was concerned about temperance. "I certainly admire the principles upon which the colony [is] founded," she wrote. "How pleasant it must be to live where there is no drunkenness and where poor society is not known."[51] Leroy agreed. He had joined the Good Templars when he was at Iowa State University, but he no longer attended their meetings. He disagreed with them only on their adamant opposition to drinking cider. "I have never thought it wrong to enjoy the reviving taste of good cider," he wrote Martha. "What is your opinion?"

Martha's response echoed conservative thinking of the times. The question one has to ask, she replied, is whether or not the cider is fresh, because if it is old, drinking it is "something like forming that habit of drinking tea or coffee. If the habit is once formed, it is hard to break. . . . Cider is something that . . . may create an appetite for something stronger."[52] Having once belonged to the Good Templars, she no longer went to meetings either, not only because their lodge was distant but because they did not seem to accomplish much in the matter of temperance. "I often think that if everyone would carry a pledge with them and induce others to sign and thus help them to keep their pledge," she opined, "there would be more good accomplished than there is by some of the orders."[53]

The temperance issue was of great importance to Martha because of her deeply held religious views. She was not fanatical or unreasonable, but the church and her faith were at the heart of the exchanges on marriage that she and Leroy pursued in their correspondence. Both were avid Methodists. Leroy was described as a "consistent Methodist, but tolerant with all other religions, firmly believing in the salvation of all devotees of all creeds."[54] He had a rich bass voice, inherited from his father, and he enjoyed singing in church and with his family. To Martha he wrote with great pleasure regarding his beliefs. "I have always regarded the Christian faith as being one of the greatest of responsibilities to act out in life," he told her. "This is, perhaps, the principal reason [for] my not being a professor of religion."[55] More of a Deist than Martha, he saw "the continual evidence of divine power" in nature. Even before he met Martha, he described the world as "continuously changing from death to life and from life to death and yet in all the workings of this vast machine, not one particle of matter is lost."[56] Leroy attended Sunday school, supported the construction of the first Methodist Church in Greeley, read the Scriptures regularly in his home and confessed to Martha that he was only a "poor erring mortal," who had "often thought when thinking of [himself] how strikingly true is the Scripture when it tells of the depravity of the human heart."[57]

Martha was determined to cultivate her own religious commitments after she and Leroy married. She wrote of her sadness when having to miss Sunday school because of bad weather or distance from home. Her love of Sunday school was so strong, she confessed, "if you don't take me, what shall I do?"[58] Singing in church was also a big part of her life. She was an alto, inheriting a beautiful voice from her father, who sang a perfect tenor at morning worship. She played a melodeon on which she took lessons from her sister Lucy.[59] When she came to Greeley she brought it with her. The primary grades of Sunday school and the Methodist Missionary Society occupied much of her time until her death in 1930.

The marriage Leroy and Martha planned was to be a sacred and solemn event, not a "sport" as some young folks regarded it. "I look upon marriage," Leroy wrote, "as the all important act of life. . . . It certainly is the *most* important ceremony that we go through on earth (aside from religious exercises)." It should not be entered into, he concluded, without considerable reflection and both parties should consent to a union based not on property, but on the admirable virtues of their respective partners.[60]

"Ah, yes!" Martha replied, "every day of our lives is a leaf in the great book of responsibility and more so than ever when we fill it with a record of our union to another for life. . . . I only hope," she added, "that I may be able to return your affections in such a manner that neither of us will have occasion to ever regret our union. . . . I am far, very far, from perfection and you may be surprised to find many mistakes attending my course through this life. . . . but one thing [is] certain: if both of us live to make others happy (by others I mean each other as well as our friends), we shall not see such great faults as we might."[61]

For two people, so inexperienced in matters of love, Leroy and Martha wooed each other with an amazing combination of seriousness, candor, and levity. Only a month after Leroy had embarked for Colorado, he told Martha of his hope that the day would come when they would be able to sustain their conversations face to face. Martha ventured that if such were to happen, "it would have to be God's will," because [we] "know not what the future may bring but we can place all our affairs in God's hands and feel that they are safe."[62] In Leroy she had found an "honest and upright man" whom she wanted to "accept as my companion." It would take her some time to get ready for marriage, because of her youth and because she had not "prepared as many things as a good many have for housekeeping." Some teased her with the nickname "grandmother," she confessed, due to her methodical and perfectionist ways, but she hoped to be ready for marriage by the end of April 1872.[63]

Leroy was impatient, but he recognized the need to get crops in the ground before returning to Iowa. The April date would be satisfactory, but the fires of love heated up in him during the cold winter of 1871 and 1872. Planning a trip to the mountains to cut some fence poles, he told Martha that he would like to have her along to keep from freezing. "[I]f you were along, I think you would have to waken me . . . as I enjoy staying in bed on cold mornings."[64] He imagined what it would be like to share his affections with Martha, sitting by her side; a pleasure of which he would never tire. "[I]f kind Providence permits," he wrote, "I hope to have both [your] kisses and affections" sometime soon.

After attending a wedding in Greeley where bride and groom kissed after the ceremony, Leroy confessed that he, too, had kissed the bride, as was the custom. He recalled that he had played kissing games as a child, but he now believed that kissing should be "between lovers when by themselves, [a]nd suitable to children when playing ring around the rosey. . . .What do you think, Miss Bennett?" he asked.[65]

Martha replied that she had no objection to a bride and groom kissing, "but now you better not kiss another bride very soon," she admonished, "unless you ask me. You see, you must love, honor and obey. I always kiss my friends when I meet them (ladies of course) and sometimes the *men* kiss *me*, but I do not like the kissing bees. . . . If anyone kisses me, I want to feel that they mean it for reasons of friendship."[66] Having broached the subject, Leroy asked if he would be allowed to kiss Martha when they meet. "Yes," she replied, "you may have a kiss when you come if it is not too public a place."[67]

In the final weeks before their wedding, Leroy admitted that while he had not read the entire ceremony in the Ritual of Marriage, he opposed a lengthy service. He considered five minutes sufficient time to tie the knot.[68] Tactfully, Martha replied that she would like the ceremony to be long enough to say all that was necessary, even though she had not attended many weddings and did not know how long that would be.[69] That was fine with Leroy. He expressed love for his "little school marm," the woman he now referred to as his "sweetest treasure," and he hoped that his affections would continue to multiply after they were married. "True love," he told Martha, "should only grow deeper the longer we are together."[70]

After sixteen months of correspondence Leroy and Martha were as well prepared for a life together as two people courting each other in the same town over the same period of time. In some ways, the love they professed in writing and their agreement to preserve the letters for posterity served as an additional commitment to the vows they were about to take. "I have all of your letters," Martha said, "and my portfolio was so full I had to put some of them in a box for safekeeping. Your mind and mine are alike about keeping them, or each other's. It may be pleasant to look them over some day which will be a very pleasant way of refreshing our memories of former days."[71]

They had addressed significant issues of companionship, ethics, and daily living. Combined with mutually complimentary family backgrounds, they were ready for both the unknown challenges of marriage and the Colorado frontier. Their correspondence had been a veritable "feast" for Martha, "richer than gold" to Leroy.[72] Letters from Martha, noted Leroy, "seem so much as if you were talking to me."[73] "My letters to you," he said, are yours forever and you may do what you want with them. I will try to keep yours in my own hands. No one to my knowledge has ever read one of your letters sent to me. They always seemed too sacred to my feelings to show other eyes to read them. I want to put them in a bundle and lay them where they will be safe as I expect to keep them through life. And if, when I am gone, others wish to know how to write a good, sensible love letter, they might do so by reading one of those letters from Miss M. A. Bennett to this boy. Good evening and good bye to corresponding.[74]

The next day he was on the Kansas Pacific Railroad heading to Iowa by way of Kansas City and St. Louis, a journey that would take him a few days longer than his trip west, but one that was cheaper than what he would have had to pay on the Union Pacific. He had written Martha's brother-in-law, H. H. Green, as she had requested, asking him to perform the marriage ceremony. He purchased a new suit, matching the dress sample Martha had sent him, and planned to take out a marriage license when he arrived in Clinton. He expressed two principal concerns: (1) the amount of time they should spend as newlyweds, visiting friends and relatives in Iowa; and (2) his rapidly tanning skin which he feared might make him appear "as dark . . . as the red man that not long since roamed over these plains."[75]

Neither concern delayed wedding plans. Martha Bennett and Leroy Carpenter were married on April 25, 1872. Except for the normal jitters associated with any marriage, the small ceremony of undetermined length conducted at the old Bennett homestead occurred without incident. After more than a month of visiting, the couple journeyed to Colorado to begin farming and to raise a family. Their partnership lasted fifty-five years. Leroy died in 1927, Martha in 1930. As with most of the early settlers in the Union Colony, they endured many privations, including a plague of grasshoppers that destroyed Daniel's fortune for the second time. But their hardships were tempered by participation in church affairs, literary societies, and local social functions. They were known for their singing talents and for generous hospitality provided to newly arrived immigrants in the community. And they rejoiced in the healthy births of three male children.

Alfred Bennett Carpenter was born first on March 6, 1873. Four years later came Delphus Emory Carpenter, on May 13,1877. A third son, Fred George Carpenter, arrived on August 15, 1881. Leroy and Martha instructed their children to be educated, literate, and proud. Leroy taught his sons the importance of forceful oratory. He took son Delph to the fields and made him practice speaking in a loud voice from a stump.[76] From both parents the boys learned about the dignity of labor, what their father referred to as "the exercise of energy." Leroy taught them that success came to those who maximized their mental abilities. "[W]e must make our wills coincide with justice and judgment," Leroy reasoned, "and undertake nothing without hope of ultimate success and when undertaken, imbue into all our actions a spirit of never fail."[77] Or, never despair! Progress was possible in all things, he taught them, but one had to have patience and a sense of justice when dealing with others.[78]

By example, Leroy and Martha showed son Delph that success in life required very hard work and attention to detail. Using an especially appropriate metaphor, Leroy spoke of little things as if they were like streams turning into mighty rivers. "The great wonders of the world," he wrote "are the result of energetic and persevering people [who] have formed them with their untiring zeal and untiring efforts."[79] But one must be tactful and modest. Approaching life with humility, rather than with bravado and overconfidence, would produce greater results than what Leroy referred to as "Yankee forwardness."[80] He and Martha agreed that the feigned superiority of certain easterners tended to produce discord. Leroy believed that with the arrival of increasing numbers of immigrants from the East, the potential for conflict in Colorado would revolve around water rights. With this in mind, he urged his son to "try and conceive of some plan whereby litigation over the water of the streams will be brought to the least possible trouble."[81] Honorable negotiation was what he had in mind. Eventually, Delph Carpenter developed his father's suggestions into the idea of interstate river compacts. By then, he, too, was a staunch Republican, a conservative in public and private affairs, a committed member of the Methodist Church, and a part-time rancher who enjoyed raising livestock to relieve the stress of legal work.

Thanks to his parents, he also possessed a strong sense of pride in the family lineage, the accomplishments of the Union Colony pioneers, and the importance of his agricultural roots. In 1920, at the age of forty-three, already experienced by appearances before the United States Supreme Court and considered in some circles to be the best candidate for the U.S. Senate, Delph asked a reporter to describe him as a simple man of the soil.

Reacting to the suggestion that he be referred to as the "Oracle of Greeley," Delph's response reveals much of the essence of his parents' nurturing:

> I want to help by improving the live stock of my country, by making farms where prairie existed before, by living and conversing with the toilers and knowing how they feel and what they desire. Their lives are my lives. My duties as an interstate water lawyer are to defend the very areas from which they "draw suck." I could not successfully represent them unless I knew them as they are and I would not care to represent them if I thereby should be denied the privilege of frequently returning to the primitive. After all, I am my birth and original environment personified. I am just a plain cow puncher, farmer and cattle raiser with all the loves and hates of my breed. I have labored long and hard to be an honorable lawyer and I try to live in my professional work in the constant atmosphere and thoughtfulness for generations yet to come in states now in the making and greater to be. But I could not, as I have said, fully realize that which is to take place or why present conditions are as they are, unless I kept my being in touch with the source of my life and breeding. So, please play me up modestly and let the credit rest where it belongs.[82]

Although Delph Carpenter was very ambitious, and sometimes disappointed when his good intentions, meticulous research, and consideration of others appeared to be unappreciated, he never forgot the example of his parents and grandparents. Unwilling to surrender when his health seemed to be getting the best of him, he continued to make a mark in his chosen profession long after he was bedridden in 1934 with symptoms of Parkinson's Disease. The Carpenters' pioneer lineage was a legacy he valued and one to which he turned frequently for strength in difficult moments.

CHAPTER 2

Education and the Beginnings of a Career

From the blackest clouds come the brightest rains.
The tree that is most exposed to wind and storm is the strongest.
The best fish come from the purest waters.
Circumstances must be turned and are not anxious to turn themselves.

—DELPH CARPENTER, 1897 DIARY

The Union Colony into which Delph Carpenter was born in 1877 was emerging from difficult times and entering a stage of relatively stable growth. Simultaneous with the end of locust attacks in 1876, extension and repairs on Canal No. 2 were completed to assure farmers a more reliable supply of water. The town of Greeley won a seven-year battle with Evans to be the county seat of Weld County as the population of the entire colony approached two thousand.

Most interesting to David Boyd, an early settler, was that life in Greeley seemed to take on different characteristics with the beginning of the 1880s. He described the first ten years as a "period of strife, struggle, experiment; of more or less of doubt and uncertainty; the last [decade, 1880–90] of fruition, attainment, definite realization and confident hope."[1] He associated this mood shift with the 1879 death of the Union Colony's founder,

Nathan C. Meeker, at the hands of Ute Indians. The patriarch's demise signaled the end of an era and the beginning of more broadly based economic development. Boyd also acknowledged that the colony's new sense of confidence resulted from the State Assembly's decision to establish a system of water administration appropriate to a semiarid region.

Colorado's recognition of the doctrine of prior appropriation in its constitution, statutes, and court cases assured Greeley farmers protection of their water rights. They were encouraged to invest more confidently in Weld County lands. Ironically, this principle of prior appropriation, which Carpenter embraced from an early age and defended as an attorney, required considerable reevaluation on his part when Wyoming sued Colorado in 1911 over rights to the Laramie River.[2] But before being selected lead attorney in that case, practical and legal experience taught him that the preservation of water rights as private property required enforcement of the priority doctrine in Colorado's district courts.

The most significant event leading to the establishment of what came to be known as the "Colorado Doctrine" of prior appropriation occurred in the summer of 1874. Up to this point, conflict over water was minimal, but when agricultural development in the Fort Collins Agricultural Colony occurred simultaneously with a drought, the Cache la Poudre River suffered lower flows than had been experienced since 1863. Greeley's principal ditch intakes were left, literally, high and dry. With forest fires burning in the mountains, "red-thighed Rocky Mountain locusts" consuming crops,[3] and orders from the trustees of the Union Colony to shut down Canal No. 2 for two days a week to benefit Greeley's town residents, farmers rebelled. They insisted Greeley's right to the reduced supply of Cache la Poudre water was greater than that of Fort Collins, because Greeley had been settled before its upstream neighbor.[4] Meeker joined the outcry and persuaded the court to issue an injunction against Fort Collins. Writing in the *Greeley Tribune*, he demanded the legal recognition of prior appropriation, "a doctrine partially formulated by the miners of California and Colorado and . . . mentioned in a territorial law of 1864."[5]

Consistent with the views of John Wesley Powell, whose revolutionary *Report on the Lands of the Arid Region* would be presented to Congress in the spring of 1877,[6] Meeker argued for the consolidation of all ditch rights on the Cache la Poudre and the appointment of a "superintendent" whose job it would be to apportion equitably the river's water to all users, including the Fort Collins people.[7] He also proposed building reservoirs to catch floodwaters and a moratorium on further diversions from the river.

One week after publication of his editorial, forty men representing twenty ditches on the Cache la Poudre met at the Eaton schoolhouse near present-day Windsor to hash out their differences. The Greeley people argued in favor of a river commissioner who would apportion water on the basis of prior appropriation. Fort Collins wanted apportionment based on need and claimed superiority because of the town's upstream location. Greeleyites countered with the argument they could and would compete with Fort Collins by constructing diversion points higher up on the river. Such a result would involve the two communities in a water war that might bankrupt them both.[8] At long last, and in return for suspension of the injunction, Fort Collins agreed to let more water flow down the river. A peaceful end to the quarrel was aided by the arrival on July 20 of enough rain to raise the level of the river and moisten the surrounding soil to a depth of five inches. This dispute ended, but Greeley farmers were scarred by the experience. They were determined not to go through a similar conflict again.

Two Weld County representatives were appointed to Colorado's nine-man constitutional committee on irrigation, manufacturing and agriculture. The committee's report to the convention was partially revised prior to adoption, but Article XVI, sections 5 and 6 of the approved constitution, recognized that the unappropriated waters of streams were public property subject to appropriation based on priority of diversion.[9] By 1876, therefore, the Colorado Doctrine of prior appropriation was constitutionally established.[10]

Meeker was satisfied with these results, but there was no administrative system in place to execute the broad constitutional principles. When Benjamin H. Eaton announced plans to construct a much larger ditch parallel to Canal No. 2 with a diversion point farther up the Cache la Poudre River, Meeker called for a meeting of water users to develop a plan that would bind all ditches to the same regulations. Delegates from twenty-nine ditch companies representing the South Platte, Cache la Poudre, St. Vrain, Big Thompson, and Boulder rivers gathered in Denver in December 1878. Some were opposed to any legislation that might impede their freedom or customary water use. Any new rule was generally unwelcome to pioneers who saw themselves as individualists, "antagonistic to laws and institutions which would control their lives and property."[11] But a majority at the meeting recognized that irrigation required a certain amount of subordination of the individual to the group. That was the nature of a community based on irrigated agriculture.

After protracted debate, committee representatives approved a "memorial" that eventually became "An Act to Regulate the Use of Water for Irrigation, and Providing for Settling the Priority of Rights Thereto."[12] This law created ten water districts, authorized the governor to appoint water commissioners for each district, and gave the commissioners authority to shut down the headgates of any ditch "which, in time of scarcity of water, shall not be entitled to water by reason of the priority of the rights of others below them on the same stream."[13] Water users were required to provide commissioners with proof of their decrees. In 1881, the Colorado General Assembly established a larger administrative category. Water divisions were "made up of all the water districts within one large drainage basin." The law also created the office of state engineer "to supervise the water districts and the water companies within them" and to measure the flow of existing streams.[14] The basics of Colorado's water administration system were complete in 1887 when the Assembly authorized the appointment of division engineers for each water division. Their job was to supervise commissioners and coordinate priorities within their districts. They were empowered to order cessation of diversion in a district with a junior priority if limited water was available on the stream.[15]

This Colorado Doctrine, copied in some form by most of the arid and semiarid western states, was the innovative response of Colorado water users to an environment in which irrigated agriculture dominated the life of its pioneer settlers. They had borrowed some ideas from the miners and the Mormons, but the administrative structure under which they would operate was developed in Colorado after the Greeley–Fort Collins dispute. The Colorado Doctrine gave irrigated agriculture a boost in the 1880s and propelled Greeley into a more confident stage of growth, easily measured by a variety of new developments.

By the 1880s, reservoir and canal owners found heretofore unavailable financial backing from foreign investors and eastern banks. New farms sprang up where water was made available through privately developed irrigation systems. Brick buildings replaced wood and adobe structures in town and the more prosperous citizens began building elegant homes.

Two opera houses offered large seating capacities for local performances and transient professionals. The Greeley Board of Trade organized to promote Greeley and Weld County, to "induce railroads to extend their lines into the city [and to] convince manufacturers to locate their companies [in Greeley]."[16] The first gas lighting was installed in entrepreneur Benjamin H. Eaton's house in 1882. A few years later the city water supply was connected to an artesian well, and the Greeley Waterworks installed fifty hydrants to protect urban residents. Boilers of a new electric light company began to generate electricity and the town's first sewer system was installed.

Even with these improvements, life was not easy for most farmers. Those residing in the potato district north of Greeley suffered frequent crop losses due to a fungus that caused blight and rust on the vines. Although the value of farmlands had increased, Meeker noted during his last visit to the colony in 1879 that farmers were not making much money and hired hands were few and far between.[17] Bricklayers were getting as much as six dollars a day. A new school had been erected but only 77 percent of the eligible student population attended. Building the town library was delayed, because of demands placed on the budget by urgent repairs to Canal Number 2.[18] These were the growing pains the Union Colony experienced as its people learned to adapt to irrigated farming. From an historical perspective, the progress made in ten years was remarkable.

The Carpenters benefited from this progress. Their lands had doubled in value and they were farming them intensely. Leroy Carpenter was doing well enough on his eighty acres in 1880 to send Martha, Alfred, seven years old, and Delphus, three, back to Iowa for a visit. It was Martha's first trip home since arriving in Greeley with her husband in 1872. She was delighted to return to her family, but the separation was hard on both of them.

Leroy wrote to her that he had cried when they left on the train, and Martha replied that she was unable to hold back the tears when she reflected on his loneliness.[19] Nevertheless, she took advantage of the return to Iowa to catch up on family doings, and she promoted Colorado's advantages as a booster of the young Centennial State: better crop yields, better quality of wheat, the ability to "control rainfall," a healthy climate, and an overall good society. Although she noted for Leroy's benefit how much cheaper everything was in Davenport, she complained about the heavy rains, attended to some dental work, and concluded that she much preferred a Colorado dam to the one the Iowa dentist put in her mouth.

Fully aware how much Leroy missed the children, Martha sent him photographs and little messages from the boys. Young Delphus missed his father and wrote him a letter, saying that he wanted to kiss his "Papa." This was the first of thousands of letters he would write later in life as Colorado's interstate streams commissioner. As a child away from home, he only wanted his mother to report that he had been good. She cooperated, of course, noting at the same time that her second-born son could be both naughty and charming when dealing with others. In comparison with his more serious older brother, she wrote, Delphus was endlessly curious, a "fiery boy" with a good supply of pluck.

Leroy told Martha he loved hearing from her. "I think more of you than [of] my life, I sometimes think. Tell Delphus I read his letter and thought of my little boy away in Davenport. If anyone doubts as to whose boy he is, tell them I have some claim." He encouraged his wife to stay as long as she liked, but he missed his family. After they had been gone for two months, he told Martha that he had cleaned out the ditch, that he was irrigating wheat, that he had put out fifteen acres of potatoes, and that he now had a hired hand. Things were going well enough in Greeley for her to know that this did not have to be her last visit to Iowa. "I often think of you and those dear boys," he wrote "and if you still enjoy home instead of visiting, of course to have you all here would be pleasant."

Martha knew that her real home was now Colorado. "I am beginning to feel my visit more than over," she lamented, "and am getting restless to get through and get home." She had visited the grave of her father, showed the boys the Mississippi River, and spent some time with her mother and favorite sister, Lucy. "I enjoy seeing my friends and relatives," she told Leroy, "but find no place like home."

Around the middle of July the travelers returned. It had been a good trip. The following summer a third son, Fred George Carpenter, was born. Their family now complete, Leroy decided to purchase his father's adjacent eighty acres with its larger house. He sold his own farm. Daniel moved to town where the infirmities of his advanced years could be better attended. The old pioneer died in 1884 at the age of eighty-eight. Leroy and Martha worked their new farm, one of the best in the county, until

Delph Carpenter (left) and his older brother, Alfred.

1925, their three sons providing whatever help they could when not attending the local schools.

Most of what is known about Delph Carpenter's education is anecdotal, but enough evidence has been preserved to note that he was a good learner who enjoyed debate, history, and writing. Carpenter's report cards for sixth through ninth grades reveal scores fluctuating between high Cs and low Bs. His teachers noted he had some difficulty in mathematics and geography, but his parents showed little concern. They knew he was learning to balance "book learning" with other experiences on the farm, that he savored time spent in the outdoors, developing a love of nature that would remain an important aspect of his character. Both forms of education, his parents believed, helped Carpenter acquire a balanced set of values.

On Christmas Day, 1887, Leroy and Martha offered their love and encouragement by writing in Delph's autograph book:

Martha: "Work for some good, be it ever so slowly; Cherish some flower, be it ever so lowly; Labor, all labor is noble and holy."

Leroy: "To Delphus our son, your race of life is now begun; With right and birth and manly vim, in life's race you will surely win."[20]

When Carpenter entered Greeley High School, Leroy and Martha advised him to be patient, to do good, to respect the dignity of labor, to have a goal in life, and to be optimistic about his chances of success. It would be hard to deny the impact of this counsel as Delph matured under the influence of more demanding teachers. Although he continued to do poorly in mathematics and received an F in Latin in his sophomore year, the worst his teachers could say about Carpenter was that he "whispers in class."[21] At the same time, his individuality began to emerge and his grades soon responded accordingly. He developed a passion for oratory and essay writing. Classmates elected him secretary of the Parliamentary Practice Association, in which he developed views on the importance of gentlemanly conduct and self-discipline. The organization's goal was to master Robert's *Rules of Order*. Membership required payment of ten cents per month and a promise to "restrain . . . from bullheadedness, profane language and all other exhibitions of anger or ungentlemanly conduct, [respecting] the rights of others in the Society."[22] In his spare time, Carpenter wrote essays and poems on love, poverty, evolution, and the importance of having a good dog. He penned a short story titled "The Fatal Gate," about a heroic cowboy who tamed outlaws. The purple prose could have

Delph Carpenter, age ten.

been mistaken for the flowery writing in one of Ned Buntline's dime novels, but the theme fit with Carpenter's uncomplicated view of right and wrong, good and evil.[23]

On behalf of his 1896 class, Carpenter spoke at graduation on the theme of "Liberty." He described man's historic struggle and ultimate victory over iniquity. He pointed to the valiant triumphs of the Jews and Greeks over their oppressors, the uprising of Roman gladiators against their masters, and the power of man to humble the most destructive forces of nature. But even with such triumphs, he noted, man needed the inspiration that comes from liberty, what Carpenter defined as "a dissatisfaction with his present state and a longing to find his nobler self." With optimism and adolescent naiveté merging in a moment of oratorical passion, Carpenter understood man to be evolving in an upward direction, "forcing each vanquished foe to aid his onward march . . . until at last with one grand shout of victory [all the nations will] reach the summit and with cheer upon cheer they [will] blend their tattered ensigns into one grand banner. . . . And now," Delph challenged his audience, "will you and I each strive in his own narrow way in this huge struggling throng, or will we put shoulder to shoulder and building on true citizenship, move on . . . with the tide of human progress, until side by side with the nations of the past and present we bear our banner pure and spotless on up the crest of glory" to live "in love and peace—and liberty."[24]

Such a speech might better remain hidden from critical eyes were it not for its expression of struggle, challenge, sacrifice, and ultimate victory. This was Carpenter's formula for success, how he viewed the life experience. It was inherited from his pioneer ancestors and it was accentuated by a middle child's tendency to be determined in pursuit of worldly accomplishments. With equal fervor, Carpenter learned to play the role of peacemaker and negotiator. He abhorred conflict, but he often found himself in the position of defending principles that he would only abandon with great reluctance.[25] Some saw stubbornness in him. Others admired his integrity. Above all, his energy and enthusiasm for hard work were directed at making himself a better person.

At this moment of graduation from Greeley High School, Carpenter was confident of his ability to obtain the education that would enable him to practice water law. He was willing to attend a university at night if necessary, and he would pay the tuition out of his own pocket. His father told him that there were no books on the subject of water. If he wanted this career, he would have to write his own texts.[26] He would also have to continue helping out on the family farm. Carpenter was happy with the plan. He liked to think of himself as a "rancher," and for reasons of practicality, he preferred evening classes because they were taught by working attorneys. The University of Denver, affiliated with the Methodist Church, accepted him. In the fall of 1896 he began his legal studies.

Over the next three years, Carpenter was fully engaged in the urban law school experience. He was nominated secretary of an organization of classmates who wanted experience in legal discussion and debate through the organization of moot courts. He organized a "quasi-employment bureau" for all university students needing work, not just those who were favored by the Methodist Church because of their religious affiliation. And in his spare time, he served as an "extra" reporter on the *Denver Republican* newspaper.[27]

When not studying, debating, reporting, farming, or helping fellow students, Delph clerked in a law office where he earned high praise from Denver attorney Arthur M. Edwards. In a letter to the *Greeley Tribune*, June 9, 1899, Edwards commended Carpenter for carrying a heavy course load while traveling throughout Colorado and Wyoming, attending to his farm work, earning high grades, and practicing law in the lower courts of the city. "He is noted for his capacity for work," Edwards commented, "both in matter of quantity and quality and his honesty and exemplary habits make him worthy of any trust which may be imposed upon him. He is liberal minded, generous and true as steel and it is to be hoped that the people of Greeley will give him the support which he deserves."[28]

Carpenter frequently analyzed himself. With ambitions to be in politics, he sought the recognition and endorsement of professionals, politicians, and community leaders. He ruminated constantly on the meaning of life and what real success would demand of him. He disclosed his deepest feelings in essays and poems, some written at the University of Denver. These musings unveiled his priorities and described the loneliness he felt for being so driven to achieve. Occasionally, he yearned for home and a chance to shoot ducks, but more frequently he challenged himself to be better, to "leave all fun and day-dreaming alone and study, study, study until I become a record smasher. There's always a place on top for the well meaning and learned," he wrote, "and that's where I'll be, that's sure. There's no use talking. I can't apply myself when [other students] are sputtering

Delph Carpenter irrigating the family farm.

Delph Carpenter as a law student, University of Denver.

around and telling jokes, laughing at my hard work and plaguing me about my hard studying."[29] Great men, he believed, are those who come "from the middle walks of life—whose lives have been molded by nature's and labor's own crude hand and who on their crude foundation have laid a lasting structure, [such men as] Lincoln, Garfield, Grant, Napoleon, Caesar, Spartacus, Moses and many others."[30]

In moments of self-reflection, he struggled over the meaning of God and nature. He could hear "golden harps and cherubs with tiny trumpets and above all the glory of God" when the Trinity Church organ was playing. But man's cruelty and inhumanity in the city disturbed him. In an essay titled, "Delph the Sunnyside Kid," he deplored how friends and relatives treated each other; how the love of God and nature were "smothered by the cram and press of everyday life." Nature's musical balm he found in the mountains, where running streams, the deep bass of rolling clouds, and the wind in the trees offered solace. "Can there be such a God as nature is?" he asked. "Is she not the foundation of all life and in [H]im do we not find the answer to all our perplexities?" If the source of true happiness was the act of making others happy, as opposed to the pursuit of "cold gold," Carpenter reasoned, one must avoid self-gratification and selfishness and search for a way to make the world a better place. Circumstances must be manipulated, he believed, because they do not alone and of themselves create opportunities. In sum, a successful man is one who effects changes courageously, winning from others the twin accolades of respect and honor.[31]

Carpenter's quest for success began when he received his law degree from the University of Denver in June 1899. While serving his clerkship as trial attorney for the office of Edwards and Royse in Denver, he was admitted to the Colorado Bar Association. Soon thereafter, Edwards encouraged Carpenter to become familiar with a high-profile probate case in which Edwards was acting as attorney for the plaintiffs. It was a chance, Edwards believed, for Carpenter to launch his career in the public limelight.

Warren Currier, at one time a Supreme Court judge in Missouri, died in 1892. He left an estate valued at $191,000 and was said to have owned "nearly one-half of the town of Greeley" at the time of his death.[32] Edwards represented Currier's sons, who sued the executors of the Currier estate for "gross mismanagement," accusing them of shoddy accounting methods, "commingling principal and income" in their reports to the court and not providing beneficiaries with their due under Currier's 1889 will.[33] According to one of the executors, who later resigned, Warren Currier was disappointed that his sons George and Henry had not been successful businessmen. He provided for his widow to receive a fixed annual income and bequeathed real estate to his sons, but he tied up the rest of the estate in a trust with somewhat vague instructions to the executors about how to distribute income from the remaining assets.

Carpenter provided some assistance to Edwards, but in 1899 he was also busy setting up his own office in Greeley. Although Carpenter participated in the Currier case, it does not appear that he used the case to make a name for himself.[34] This may be explained by the fact that he was beginning to focus on his own political agenda. The attorney for the Currier estate executors was James W. McCreery, a Republican already established in Weld County politics. Carpenter would not want to appear an adversary of McCreery when his goal was to advance up the political ladder. Carpenter had mixed feelings about getting too involved in probate estate work. An interest in water was already paramount, but he was not sure such a specialty would produce enough business to guarantee a satisfactory living for his family.

To better understand the talents and capabilities that would lead to success, Carpenter submitted himself to a brain analysis. Known as a phrenology exam to many young professionals in the late nineteenth century, the test's purportedly measured the size of brain compartments in order to "learn your best power and use it, and thereby insure success in life."[35] Dr. J. R. McHugh, "phrenologist and physiognomist," administered the exam. According to his evaluation, Delph's strengths were in parental love, friendship, and a good memory. Not far behind were a love of words, an interest in history and general order, a love of home and country, and a desire to marry. At the age of twenty-four, without knowing any more about how his legal career would evolve, he offered these unscientific but revealing qualities to Anne Michaela (Dot) Hogarty in the form of a marriage proposal. She had been a high school classmate and was the daughter of another Greeley pioneer family. His offer was accepted. They were married at Trinity Episcopal Church in Greeley on June 5, 1901.

Dot Hogarty was fourteen months younger than Delph, but they graduated from high school in the same year. Her father, Michael Joseph Hogarty, was born in County Kildare, near Dublin, Ireland, in 1835. Her

Dot Hogarty on her wedding day.

mother, Sarah Ann Carr, was born in Horseheads, New York, in 1844. Michael stayed with his grandmother when his parents came to the United States early in the 1840s, but following her unexpected death, Michael's mother returned to Ireland and brought her son to New York. Unfortunately, his parents died two years later. Michael went to live with a guardian. He attended public schools in the winters and helped around the farm in the summers.

Michael was bright. Hoping for a career in medicine, he studied at Alfred Academy and University, but the outbreak of war in 1861 changed his plans.[36] Although he was able to continue his studies for two more years while teaching at a district school, he decided to enlist in the 141st New York Infantry in 1863. After holding various clerical positions, he saw action at the battle of Resaca, Georgia, on May 15, 1864. During this engagement a minié ball hit him below the left eye, destroying the eye and fracturing the cheek bone.[37]

Michael Hogarty was discharged from the service in the fall of 1864. He married Sarah Ann Carr after returning to his former home near Elmira, New York. When his wounds partially healed, he was able to reenlist as a commissioned officer, commanding a company until the Confederates surrendered in 1865. He continued in various military posts until 1870 when he applied for a leave of absence, complaining of vertigo, dementia, and other problems related to his wounds. Referred to a retirement board at Fort Leavenworth, Kansas, Hogarty was told that he had only a few years to live and that he was unfit for military duty. He was retired from the military and later promoted to the rank of captain. In 1871, he moved Sarah and their two children to the Union Colony, hoping to regain his health. The climate and outdoor life gave Michael renewed vigor. Three more children were born to Michael and Sarah. Dot Hogarty, the fifth and last, arrived on July 31, 1878.

Dot grew up on the Hogarty farm north of Greeley in what was known as the LaGrange district. In addition to the hard farm work that characterized rural life, she experienced her father's warm hospitality, his steadfast support of Union Colony principles, his uncompromising Republican political views, and his staunch defense of law and order. Dot became an accomplished musician. After graduating from Greeley High School, she earned a degree from the University of Northern Colorado (Greeley Normal School). Friends commented on her contagious sense of humor,

Captain Michael J. Hogarty, father of Michaela "Dot" Hogarty.

intelligence, and devotion to community. She manifested an early and ongoing interest in the Daughters of the American Revolution, the Trinity Episcopal Church, and the Women's Christian Temperance Union —organizations and causes that paralleled those long embraced by the Carpenter family.[38]

The union of Dot Hogarty and Delph Carpenter, merging two pioneer families, was a marriage of great promise: similar values, similar histories, similar aspirations. Michael Hogarty gave his daughter away in a simple ceremony attended by a small group of family and friends. Following a lunch and reception at the Hogarty home, the newlyweds boarded the afternoon train for Denver.

The first leg of a three-week honeymoon was to St. Paul, Minnesota, where Carpenter served as one of two delegates from northern Colorado at a convention of the Modern Woodmen of America (MWA). In a manner suggestive of his emerging political skills, Carpenter successfully thwarted Denver's plans to appoint all MWA delegates from their own city. He also managed to get his travel paid by the Poudre Valley Camp of the MWA. Youngest of the four-member delegation, Carpenter won respect from other participants as an "organizer and a gentleman."[39] After the convention, the newlyweds traveled east to an exposition in Buffalo, New York, returning to make their home in Greeley in early July.

Carpenter came back to his practice as the senior partner with Charles Townsend in the firm of Carpenter and Townsend. He had already developed an "enviable" reputation as a "promising young attorney" and had shown an interest in local politics by announcing his candidacy as Republican challenger in an unsuccessful bid to unseat a local county judge.[40] His search for recognition and success had begun in earnest.

For the next five or six years, he took whatever cases he could get, looking for opportunities to make a name for himself, complaining frequently about a shortage of cash, and urging litigants to settle out of court. To some extent, his financial woes were brought on by land purchases, but Carpenter enjoyed livestock and he wanted to own a ranch where he could develop blooded cattle.

The spot he selected was located fifteen miles northeast of Greeley on Crow Creek, one mile and a half south of the Barnesville station on the Union Pacific Railroad.[41] In addition to the cost of the land, he paid $600 to the newly incorporated ditch company as his share to extend the original Union Colony Canal No. 2 eastward to Crow Creek. When completed,

Delph Carpenter as a young attorney.

the extension gave him the right to five shares of irrigation water. Although these expenses were burdensome, he risked the investment in raw land with the same expectations his father and grandfather had shown a generation earlier. Irrigated agriculture in Weld County was the only sensible way to farm, he believed, and sooner or later land values would increase as irrigated property became harder to find. Responding to an inquiry from a widowed Kansas farmer in 1906, Carpenter noted that "the land in this country is absolutely worthless when it comes to making a living upon it unless you are able to irrigate." A quarter-section homestead with water would cost up to $6000, he noted, "but as a matter of fact, all of the land situated under canals, either prospective or constructed, has already been filed upon."[42]

Initially, Carpenter was unable to devote much time to the Crow Creek Ranch. He was building up his law practice and his cash flow was inadequate to buy livestock. When he did have money, he purchased steers, fattened them up on a mixture of potatoes, ground corn, and alfalfa and sold them in Denver for more than he could have gotten for the potatoes on the open market.[43] The old days of the open-range cattle industry were just about over, but his romantic notion of cowboy life further defined the values he embraced in his professional life.

Being a cowboy in the old days, he wrote, "demanded nerves of steel, a cool head and rugged constitution, coupled with dash and daring unknown to any class or race of men, except, perhaps, the Arabs of the desert."[44] By the early twentieth century, however, cowboying was just another job. Cattle were being fenced in and sheepmen competed for the remaining free grass on public lands. Carpenter knew he would never punch large herds of cattle on the open range, but he could play cowboy in the wide-open spaces by organizing and participating in coyote hunts. This activity connected him to the romance of the Old West, nurtured his nostalgia, and provided relief from the rigors of office work.

Coyote hunts were a regular winter ritual. By January farmers had sold their crops or stored them in underground dugouts. They faced a relatively quiet period for two months prior to spring planting. If snow did not cover the ground in January, a coyote hunt would enable men and women to enjoy the outdoors, test their horsemanship and gather briefly as a community.

The event was viewed by participants as more than a chance to kill a few predators. It was a form of cultural regeneration. From the small towns

Delph Carpenter on his bronco during a coyote hunt.

around Greeley, hundreds of people gathered with similar objectives. Those who did not participate on horseback joined the hunters afterwards in a victory celebration. Food and beverages were served around a fire and prizes were awarded to men and women for various skills. Around the coyote hunt, the community's ties to the past were strengthened, old values were tested, and man's perceived dominance over nature was ritualized.

The first few years of the twentieth century were propitious for support of such a gathering. Theodore Roosevelt was in the White House, urging Americans to follow the rugged outdoor life. Owen Wister's *The Virginian* (1901) and Andy Adams's *Log of a Cowboy* (1902) provided the national culture with a new American hero. Aspiring to cloak their actions in elegance, the coyote hunters saw themselves as descendants of southern aristocrats who engaged in a type of fox hunt with hounds. Their undisguised enthusiasm for the hunt was an expression of militarism, machismo, Manifest Destiny, and an obsession with the romantic and mythical West.

Carpenter was a frequent leader of these hunts. In an essay written for *Cosmopolitan* in 1903, he described the "wonderful freedom, exhilaration and ever varying cycle of adventure and panorama of scene" associated with the hunts. Organized in a circle with a twenty-mile radius, groups of riders were divided into four divisions and assigned to the four compass points of the perimeter. Each division was charged with the responsibility of moving towards the center at a designated time in the early morning with "Russian stag hounds, English grey-hounds and a few Great Danes" following the horsemen in packs of six to ten animals. As the four groups came into sight, they could see coyotes looking to escape the trap. Some would break for freedom, the riders in hot pursuit with their dogs. No firearms were allowed on the hunt. The animals had to be killed by dogs or roped by the riders. As Carpenter described it, the "grand finish" was a stirring moment, not unlike a cavalry charge, in which one's blood was "stirred to red heat, leaving a sense of exhilaration seldom experienced and often longed for."[45]

After each division counted its trophies, prizes were awarded, sandwiches, coffee, and other libations were consumed; and bronc riding exhibitions finished off already exhausted horses. Under the January sun on the Colorado plains, the Old West was momentarily reborn, but as shadows lengthened and the temperature dropped, hunters and their families returned to life's realities, fully aware that in future years hunts would probably be restricted by the wheels of progress. "Fox hunting," Carpenter concluded, "is the sport of princes, but wolf [coyote] chasing [is] its formidable rival. Both have their glory, but while the one lives on the other will pass as the 'Virginian' of the West vanishes before the dawn of a greater civilization."

Back in his office, Carpenter faced his own reality of making ends meet. Michaela H. Carpenter, born in 1902, and Donald A. Carpenter, arriving

in 1907, added to his financial responsibilities. He worked the legal profession with little respite, pursuing debtors, providing help to Homestead
and Desert Land Act entrymen, probating wills, examining land titles,
researching ditch rights, settling livestock disputes, and supervising the
senior Hogartys' property after they moved from Greeley to National City,
California, in 1903. He championed rights of the poor and falsely accused,
accepted responsibility for abandoned children, and defended an impo-
tent man accused of rape. He knew full well that a jury would probably
side with the little girl in question, but his sense of justice demanded that
he represent a man he thought was innocent. In another case he assisted
a woman unable to collect from her debtors, aware that "there [was] practically nothing in it for [him] except a whole lot of centure" [*sic*] if he
failed.[46] Paid irregularly for his work, he became frustrated as expenses
continued to exceed income. "[I]t is cold cash," he told a friend, "glittering
in the palm that has the most enticing power for mankind as a rule . . .
[P]eople get tired of hot air and want 'the real thing' once in a while."[47] His
best chance for both fame and fortune came when he agreed to defend
an accused murderer who admitted killing a man in self-defense. The case
gave another boost to Carpenter's career.

Charles Simonsen took the life of Charles R. Lewis, editor and publisher
of the *Kersey Enterprise* on the night of August 24, 1907, in the town of
Kersey, Colorado. In some ways, the clash between these two men reflected
the morality battles that had been going on since antitemperance advocates established the rival town of Evans in protest against Greeley's strict
rules regarding the manufacture and sale of alcoholic beverages. The
Kersey faction opposed drinking and gambling. It was headed by Lewis,
the "self-appointed guardian of morals at Kersey."[48] According to the *Weld
County Republican*, "the saloon class" supported Simonsen.[49] He had been
the subject of a series of Lewis's articles implying that Simonsen's wife was
an adulteress. Offended by these attacks, Simonsen protested, but Lewis
laughed him off. One August day Simonsen came to Kersey with his wife,
daughter, and mother to do some errands. Lewis, who was apparently in
his cups, followed them from store to store, hurling insults at the women
and threatening violence. Simonsen went to the justices of the peace for
help. They pleaded ignorance of the law and refused to issue a warrant for
Lewis's arrest without prior approval from the district attorney in Greeley.
Depressed and fearing for his life, Simonsen returned to his home, armed

himself with a pistol and went back to Kersey to finish his errands. Coming down the main street, he ran into Lewis, who approached him shouting obscenities and waving his arms. Simonsen fired his pistol, killing Lewis in his tracks. He then surrendered to local authorities.

During a four-day trial in December 1907, the state tried to show that the murder was premeditated and that Simonsen had returned home with the specific intent of arming himself to kill Lewis. As defense attorney, Carpenter argued that the accused had acted in self-defense and that Lewis had boasted to many of his friends that he was intent on "killing that Swede" even if he lost his life in the attempt. The jury deliberated for eighteen hours before finding Simonsen not guilty. Because the trial generated so much interest in Weld County, it significantly enhanced Carpenter's reputation.[50] His name and legal talent became known throughout the county. Even better, he had earned $750.

Expressing the incredulity of many who had been expecting a different verdict from the jury, Captain Hogarty congratulated Carpenter, but at the same time he expressed his opinion that Simonsen should have been hanged. "The jury must have known that he willfully and deliberately killed Lewis," Hogarty wrote sarcastically to his son-in-law, "and yet you must have convinced them that he didn't . . . hence Lewis must still be alive. I looked over that jury and I never thought that you would be able to hypnotize them, but there is no telling what the average juror will do."[51]

With victory in hand and the 1908 election year just beginning, the thirty-year-old Carpenter decided to take advantage of his notoriety by attempting another sortie into politics. "I will be a candidate for the State Senate this fall," he wrote Hogarty, "the fight being between me and Charles Southard [with] Statler and the machine favoring Southard [for the Republican nomination]."[52] Although he had immersed himself in his law practice during the previous five years, Carpenter had found time to ingratiate himself with the party leadership. In 1906 he was a delegate to the Republican state convention, a delegate to the judicial convention, and a representative from Greeley on the Weld County Central Committee.[53] In 1908, contrary to Carpenter's expectations, the Republicans endorsed his candidacy for the state senate and sent him off to battle William L. Clayton, his Democratic opponent, in the fall election. Carpenter won easily and became the first native-born Coloradan to be elected to the state senate. There were few Democrats in Weld County, and Clayton's chances were further diminished by accusations of having neglected the State Normal School (now the University of Northern Colorado in Greeley) during his term as senator.[54]

Identified with the farming and livestock interests of northern Colorado, Carpenter was placed in charge of the senate committee on agriculture and irrigation. Before his election he had begun to specialize in water rights cases. The Seventeenth General Assembly appointed him head of a special committee of three senators to investigate the condition of Colorado's surface water, especially in regard to the status of interstate streams. The senate was concerned about the possibility of legislation that might undermine the "Colorado Doctrine" at a time when irrigated agriculture was expanding. In 1911 Carpenter was elected chairman of this committee by the other two committee members who represented the Arkansas River and the West Slope.

Colorado had reason to be concerned about the status of its interstate streams. The U.S. Supreme Court announced in 1907 that it had the authority to intervene in interstate water conflicts if it could be shown that headwaters states were denying equity to their downstream neighbors.[55] In 1901, Kansas had accused the state of Colorado of appropriating more than an equitable share of water from the Arkansas River. Six years later, the High Court rendered a decision which implied that Kansas was entitled to an equitable amount of Arkansas River water. If Kansas could ever prove injury, said Justice David Brewer in his decision, the High Court would intervene and make a determination for the equitable apportionment of water between the states in litigation.

This was a shocking revelation to smug Coloradans who believed that all water originating within their boundaries belonged to the people of Colorado. The *Rocky Mountain News* recognized the potential danger, calling the *Kansas v. Colorado* case "the most important . . . that ever reached the Supreme Court from a state west of the Mississippi."[56] Not only had the Court asserted its power to intervene in interstate water disputes, the national government through the Department of Interior had claimed its right to control and administer the waters of western states, thus bringing to the fore a matter of states' rights. Carpenter was deeply suspicious that the newly formed Reclamation Service (Bureau of Reclamation after 1923) would continue to insist on federal control of surface waters in the West.

In every sense, therefore, the committee to which Carpenter was appointed had enormous responsibilities. According to the senate resolution that created their committee, the three men were to "inquire into and investigate" stream conditions, watersheds, diversions, storage facilities, return flows, and water supplies. They were to call witnesses, if necessary, take testimony, and produce written reports. All of this was to be done without compensation, except for reimbursement of expenses, prior to the beginning of the Eighteenth General Assembly in 1911.[57]

Carpenter delivered his report on January 31, 1911. He protested the absence of funding to accomplish fully the committee's task, but his report reflects the seriousness with which he accepted the assignment. Additionally, what he wrote reveals the extent to which Carpenter believed that state government should not tamper with Colorado's existing constitution and laws. He defended "the fundamental doctrine of the acquisition of title to water rights by priority of appropriation and beneficial use." He warned legislators of their need to be vigilant against encroachment by the federal government on the state's right to control its own water. He commended the Department of Interior for the fine works it was building and for the reclamation of lands in the arid West, but he reminded lawmakers that the Reclamation Service was required by law to operate "entirely under and subject to the constitutional provisions, statutes and judicial decisions of the several states." The Reclamation Service, he noted, would have to be watched. They had refused "to grant rights of way for ditches, reservoirs and power sites"[58] in the San Luis Valley, and the National Irrigation Congress, meeting in Pueblo in 1910, had resolved to seek federal control of interstate streams.[59]

Carpenter was troubled by these trends. He wanted Colorado to establish a water defense fund. With regular appropriations the state could respond to all kinds of encroachments, whether from the federal government or from neighboring states. "Too serious consideration cannot be given this most important topic," he wrote.

> The motto "Millions for defense, but not one cent for tribute" may well be borne constantly in mind. Our position on the crest of the continent not only invites attack, but compels constant vigilance coupled with readiness to respond to any and all attacks. Every facility should be provided for constant preparation and immediate action on our part.

Through his report to the Eighteenth State Assembly, Carpenter showed that he championed the Colorado Doctrine as a sacred legal and administrative principle. It also revealed him to be a determined advocate of states' rights and an opponent of federal "Boards of Control and other like Elwood Mead machinery."[60] Those who were aware of his passion viewed him as the Colorado "watchdog of the agricultural interests."[61]

Carpenter was soon preoccupied almost exclusively with issues related to the defense of Colorado's water rights. It was the single cause with which he most readily identified; the one that would allow him to define himself as an accomplished attorney, prepared to achieve goals that would garner both recognition and appreciation from others. He felt so strongly about his new identity that he did not charge Colorado the cost of his 1911 investigation. "[We] desire to state," his report concluded, "that your committee makes no claim for reimbursement for traveling and other expenses. The expenditures made by the several members of the committee are gladly contributed to the good of the cause."

Opportunities soon landed on his doorstep. "I have handed in my report of the irrigation committee," he wrote Captain Hogarty, "and will send you a copy as soon as printed in pamphlet form. It has done me a great amount of good already among the irrigationists of the state, whose business, as you well know, I most desire."[62]

Recognition for Carpenter came in the form of appointment as attorney for the Greeley-Poudre Irrigation District at an annual salary of $4,000. Organized in 1909, the District constituted 125,000 acres of raw land north of Greeley in the vicinity of Nunn, Colorado.[63] The plan for development was conceived in 1904 by D. A. Camfield, one of the most successful land developers of the period. Camfield's profits were to be realized when the land was sold at ten times its cost, following delivery of irrigation water to holding reservoirs in the area. Because the Cache la Poudre River was already oversubscribed to farmers and towns, Camfield designed a scheme in which 180,000 acre-feet (900 cfs) of Laramie River water would be brought through a two-and-one-quarter-mile tunnel into the Cache la Poudre River and thence by canals to reservoirs in the vicinity of Nunn. Funds for tunnel and canal construction were raised by the sale of bonds secured by liens on the farmlands. When Camfield died unexpectedly, expenses for the Laramie-Poudre Tunnel consumed most of the cash raised. The reservoirs and canals remained to be built, resulting in a loss of momentum for the project. Even though the tunnel had holed through in 1911, Delph's efforts to maintain interest in the Greeley-Poudre Irrigation District were handicapped by fears that, without Camfield, the project would never be completed. Potential investors sensed real trouble when Wyoming objected to the potential loss of so much water from the Laramie River into Colorado. In 1911 Wyoming attorneys filed suit against Colorado in the Supreme Court.

Referencing the Court's decision in *Kansas v. Colorado*, Wyoming argued that under the principles of prior appropriation, generally accepted in the West, and the definition of equitable apportionment as stated by Justice David Brewer in the *Kansas* case, Wyoming had every right to object to the loss of 180,000 acre-feet of water out of the Laramie River basin to Colorado.[64] Colorado responded to the suit by naming Carpenter lead defense attorney. The resulting legal battle was one that defined both his career and the course of western water law.

For another year, however, Carpenter focused most of his energy on senatorial obligations. Gathering evidence, finding witnesses, and developing a legal argument for the *Wyoming* case would take time. What he failed to realize was that Colorado was ill-equipped to defend itself properly. The pressures of preparing briefs, locating experts, and formulating a legal plan would fall largely on his shoulders, and this weight would increase in 1916 when Nebraska sued Colorado in federal court, demanding more water out of the South Platte River.

Because Carpenter had sensed after the *Kansas* decision that the Supreme Court was unlikely to uphold Colorado's long-standing claim to all waters within its boundaries, he began searching for alternatives to litigation between states. Gradually, he devised a logic enabling him to apply the compact clause of the Constitution to conflicts on interstate rivers. At the same time, however, he was forced to prepare priority arguments against Wyoming's claims on the Laramie River. Carpenter hoped the High Court would recognize Colorado's geographical location at the headwaters of the Laramie River and honor the "superior" beneficial use to which the Greeley-Poudre Irrigation District would put water taken from this river. But he knew it would be a tough sell. The Supreme Court seemed to be leaning toward a recognition of priority on interstate streams and Wyoming had a better case.

The internal strain of working with conflicting theories, combined with inadequate support from the state, eventually broke his health. Before his collapse, however, Carpenter managed to obtain additional recognition as a state senator. One of the younger leaders of the Republican party, Carpenter identified a flaw in the application of the Colorado Doctrine that allowed ditch owners the right to take water away from senior reservoirs. Addressing this issue, and speaking out against what he viewed as some of the more reprehensible aspects of the Progressive reform movement—such were the tasks Carpenter embraced during his remaining years in Colorado politics.

The national reform movement known as Progressivism peaked in Colorado between 1908 and 1912 when Democrat John F. Shafroth was governor. His administration coincided with Carpenter's senatorial term, but some of Shafroth's political objectives were abhorrent to the Greeley Republican. Philosophically, Carpenter was a William H. Taft supporter. He viewed Teddy Roosevelt Republicans as boors and wondered how pioneers would have settled Colorado Territory if Gifford Pinchot, chief of the U.S. Forest Service and the "nation's most visible conservationist," had implemented policies on national forests during the 1870s. Pinchot believed in federal regulation of the nation's natural resources. Progressives wanted to treat rivers as units administered by federal agencies, and they felt called to develop the nation's water supplies as rapidly as possible. Carpenter opposed these objectives. His training in constitutional law led him to view the federal system with awe and reverence, but when Pinchot's plans appeared to threaten the autonomy of Colorado and other western states, he bristled.[65]

Most objectionable, Carpenter believed, was the Progressive advocacy of centralized control of western water. Pinchot's objective was to target monopolistic water power companies,[66] Carpenter, on the other hand, viewed the government's attempt to control any aspect of natural resources as an abomination, a violation of states' rights. He failed to distinguish between the potentially constructive results of reducing the influence of the water companies and what he determined to be more harmful consequences of states losing control of their forests and streams. "No pains or effort should be spared," he said, "to curtail the many attempts made during the past ten years to centralize the control of waters and water supplies

of the various states in the central government at Washington." If the federal government's attitude were to continue, he predicted, it would be "bit-
terly resented by all of the arid states."[67]

Carpenter exercised a literal and straightforward interpretation of the
Constitution. Consequently, he considered unconstitutional much of the
Progressive platform. Although he sympathized with the plight of workers,
especially women in the labor market, he belonged to a group of regular
Republicans and conservative Democrats who saw some of the Progressive
reforms as potentially dangerous. Specifically, he disagreed with Shafroth's
efforts to amplify state power through creation of regulatory commissions.
Nor did he favor diffusing the political power of duly elected state officials.
When the initiative and referendum act was passed as an amendment to
the state constitution, Carpenter was in the midst of clarifying the priority
rights of reservoir owners. Unexpectedly, his reservoir legislation became
the first law challenged by proponents of the newly approved referendum
process.

This incident began in the fall of 1910 when Carpenter received a query
from a constituent Windsor farmer who complained that the rights of
reservoir owners appeared to be inadequately protected by Colorado water
law and its administrator, the state engineer. Carpenter expressed sympathy for the man's dilemma. The existing state engineer, he replied, "is a
fine gentleman but knows no more about irrigation than a bull does about
cut glass. . . . [The] problem of direct irrigation vs. storage has come before
me a number of times during the past two years, and I must frankly express
that I am still at a loss to find a definite mode of meeting the situation without doing great injury to some of the appropriators of the state."[68]

As chairman of the senate committee on irrigation, Carpenter reviewed
a 1901 law that contained a sentence preventing senior reservoirs anywhere in the state from storing water when needed by junior ditch appropriators. Because of confusion surrounding its meaning and his own belief
that the sentence was in violation of Article XVI of the state constitution,
Carpenter recommended repeal of the sentence. He drew up a bill amend-
ing the law of 1901 with the objectionable sentence left out. After being
redrafted by a colleague from Lamar, the bill came to the floor with a substitute sentence known as the Parrish Amendment.[69]

Carpenter's objective was to clarify the priority rights of reservoirs so
they were in conformity with Colorado water law. The Parrish Amendment

Delph Carpenter at his seat in the Colorado State Senate, ca. 1910.

accomplished this objective by making junior ditches and reservoirs subject to their senior equivalents. However, local newspapers accused Carpenter of favoring corporate reservoir interests. Echoing Progressive sentiments, they warned that if his bill were to pass, it would create a giant reservoir trust.[70] In fact, Carpenter was trying to eliminate an injustice that had allowed junior ditch appropriators to take water away from senior reservoir owners, but newspaper suspicions fueled the debate with front- page stories.[71] His sole purpose, he said, was "to correct an error of a previous legislature, to prevent unnecessary and disastrous litigation, and to sweep away all foundation for unwise and fraudulent speculation and representation."[72]

Members of the Direct Election League of Denver were ready for legislation upon which they might apply the referendum. They knew that Carpenter had been an outspoken opponent of both the initiative and referendum, so they aimed their guns at his 1911 Reservoir Bill. It had passed both houses of the state legislature and was ready to be signed into law. The League described this bill as a "thief in the night . . . a most dangerous law, leading to endless litigation, [giving] promoters of 'wildcat' reservoir schemes a chance to swindle investors," and they successfully obtained the eleven thousand signatures needed to refer it to the people in the 1912 election.[73]

In the year and a half of public discussion preceding the vote, Carpenter spoke repeatedly about his opposition to the initiative and referendum. Echoing the fears of Alexis de Tocqueville, he expressed concern that 8 percent of the electorate might initiate a bill without any discussion and if only ten people voted on it and six approved it, the initiative would become law. The minority would have imposed its will on the majority.[74]

For Carpenter, this possibility represented a shocking development in the course of American democracy. He anticipated Denver's urban population bullying the rest of the state repeatedly. Worse still was the threat to governmental stability, he said, if "life, liberty and property of citizens [were] entrusted to the confusion and turbulence of elections and to the caprice and whims of the hour. Even the spirit of true democracy [would be] violated," he argued, "and so long as I am a member of this body I shall never permit myself to violate my duty and the dictates of my conscience. . . . The people in my portion of the state have two don'ts—'Don't fool with our water right laws or the constitution.'"[75]

Here was the essence of Carpenter's obduracy. Constitutions were sacred documents and should not be easily amended or broadly interpreted. Good law and legislation required debate, confrontation, discussion, and ample time to present evidence. The initiative and referendum, he believed, put power in the hands of municipalities, corporations, and other groups with the means to influence voters, thus circumventing the democratic process. "Newspaper graft" would be encouraged and well-established principles, such as the doctrine of prior appropriation, would be endangered by ignoring legislative authority.[76] Unfortunately, the voting public wanted to flex its newly discovered political muscle.

In the 1912 general election, the Parrish Amendment was defeated. The rest of the Carpenter Reservoir Bill, however, remained intact without the objectionable sentence. Its passage guaranteed to every farmer who obtained a water supply from a reservoir that his rights in order of priority were equal to the rights of those who irrigated directly from ditches. What Carpenter had to explain to perplexed Coloradans was that his bill, as it stood, shorn of the Parrish Amendment in 1912, effectively repealed the objectionable language of the 1901 law,[77] restoring the constitutional guarantee "that among those using water for agricultural purposes, the first in time shall continue to be the first in right."[78] This meant that reservoir water rights were now on the same legal basis as direct appropriation rights from ditches. The legislation also required ditches, canals, and reservoirs to be kept in good repair along with the installation and maintenance of proper measuring devices. Owners and operators would be liable for any damages occurring and for criminal penalties if they neglected maintenance of their property. Water officials and citizens now had the means to enforce responsible conduct by appropriators.

Carpenter had been in the vanguard of a tough political battle, but he was rewarded when state engineer Charles W. Comstock issued a general order establishing the Carpenter Reservoir Bill as the rule of official conduct for water officials. Reflecting on his accomplishment in a letter to state engineer M. C. Hinderlider in 1932, Delph revealed how the experience affected his thinking about interstate priorities when, in 1922, Colorado was in a position vis-à-vis California that was similar to the tension between Colorado ditch companies and reservoirs prior to 1912:

> A moment's reflection is sufficient to convince that it would be both unconstitutional and unconscionable to permit the water supply of an expensive reservoir system to be taken away without compensation and given to a subsequent, junior, cheap and wasteful ditch

system. Such a procedure would put the instrumentality and method of making *uses* [author's emphasis] as the sole criterion and not *priority of appropriation* [author's emphasis]. Under such a system of law, a ditch constructed one hundred years hence could dry up a whole Cache la Poudre reservoir system.[79]

The Carpenter Reservoir Bill's significance is that it shows how entrenched in Carpenter's mind was the western system of prior appropriation and how difficult it would be for him to abandon this system in favor of negotiated compacts. Looking ahead briefly to 1922, when upper basin states of the Colorado River, including Colorado, demanded protection for undeveloped water rights at a time when California's irrigated agriculture was expanding, the upper states' principal concern was the potential for California to establish senior reservoir rights by means of a dam on the lower end of the Colorado River. When the Supreme Court handed down its decision in *Wyoming v. Colorado* that same year, recognizing the legitimacy of interstate prior appropriation, Carpenter knew that the upper basin's only hope for equity was agreement on a seven-state compact plan that relied on comity, not priority or competition. It was the only way he could see to preserve Colorado's right to Colorado River water in the future and it was a plan that matured considerably while Carpenter served in the Colorado senate.

By 1912 Delph had become increasingly caught up in the Greeley-Poudre Irrigation District's financial problems. His salary had been reduced to $175 a month and he was forced to travel frequently to Chicago to meet with the bond brokers. Although he had been stung by criticism during the Carpenter Reservoir Bill fight, he decided to run for another term in the senate. He was proud of his record: a major report on Colorado's surface water; the Carpenter Reservoir Bill; a bill to extend the life of the Union Colony for twenty years; election to the post of minority leader of the senate in 1911; recognized sponsor for the offices of state engineer, attorney general, and superintendent of public instruction; sponsor of a bill creating a state traveling teacher for the adult blind; and a host of other accomplishments. He concluded, somewhat immodestly, that with the exception of Senator James W. McCreery, he had achieved more in four years than any of his predecessors had in eight, notwithstanding the fact that, throughout his term, he was a member of the minority party.[80]

Denver Daily News cartoon of Delph Carpenter as state senator.

Even so, Carpenter doubted he could win reelection at a time when Bull Moose Republicans were splitting the party vote. He was appalled by the behavior of the "drunk and crazy" followers of Teddy Roosevelt. At their national convention in Chicago, they flippantly spoke of promoting amendments to the Constitution. Taft men, he noted, were attending strictly to business, but the followers of Roosevelt seemed to believe that the country was going to the dogs and major constitutional changes were in order. "To them," he wrote, "a Constitution of a great commonwealth or of the nation is of no more value than a mere dime novel."[81]

As much as he wanted to fight the Bull Moosers, Carpenter was afraid the campaign would subject his family to vilification and abuse. Torn between serving a "just cause" and protecting his family, Carpenter spent time in Chicago, focusing on Greeley-Poudre problems and trying to distance himself from any possibility of future campaigning. "I would rather retire to private life and practice," he wrote his friend D. E. Gray, "than to be compelled to voice the cry of the rabble."[82]

But when Gray telegraphed him to the effect that Weld County Republicans had unanimously nominated him for reelection, he was ecstatic. The political war horse in him came to life. He expressed willingness to go out on the firing line at any time and he pledged to his opponent, Hubert Reynolds, he would wage a "gentleman's campaign in every particular."[83]

It was indeed a clean campaign. Carpenter worked diligently to make up for lost time, on one day driving seventy miles and giving four speeches after seven o'clock in the evening. He lost eight pounds during the summer, pledging to protect Laramie River water for Weld County and vowing to keep Denver from dominating affairs in the rural parts of the state.

When the vote was tallied, however, he was in second place, 816 votes behind the winner, Democrat Reynolds. In third place was the Progressive candidate, R. M. Haythorne. The defeat hurt, but Carpenter congratulated his opponent and commended him as an honorable man. It was a year for Democrats from the White House (Woodrow Wilson) to the State House (John Shafroth), but it was the third-party candidate that did him in. "I was kicked by the Democratic mule," Carpenter observed, "stepped on by a bull moose and left for dead owing to bad decisions in the Republican ranks in this country." He did not like to lose, especially because he had "hoped to be of material service to the state in the matter of the defense of the waters of our interstate streams."[84] But he was now free from political activities and felt some relief over the fact that he had the opportunity to get his own financial affairs in order.

As Denver's *Daily News* reported in 1911, Carpenter had been a very determined "Give-a Damn" senator whose philosophy of "I Will" spoke well for his determination and commitment to any job assigned him. He never wreaked vengeance on an enemy, tried to give others a "square deal," and demanded nothing more of others than he asked of himself. Having grown up in a household representing the best traditions of pioneer Yankees and Virginians, Carpenter learned how to treat people—with integrity. His heroes were the "conquerors' of the arid West who had the "foresight" to build ditches and reservoirs for the Union Colony and who "forced Congress to recognize that the [West's] arid lands *must* be reclaimed."[85]

He borrowed the "I Will" attitude from his parents and from the pioneers who had risked everything to reclaim western lands. Their example stimulated in him a strong desire to pioneer in the field of water law. But none of the challenges he was about to accept would have been viable without the loyalty, patience, and intellectual stimulation provided by his wife. She encouraged him to believe that he could do anything to which he committed himself fully.[86] This self-assurance served him well as he attempted to save the troubled Greeley-Poudre Irrigation Project while simultaneously preparing Colorado's defense against Wyoming in the suit involving the Laramie River.

CHAPTER 3

The Making of an Interstate Streams Commissioner

If I can keep my head above water for the next ten years I will be comfortably fixed for the rest of my life, although the present financial depression is pinching me like it has everybody else.

—DELPH TO COUSIN ALFRED, OCTOBER 30, 1914

Carpenter congratulated his cousin Alfred G. Carpenter in the fall of 1914 on the strong newspaper endorsement Alfred received during his campaign for election as a court of appeals judge. Predicting his election, Delph wrote, "I sincerely trust that . . . you will have as interesting a line of experiences as it was my fortune to enjoy during my four years of public life in this state." Reflecting on his tenure as senator, Carpenter added:

> While I was forced to bear the brunt of a great many political attacks and had many unpleasant things said about me by political adversaries, nevertheless, I thoroughly enjoyed my work and, I believe, came off with a record as good as could be expected. Professionally, it was a great advantage to me and I am now enjoying its fruits by having the privilege of trying the interstate water case between Wyoming and Colorado, and also enjoying a practice of the best class in this portion of the state, although not as large as yet as I hope in time to

enjoy. This condition of my practice I attribute primarily to my public career and coming, as it has, in the earlier years of my life, I ought
in time to reap at least reasonable compensation for the tortures I
was compelled to endure.[1]

Carpenter's appointment as lead attorney in *Wyoming v. Colorado* was,
indeed, attributable to his good record in state politics. No one else had
a firmer commitment to preserving Colorado's sovereign rights in the
United States or a greater interest in protecting the state's water resources.
But if Carpenter had expected some relief from the "torture" of politics,
he was unprepared for the "Hell" he would have to endure in defense of
Colorado's priority claims on the Laramie River.[2] The lessons he learned
were sobering but fundamental to his expectation that interstate water
compacts would be more effective than interstate litigation.

Wyoming's 1911 suit against Colorado was based on the undeniable fact
that any water removed from the Laramie River into another watershed
would be lost permanently for existing and future use in Wyoming. The
Greeley-Poudre Irrigation District in Colorado had raised enough money
through the sale of bonds to contract with the Laramie-Poudre Reservoirs
and Irrigation Company for the construction of the Laramie-Poudre
Tunnel under Green Mountain. This tunnel, connecting two separate
watersheds, holed through in the spring of 1911. Its completion threatened Wyoming with the annual loss of more than 100,000 acre-feet of
Laramie River water.

Carpenter was in a unique position. As attorney for the Greeley-Poudre
Irrigation District, he was required to be a strong protagonist for this diversion project. In 1911 it was 60 percent finished. Successful completion
would depend on raising additional money and on the confidence of
prospective bond investors willing to purchase the balance of a $5 million
offering.[3] This confidence was shattered by Wyoming's lawsuit. Bond sales
after 1911 all but ceased because of fears that the Supreme Court would
find in favor of Wyoming's complaint. The Greeley-Poudre Irrigation
Project would fail without water from the Laramie River.

Carpenter's work as lead counsel for the State of Colorado had official
sanction, but the lack of a legislative appropriation in the early phase of
litigation indicated that state officials, especially the attorney general, simply assumed that the interests of the state and the Greeley-Poudre Irrigation

District were analogous.[4] Carpenter was expected to hammer home the standard view: Colorado owned all water originating within its boundaries and the Greeley-Poudre Irrigation District had a right to remove that water from the basin of origin in Colorado's North Park to another basin in Colorado, provided it did not injure senior appropriators in Wyoming.

Unfortunately, this assumption by most state officials was flawed. Carpenter's legal challenge was complicated by the fact that his commitment to prior appropriation as a legitimate basis for watering the Greeley-Poudre Project was contrary to the Supreme Court's view of equitable apportionment as enunciated in *Kansas v. Colorado*. A student of this Arkansas River case, Carpenter suspected that because both Colorado and Wyoming were prior appropriation states, the Court might be tempted to favor the state with the earliest priorities on the Laramie River. This impression required him initially to formulate an argument based on a different kind of priority, one that stressed Colorado's prior sovereignty as a state in the federal republic. If he could keep the case from going to trial by convincing Wyoming that Colorado might be able to claim this form of senior priority, he might be able to get an out-of-court settlement, thus fulfilling his obligations to Colorado and to the Greeley-Poudre Irrigation District. But if Wyoming insisted on litigation and the Supreme Court decided to hear the case, he would have to compromise or run the risk that the High Court would favor Wyoming with a decision that supported interstate priority as the best form of equity on the Laramie River. These conflicting thoughts and interpretations created a great deal of stress, some inconsistency in Carpenter's briefs, and ultimately a new set of principles he would apply to Colorado's interstate streams in later years.

Carpenter had no difficulty fighting for the Greeley-Poudre Irrigation Project. His pioneer background encouraged him to believe it was a "grand enterprise" whose failure would "permanently impair the value of irrigation securities over the entire arid West."[5] He hoped that within a year, after the facts were brought to light, the High Court would recognize the lawsuit as politically motivated.[6] If this happened, the justices would refuse to hear the case. The equity of Colorado's claims would be revealed, and water would be allowed to flow through the Laramie-Poudre Tunnel for the benefit of settlers in the Greeley-Poudre Irrigation District.

To this end, he introduced a demurrer, hoping to persuade the High Court to throw out the case entirely, but it was overruled. In the fall of

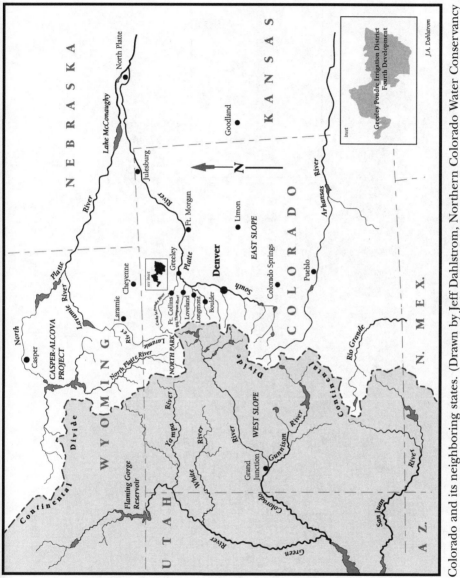

Colorado and its neighboring states. (Drawn by Jeff Dahlstrom, Northern Colorado Water Conservancy District, reprinted from Tyler, *Last Water Hole in the West*)

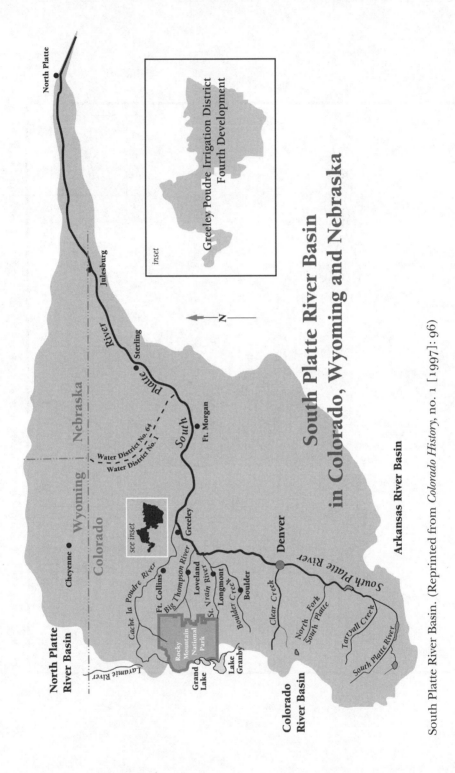

North Platte
River Basin

North Platte

Julesburg

River

Sterling

Nebraska

Platte

Ft. Morgan

Wyoming

South

Water District No. 64
Water District No. 1

Colorado

Cheyenne

see inset

Greeley

Denver

South Platte River

N

inset

Greeley-Poudre Irrigation District
Fourth Development

Cache la Poudre River
Ft. Collins
Big Thompson River
Loveland
St. Vrain River
Longmont
Boulder Creek
Boulder
Clear Creek

Laramie River

Rocky
Mountain
National
Park
Grand
Lake
Lake
Granby

North Fork
South Platte

Tarryall Creek

South Platte River

Colorado
River Basin

Arkansas River Basin

South Platte River Basin
in Colorado, Wyoming and Nebraska

South Platte River Basin. (Reprinted from *Colorado History*, no. 1 [1997]: 96)

1912 the Court gave Colorado, the Greeley-Poudre Irrigation District, and the Laramie-Poudre Reservoirs and Irrigation Company ninety days to answer Wyoming's charges. A trial seemed inevitable. Carpenter dreaded "the long, tedious task of taking the evidence," but he had no choice.[7] What had begun as confident assurance that Colorado's geography and history would serve as a valid priority claim became, in Carpenter's mind, a confused mixture of contravening arguments involving states' rights, intrastate priorities, and federal powers. Carpenter began questioning the implications of interstate priorities determined by the Supreme Court, a process that eventually led him to center his thinking on the constitutional meaning of state sovereignty. This conversion emerged gradually during preparation for trial, but his early briefs reveal that he had difficulty breaking away from the priority principle that had so dominated Colorado and the West during his formative years.

Testimony for *Wyoming v. Colorado* began in August 1913. It continued for 257 days in Cheyenne, Denver, and Greeley. Carpenter complained of being financially stretched and "dead tired." His offer to work for a reduced salary was accepted by the Greeley-Poudre Irrigation District, but the strain of pre-trial preparation continued unabated. Against the advice of many, he began formulating the geographical priority issue in response to the High Court's order, hoping to prove that Colorado, not Wyoming, had the most sovereign and senior claim to the Laramie River. "I *must* do it," he wrote in his diary, "or we may lose the case."[8]

To this end, he advised Governor Elias Ammons that the Greeley-Poudre Irrigation District would continue to furnish counsel to the state, but "[e]xperts of international reputation must be employed," he pleaded, "and their continuous service will be necessary from now until the evidence is concluded."[9] Searching for international precedents that would match Colorado's claim to senior water rights, Carpenter launched inquiries abroad. To the United States consul-general in Paris he inquired about an alleged river dispute between Switzerland and France, settlement of which supposedly "gave the first use of the water of the stream to the country of origin, in that case being Switzerland."[10] To the American minister in Berne, Carpenter noted that Colorado was very much like Switzerland "in that it is the country of origin of the water and inasmuch as international law in a large measure controls between states in litigation pending . . . before the United States Supreme Court, this precedent will be of value to me if the decision was in favor of the country of origin."[11] It is not known how the minister replied, or if he replied at all, but it is clear from this tactic that Carpenter believed Colorado would have a better case if its situation vis-à-vis Wyoming could be compared favorably to established international precedents.

Seeking out the most reliable experts locally, Carpenter selected Louis G. Carpenter to be a key witness because he had international experience. No relation, Louis Carpenter had studied water systems around the world. He was an engineer who taught the first class in irrigation engineering in the United States at Colorado Agricultural College in Fort Collins. On leave and during the summer months he traveled throughout southern Europe, Africa, and India. He read French, Portuguese, Spanish, German, and Italian, served as Colorado's state engineer for two years; and specialized in transmountain diversion.[12] It is "necessity," Louis Carpenter testified, that "universally cause[s] inter-watershed diversions. When people need water, they get it wherever they can and the only limitation on 'intra- and inter-watershed' diversions" has been that "he who is first in time shall forever be first in right as against all who shall claim from the same source *within his respective sovereign jurisdiction.*"[13] In other words, Louis Carpenter believed that Colorado's right to Laramie River water was already proven by its geographical position on the Laramie River and by "necessity."

Delph Carpenter was pleased with Louis Carpenter's testimony, but after a year of research and ample time to assess the strength of Wyoming's claims, Delph began to shift the emphasis of his argument to state sovereignty. He felt uncertain about the High Court's possible reaction to the idea of state-of-origin priority. By the time he began formally dictating briefs in 1914 and 1915, he was truly concerned about establishing a precedent of prior appropriation as an administrative guideline for interstate rivers in the West. States have full jurisdiction over their own lands, he reasoned. They can modify their water doctrine at any time. They are sovereign and equal entities in the federal republic and they would surely reject the notion of a third party administering their water rights.[14] Priority, he concluded, belongs to "*intra state* law and usufructuary rights are under control of the state using its police power." If priority were applied to interstate streams, it would "impose exclusive and perpetual servitudes upon the territory and natural resources of one state [over another]." This case, he observed, "should be governed by the principle that each state has the sovereign right to enjoy the waters of the streams within its territory . . . and the Court should not intervene unless one state is unreasonably injuring another."[15]

Carpenter's thinking had changed significantly. From an earlier claim that Colorado's right to all Laramie River water was based on the geographical origin of that river in Colorado, he was now arguing that Colorado as a sovereign state of origin was entitled to an *equitable* amount of Laramie River water for agricultural development in the Cache la Poudre watershed. The transmountain diversion system through the Laramie-Poudre Tunnel was a universally accepted delivery technique to which Louis Carpenter testified at great length. Furthermore, the diverted water would be put to better use in Weld County, Colorado, than on the high plains of Wyoming. Even with the diversion of 100,000 acre-feet, ample water would remain in the Laramie River to satisfy Wyoming's senior water rights.[16]

These points covered most of the issues that the Supreme Court asked both sides to address in trial.[17] Rushing to get his briefs in on time, Carpenter went through several stenographers, finally speaking thousands of words daily into a new dictaphone. He sent the wax rolls to Denver where they were transcribed at the rate of one hundred pages a day. The process consumed most of a year, including corrections and additions. His briefs went to the printer in November 1916. One month later he was in Washington to present Colorado's argument to the justices of the Supreme Court.

Carpenter arrived at his Washington hotel on December 2 with an infected wisdom tooth. It was pulled the following day, but complications forced him to return to the dentist several times prior to his scheduled appearance before the justices on December 7. Enduring considerable pain, he presented his view of the legal issues for a day and a half. "On the whole," Carpenter confided to his diary, " [I] feel satisfied at having done our best—Wyoming unfair in injecting new water measurements and misquoting record—otherwise, everything O.K." Colorado Senator Charles S. Thomas, who watched the entire proceedings, told him that "at the close of the session, Chief Justice [Edward D.] White [remarked] I had made one of the most interesting arguments he had heard in many years— Several others in attendance congratulated me and said many pleasant things of my argument, including Deputy Attorney General of California, Al Craven."[18] Thomas concluded that if Colorado were to lose, it would not be the fault of counsel.[19]

Feeling positive about his presentation to the Court, Carpenter took advantage of being in Washington to speak with Arthur P. Davis, director of the United States Reclamation Service, about the possibility of federal aid in the construction of the Greeley-Poudre Project. Given his aversion to federal intervention in water-related matters, this request might appear unusual. But Carpenter was politically astute. He enjoyed associations with powerful people and he wanted the Greeley-Poudre Project to succeed.

Carpenter had met Davis, nephew of John Wesley Powell, at a national irrigation conference in Denver in 1914 under less than optimal circumstances. At that time, Carpenter criticized an article Davis wrote. The subsequent row had gotten into the newspapers. Following a face-to-face discussion, the two men patched up their differences and began a friendship that would last for many years. "I believe [the incident] did me good," Carpenter confessed, "and made them [the Reclamation Service] think more of me."[20] Carpenter congratulated Davis on his appointment as head of the Reclamation Service in December 1914. Davis responded with warmth. "I wish to thank you most heartily," Davis wrote, "for your proffer of service towards bringing about better feelings between the Federal and State authorities." To this, Carpenter replied that he hoped "no unfortunate friction [would] develop which [would] impede [Davis] in rendering the most efficient service. If any Ballinger-Pinchot affair begins to develop, I trust that you will call on me if I may be of any possible service to you, remote as I am from the capital and insignificant as my services may be."[21] This cordial exchange, and the relationship that flowered in subsequent years, proved significant during Colorado River Compact negotiations in the early 1920s.

Business completed in Washington, Carpenter took some vacation time. He visited Gettysburg, Harper's Ferry, and Niagara Falls, stopped in to see cousins in New York and Ohio, and returned to Greeley by way of Chicago. He arrived home just before Christmas, optimistic about the outcome of the litigation with Wyoming, but worried about the loss of income now that *Wyoming v. Colorado* was supposedly over. Providing adequate support for his family nagged at him, even though his career seemed to be progressing nicely.

Because his assets were tied up in land, cash was in short supply. The Greeley-Poudre Irrigation Project's finances were in such terrible shape that interminable squabbles over Carpenter's expenses had resulted in annoying reimbursement delays. At times he viewed Greeley-Poudre board members as a "bunch of ingrates,"[22] and in a moment of pique he allowed that he had been "running a law school" in Chicago to educate brokerage attorneys on the financial and legal status of Greeley-Poudre bonds.[23] It was clear to him the Wyoming litigation was causing a domino effect and he was one of the victims. The market for irrigation securities was flat; the Chicago brokerage company could not sell bonds as long as the Supreme Court was in deliberations. This meant that the Laramie-Poudre Reservoirs and Irrigation Company had insufficient funds to finish the water delivery system for which it was contracted. Without works in place for delivery of Laramie River water to the 125,000 acres of Greeley-Poudre Irrigation District lands, bonds went into default for lack of revenue from land sales to pay interest.[24] Consequently, the District's attorney did not get paid.

Carpenter's financial woes were exacerbated by his interest in developing his Crow Creek Ranch. He failed to build a decent ranch house and because he was absent so much of the time, he could not attend to the business of running the ranch with any kind of efficiency. His hired hand went insane, planted crops were neglected, and he was threatened with litigation by cattlemen to whom he owed money for breeding stock. Charles Lory, president of Colorado Agricultural College, had to remind Carpenter to pay his debts. Eventually, he paid and apologized, blaming the "bad conditions in this part of the country" for his tardiness.[25] Livestock ranching began as a hobby for Carpenter, but he had researched the Bates strain of milking Shorthorns and was convinced that if he provided bull calves to local stockmen, the quality of life in the agricultural community would improve rapidly. "This Shorthorn business is not a fad with me," he told a rancher.[26] Financing the Bates operation was problematic, but Carpenter was convinced that a connection existed between a healthy farm and ranch environment and a secure water supply.

For the state of Colorado, that security was challenged by a lawsuit filed by Nebraska against Colorado on April 16, 1916, when Carpenter was most preoccupied with the Wyoming litigation. The suit was aimed at Colorado appropriators on the South Platte River. Nebraska alleged that the development of irrigated farms in Colorado was drying up the river at the state line. Carpenter traveled to Fort Morgan to help ditch owners draw up articles for an organization—The Colorado Water Users' Association—that would lead the defense of their water rights. With unanimous approval, the association officers selected Carpenter to be their managing and directing attorney at a salary of twenty-five dollars a day plus expenses. He accepted promptly. "I am to be boss of the legal and business end of the suit," he wrote, "and to present pleadings, briefs, etc. to counsel for the state, the sugar company, etc. My services are to begin at once."[27] Unquestionably, he was relieved to have remunerative employment.

Juggling other responsibilities, Carpenter traveled to Lincoln to discuss the case with the Nebraska attorney general and state engineer. Conversations with both men convinced him the case was politically motivated. He did not believe agricultural development in Colorado was a threat to Nebraska farmers. Quite the opposite: the increase in acreage and number of reservoirs in the Colorado section of the South Platte River had resulted in a constant return flow to the river that stabilized its course even in drier months and years.[28] As he had done in preliminary stages of the Wyoming litigation, Carpenter set off to explore the length of the river and to evaluate the irrigation ditches. He was surprised by the deep wells and irrigation pumps used by Nebraskans. He became convinced that Colorado development had actually improved the river. All he needed was a reliable historical record, showing what the river had been like in the days of the early pioneers before irrigated agriculture. If he could prove to Nebraska legislators that the river was getting better, he might succeed in having the lawsuit withdrawn.

Carpenter began searching libraries for old maps, books, and manuscripts containing recollections of freighters, buffalo hunters, soldiers, and other sojourners who traveled the old South Platte and Mormon trails before the days of agricultural development in Colorado. He became acquainted with Frank A. Harrison, a Nebraska historian, who seemed to know much about the South Platte. "I made up my mind," Carpenter wrote in his diary, "that he is the man I am looking for to take up the processing of evidence in Nebraska re[garding] [the] history of the South Platte."[29]

Not surprisingly, Carpenter took to Harrison. He was the "I Will" type, a man who had trained as a lawyer, practicing in Grand Island after working with the Union Pacific Railroad in the "postal service." He traveled frequently to Honduras and Guatemala. In addition to being a photographer and lecturer on Central America, he was a trader among the Indians of those countries. Harrison's "zeal and potential active energy [are] more than double [that of] any character I have met in years," Carpenter noted. A trustworthy research assistant was needed, Carpenter believed, but the man chosen also had to understand Nebraska politics. Two prominent Nebraskans were using the South Platte issue to maneuver for position in the coming senatorial contest. Carpenter had to understand what was going on, so paying Harrison $500 plus expenses was a good investment. "Maybe he will do me double," Carpenter conjectured, but "some way I feel that I have, by accident and without warning, found a valuable aid. In any event, I told him nothing that would do us any harm and may do a great deal of good."[30]

Returning to Colorado on the train, Carpenter observed how much water the Nebraska ditches contained. He spoke with men at Scottsbluff who said that irrigation in Wyoming had steadied the flow of the North Platte River. He heard from Nebraskans who thought Harrison might be a "double-crosser in politics," but he remained convinced that he "could not have made a better choice for a Nebraska agent and information source."[31] Before returning to Greeley, he stopped briefly in Julesburg, Colorado, on the South Platte River to do more research and to interview old-timers about the condition of the river. When he arrived at his office in Greeley, he was feeling good about the Nebraska case, but a depressing telegram from Washington arrived the same day. It stated that the *Wyoming v. Colorado* case had been redocketed for further argument on certain points. The Supreme Court had decided to allow the federal government to enter the case.

Carpenter felt overwhelmed and dejected. The news "greatly depressed me," he wrote in his diary. "Somehow I felt the crushing weight of that litigation harder than ever before. Even before, my nerves seemed to grip me and my hair turn[ed] white. I hate to go into it all again and this time against the government as well."[32] A few months later he confided to an attorney that the prospect of rearguing the *Wyoming* case was having "a very oppressing effect upon [him], owing to the fact that [he] had considered the matter concluded and congratulated [himself] upon being able to devote [his] energies to the Nebraska case which [would] involve far greater preparation than that connected with the Wyoming litigation."[33]

At the very least, Carpenter would do his best to position Colorado for a successful defense. He began lobbying in Colorado for an adequately funded water defense bill. Although legislation of this sort was pending in

the State Assembly, it seemed in danger of being eliminated due to squab-
bling between senators and the attorney general. But Carpenter had allies.
The state engineer's office was concerned about the prospect of losing
funds for the preparation of hydrographic studies on the South Platte and
Laramie rivers. Armed with credibility, experience, and conviction, Carpenter appeared before Colorado's senate and house committees on agriculture and irrigation. He answered questions, ironed out difficulties, and
persuaded senators and representatives that the outcome of litigation on
these two rivers would have unprecedented importance to the future of
the state. After a few days of testimony, the senate adopted Carpenter as
its legal counselor and both houses approved a $50,000 appropriation for
defense of Colorado's rights on all of its interstate streams.[34]

Carpenter was proud of this accomplishment. When Governor Julius C.
Gunter signed the water appropriation bill, victory was in the air, and
Carpenter was unable to restrain his enthusiasm:

> This is a great triumph and I believe [it] marks a new epoch in our
> Colorado water claims. I feel as though (having drawn and champi-
> oned the bill) I have had my share in the great constructive legisla-
> tion of Colorado. . . . During the last two weeks of the legislature, the
> senate committee practically gave me despotic control of their work
> and passed all bills as I amended them or rejected bills I opposed.
> [It] was rather remarkable, considering I am a Republican and they
> largely Democrats. . . . I should feel complimented . . . but somehow,
> I simply have the satisfaction of having served my beloved state in a
> time of great need.[35]

His real service to Colorado and the West, however, was just beginning.
With the Wyoming and Nebraska litigation, as well as right-of-way filings
for the Greeley-Poudre Irrigation District and investigation of water
decrees for Lake Cheeseman by request of the Denver Union Water
Company, events were unfolding that would require Colorado's defense
of rights on a number of streams involving other states.

Carpenter was overloaded with work, and he complained frequently of
fatigue. Many nights he missed the last train home after a full day in Denver,
where he worked until after midnight in his room at the Metropole Hotel.
He tried easing the burden through use of the telephone and automobile,
but long days turned into weeks without relief. A partial Sunday with the

family was his only respite. When war was declared against Germany on April 7, 1917, life became even more complicated. Stress began to wear him down physically and emotionally. He complained of "terrific strain," but had a hard time delegating responsibility to those whose work failed to meet his perfectionist standards. Although the attorney general assigned him some help to write the extensive legal briefs required for the new phase of the *Wyoming* case, Carpenter felt obligated to rewrite much of what he was given, almost always in longhand. In his diary he stated that he had treated the subject (of interstate streams litigation) in his own way and in a manner foreign to the books.[36] Few possessed his knowledge and no one equaled his zeal.

Here was a pioneer at work, one who believed that proper application of the law would preserve the natural resources of his native state for future generations. Exhausted as he was from preparing for litigation, he could still be touched by Colorado's natural beauty. It was a tonic for him and gave meaning to his legal investigation. Returning from one of his trips to Nebraska, he became enraptured by the sun setting over Longs Peak. It was, he wrote, "the most gorgeous sunset, set in a bank of brilliant red clouds over which was clear blue sky, over[lain] with heavens of golden hue, mountains purple beneath [the] foreground, green trees, etc." Brief forays into the country, vistas from the train, time spent hunting ducks with son Don, and occasional visits to Crow Creek Ranch probably kept him sane. But by any measure, he was overcommitted, overworked, and unusually determined to make a mark on the West. He was ambitious.

On May 13, 1917, his fortieth birthday, Carpenter expressed pleasure with what he had accomplished so far in life. In addition to being Colorado's interstate streams commissioner, he was a member of local and state bar associations. He had been asked to be a candidate for a seat in the United States Senate. He was a Mason, secretary of the Union Colony of Colorado, and a recognized stockman and farmer. Reflectively, he noted:

> Perhaps, I have accomplished more than most men at my age, but not so much as many. I was admitted to the bar at 22, elected to the Senate at 31, became an interstate water lawyer at 33 and argued one of the greatest cases of western times (Wyoming v. Colorado) before the U. S. Supreme Court with favorable mention by the Chief Justice at age 39. I hope I do as well in the years to come.[37]

Unexpectedly, the Supreme Court announced that it was limiting arguments in the next round of the *Wyoming* case to the priority and state-lines issues. Although this pronouncement narrowed the focus of Carpenter's research, the Supreme Court's order seemed to suggest that the state-of-origin priority argument would fall on deaf ears. Colorado might have difficulty obtaining sufficient water for the Greeley-Poudre Project. If all the justices wanted to hear was a discussion of whether or not the first-in-time-first-in-right principle should be recognized across state lines, Colorado's quest for its version of equity on the Laramie River might be in jeopardy.

Still, Carpenter was opposed to any compromise with Wyoming. He was determined to win the lawsuit on the basis of what he believed to be Colorado's legal right to water originating within its own boundaries. By December 1917, he had finished preparing the briefs and had responded to the brief of the United States. With his second date at the Supreme Court less than a month away, he looked back at what had been accomplished in the past twelve months:

> Year 1917 has been a busy and prosperous year for me. [I] have made more money this year and had more peace of mind than ever before. I am reaching full strength as a lawyer, but feel somewhat the strain of the interstate water suits, and feeling a little older. [Attorney] General Hubbard has been very fine to work with. He knew enough to know that he knew nothing of the cases and left off leaving everything to me. If the cases are won, it is my winning. . . . [I] feel that the year has been well and profitably spent.[38]

On January 1, 1918, Carpenter departed Greeley for Washington by train. He arrived in the capital with sufficient time to do some sightseeing before boning up for his presentation before the Supreme Court justices. Dot sent him a letter. Anticipating his "fateful day," she told him, "If you don't get what you go after, it will be the first time. I see laurel wreaths and great big headlines in the papers."[39] Consistent affirmation of her husband's career was Dot's way to offer assistance at a time when her husband needed emotional support.

The oral argument commenced on January 9 with the facts of the case delivered by Colorado Attorney General Hubbard and his predecessor, Fred Farrar. On the second day, Carpenter was expected to argue the law

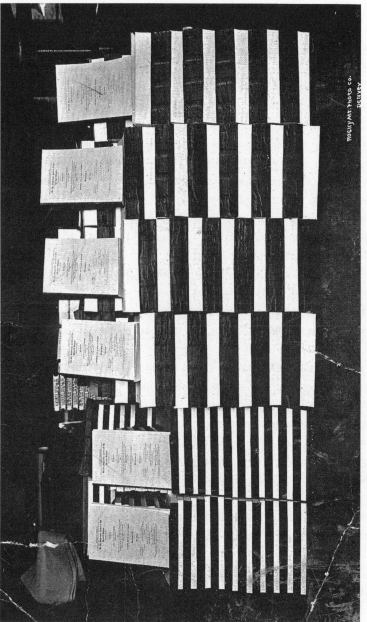

Re-argument brief, *Wyoming v. Colorado*. Printed by Rocky Mountain Photo, Denver, Colo.

of the case. When his turn came, he was "showered with questions" by the justices and felt that his argument had been "badly broken." Although he was satisfied that he had done "fairly well," he was not as pleased with his performance as he had been a year earlier.[40] Carpenter returned to the Shoreham Hotel where the Colorado delegation was staying. He discovered that his Denver colleague, Platt Rogers, had become sick. Although medicated and assured by a doctor that he would be fine in the morning, Rogers awoke too feeble to get out of bed. With "broken rest and only one hour to prepare," Carpenter was forced to pick up the thread of Rogers's argument before the justices. He was such a master of the material and such a student of all aspects of the case that he was able to lay out the essence of his colleague's planned presentation in the time allotted, receiving "many compliments" when it was over. "I am more true to the form of December 1916 argument," he wrote, "by reason of limited interruptions. [I] felt consoled and well repaid for undertaking [the] difficult task of completing another man's argument."[41]

But Carpenter was less than sanguine about the outcome of the case. In his view, litigants for Wyoming had "grossly misstated the facts, so much so that [he] became very bitter." He feared that their tactic of providing gifts in the form of stuffed elk meat to the clerk and to Justice Willis Van Devanter was as iniquitous as the "falsehoods" they imposed on the High Court during trial. And when the United States endorsed Wyoming's plea for recognition of priority rights across state lines, he had to conclude that "it makes hard going for us and we may expect most any kind of decision."[42]

The solicitor for the Reclamation Service also made a solid presentation, but in Carpenter's eyes he seemed to be ignoring the letter and spirit of *Kansas v. Colorado*. The government's ambition to "obtain complete administrative control over all western streams" appeared conspiratorial, but there was nothing more the Colorado camp could do to influence the Supreme Court. Carpenter was worn out and frazzled. He admitted he had nothing left to give. If justices were to ask for more argument, the estimated workload and mental strain would "strike terror into [his] heart."[43] It would be far better, he mused, if everyone could gather around a table to "talk in a natural and easy way."[44] Litigation would be avoided and sustainable equitable apportionment could be hammered out between states without Supreme Court intervention. This was the approach he hoped to take with Nebraska over the South Platte River, but before he could present his ideas to the Nebraskans, the state of Colorado engaged him in another priority challenge from Nebraska on the Republican River.

The main stem of the Republican River flows in Kansas and Nebraska, but Colorado supplies water through three tributaries: the North Fork, the South Fork, and the Arikaree. The Pioneer Irrigation Company of Nebraska was demanding an 1890 priority right to water diverted from the North Fork within the state of Colorado for sale and use in Nebraska. The Colorado state engineer refused to recognize Nebraska's demand.[45] He adhered to the principle that, under Colorado's constitution and statutes, water in natural streams belonged first to Coloradans and could not by law be appropriated by another state, regardless of priority of appropriation. Nebraska sued in United States District Court and won. Colorado's appeal landed in the Supreme Court by way of the United States Circuit Court of Appeals for the Eighth Circuit.[46] Carpenter's brief for the Supreme Court paralleled the argument he used against Wyoming.

Priority of appropriation across state lines was inequitable, and Carpenter's briefing of the case in the fall of 1918 stressed this point. The additional salary he earned from the water defense fund was welcome, but more important to Carpenter, the Republican River investigations were certain to help Colorado on the South Platte River case and might even influence the outcome of *Wyoming v. Colorado*. Once again, however, the additional workload exhausted him. On November 11, 1918 (Armistice Day), he wrote in his diary that there were "great celebrations" in Denver, that it took his streetcar forty minutes to get from the train depot to his office, that the fighting was over, but "Sorry, I had to work."[47] By the time of his departure, once again, for the Supreme Court in Washington, his stenographer had taken ill with the "Spanish influenza," a disease that had already reached epidemic proportions nationwide.[48] Carpenter was vulnerable because he was so tired, but he was also proud of his accomplishments. In his diary he wrote:

> This brief has made a nervous wreck of me. I have given it my very life, realizing how desperately vital it is, but [I] have done my very best. My stenographer took ill . . . and I typed the last of the brief myself. I have worked it out all alone, no help from anyone . . . . Neither the attorney general nor . . . his department had anything to do with it.[49]

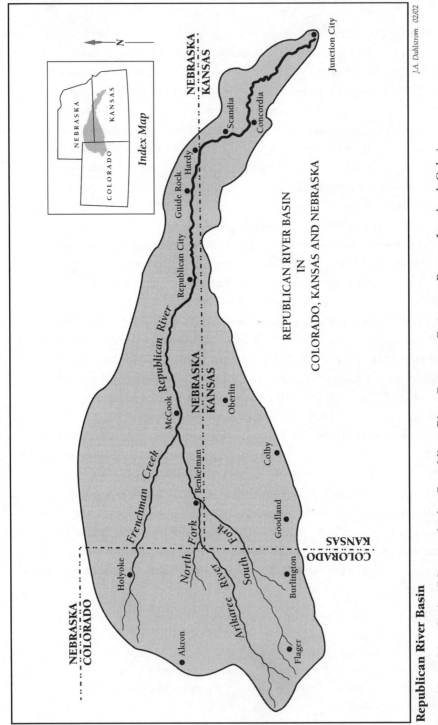

Republican River Basin

Republican River Basin. (Map attached to Republican River Compact, Carpenter Papers, Loveland, Colo.)

J.A. Dahlstrom 02/02

The feeling of isolation, loneliness and sacrifice surfaced in Carpenter most frequently when he was overworked. Passionate as he was about the importance of settling disputes on interstate streams, he also felt that too few people comprehended the importance of his efforts to defend Colorado's natural resources for future generations. The Supreme Court, in his opinion, was "badly confused' by these western water issues. Judge Willis Van Devanter (who was not at the Supreme Court when the Republican River case was heard) seemed to have his own "preconceived opinion," and the rest of the Court appeared to be "desirous of settl[ing] interstate water problems by fiat in the Wyoming case."[50] Nevertheless, befitting his sense of loyalty to the state, he invested every intellectual and emotional strength he possessed into his presentation. As he later recalled:

> I argued the Republican River case, with the deliberate purpose of throwing a side light upon the Wyoming case and, while my time was so limited that I could barely touch upon the law of the case, nevertheless, I believe the effect may have been to cause the Court to pause before rendering a possible decision along the lines of priority irrespective of state lines. I laid particular stress upon the fact that the enforcement of the doctrine [of interstate priorities] would be an invasion of the local jurisdiction of the upper [headwaters] state, an interference with the sovereign control of the resources within its border, and, above all, would compel the State officials to violate, not follow, the law of their own State.[51]

But his argument failed to convince the justices. When the Supreme Court issued the long-awaited decision in *Wyoming v. Colorado* (June, 1922), it recognized interstate priorities on streams where states endorsed the principle of prior appropriation. On that same date, the High Court disposed of the Republican River case by referring to the *Wyoming* decision as an authoritative precedent.[52]

Colorado lost the priority battle, but Carpenter learned certain lessons from his work on the Laramie and Republican rivers. Headwaters states, such as Colorado, would not fare well in interstate stream conflicts if the Supreme Court decided the outcome. If he could effect the apportionment of water among states through negotiations leading to compact agreements prior to a trial, the impact of a Supreme Court decree could be minimized or altogether avoided.

The Republican River Compact of 1942, even though it was signed twenty years after the High Court's verdict, proved this point. It is one of many agreements on interstate streams, resulting from Carpenter's vision of Colorado's future, all of which led to his being known as "the father of the compact idea."[53] The Republican River Compact allocated surface water to Colorado, Kansas, and Nebraska, and specified that the waters allocated to each would be subject to the laws of the state in which they were put to beneficial use. It proved effective in deterring litigation until advanced technology made possible the removal of water from deep wells in the Republican River basin.[54]

The real victory for Carpenter was the statement in Article V of the compact that "Colorado, through its duly authorized officials, shall have the perpetual and exclusive right to control and regulate diversions of water at all times by said canal [Nebraska's Pioneer Irrigation Company] in conformity with said judgment."[55] In other words, Colorado would control its own water and would not have to accept an odious and constricting servitude imposed by neighboring states claiming senior priorities.[56] Since the end of his senatorial career, Carpenter had been developing this concept gradually. It was the guiding principle he hoped to pursue when he returned to South Platte River discussions with Nebraska after his Court appearance in Washington regarding the Republican River.

His first task was to find a solution to Nebraska's claim for an 1897 priority date on the South Platte River. Carpenter sensed he was making history. Negotiations with Nebraska's interstate streams commissioner, R. H. Willis, established principles and precedents later used in resolving the seven-state conflict on the Colorado River.[57] The key to success was proving to Willis that irrigation in Colorado created a vast land sponge through which water gradually returned to the river year round, making the South Platte a more constant and dependable source for downstream Nebraskans. Carpenter was willing to offer the Nebraskans some water if they would agree to stop fighting and look for a constructive solution to the conflict.[58]

Throughout 1918, he continued to read memoirs, reflections and diaries of early travelers on the South Platte Trail. He took affidavits from dozens of oldsters who remembered the river before Indians and buffalo disappeared from the plains; he took photographs of used and unused ditches; and he continued to travel up and down the river, blowing out tires on his Dodge in "blast furnace" weather. He looked for good reservoir sites and concluded that, for the most part, Nebraskans were content to gamble with the weather, ignorant of irrigation, and misled by politicians who were nothing more than purveyors of misinformation.[59]

Ever the consummate diplomat, however, Carpenter kept these opinions in his diary. More openly, he designed a plan whose simplicity belied the extensive historical, hydrological, and engineering data accumulated over a five-year period. What he discovered was that the South Platte River had an upper and lower segment. The upper part of the river, into which most of the tributaries fed and where most of Colorado's irrigated agriculture was located, terminated for all intents and purposes at a point where Washington and Morgan counties came together. The lower part of the river, Water District 64 in Colorado, stretched across the state line into Nebraska to a point where the North and South Platte rivers joined. Carpenter was convinced that topography in the lower river was an obstacle to further irrigation and reservoir development by Colorado, but Nebraskans could benefit from return flows generated by expanded irrigation on the upper river. Capitalizing on a cordial relationship with Willis, he drew up a compact guaranteeing a mean flow of water across state lines into Nebraska while denying Nebraska's claims to an unqualified 1897 prior appropriation date within Colorado boundaries.

The final compact was signed in Lincoln, Nebraska, on April 27, 1923. It represented the first effort of two states to use the treaty power of the Constitution for the settlement of interstate stream conflicts. Although the Colorado River Compact was actually signed four months earlier, the principles and objectives of interstate compacts were first tested and found acceptable on the South Platte River. From Carpenter's point of view, he had been able to persuade Nebraska that water users on the lower river would be protected "without injury to present and future users in Colorado," thus permitting "practically unlimited expansion and development in Colorado."[60] Carpenter believed the compact provided a *permanent* solution for both states, one that would establish peace between neighbors while encouraging entrepreneurial activity without risk of litigation.

His inability to build the same relationship with Wyoming was troublesome. The Greeley-Poudre Irrigation Project was all but defunct. Even though some water was flowing through the Laramie-Poudre Tunnel, district bonds were selling for twelve cents on the dollar. The longer the Supreme Court sat on the *Wyoming v. Colorado* case, the more investors

doubted that enough water would be adjudicated for Colorado to fill the
project's needs. Parts of the project had been purchased already by outside interests and there were liens on many of the lands where taxes were
unpaid. Still, amidst criticism and waning support, Carpenter defended
his client. He believed in the future of irrigated agriculture. When another
attorney attacked him for filing a condemnation suit that would prevent
a competitive group from owning the first sixteen miles of the Greeley-
Poudre ditch system, Delph replied:

> Get as mad as you wish, say all the unkind things about me you can,
> post my name in red letters on the bill boards and throw rocks at it
> and get it off your system, but believe me, friend Russell [Fleming],
> I am going to stay with the people that have made possible the value
> of your properties and are developing a great desert into beautiful
> fields. These people have been my loyal clients and I will not quit
> them now or at any other time.[61]

Clearly, Carpenter was having to choose between the kind of adversarial combat that might benefit local irrigation interests and allegiance to
the broader constitutional theories whose application could reduce the
potential of interstate litigation over a period. Because he saw the opportunity to enhance his career, and because the prospects for successful litigation now seemed doubtful, he chose to embrace the broader theories
that would help him make his mark. In a letter to F. W. Harding, secretary
of the American Shorthorn Breeders' Association, he admitted that "a successful defense of [interstate] suits causes one to take a position almost as
foreign to his own business as though he were engaged in a foreign war
upon foreign soil."[62]

Considering the fact that Carpenter had begun the South Platte litigation by accusing Nebraskans of waging the equivalent of war on the sovereign state of Colorado, the South Platte Compact represented a change
in his thinking about conflict resolution. When states began to rely on the
Supreme Court for the solution of interstate water problems, they were
engaging in the equivalent of war without first exploring the possibility of
diplomacy. The sovereignty of states under the U.S. Constitution, he argued,
should be more widely understood. Few public officials were familiar with
comparable international circumstances or the language of the American
Constitution. Consequently, they did not appreciate the powers that states

already possessed to solve interstate water conflicts by treaty. The Supreme Court, he charged, was especially remiss in not requiring diplomatic negotiations between states "as a condition precedent to the granting of leave to institute interstate suits."[63]

When applied to disputes on interstate streams, Carpenter's thoughts were innovative, but the intellectual endeavor took a lot out of him. As he looked into the future, he foresaw problems that could easily keep Colorado on the legal defensive for a long time to come, principally because of the state's geographical location at the headwaters of major western rivers. The seemingly endless work he accepted on behalf of Colorado and the Greeley-Poudre Irrigation Company forced him into a state of almost constant exhaustion. At some point in later 1918 or early 1919, he succumbed to the Spanish influenza virus. After repeated entries in his diary to the effect that he was "very, very tired," Carpenter confessed that his health was "slightly impaired from overwork on interstate water litigation," and that he was in "semi-retirement."[64] He thought he had a neuritis condition that would go away with rest, but doctors' examinations later concluded that the unusually severe influenza had settled into his body as a form of Parkinson's disease. Tragically, Carpenter's health had begun to deteriorate at the very moment when serious and unsettling developments on the lower Colorado River demanded more of him than at any other time in his career.

California's Imperial Valley was the center of the new controversy. It was one of the nation's richest agricultural areas. It had come close to total annihilation between 1905 and 1907 when the Colorado River built up a silt barrier at the head gate of the Alamo Canal and diverted itself entirely into farmers' fields and homes, creating the Salton Sea. Trains of the Southern Pacific Railroad loaded with large boulders ultimately stemmed the rush of water, saving something of the farming community. A new diversion point for the canal was constructed and levees were put in place to keep the river between its banks, but predictions of future floods worried the valley's inhabitants. The Colorado River's relentless cutting force, its uncontrollable power during spring run-off, and the incessant deposit of silt threatening the canal's new head gate created an incessant demand for flood control.

Economic and demographic expansion continued in the Imperial Valley in spite of concerns about the river. Los Angeles and San Diego boomed, but southern California felt isolated and disconnected from the economy of the rest of the United States. In order to call attention to the Colorado River's vital role in the area's development, San Diego publicist Arnold Kruckman organized a group of businesses and local governments to promote economic growth by trumpeting the beauties of the area and waving the flag of patriotism for America's participation in World War I.[65]

The League of the Southwest was born in San Diego in 1917, seven months after the United States entered the war. Delegates at the first convention included representatives from eight western states and six foreign countries, all of which were interested in transforming the Colorado River basin into a unified, habitable, and productive community. Mexico was one of the countries represented, but both Mexicans and Indians were ineligible for membership in the League. Municipal, cultural, commercial, industrial, county, and state organizations were invited to join the organization. Individuals were denied the right to vote, but member organizations could obtain a number of votes equal to the number of memberships purchased at $25 each.[66]

Kruckman's objective was to establish a unified power base capable of sustaining a partnership with the federal government. Convention-goers passed resolutions, emphasizing the importance of the Colorado River to regional development and calling on Congress to solve the "ever-present problem of the refractory" stream while promoting "reclamation of lands along the river." They also urged the government to build more highways and called on more Hispanics to enlist in the war.[67] The convention was a mixture of patriotic pageantry and a declaration that federal assistance would be needed if the Southwest was to advance economically.

The League conducted a second meeting in Tucson in January 1918, the same month Carpenter presented oral argument in the second phase of the *Wyoming v. Colorado* litigation in Washington. Compared to the four hundred delegates who showed up in San Diego, only fifty made it to Arizona. They addressed drought relief, discussed the "vital need" for federal assistance in eliminating the annual flood menace, and urged Congress to survey potential storage sites in the Colorado River basin. It soon became clear that Kruckman's goal of unity would be difficult to achieve until all participants agreed to a workable system of water law.

Most western states had adopted some form of the Colorado Doctrine, but California also recognized riparian rights. Additionally, each of the seven Colorado River basin states had questions about international and interstate law that required answers before agreement on any potential projects could be obtained. As of 1918, most states acted on a basis of premeditated self-interest. They assumed that conflicts would end up in the Supreme Court, but the Court had yet to give clear direction. As noted above, the High Court handed down only one relevant decision, *Kansas v. Colorado* in 1907, but that decision failed to address the issues of transbasin diversion and interstate priority. Furthermore, rights of the federal government on western streams were still being contested. These were the issues with which Carpenter had been dealing in his work on the Laramie, Republican, and South Platte rivers.[68]

Tucson delegates called for an interstate conference to address the lack of consensus on water law. Due to postwar problems, however, the next official League meeting did not occur until 1920. In January 1919, all Colorado River basin states sent representatives to Salt Lake City for the purpose of considering legislation proposed by Secretary of the Interior Franklin K. Lane to reclaim four million acres of land in the Colorado River basin for World War I veterans and other interested persons. Lane was convinced that a "National Soldier and Settlement Act" would provide jobs, attach the best sort of Americans to the soil, reduce the rate of flight to cities, and put neglected, but potentially valuable, lands to good use. He supported legislation to achieve this objective and was pleased to announce that Arthur P. Davis, the Reclamation Service's director and chief engineer, was preparing the necessary data concerning land resources in this region.[69]

The United States Reclamation Service was enthusiastic about Lane's proposal. Its engineers had shown considerable interest in building storage and flood control projects on the Colorado River since 1915. From that year forward, annual reports consistently listed sites available for dams and reservoirs, the advantages of irrigated agriculture, and statements underscoring the need for a federally supported reclamation program that would sustain the national "return to the farm movement." By 1921, Reclamation Service engineers were sufficiently impressed with possibilities at the Boulder Canyon site to make an agreement with Los Angeles, Pasadena, and the Coachella Valley to carry on further investigations. Another area of interest was the Alamo Canal. Diverting water from the Colorado River just above the international border, the canal dipped into Mexico for fifty

miles before crossing back into the U.S. Imperial Valley farmers feared the
Mexicans would not maintain the canal properly, thus putting at risk the
water required by their crops. Davis favored an All-American Canal and also
believed there was sufficient water in the Colorado River to supply all the
basin's needs. He was eager to engage in construction of works that would
put this water to reliable and beneficial use.[70]

Government officials wanted to prevent another Imperial Valley disaster and hoped to provide a safe and secure environment for these new
settlers. Eventually, they agreed to pay one-third of the cost of a study to
determine the feasibility of an All-American Canal from the Colorado
River to the Imperial Valley.[71] Although the government's enthusiasm for
such a project appeared on the surface to be well-meaning and constructive, representatives of upper basin states began to suspect that southern
California and the Department of Interior were moving forward in a
potentially powerful partnership without consulting the Colorado River's
states of origin: Wyoming, Colorado, New Mexico, and Utah. From their
viewpoint, construction of works on the lower Colorado contained the
potential for large claims of priority at a later date.

This fear was addressed for the first time at the Salt Lake City meeting.
With support from the National Irrigation Congress, whose principal journal mouthpiece, the *Irrigation Age,* had relocated from Chicago to Salt Lake
City, delegates considered the Lane bill in a discussion that involved all of
the Colorado River basin states. The *Irrigation Age* had also become the
official organ of the League of the Southwest. Although its editors had
been critical of the Reclamation Service's past policies, they, too, had
begun to support legitimate government projects that would advance irrigated agriculture.

Carpenter, however, was unenthusiastic about Lane's proposals. He
remained convinced that the federal government would try any scheme
to win legal control over western water. He hoped that "great caution and
prudence [would] be exercised in order that the rights of the state[s]
should not be inadvertently bargained away."[72] He shared these views with
Louis Carpenter, Colorado representative at the Salt Lake City meeting
and the engineer on whom he relied during preparation for argument in
the *Wyoming* case. Louis Carpenter saw how the League might play a major
role in future developments on the Colorado River, and he encouraged
Colorado officials to take a more active interest in this organization. More

particularly, he noted, Colorado should understand "the extent to which the construction of a reservoir at the lower reaches of the Colorado River, and the rulings that might be made, [could] affect the development of Colorado."[73]

Here, then, was the central issue for the Colorado River basin states. Although still not an official member of the League, Colorado had called attention to the threat to future development in the upper basin states if federally constructed works were placed on the lower Colorado River. Because of his experience with Nebraska and Wyoming over the issue of interstate priorities, Carpenter understood how dam construction on the lower Colorado River could obligate Colorado to future water deliveries. He also understood that if the threatened levees broke again on the lower Colorado, the lower basin states would quickly find federal agencies interested in controlling western rivers, regardless of upper basin pleas for equity. For these reasons, he was pleased by the outcome of events that transpired at the Salt Lake City gathering.

At that meeting, the advocates of immediate reservoir construction on the lower reaches of the Colorado River urged a united effort to secure federal aid, but upper basin representatives objected. Logically, they argued, the first works on the Colorado River should be constructed in the headwaters states so that these states would have "protection against adverse claims which might result from immediate development upon the lower river."[74] In spite of Reclamation Service assurances that development along the lower river would in no way injure the upper states, a number of delegates reminded government officials of the "illegal federal policy of refusing to grant rights of way for irrigation works over the public domain" in New Mexico, Colorado, and Wyoming.[75]

A resolutions committee responded accordingly. It composed a declaration endorsing the idea that flowing water is most efficiently used when it is first captured upstream in order that its reuse can occur as it flows downstream and back into the basin. The resolution further urged the Interior and Agriculture departments to develop a "liberal and sympathetic policy" in which rights of way for reservoirs and ditches would be granted on the public domain with the objective of "placing the lands of the United States in the actual possession and occupation of its citizens." In conformity with these guidelines, conferees pledged themselves to a "hearty cooperation" with the federal government so long as government activity conformed to the laws of the states, including laws dealing with "appropriation of water," from which projects were to be developed.[76] For Carpenter, this guarantee of states' rights, especially in the upper basin, and the endorsement of what he believed to be the most efficient method of utilizing river water in arid states were huge votes of confidence in the principles he had been espousing for some time.

But the upper basin's euphoria was short-lived. At the first postwar meeting of the League in Los Angeles in the spring of 1920, the delegates, 80 percent of whom were Californians, exhorted the government to begin development on the lower river rather than at the headwaters. They requested the government to complete its hydrographic studies so that "prompt construction" could begin of a "great dam . . . at or near Boulder Canyon."[77]

Kruckman believed that the "psychological" moment had arrived to present these demands to Congress. His enthusiasm was shared by Director Davis, who told the conference that a dam, "possibly 500 or 600 feet high," could store as much as 25 million acre-feet of water, enough to "control the floods . . . and the silt deposits," thus preventing "any material damage [along the lower Colorado River] for hundreds of years." Additionally, Davis noted, "a large amount of power could be developed to operate several thousand miles of railroad which are within the limits of practical power transmission."[78]

This eagerness to build a large dam on the lower Colorado was not what officials of the upper states wanted to hear, at least not without some guarantee of protection. Victor Keyes, Colorado's attorney general, informed the conference that his state contributed 85 percent of the water of the Colorado River. Colorado was anxious to retain part of that runoff for its own development, a principle embraced in the Salt Lake City resolution and calculated "to assure prosperity for 'the whole of the great Southwest,' not simply for his state."[79] If a dam were to be built, Colorado's preference would be for one on the Green River or the Grand River, both of which were considered principal sources of the main stem of the Colorado River.[80]

Not all of the spokesmen for the upper basin states agreed. Governor Simon Bamberger of Utah vetoed any idea of a dam on the Green River because he felt it would actually "hamper, not further, the economic development of northeastern Utah and northwestern Colorado."[81] Other delegates from the upper river voiced sympathy for the plight of Imperial Valley residents. Additional support for dam construction at Boulder Canyon came from Harry Chandler of the *Los Angeles Times,* whose 250,000 acres of farmland south of the Mexican border would benefit immeasurably from flood control on the lower Colorado River.

The Reclamation Service reassured everyone present there was ample water in the Colorado River for each state's needs. Even Keyes agreed that the League's immediate focus should be on a dam at Boulder Canyon. Delegates approved a resolution to this effect and created a committee of state and Reclamation Service engineers to map out a comprehensive development plan for the entire Colorado River basin. At meeting's end, the seven states of the Colorado River basin enjoyed a felicity of purpose, the likes of which they would not experience again until they signed the Colorado River Compact in the fall of 1922.

Suspicion and doubt surfaced unexpectedly following adjournment of the Los Angeles meeting. Lower basin proponents of an All-American Canal feared that Director Davis's repeated assurances of ample water in the Colorado River for all claimants would lead to United States recognition of Mexico's claims to half the water diverted from the Colorado River below the international border. In reality, however, members of Congress were more concerned about the impact of further agricultural development on already deflated farm prices. Hoping to obtain more information, they passed the Kinkaid Act in May 1920, directing the secretary of the Interior Department to complete surveys of the river and to investigate the Imperial Valley's problems. This legislation authorized the government to provide part of the survey costs if local groups, particularly those in the Imperial Valley, would provide the balance.[82]

It was really Davis who drove this project forward. Even before becoming Reclamation's director, he had what professor Norris Hundley, Jr., refers to as "almost an obsession" with development of the Colorado River.[83] In response to California's concerns, he met with the Los Angeles Chamber of Commerce in July 1920, promising his support for an All-American Canal and a large reservoir on the lower river. Upper basin leaders viewed Davis's actions as conspiratorial. Attempting to gain admittance to the meeting, they were at first denied, and when the doors finally opened to them, no one was interested in their views. The rebuff was exacerbated a month later when a large group of Californians met with Davis in San Diego to discuss financing the surveys authorized in the Kinkaid Act.[84]

To Coloradans, the train seemed to be leaving the station without them. The government appeared to be ignoring upper basin concerns, while wooing California's support for projects the Reclamation Service desperately wanted to build. Director Davis repeatedly opposed building projects on the upper Colorado River until the danger of potential flooding could be addressed downstream. From his perspective, the upper basin states simply had nothing to worry about. There was plenty of water in the river and he was "willing to stake [his] reputation upon the belief that it is feasible . . . to store the waters of the Colorado River below the cañons of the Colorado . . . and not interfere in any way with the use of the water in the basin above."[85]

By August 1920, so much interest had been generated in the future of the Colorado River that what was supposed to be a meeting of the League's engineering committee turned into its fourth, and most significant, official gathering. From all seven states of the Colorado River basin, representatives convened in the senate chambers of Denver's capitol. They listened intently as Coloradans expressed anxieties shared by Wyomingites, Utahans, and New Mexicans. To some degree, they all sensed a cabal developing between California and the Reclamation Service. "Our main fear," stated Colorado's state engineer, A. J. McCune, "is that Los Angeles and the Imperial Valley will get the government committed to a policy that will interfere with our development."[86] Colorado hoped to cooperate with the other states, but wanted to be left alone to develop its own irrigation projects.

The moment was portentous, not only because most of the states were represented by their governors but because there was a "frank and serious undertone" reflecting the near stalemate at which they had arrived. Most importantly, an acceptable solution was found to the growing polarization between the upper and lower basin. Colorado Governor Oliver Shoup turned to Carpenter for a plan that would combine protection for the upper basin's freedom to develop at its own pace with a dam and reservoir for flood control on the lower river. Drawn up in the form of a resolution for League delegates, Carpenter's proposal urged application of the states' treaty-making powers under Article I, section 10 of the U.S. Constitution. In terms of western water history, this was a watershed event. Although it was something he had been working over in his mind for nearly a decade, this was the first time the idea was openly suggested to a large delegation of western states.

In his welcoming remarks to League members in Denver, Governor Shoup indicated that he wanted a different approach to Colorado River issues. He also insisted that upper basin states would not give up any of their rights "for any reason whatever. . . . It is important to us," he said, "to make this clear to the country at large, so that our future may not be jeopardized."[87] Former Colorado state engineer John H. Field echoed these sentiments. He regretted Colorado's earlier endorsement of a high dam on the lower Colorado River. All he asked of fellow delegates was that Colorado "not be dealt with in ignorance. . . . Colorado does not fear anything if proper investigation and proper consideration has [sic] been had."[88]

Retiring to his office in the capitol on the evening of August 26, Carpenter drew up the draft resolution, calling on his collective experiences with other states and the federal government. His 1912 discussions with Colorado engineer Royce Tipton, regarding the federal government's embargo on irrigation projects in the San Luis Valley, had started him thinking about interstate compacts. While constructing Elephant Butte Dam on the Rio Grande in New Mexico, the Department of Interior had shut down development upstream in Colorado. This embargo caused Carpenter to become an impassioned advocate of states' rights. His suspicions of the federal bureaucracy were strengthened after working with solicitors from the Reclamation Service in the *Wyoming v. Colorado* litigation. The federal government seemed determined to undermine state autonomy by seizing control of western rivers.

A solution could be found in the compact clause of the U.S. Constitution. States were allowed to negotiate treaties among themselves with congressional permission. Heretofore, fishing rights and boundary disputes had been resolved by means of interstate treaties, but no interstate stream conflict had been settled in this manner. As of 1920, conflicts on interstate streams were supposed to be resolved through litigation. Carpenter's compact ideas had been ridiculed in the past by those who sought a clear-cut victory in court, but the potential for disaster on the lower Colorado River in the summer of 1920 provided an opportunity for change.

Carpenter was aware the League had run out of ideas. He saw Shoup's challenge as a chance to leave a lasting legacy for himself and for his beloved state of Colorado. Because he had developed an acute sense of history, he knew that the moment had arrived to attempt public approval of the interstate compact idea. But he was also a politician, and he was aware that any innovative plan would be most likely to succeed if it were presented to League delegates as an already approved resolution. Therefore, when the draft was ready, he submitted it to the resolutions committee as follows:

> Resolved, That it is the sense of this conference that the present and future rights of the several States whose territory is in whole or in part included within the drainage area of the Colorado River, and the rights of the United States, to the use and benefit of the waters of said stream and its tributaries, should be settled and determined by compact or agreement between said States and the United States, with consent of Congress, and that the legislatures of said States be requested to authorize the appointment of a commissioner for each of said states for the purpose of entering into such compact or agreement for subsequent ratification and approval by the legislature of each of said States and the Congress of the United States.[89]

Carpenter persuaded New Mexico's state engineer, L. A. Gillett, to father the resolution before the committee. Some discussion ensued, but it was so strongly supported by Shoup and Gillett that it was soon approved unanimously and included as part of the committee's report to the full body of the League.

Approval came quickly. As Carpenter later recalled, "None comprehended the full import of the resolutions which were adopted as a matter of course, and the meeting adjourned."[90] It was clear, however, that for political reasons, the lower basin states had come to appreciate the need for cooperation with the upper basin. Approval of Carpenter's resolution represented a trade-off. A dam on the lower river would require approval by congressional representatives on key committees representing all seven states; in return for flood control, a promise of protection for future upper basin development would eliminate upper basin fear of a California-imposed servitude.

A *Denver Post* reporter was the only representative of the press to interview Carpenter after approval of the resolution. Consistent with the tone of another article in the *Rocky Mountain News*, the reporter's comments were matter-of-fact and uninspired. Response from Reclamation came from Davis, who expressed some concern at what appeared to be a "complete change in policy respecting reclamation matters." But Carpenter had a "satisfactory" interview with him, after which Davis offered his "unqualified support."[91] As Professor Hundley insightfully observed, the stage was now set "for a pioneering adventure in interstate diplomacy."[92]

It is not hard to imagine Carpenter's sense of pride. His 1920 diary suggests he thought mostly about how he was going to save his purebred herd of Bates Shorthorn cattle. But an article in the October 1920 issue of *Country Gentleman*, and related correspondence between Carpenter and author E. V. Wilcox, shed some light on what the Coloradan felt about his role in preserving Colorado's water.

Wilcox wanted to refer to him as "The Greeley Oracle." But Carpenter asked that he be seen in a more humble light. He had been given the chance to advance the cause of reclamation first defined by pioneers such as Nathan C. Meeker, Governor Benjamin H. Eaton, and Daniel A. Camfield. All were "vilified and abused," Carpenter wrote to Wilcox, a generation before their time, but they built visionary projects appreciated by those who followed. Carpenter's grandfather, Daniel Carpenter, spent a fortune "fulfilling the Meeker ideal." His father "continued the struggle" and broke under the strain. "Could the son and grandson do other than continue the drive," Carpenter asked, "if he were American and were the true descendant of such men?"[93]

Obviously not! "To those of us who make up the second generation," Carpenter noted, must fall the task of "overcoming original mistakes or reconstructing financial blunders. . . . Ours is the duty of . . . defending what we have, as well as that of pioneering in fact and in law." To understand "why my life is devoted to interstate water litigation," one need only look at Colorado's location on the crest of the continent. The lower states look at the origin states with jealous eyes and seek ways "to break down the barrier of the State boundary." The Reclamation Service is prone to join with them, hoping to become an administrative agency for distribution of the water of our streams. The "future welfare of mankind forbids" this. Even though we are "attacked from various quarters," Carpenter wrote, Colorado had to defend its property rights. Agricultural growth in the upper basin "dissipates the disastrous floods and brings back [the] water in [a] steady flow to the same general drainage in the form of seepage water from the great land sponge."[94] Lower states actually benefit from basin-of-origin development.

Through the police power of the state, Colorado developed the administration of its public waters, "long prior to other states." And as a sovereign state, Carpenter argued, Colorado has the right to regulate and administer its own natural resources. "We cannot concur with the hidden ambition of the Reclamation Service to become a perpetual body for interstate regulation of waters of the streams. No such power exists under the Constitution and Colorado needed no help from that quarter." But the actions of the government and lower states placed Colorado on the defensive. If other states wanted some of Colorado's water, an interstate compact would allow each party to take a "reasonable portion, whatever it [might] be under all the facts and circumstances, which materially differ[ed] on each interstate stream. . . . [I]t is the duty and privilege of some of us of the second generation to defend, never attack, the water rights of our farmers now and to be."[95]

Nothing that Carpenter wrote at this time better illustrates his pride of accomplishment at the League meeting in Denver, his passion for interstate water work, his dedication to state sovereignty, and his determination to honor the memory and add to the works of earlier pioneers. With a strong sense of regional history, a love of constitutional law, and a determination to protect Colorado's future, Carpenter accepted the challenge of organizing the Colorado River Compact Commission. Within months of his success at the Denver meeting, Governor Shoup named him "ambassador" for Colorado on the states' major streams. His assignment was to negotiate treaties and avoid interstate water litigation.[96] A career, which his father had told him he would have to invent, was now defined as much by his own drive to succeed as by economic and political circumstances on the West's major rivers.

CHAPTER 4

The Colorado River Compact: Phase I

Herbert Hoover: We have not been able to get any agreement on a general single idea for a compact. Therefore, this session has no result except to define differences. The question arises, is it worth while to have another session? Or shall we make the declaration now that we are so hopelessly far apart that there is no use in proceeding? Do the commissioners think there is any basis of arriving at an agreement?

Delph Carpenter: I feel frankly that this is a matter requiring very prudent and thoughtful treatment. Hasty treatment would be unwarranted. We are here with a pretty sacred trust and it should not be treated lightly. I really believe that in the months and weeks to come many small matters of difference can be argued out.

—MINUTES, COLORADO RIVER COMPACT COMMISSION,
SEVENTH MEETING, JANUARY 30, 1922

From the August 1920 meeting of the League of the Southwest in Denver to the signing of the Colorado River Compact in November 1922, Carpenter's career reached its apogee. Although his health and financial affairs were at times unstable, no other period of his life was so filled with intellectual and physical vibrancy. From his perspective, the League's 1920 resolution, committing seven Colorado River basin states to the treaty

process, was a clear vindication of his endorsement of negotiation over litigation and state sovereignty over centralized government. With support
from the other commissioners and encouragement from Secretary of
Commerce Herbert Hoover, the United States' representative on the Colorado River Compact Commission (CRCC), Carpenter eventually succeeded
in effecting a seven-state compact that he later referred to as "the first
exemplification of interstate diplomacy in the history of the United States
on so large a scale."[1]

He had been immersed in the struggle for interstate river compacts
since Nebraska's 1916 suit over appropriative rights on the South Platte
River, and he had discussed compact negotiations with other states that
shared surface water with Colorado even earlier. But most of his counterparts in the field of water law expected the courts to resolve interstate problems. The thought of negotiation, compromise, and the equitable sharing
of a jointly used natural resource was anathema to them. For the most
part—and with the notable exception of Nebraska—Carpenter usually
argued his compact theory with attorneys, engineers, and government officials who preferred to risk all in long, drawn-out legal battles.

Not so Carpenter. When preliminaries of Colorado River negotiations
began in 1921, he doubted the Supreme Court's willingness to grant jurisdiction of origin priority to any state located at the headwaters of a major
river system. He feared the High Court would soon recognize the principle of interstate priority, thereby placing basin-of-origin states in a condition of servitude to faster growing downstream states. He was determined,
therefore, to lead the CRCC through the legal mine field of treaty-making. At the age of forty-five, convinced that he could make a difference in
how the West developed, Carpenter embraced the idea of a Colorado River
Compact with evangelical fervor, not only as a necessary antidote to interstate litigation but as his own, self-defining cause.

Although Hoover eventually pronounced in favor of the compact plan,
Carpenter's zeal and inflexibility were initially offensive to him. The two
men came from very similar midwestern roots. Both believed that certain
praiseworthy character traits appeared in those who worked the land, especially the first generation of sod busters. Part of this legacy caused them to
be suspicious of change proposed by others. Although both saw strong
state and local government as the sine qua non of a healthy federal republic, their black-and-white approach to certain issues bred suspicion of each

other. They were inclined to oppose suggestions that seemed to be inconsistent with their own core beliefs. Sometimes their egos got in the way,
causing stubbornness and inflexibility to rule their relationship. In retrospect, however, both men were also innovators in their respective careers.
When they finally learned to appreciate each other's intellectual acumen,
integrity, and mutual interests, a friendship was born that lasted until
Carpenter's death in 1951.

Colorado engineer Ralph I. Meeker developed an appreciation of Carpenter's unique talents more rapidly. The two men had known and
respected one another for more than a decade. Referring to him as "Mr.
Ambassador of Liquid Gold and Salvation of Colorado,"[2] Meeker frequently
commented on Carpenter's skills as intellectual, politician, man of the soil,
principled debater, negotiator, and man of vision who was capable of bringing about agreement among adversaries with parochial and proprietary
interests. Meeker was a talented engineer. His data proved invaluable to Carpenter, and was good enough to be accepted by other state officials as well
as the federal government. As the relationship bloomed between these two
men, so did their mutual admiration. Meeker began referring to Carpenter
as the "Silver Fox of the Rockies," probably because he saw him as sly but
also because he firmly believed his talents were rare and of great value to
the future of the West.[3] For his part, Meeker became "The Lone Wolf," a
force to be reckoned with during debates on interstate river hydrology.

While the two men complimented each other's skills, Meeker was probably unaware that Carpenter wrestled with his own demons. Formation of
the CRCC represented the professional chance of a lifetime for Carpenter,
but he was profoundly aware that failure could end his career. He saw himself as possibly "the only lawyer in America, if not in the world, whose practice was confined exclusively to litigation and disputes between states
respecting the use and disposition of waters of interstate rivers."[4] Because
the other commissioners and western state governors tended to view him
in the same light, he eventually accepted a leadership role, but he remained
vulnerable and sensitive to criticism. Committed to the goal of a seven-state
compact, he drew on proven strengths of oratory, legal analysis, and common sense, all learned from his parents and refined in the public arena
of adversarial politics. Demanding what was best for Colorado and the West
required an extraordinary amount of perseverance, but Carpenter believed
so deeply in his mission that it became an obsession.

Carpenter needed to find Colorado River solutions that enabled his state and the upper basin to develop at a pace consistent with geographic and economic realities. He defined his duty as that of "correcting [past] mistakes and defending what we have, as well as that of pioneering in fact and law."[5] In a tone that now sounds defiant, he noted that Colorado, on the crest of the continent, was the birthplace of the Colorado River. "We claim no right to entirely shut off our streams from other states," Carpenter stated.

> All we ask is to be let alone. . . . We have originated and developed administration of public waters through the police power of the state, long prior to other states. . . . We cannot concur with the hidden ambition of the Reclamation Service to become a perpetual body for interstate regulation of waters of the streams. . . . If other states have a grievance we will gladly meet and treat and will enter into inter- state compact in manner as provided by the federal constitution. We do not ask for the whole, as probably we have a right to do, but are willing to take our reasonable portion, whatever it may be under all the facts and circumstances. . . .

No one questioned Carpenter's sincerity, but few understood the rea- son for his zeal and the extent to which his family's pioneer past influenced his thinking. He was an interstate water lawyer who had argued cases before the United States Supreme Court. But he was also a "cow puncher, wrestling with the calves, cussing at the men and indulging in the ordinary modest undertakings of an agriculturist." The rural West was Carpenter's environment. He wanted to improve the quality of farming and livestock raising and he felt an affinity with those who made their living in agricul- ture. His duty as an interstate water lawyer was to represent the people who worked the land and who would build better western communities if inter- state agreements reflected their needs and values.[6]

Carpenter was at best an absentee rancher who grew up believing that land ownership was the key to wealth, but raising livestock on his own land was more than just a hobby. No matter how much he enjoyed the limelight of politics and the excitement of the courtroom, in his own eyes he was still a cattleman and farmer. Early success in showing his herd of Bates Shorthorn cattle gave him great satisfaction, but the postwar depression in agriculture made it difficult for him to keep his herd and pay off loans.[7]

As he prepared to begin CRCC negotiations, he referred to his financial situation as "desperate." Sheep and cattle feeders were losing money all around him. Banks were unwilling to make loans and his few legal clients failed to pay bills. "I must work my clients with all my might," he concluded, "[or] the ammunition wagon will be worse than empty."[8] But he refused to abandon the ranch. It represented continuity with his past and a fantasy of the Old West to which he could always retreat when the pressure of litigation wore him down.

As with his legal work, Carpenter's livestock operations reflected an obsession with perfection. Interstate water was his business; cattle were his avocation.[9] He approached both with the same vigor and enthusiasm. He wanted to shape the West's future and he chose the Bates Shorthorn breed because he was convinced their offspring would most quickly improve farmers' herds in Colorado and Wyoming. His dams and sires were "inferior to none in America" and were capable of enduring "sundry changes of weather" in the Rocky Mountain region. Most importantly, the animals were good milkers and easy to breed.[10]

Carpenter developed an interest in Bates Shorthorns when he was a boy. One of Weld County's pioneer ranchers was an Englishman whose Shorthorns served the dual purpose of being good beef cattle and good milkers. By 1919, Carpenter had a herd of eighty-five carefully selected animals. Nothing rewarded him more, he stated, than the "satisfaction of doing something worthwhile for this God's garden of plain and mountain that gave [him] the boyhood inspiration to found a herd of [Bates Shorthorn] cattle."[11]

The Bates line of Shorthorns almost became extinct in the United States, following an attempt by breeders to merge the beefy Scotch Shorthorns with the English milk strains. Carpenter struggled to find bulls and cows with pure Bates bloodlines. He located stocker animals in Texas and Kentucky, convinced that pairing his bulls with the "scrub cows" on most Colorado farms would produce superior offspring. Eventually, he established a foundation herd that served the local community and earned praise from the land grant university in Fort Collins.[12]

When the CRCC began its meetings in 1921, Carpenter came to the table with a compact philosophy that intertwined with his views on the future of western farmers and ranchers. Irrigated agriculture was linked to his theory of interstate compacts. He imagined the West not unlike

Thomas Jefferson's nation of yeoman farmers, with families committed to the land, improving their livestock with quality bloodlines and enjoying security with a guaranteed supply of water for crops. If Colorado could mature gradually along this course without having to compete with other western states for available water supplies, stable economic expansion would occur and communities would enjoy permanence. With this sense of what the future might be, Carpenter commenced two years of discussions that culminated in the Colorado River Compact.

First order of business was to draft a bill for the legislatures of all seven states that would authorize governors to appoint Colorado River Compact commissioners. The Arizonan Sims Ely, secretary of the League of the Southwest, had come to know Carpenter and Colorado Governor Oliver Shoup during the League's Denver meetings. He recommended Carpenter to craft this legislation and to draw a bill for Congress that would give formal recognition to the CRCC.[13] "I know of nobody who is so well qualified as Judge [sic] Carpenter for the task," he told Shoup. "I was . . . impressed with Judge Carpenter's broadness of view and with his sincere desire to arrive at an equitable and permanent settlement of all questions relating to the conflicting water rights in the basin states."[14] Shoup agreed and urged Carpenter to draw up the documents as soon as possible.

Carpenter began work promptly, but he was handicapped by other demands on his time. Authorities in Nebraska, Kansas, Wyoming, and New Mexico wanted him to begin work on agreements relating to the South Platte, Arkansas, Laramie, and La Plata rivers. As interstate streams commissioner for Colorado, he had a responsibility to honor these requests. He also had an obligation as chairman of the Weld County Republican Party to speak in support of candidates in the 1920 election. Recognized as an able orator, Carpenter compared the rival Democrats and their Non-Partisan League to a rattlesnake, waiting to suck the blood out of Colorado farmers.[15] He opposed the Dakota-based League's plan of "socialist" aid to agriculture and enthusiastically supported Republican gubernatorial nominee Oliver Shoup as "the exponent of law and order." He blamed the Democrats for high taxes, low sugar beet prices, and radical views on labor.[16] In addition to these time-consuming commitments, Carpenter continued to represent the Greeley-Poudre Irrigation District[17] and the state of Colorado in unresolved interstate litigation.

Colorado River Compact Commission. Standing from left to right: Delph E. Carpenter (Colo.), James G. Scrugham (Nev.), R. E. Caldwell (Utah), Frank C. Emerson (Wyo.), Stephen B. Davis (N. Mex.), W. F. McClure (Calif.), and W. S. Norviel (Ariz.). Seated from left to right: Governor Emmett D. Boyle (Nev.), Governor Oliver H. Shoup (Colo.), Herbert Hoover, chair and federal representative on the commission, and Governor Merritt C. Mecham (N. Mex.). The governors were not members of the commission. *Denver Post* photograph.

With all he had to do, Carpenter still found time to circulate the sample appointment legislation to each of the Colorado River basin states. It authorized governors to name commissioners who would meet "for the purpose of negotiating and entering into a compact or agreement between said states and [the] United States, with consent of Congress, respecting the future utilization and disposition of the waters of the Colorado River and all the streams tributary thereto." A disclaimer stated no compact would be binding on any of the states unless it was ratified by the seven state legislatures and Congress.[18] The other states appointed commissioners as follows: W. S. Norviel, Arizona; W. F. McClure, California; J. G. Scrugham, Nevada; Stephen B. Davis, New Mexico; R. E. Caldwell, Utah; and Frank C. Emerson, Wyoming. Shoup also authorized Carpenter to negotiate compacts on all of Colorado's interstate rivers.[19]

In preparation for a meeting of the governors and their commissioners in Denver before the onset of formal discussions in Washington, Carpenter sent Shoup a draft of legislation that the governors would take to Congress. This draft would be offered to congressmen who might need assistance and some background in the constitutional, international, and legal precedents involving the application of reserve treaty powers of the states to interstate water controversies. In a cover letter to Shoup, Carpenter stated he had made "an exhaustive review of the authorities upon interstate treaties, compacts and agreements, limitations of the rights of the states and limitations of federal power. . . . I greatly esteem the honor of having been called upon to draft this measure, and hope [it] may be a stepping stone in the preservation of the comity between the states of the Colorado River drainage."[20]

Carpenter included a memorandum to Shoup, outlining how the seven states should proceed. The subject was so important, he noted, it should be taken up "through the executive and legislative departments of our national government."[21] Congress needed to understand the upper basin states would only feel protected if a compact were signed prior to legislation authorizing reclamation works on the Colorado River. "Colorado should carry leadership in this presentation," he argued, and "should be prepared to lead off in the discussion of the problems involved after the formalities of the interviews with the executive officers of the Government have been cared for by the President of the League."[22] Carpenter urged Shoup to exclude the public, to avoid publicity and to limit the press to authorized statements. The press, he feared, might distort the issues and force commissioners to engage in political posturing. He had begun to exert leadership on Colorado River matters and he was fully prepared to explain his views of the need for interstate compacts to anyone who would listen.

In January 1921, at the annual meeting of the Colorado Bar Association in Colorado Springs, Carpenter delivered a lengthy and impassioned speech, summarizing his reasons for believing that compacts on interstate streams were necessary for the preservation of state sovereignty.[23] Each state, he argued, entered the Union on equal footing with all the others. Under the Constitution, some sovereignty had been conceded to the federal government, but the states' treaty-making powers were limited only to the extent congressional consent was required. If states allowed the Supreme Court to determine the allocation of waters that flowed between them, they would be inviting control of their natural resources by a politically motivated federal entity staffed by government employees unfamiliar with western conditions. Their time in office was tied to the patronage of constantly changing administrations. The net result of abandoning conflict resolution to the federal government would be the states' loss of control of natural resources. It could also mean adoption of prior appropriation as an administrative rule for the regulation of western rivers across state lines.

Under such circumstances, Carpenter reasoned, states would fall under a "galling yoke of bureaucratic oppression," as already witnessed on the Rio Grande and North Platte River. In each case, the headwaters state—Colorado—found itself under a servitude, or obligation, to deliver water to a federal project with no consideration by the government of Colorado's present and future needs. To preserve the peace and harmony of the federal union, to promote comity and equity between the states, and to prevent the "un-American" and "un-Constitutional" abuse of power by the federal government, Carpenter concluded, western states would have to map out a plan of equitable apportionment between them before allowing the government to begin construction of reclamation works.

Soon after his speech, the commissioners met in Denver under the leadership of Arizona Governor Thomas E. Campbell, president of the League of the Southwest. Joined by six of the seven governors, they reviewed the draft legislation Carpenter had prepared for Congress. Impressed by his research and reasoning, they passed a resolution asking Congress to appoint a representative of the United States to act as a member of the CRCC. The resolution further stated that "the proposed draft of a bill for presentation to Congress . . . be offered as a suggestion for legislation" and that "Governor Thomas E. Campbell of Arizona, and the Governors of the other States of the Colorado River basin, or such representatives as they may severally designate, be . . . authorized to present this resolution to the President and to the Congress of the United States."[24]

The group of governors and commissioners arrived in Washington in May. They met first with Secretary of the Interior Albert E. Fall, who approved the draft legislation that Carpenter and S. B. Davis, Jr., had revised since the Denver meeting. Carpenter was pleased with the Fall interview, but he was naive about the political atmosphere that surrounded the secretary. He commented that Fall "has no sympathy with bureaucracy [and] [i]f given a free hand, he can accomplish wonders in his department during four years."[25] Unfortunately, the Teapot Dome scandal, exposed in 1922, showed that the "wonders" to which Carpenter referred were self-serving interests that landed Fall in deep trouble.

President Warren G. Harding had been informed of the plans for a Colorado River Compact before the governors and commissioners arrived at the White House. He received the men cordially and expressed "hearty approval of their purpose . . . assur[ing] them of his unqualified support."[26] Following the meeting, Carpenter felt almost reverential. He was impressed by Harding's "dignity and charm," but his assessment of the administration was flawed by the bureaucratic stereotyping to which he had succumbed in recent years. The "new ambiance" in Washington, he noted, was free of "[t]he old timidity and restraint . . . so noticeable a year ago [which] has [now] been replaced by an air of freedom and action. The governmental departments are functioning normally. Radicals and bureaucrats are both in situations where they can do little harm."[27] Carpenter failed to note that the president's own cabinet included men who favored the expansion and centralization of federal power in the area of natural resources. He preferred to believe that Harding's reputation for laissez-faire leadership would mean the diminution of a national presence in the West.

Carpenter was too preoccupied with moving forward with the process of interstate compact authorization to be an objective observer in Washington. His mind was also clouded by the flare-up of his "neuritis." It was a health problem that would be diagnosed as Parkinson's disease in 1926, but at the time he attributed the extreme discomfort in his writing hand to the pressure he was feeling as the most knowledgeable member of the Colorado River Compact delegation. The tensions increased when Governor Campbell asked him to remain in Washington with Commissioner Davis to present the draft legislation to Congress. The seven western governors believed that Harding would urge Congress to adopt the legislation, so they decided not to remain in the capital at taxpayers' expense if Carpenter was willing to represent the CRCC at any and all congressional hearings.

Carpenter acceded to Campbell's request. He had been informed that all senators and representatives from interested states had been interviewed and properly briefed, and for the most part, he was told, they favored legislation that would enable the seven states to begin compact negotiations. But when Davis went to New York, Carpenter found himself the lone CRCC representative in Washington. Believing that congressional approval was a mere formality, he prepared to testify before the House Judiciary Committee while New Mexico Senator H. O. Bursum introduced the compact bill in Congress.

Problems developed when Wyoming's Franklin Mondell, house majority leader and senior congressman from the Colorado River basin, opposed the bill.[28] Mondell took a proprietary view of legislation that would have a major impact on his state. Other congressmen objected to the bill on grounds that funds should not be spent on a federal representative to the commission.[29] The political ground rules and congressional turf battles were not at first apparent to Carpenter, but he learned quickly that congressmen had territories and eastern representatives were unconvinced that spending money on the West was in the national interest. Having experienced rapid approval of his compact plan by western governors, Harding's cabinet, and Reclamation Service director A. P. Davis, he was unprepared for these setbacks.

Taking the offensive in his appearance before the House Judiciary Committee, Carpenter addressed the political, economic, legal, and philosophical arguments in favor of a Colorado River Compact. He wanted to prove to Congress that it was good for the entire country. After reviewing the history of Colorado River problems, Carpenter cited hydrological studies of the Geological Survey and Reclamation Services. He compared the task at hand to negotiations he had already begun with Nebraska on the South Platte River, giving two reasons why the federal representative on the CRCC should not be a bureaucrat: (1) this person would have to be "someone of more than ordinary ability. . . . a man capable of sitting upon the Hague Tribunal . . . because he would be in a position not only to protect the United States in its interests, but primarily to assist the States in entering into a compact that would put at rest all future contentions upon that river"; (2) the individual selected by Harding would "stabilize the water titles . . . within the States, so that the United States Reclamation Service, in building further projects, or private interests in building their projects, would know where they stand."[30]

Responding to questions from the committee, Carpenter noted that it would be "wild folly" to enter into litigation without first trying the compact method. He had experienced personally the effects of 267 days of testimony, endless hours of writing briefs, two appearances at the U.S. Supreme Court and ten years waiting for a verdict in *Wyoming v. Colorado*. During this time judges had died and conditions had changed in both states. By contrast, the compact method of settling interstate water disputes would preserve the integrity of states' rights. It would leave the rights of Mexico on the Colorado River to the treaty-making powers of the Senate and it would allow an agreement between the seven states to conform to topographical conditions peculiar to the Colorado River basin. Within a year to a year and a half, Carpenter predicted, the CRCC could have a compact drawn that would permanently resolve the question of water rights and enable the federal government to launch reclamation programs.[31] If Congress hoped to see the arid West grow into a productive sector of the country, a reasonable division of Colorado River water was a crucial first step.

Carpenter took nothing for granted in his appearance before the committee. He provided the members with an exhaustive analysis of the power of states to enter into compacts, accompanied by charts providing hydrological data on the Colorado River. Having learned from experiences at the Supreme Court, he knew easterners would need instruction regarding the needs of arid lands, the importance of states' rights in the West, and the precedents already established on international rivers. He cited numerous examples of interstate boundary, harbor, and fishing disputes settled by compact in the United States, and he quoted the opinion of

Attorney General Judson Harmon, who ruled in 1895 that the United States had "the right to utilize the total flow of the Rio Grande." For the sake of comity with Mexico, however, Harmon had recommended that "the matter be treated as one of policy and settled by treaty."[32] Carpenter wanted it known that he, too, believed that states of origin had a jurisdictional priority to water flowing across their boundaries, but he agreed with Harmon's reasoning regarding the importance of international and interstate comity, and he favored this same approach on the Colorado River. It was consistent with common sense, fairness, and the very general principle of equitable apportionment announced by the High Court in *Kansas v. Colorado*.

Achieving a seven-state compact, Carpenter concluded, was also a realistic objective. He called attention to the average annual flow of the Colorado River, 16 million acre-feet at Yuma. He described the potentially irrigable lands in the Colorado River basin, 5.2 million acres, and he assured the committee that because "20 to 50 percent of the water applied to land for irrigation ultimately returns to the stream channel," there would always be sufficient water in the system to support the needs of all seven states.[33] Furthermore, he noted, A. P. Davis shared his convictions regarding the adequacy of water in the Colorado River for everyone in the basin.

The testimony was well received. Under the leadership of chairman Andrew J. Volstead of Minnesota, the committee approved the CRCC bill and sent it on to the House, where it passed overwhelmingly two days later. Senator Bursum graciously accepted Mondell's name on the legislation and guided it through the Senate. It was signed into law by President Harding on August 19, 1921.[34]

Carpenter's political instincts had served him well. He discovered that Mondell's objection to the Bursum Bill was based on more than political jealousy. Mondell genuinely opposed language that required the federal representative on the CRCC to sign the compact once it was completed. He insisted that the United States had no right to sign a compact with a state.[35] The novelty of a compact among seven states, Mondell argued, could result in resistance and possible defeat in the House, especially if the United States was tied to the agreement. It would be far better if Harding's appointee in the negotiations protected federal interests and reported back to Congress when negotiations were completed. Senators and representatives would then be able to express approval or disapproval of the compact through appropriate legislation.

In spite of the physical pain he had to endure, Carpenter managed to play a significant role in bringing about congressional consensus. He conferred extensively with Bursum and Mondell and he sought advice from congressmen Edward T. Taylor (Colorado) and Andrew Volstead (Minnesota), as well as from Coloradan Hubert Work, Fall's successor as secretary of the Department of the Interior from 1923 to 1928.[36] Responding to what he learned from these connections, Carpenter revised the original bill to meet their concerns but changed only its form. From his own point of view, he had compromised none of his major goals, while Congress, in approving the legislation, "established the principle of equitable apportionment of the waters of interstate streams . . . by compact as the federal policy."[37] Carpenter's experience in the political arena paid dividends. He enhanced his own credibility, directed the CRCC legislation toward a speedy conclusion, and commenced the education of congressmen regarding the needs of western states.

There was little time to celebrate. The day after his testimony he checked out of Washington's Shoreham Hotel and headed west on the B & O Railroad. Before returning home, he conferred with attorneys in Chicago over Greeley-Poudre Irrigation District matters, met with counterparts in Lincoln, Nebraska, to review the status of negotiations on the South Platte River, and stopped in Topeka, Kansas, to discuss Arkansas River matters with the state's attorney general.

For the balance of 1921, Carpenter juggled these responsibilities skillfully. He also initiated discussions with New Mexico commissioner Davis regarding the future of the La Plata River. These conversations, which led to a La Plata River compact between New Mexico and Colorado, equipped Carpenter "for better consideration of the greater problems of the Colorado River."[38] In fact, La Plata River negotiations with Davis had a significant impact on Carpenter's tactics during Colorado River Compact negotiations.

Stephen B. Davis was easy to like. A Yale Law School graduate, experienced in land and water law issues, refined and diplomatic in his professional relations, he matched Carpenter in intelligence and political acumen. The two lawyers had already joined efforts in drafting the legislation taken to Washington by the CRCC. They respected each other. And they faced a dilemma on the interstate La Plata River, whose history presented challenges similar to those on the Colorado River. By virtue of Spanish and Mexican settlement in New Mexico, a priority of right based on first in time, first in right belonged to downstream New Mexico. Colorado's diversion of La Plata River water occurred in the second half of the nineteenth century. Colorado, however, was the basin of origin for the La Plata River and some Coloradans continued to believe that this geographical fact gave Colorado an indisputable right to an unlimited diversion of La Plata River water.[39]

Carpenter thought otherwise. He was ready to compromise. In light of his experience with Wyoming and the forthcoming negotiations with Colorado River basin states, the old jurisdiction of origin priority no longer seemed tenable. He compared the controversy between New Mexico and Colorado to the international conflict between Mexico and the United States over the Rio Grande, a struggle settled by treaty in 1906.[40] Carpenter reasoned that states were commonwealths with somewhat less sovereignty than nation states. Even though "self-preservation [was] the first law of nations," he noted that "from considerations of comity, the [La Plata] question should be decided as one of policy and settled by treaty. . . . While New Mexico may not justly require that Colorado shall yield all that New Mexico might desire, upon the other hand, Colorado cannot utterly ignore a reasonable benefit to New Mexico."[41]

Carpenter worked with Davis for five months in this spirit of compromise. He emphasized the importance of collecting accurate data. He educated Davis on the principle of return flows, water that returned to the basin after initial use upstream. He led Davis on a tour of the river itself, discussing possible reservoir and dam sites. He emphasized the importance of patience, exhaustive investigations, the possibility of transbasin diversion,[42] and the precedent-setting nature of their task. Above all, Carpenter persuaded Davis that a compact would preempt a free-for-all race to develop industry and agriculture in both states. If it worked as designed, the compact would eliminate the need for costly litigation, preserve state sovereignty, assure equitable apportionment of the river, and avoid future embargoes by the Reclamation Service.[43] This was his mantra, one that would be repeated frequently in subsequent negotiations involving other rivers. The intensity of deliberations with Davis gave final expression to his compact philosophy and strengthened his vision of a future in

which limited intrusion by the federal government and the priority of
states' rights would prevail in the American West.

La Plata Compact negotiations were Carpenter's dress rehearsal for
meetings with the seven-state CRCC. The contact with Davis also provided
him with an opportunity to gain the respect and friendship of an upper
basin commissioner who would prove to be a strong ally in Colorado River
discussions. But unlike the La Plata River, the Colorado River was international. President Harding would have to choose a sophisticated and well-
informed federal representative with impeccable credentials if CRCC
negotiations were to succeed.

Carpenter favored Elihu Root for this position. Root was a prominent
attorney who had specialized in corporate affairs before serving as secretary of war and secretary of state under presidents William McKinley and
Theodore Roosevelt. In addition to his work in Cuba, the Philippines,
South America, and Japan, Root negotiated forty reciprocal arbitration
treaties, formulated a plan to create the Central American Court of Justice,
and participated in the establishment of the Court of International Justice
at The Hague. As the first president of the Carnegie Endowment for
International Peace, he believed international law represented mankind's
best chance to achieve world peace, but he also knew that overcoming
national tensions, prejudices, and jealousies would take much hard work,
time, and wisdom.[44]

Carpenter appreciated Root's talents. For the CRCC, Carpenter wanted
a federal representative with international experience who was capable of
comprehending California's interest in developing Mexican lands and who
was free of obligations to the federal bureaucracy. Carpenter's general fear
of the monopolistic tendencies of government bureaus and his extreme
suspicion of the Reclamation Service motivated him to suggest Root for
the position.

"An Elihu Root," Carpenter argued before the Colorado Bar Association, "could readily comprehend the opportunity of concluding by one
convention, the respective permanent positions of the States and of the
United States and of determining for all times the equitable apportionment of the waters of this great river." His leadership would "assure free
interstate exercise of self-preservation and development, without interfering with a similar enjoyment by other states, free from imposition of any
foreign control or servitudes except those conceded by compact."[45] Less

experienced individuals, Carpenter firmly believed, would fail to achieve consensus among the seven disparate states.

Carpenter was confident Harding would make the right choice, but he activated connections already established with the League of the Southwest to influence the outcome. Hoping to inform the president of the urgency of a proper appointment, he sent a copy of his bar association speech to the League president, Arizona Governor Campbell, explaining in a letter that the federal representative should function as both "umpire and advisor."[46] As expected, Campbell took the speech to Washington and presented it to Harding.

When an appointment was not immediately forthcoming, Carpenter attempted other forms of persuasion. He told Commissioner Scrugham that, instead of suggesting specific names to Harding, he would advise the president on the "type" of federal representative most desired, "leaving the President and secretaries of state and interior to find the actual man."[47] James Brown Scott, secretary of the Carnegie Endowment for International Peace, was very much on his mind as a substitute for Root. He was "someone thoroughly advised on matters of interstate and international law."[48] Even though Scott had made clear his interest in remaining at the Endowment, Carpenter hoped to convince him to accept an appointment if tendered.

Throughout the summer and fall of 1921, Carpenter corresponded frequently with the other commissioners on the importance of an experienced and impartial federal representative. A CRCC meeting was unthinkable, he stated, until this post was filled. He considered other possible candidates: Denver Judge James Platt Rogers who had participated in *Kansas v. Colorado*; Elwood Mead, who had achieved a reputation as an international consultant in irrigation; and A. C. Campbell of Wyoming, whom he described as having a "fearless judicial intellect." All were flawed by one thing or another. Rogers was in retirement, Mead had too many connections to California, and Campbell was unknown to the Congress.

When League secretary Arnold Kruckman called for a December 1921 meeting in Riverside to recommend a federal representative to the president, Carpenter was alarmed by what appeared to be a California initiative and accepted Kruckman's invitation to speak. In addition to his conviction that the seven states needed to sign a compact prior to construction of a Colorado River dam, Carpenter was also suspicious of the Californians, and he wanted to visit first-hand both the Imperial Valley and the Boulder Dam site.[49] He had learned from Sims Ely of Arizona that Los Angeles was offering to finance a Boulder Canyon dam in return for a share of hydroelectric power.[50] Other rumors were circulating that the Reclamation Service was out of funds and was encouraging states to provide money so that Boulder Canyon studies might continue. In response, Carpenter urged Nevada and Arizona to "sabotage federal efforts" until the CRCC met to consider all aspects of the alleged proposal. From his vantage point, the federal government viewed with scorn and arrogance any plan to negotiate a compact prior to building a dam on the river.[51] He suspected collusion between California and the Reclamation Service, and he showed very little tolerance for any partnership that would undermine the chance for a Colorado River Compact.

Arriving at Riverside, Carpenter could see that California interests had taken over the League machinery. Existing rules of membership enabled California delegates to establish a solid majority and to insist all resolutions be approved by their delegation. Upset by such "steam roller tactics," delegates from other states refused to participate unless voting was by state. As debate on this issue heated up, Secretary Fall arrived to say that President Harding had selected Secretary of Commerce Herbert Hoover to be the federal representative on the CRCC. Hoover had accepted. The central purpose of the Riverside meeting was now moot. With non-California delegates ready to walk out of the resolutions committee, the Riverside meeting ended. For all intents and purposes, it was the last meeting of the League of the Southwest. Among other lessons, it revealed some Californians ready and willing to use political muscle to push for early construction of a dam. These people demonstrated little regard for the upper basin protection desired by Carpenter and other representatives from the basin-of-origin states. They gave warning by their actions that California would pursue its goals vigorously, behind the scenes if necessary, until they were assured of flood control and storage on the Colorado River.

How Hoover would react to California's aggressiveness was unknown. His appointment evoked a lukewarm reaction in all seven Colorado River basin states. He was an adopted Californian, an engineer, not a lawyer, and a man who knew more about mining than western water. His selection by Harding was something of a mystery. Most likely, Secretary Fall played the key role in tapping him for the job, but Carpenter's importuning might have influenced the decision. Carpenter had conferred with Fall in Denver before his trip to

Riverside and had reported to Governor Campbell that Fall understood the importance of a signed compact prior to dam construction and the need for an experienced federal representative on the CRCC.[52] Before leaving for California, Carpenter was informed by Kruckman that the secretary of commerce had provisionally accepted an invitation to the League meeting.[53] But Hoover did not attend, most probably because he was discussing the nomination with the secretary at that time. The official appointment from Harding came on December 17, 1921. In response, California's Congressman Phil Swing made the most accurate observation when he noted that Hoover's cabinet post and his experience as an international negotiator and administrator during World War I gave him the credibility needed to represent the federal government.

Hoover's appointment to the CRCC worked out remarkably well. Although not on Carpenter's list as a possible representative of the United States, he made a good teammate for Carpenter. When they came to know each other, the two men created a synergy of direction and leadership for commissioners who came together with vastly different levels of experience and very diverse agendas. The teamwork of Carpenter and Hoover contributed enormously to the unanimity among the seven men who signed the Colorado River Compact on November 24, 1922.

Hoover had the ability to think broadly. He had already spoken out on the need for national planning regarding natural resource development. Transportation, water supply, reclamation, and electric power, he believed, required coordination by a central authority. Hoover's goal, as he described it, was a "program for the full utilization of our streams, our rivers, and our lakes. . . . Every drop of water that runs to the sea without yielding its full commercial returns to the Nation is an economic loss."[54] Rivers should be viewed in their entirety; science and technology would help bring them under control; and power would be developed and distributed by private enterprise.

While he argued for coordinated planning between business and government, Hoover also stressed the importance of local control of reclamation projects. This is what Carpenter found most appealing. "I want to see more local responsibility," Hoover said. "We are a democracy and we must proceed by persuasion."[55]

Persuasion, in fact, was Hoover's hallmark. Raised a Quaker with strong views against force and violence, Hoover believed he could influence others to oppose waste, social irresponsibility, corporate bullying, and bureaucratic ineptitude. In many ways a Progressive, he wanted all Americans to share in the nation's largesse.[56] Combining "scientific management, organized cooperation, and private initiative into a new and superior political economy" was the Department of Commerce's chosen course under Hoover. Through national commissions and conferences, he hoped to encourage a broad level of participation by the American people in all forms of commerce. The net result would be cooperative, rather than marketplace, capitalism.[57]

As a person, Hoover was shy and awkward, sensitive, temperamental, opinionated, and politically driven. As described by historian Robert K. Murray, he was "a peculiar blend of opposites . . . an aggressive introvert."[58] In contrast to other cabinet members, Hoover was an empire builder, expanding the reach of the Commerce Department into areas selected for control by the other secretaries. He "was secretary of commerce and 'assistant secretary of everything else,'" Murray concludes.[59] He was probably closest to Secretary Fall, but his greatest supporter was the president himself. Hoover's belief in economic opportunity for every American and his outspoken commitment to "rugged individualism" matched Harding's philosophy. The two were especially close in their views of government-business cooperation. Aware of the growing controversy regarding public and private power development, they also wanted Congress to encourage both private and public sectors of the American economy.[60]

When Hoover accepted Harding's nomination to the CRCC, therefore, it was with the conviction that agreement on a Colorado River Compact would lead to a more efficient use of western lands that would provide opportunities to war veterans and others with ambition to settle a new frontier on the Colorado Plateau. Hoover had not yet given much thought to how such settlement and accompanying reclamation projects might threaten the upper basin states. In the fifteen months since the League of the Southwest had approved Carpenter's compact plan, Secretary Fall and Reclamation director Davis had spoken repeatedly about a federally constructed dam at Boulder Canyon and the possibility of hydroelectric power generated by private and public entities. Encouraged by their statements, spokesmen from California, Arizona, and Nevada assured representatives of the four upper basin states that they had no interest in developing priority rights that would establish a servitude on the Colorado River.[61] But suspicion of the federal government and each state's proprietary view of

Colorado River water were concerns of CRCC commissioners when they received Hoover's invitation to a preliminary meeting in Washington on January 10, 1922.

Carpenter responded to the invitation with uncharacteristic petulance. His telegram to Hoover stated that he had an engagement on that date at the Supreme Court. Furthermore, he noted, "Colorado law under which I was appointed [to the CRCC] provides that the Governor of Arizona call the first meeting of [the] interstate commission, and commissioners of [the] seven states recently agreed upon [a] tentative date for [a] call as of Phoenix [in the] latter part of January." He then wired Commissioner Scrugham to say that Hoover mistakenly expected to be elected chairman of the CRCC and was "laboring under [an] erroneous impression [as to] both his powers and character of commission."[62]

Carpenter's attitude toward Hoover was similar to that of Commissioner Caldwell, who was also surprised that the secretary would automatically assume the chairmanship. Upon reflection, however, Caldwell joined Scrugham in advising Carpenter not to oppose Hoover and to accept the secretary's second offer to meet in Washington later in January.[63] Scrugham concluded that Hoover might actually make the best chair, "for the reason of his position as a cabinet officer,"[64] but Carpenter advised fellow commissioners not to make any commitment as to the chairmanship of the CRCC until they all convened in Washington. There had even been talk of nominating Carpenter to this position, not so much to honor him as to neutralize a "very good talker" from Colorado.[65] There is no evidence that the Coloradan coveted so much responsibility, and after meeting personally with Hoover, Carpenter recognized the value of the secretary's international experience and his standing with the Harding administration. He telegraphed Caldwell that it might "be wise [after all] to elect Hoover chairman."[66]

Accompanied by his engineer friend R. I. Meeker, Carpenter arrived in Washington on January 25, 1922, where he settled in once again at the Shoreham Hotel. CRCC meetings began the next day at the Department of Commerce. Hoover welcomed the commissioners with a speech that described the purpose of the CRCC and the government's interest in irrigation, treaty obligations, and power development on public lands. He noted the importance of the Colorado River as a national asset and emphasized the need to provide an equitable division of the water and development of resources "so as to give the greatest benefits to the nation."[67] He alluded to the complexities of the work at hand and the "extreme jeopardy" in which the river had placed populations on the lower end of it. Joint consideration of the seven states' common interests, he advised, would determine how successful they would be in their pursuit of a compact. Carpenter responded by nominating Hoover as CRCC chairman. The motion was approved unanimously, and Hoover immediately accepted. He then asked to hear from all the commissioners as a first order of business and turned to Carpenter to present "the basis on which the [commissioner from Colorado] consider[ed] our work could most expeditiously proceed."[68]

Carpenter was best prepared of all the commissioners to discuss the CRCC's objectives and the constitutional background of interstate compacts. Hoover's request that he lead off the discussion was a courteous recognition of this expertise. The men who sat around the table had some understanding of the task at hand, but each arrived with a strong sense of duty to his own state and little experience in interstate litigation. Carpenter, too, was conscious of what these negotiations could mean for Colorado. The future of Colorado, where ran the headwaters of so many rivers, would be affected by precedents established by CRCC commissioners. If the seven states were going to cooperate in an unprecedented distribution of the water in which all were keenly interested, each would have to accept some form of compromise, but Colorado should not have to give up its right to future economic development. The great volume of water in the Colorado River, Carpenter believed, combined with the topographical and geographical uniqueness of his state, meant that any compromise among the seven states should not have to infringe significantly on Colorado's free and unlimited use of the river.

The other commissioners were surprised by Carpenter's claim that Colorado should be exempt from restrictions, but his response probed in the direction of finding a common basis for agreement. "The prime object of the Commission," he suggested, was "to avoid future litigation among the states interested in the Colorado River . . . [and] to settle in advance those matters which otherwise would be brought into court." Each commissioner represented a sovereign state in the federal republic. Interstate cooperation demanded that some of this sovereignty would have to be abandoned. Commissioners would need reliable facts on which to base decisions that would affect their states for years to come. They would need

Delph Carpenter in Washington, D.C., January 1922.

to know how much water flowed in the Colorado River, the present and future water needs of each state, and accurate data on the location and types of control structures desired. Carpenter warned commissioners not to address matters "purely within the province of Congress" and not to get bogged down in too much detail. What he most wanted to discover was the hidden agenda with which each commissioner arrived at the meeting. "They have made a long pilgrimage," he noted. "Their time is valuable and they need to be heard."[69]

Carpenter's invitation to learn from the other commissioners was genuine. He was not ready to dominate discussions and he very much wanted Hoover's respect. But he also needed to assess the nature and extent of opposition to his compact plan while the meeting was still young. He did not know the commissioners well. By encouraging them to discourse openly with him, he would give the impression of being pliable and cooperative while they, in turn, would expose those elements of their agenda that would require his most diligent consideration.

The tactic worked. Hoover endorsed "the great force of what Mr. Carpenter has stated as to the limitation of the functions of this Commission and of the undesirability of getting too far afield." The chairman also echoed Carpenter's interest in accurate factual data, especially regarding the amount of water in the river and the quantity of storage required to control seasonal surges. He urged commissioners to think broadly of developing the entire river, to see their task not as competition for advantage between states but as an "opportunity to advance national thought on what is one of the greatest assets [the Colorado River] of the United States."[70]

Having set the tone, Hoover invited the other commissioners to speak. None presented a comprehensive plan, but each gave the impression that he was interested in cooperation, so long as adequate factual information was provided on the hydrology of the Colorado River. Commissioners Norviel of Arizona and McClure of California reminded colleagues that time was of the essence, that existing levees could break at any moment. Wyoming Commissioner Emerson responded with a plea for cooperation. His state's ten-year battle in the courts over the Laramie River convinced him that litigation of interstate water issues was senseless, but he challenged the lower basin states to recognize that any cooperative agreement must acknowledge the upper basin's need for "assurance that we may go ahead with our development as it does become feasible."[71] Stated simply, Emerson wanted the "protection" that Carpenter was so eager to achieve for all the upper basin states.

Brief and to the point, the commissioners' first comments outlined the crux of the conflict that lay ahead. California favored action to avoid another devastating flood. Commissioners representing the upper basin agreed to cooperate with those of the lower basin in seeking appropriate legislation to build a dam and reservoir if they were guaranteed the right to grow at their own pace without worrying about losing a priority battle to the more rapidly growing states on the lower river. Essentially, it was a conflict between flood control and storage on the one hand and protection for future growth on the other. In Emerson's view of what would represent an equitable compromise between the two basins, Wyoming would "surely go to the limit in helping developing [*sic*] the lower river or any other part of the river" if development in the upper basin could happen later on when it became feasible.[72]

Ironically, Emerson was arguing against the same concept of interstate priority that he had embraced in one form or another during Wyoming's ten-year fight with Colorado over the Laramie River. But such is the inconsistent and convoluted nature of western water law. Emerson was sick of legal wrangling. He was ready to support a compact with the other states, provided he had accurate information and assurance that Wyoming's future would not be penalized by a rapidly constructed dam on the lower river.

Hoover turned next to Director Davis, the man most qualified to address the hydrological facts in which all commissioners had expressed a paramount interest. Clearly, no one present had a greater interest in effecting a development plan for the entire Colorado River basin. Davis came to Washington with a preliminary draft of the Fall-Davis Report. This was a study authorized by the 1920 Kinkaid Act that directed the Reclamation Service to study the Imperial Valley's needs and show how storage on the Colorado River might alleviate the threat of floods and expand irrigated agriculture.[73] By 1922, Davis had twenty years of experience with the Service. He had begun by taking several trips to the Colorado Plateau, eventually accepting a job from his uncle, John Wesley Powell, as assistant topographer with the United States Geological Survey. After earning an engineering degree, Davis was given the task of measuring stream flows in the arid Southwest. When the Newlands Act created the Reclamation Service, he was appointed assistant chief engineer. From 1914 to 1923, Davis was chief engineer and director of the Reclamation Service.

Carpenter understood that his relationship with Davis was critical to the success of compact negotiations, but he was uncomfortable with the director's commitment to comprehensive control of the Colorado River. Since the summer of 1921, both Carpenter and Scrugham had shared this concern about Davis, and when the preliminary Fall-Davis Report was released, Scrugham expressed his disgust. He wrote to Carpenter that the Service's plans contained "such a gross partisanship and disregard for states' rights that I consider them to be a menace to the sane development of the [Colorado] stream system."[74] The Service, Carpenter replied, "is making stupendous efforts and doubtless constantly working through secret channels to the objective of planting and firmly fixing their Boulder Canyon Reservoir before the states may act on the compact." As noted earlier, Carpenter had learned that Davis was trying to contract with Los Angeles over the power rights to be produced at Boulder Canyon and that Los Angeles was planning to build the dam and the power plant with its own resources if the federal government declined to intervene.[75]

Carpenter's suspicions grew during the Washington meetings. He was vulnerable to rumors and convinced the Reclamation Service planned on using the West as a laboratory for social and economic reform. His loyalty to states' rights was tied to a powerful respect for the Constitution's Tenth Amendment, a perspective in which the federal government abandoned rights to western streams in the territories as soon as they were accepted as states in the Republic. It was a position that had been articulated by Wyoming Congressman Mondell during debates on the 1902 Newlands Act,[76] and Carpenter was in strong agreement. In his mind, state sovereignty was only limited by powers the Constitution specifically ceded to the federal government. If any argument was ever proposed in support of federal rights in western waters, it was declared null and void by the Supreme Court's ruling in *Kansas v. Colorado*. More importantly, Carpenter insisted, if the federal government were to have its way, the very basis on which the Republic was founded would be undermined. The dual sovereignty (state and federal) inherent in the republican form of government would be eclipsed by a dominant federal presence on western streams. His defense of states' rights, therefore, was a defense of the federal system itself, a system he believed to have been fairly conceived in the minds of the Founding Fathers.[77]

For his part, Director Davis knew that any attempt at bullying by the federal government would defeat his objective of centralized river planning. A scheme to develop the Colorado River would have to please both basins. His experience with Uncle John (Wesley Powell), and his career as a Progressive in the Reclamation Service, had convinced him that only the federal government could bring about efficient and coordinated development in the arid West. Furthermore, as an engineer and disciple of single-taxer Henry George, Davis deplored inefficiency and waste. America's moral fiber could be restored, he believed, if government programs opened up new lands in the West for independent farmers.[78] Like Carpenter, he embraced the agrarian myth and was an advocate of local control of projects once they were constructed. Both men thought reclamation would make the desert bloom and in order to achieve their objectives they needed to be politically astute. Far too many of the twenty-four government-built reclamation projects in the West were seen as failures, either because beneficiaries of federally subsidized water had defaulted on their obligations or farmers had abandoned projects for lack of ongoing support. As of 1922, less than 10 percent of the $135 million spent on reclamation had been repaid and only 7 percent of the West's irrigated acres were attributable to federal reclamation.[79] This was not a good record.

When Davis addressed the commissioners, therefore, he was fully aware of their diverse opinions about the merits of a federally constructed project. He and Carpenter both wanted to settle potential disputes on the Colorado River prior to construction, but each man had different reasons for wanting the compact process to succeed. Ultimately, Davis's perspective on the role of the federal government would have to overcome the Coloradan's narrow interpretation of federal authority in the West if both were to realize their goals. And Carpenter would have to soften his rigid opposition on states' rights issues to facilitate an acceptable partnership between the states and the federal government.

Noting that the first step toward a partnership was agreement on the critical data, Davis introduced the preliminary draft of the Fall-Davis Report. He assured commissioners that, even though much work remained to be done, evidence gathered to date indicated ample water was available in the Colorado River for the present and future needs of all seven states and

Mexico, "not only by gravity but by reasonable pumping." Storage of some form would be essential. Although he liked the idea of building reservoirs in the upper basin to reduce evaporation losses, the dangers of flooding could not be eliminated unless dams were constructed on the lower river. Silting behind the dams would be a problem, but the flood danger had to be eliminated. Davis understood the desire of upper basin commissioners to develop dam projects slowly. As much as he favored immediate dam construction on the lower Colorado River, the Reclamation Service's advocacy of this project would have to be tempered by the needs and concerns of all seven states. Furthermore, to win congressional approval, a reclamation project would need to have broad national appeal and provide "the greatest possible benefits to the country" as a whole. He displayed maps and charts to indicate areas where irrigation might be developed in the future and he reiterated his desire to eliminate waste and to do nothing on the river that might harm Mexico. Although his report did not consider the impact of out-of-basin transfers, it dealt with hydroelectric power and concluded that power needs should be subservient to irrigation. A high dam at Boulder or Black Canyon would be recommended, he said, when his report was finalized.[80]

Davis admitted that the results presented in his report were uneven. The river's hydrology and estimates of acreage that might be brought under irrigation were approximate, although he assured commissioners that his figures were "liberal." Davis concluded that 6.9 million acres in Mexico and the United States could be irrigated in the Colorado River basin. This included 2.7 million acres already irrigated and 4.2 million reclaimable acres if storage and diversion projects were constructed. He estimated full development of these lands would require about 16.7 million acre-feet of water from the Colorado River, 10.8 million acre-feet of that figure being the "probable additional required" under reclamation.[81] Using this data, Davis presented what he believed to be a fair proposal to diffuse the principal fears of all seven states. He urged that no state should obtain a priority or right against another state as a result of the construction of works on the river and that existing claims of priority be waived. He also recommended the organization of a permanent Colorado River Commission that would empower states to appropriate additional water for new lands under irrigation.[82]

Protective of their own estimates regarding future agricultural development, some commissioners disputed Davis' calculations of reclaimable

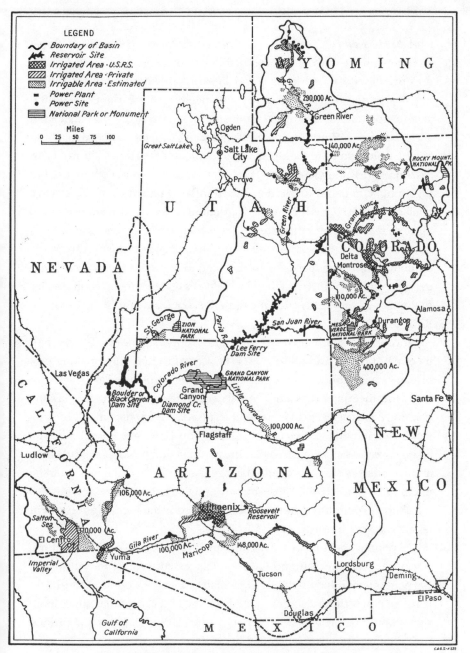

THE AREA AFFECTED BY THE COLORADO RIVER PROJECT
Hundreds of thousands of acres of arid land will be made into fertile farms by the development of the Colorado River, and great hydro-electric plants will distribute power from Los Angeles to Denver

1921 map of Colorado River Basin. (Carpenter Papers, Loveland, Colo.)

land. At Hoover's suggestion, an ad hoc committee was charged with doing an independent study of water availability in the Colorado River. The figures presented showed Mexico and the United States capable of irrigating nearly 7.2 million new acres and needing more than 20 million acre-feet of water if each of the states and Mexico were to fully irrigate old and new lands. It became apparent that using irrigable acreage as a basis for the Colorado River Compact would bankrupt the river. California and Arizona were willing to accept Davis's figures with minor adjustments, but Wyoming, Utah, and Colorado offered inflated estimates of the acreage available in their states for irrigated agriculture. New Mexico alone claimed more than three times the acreage Davis had arrived at. Because none of the states in the upper basin wanted a compact in which their future development would be jeopardized by the need to deliver water to faster growing states in the south, they felt obligated to exaggerate their requirements. In doing so, they far exceeded the most liberal assessments of the Colorado River's flow.

Hoover was clearly upset by the commissioners' knavery. By the sixth meeting of the CRCC, all he could see was individual states making proprietary statements with little interest in the bigger picture. "We ought not to let this meeting break up," he warned, "without bringing in a broad–visioned constructive plan in general terms so as to advance the whole subject." Worried about the critical situation on Colorado River levees, he asked commissioners to agree that the construction of works should begin at the earliest possible moment; that the construction of a dam should be undertaken by the federal government; and that private, state, and municipal sources of funding should be investigated if the federal government failed to approve construction.[83]

Carpenter was not present at the meeting when Hoover asked for a response. But Emerson and Caldwell expressed sentiments with which Carpenter would have agreed. They made clear their opposition to dam construction without a commitment from the lower states that upper basin rights would be protected in years to come. Although Davis had pushed for a compact based on an equitable division of water to each of the seven states, the principal problem blocking success was a familiar conflict, in which those at the headwaters and those at the river's lower end had different needs, fears, and ideas of how to achieve security in their respective locales.

Hoover was frustrated by the stalemate. He did not yet grasp the reason for the states being so self-centered. "I have to look at this matter from a more national point of view than some of you," he argued. The CRCC was set up after great effort, and considerable expectations were riding on its ability to resolve conflicts and to provide "immediate relief" to the lower basin. "It would seem a great misfortune," he said, "if we dissolved the Commission without at least agreeing upon so primary a necessity as a control reservoir. This whole business is utterly fruitless if we cannot agree on a simple statement of an obvious fact."[84]

Carpenter saw his chance to be assertive at this juncture. He had been preparing a proposal, one recognizing that progress on a compact required an understanding of river basin culture. Hoover was pushing for agreement on a dam, but Carpenter wanted the compact to proceed on a more general basis that would guarantee the basin-of-origin states ample time and water for complete economic development. His proposal did not win immediate converts and even alienated some of his fellow upper basin representatives. It also annoyed Hoover. But the proposal did shift the debate away from the quagmire of irrigable acreage by state to a more general concept of equitable apportionment for the two competing basins. It gave Hoover and the other commissioners a better chance to understand why Carpenter was so opposed to any dam construction for the benefit of California without reciprocal and meaningful commitments to the basin- of-origin states on the upper river. It also helped commissioners redirect their thinking, from a singular and selfish focus on their own states to ways in which the upper basin might cooperate with the lower basin for the mutual benefit of all.

The essence of Carpenter's plan had to do with the limitations of nature. He pointed out how difficult it would be for Colorado to utilize existing water and to achieve rapid growth because of the mountains and deep canyons in which surface water flowed. The states of origin, he noted, "will never be able to beneficially use even an equitable part of the waters rising and flowing within the respective territory of each, and the major portion of such waters will flow from such states irrespective of the uses and development within the states of origin."[85] Colorado, Carpenter noted, produced between 60 and 70 percent of the water annually passing Yuma in the Colorado River. As a sovereign state, Colorado might try to claim all the water it produced, but because he espoused the principles of equity outlined in *Kansas v. Colorado,* and because Colorado desired comity between the states, a better solution needed to be found. Colorado should abandon such claims, asking in return that a compact should not limit water use in the upper basin if the states of the upper basin, in return, would endorse a storage dam on the lower Colorado. The basin-of-origin states would forsake any claim to "absolute dominion and exclusive use of all water within its domain" in favor of some sort of scheme that would consider the rule of "continuous uninterrupted flow" as proposed in *Kansas v. Colorado.*[86]

In what turned out to be the longest speech of the seven Washington meetings, Carpenter apologized for the "impromptu" nature of his remarks, noting he would have preferred time to consult with his colleagues in the upper basin. But he made no apology for his proposal, underscoring his strong belief that limitations on water use in the upper basin would be in conflict with the realities of nature and with the Reclamation Service's findings that enough water existed in the basin for the needs of each state. His views on limitations were supported by his lengthy discourse on state sovereignty, the meaning of Article I, section 10 of the Constitution, the status of federal rights to water in the West, and the applicability of international law. The speech was received by Hoover and the commissioners with mixed emotions, but Carpenter was speaking from the heart and from more than ten years of practical experience gained in and out of court.

For too long Colorado had been on the defensive in interstate-streams litigation involving Wyoming, Kansas, Nebraska, and New Mexico. Regarding each of the streams connecting Colorado to one of its neighbors, Carpenter had argued that upstream development enhanced and stabilized return flows in the lower basin. In the course of his investigations he had become convinced that any limitation on Colorado appropriations would have a negative impact on downstream neighbors, unless water was diverted out of the basin. Additionally, he had been unable to forgive the Reclamation Service for the embargoes established on the North Platte and Rio Grande when Pathfinder and Elephant Butte reservoirs were constructed. Not only did these projects violate his understanding of states' rights, they also impeded development in the poorest parts of the state.

Carpenter's seemingly inflexible pronouncements on the role of nature and his opposition to water-use limitations in the upper basin must be bal-

anced with an understanding of how much he wanted the CRCC to formulate a compact that state legislatures could actually approve. From close
experience with Colorado's State Assembly, he knew legislators in Denver
would reject any plan that imposed use limitations on the state. But Hoover
questioned Carpenter's logic. How could the Coloradan reject the principle of interstate priority and then deny to the lower basin a dam that
would save their agriculture?

The problem, Carpenter replied, was that the federal government was
already involved in proposed construction plans. Even though the decision in *Kansas v. Colorado* had specifically denied federal rights in western
waters, government officials from the Department of the Interior continued to assert their alleged authority on both navigable and non-navigable
streams. The upper states did not want to retard development in the lower
basin, but neither did they want to be penalized in the courts for sup-
porting this development.[87] Because California supplied no water to the
river, Carpenter argued, that state should make the "greater yielding."
Likewise, because the upper basin provided "the greater part of the water
that flows for the benefit of all of us . . . we are entitled to freedom from
attack from below."[88]

With only Caldwell solidly in his camp, Carpenter eventually recognized
the need to soften his stand. He offered to limit out-of-basin transfers by
Colorado and expressed a willingness to later reconsider his statement that
the upper basin would need fifty to one hundred years of development
time without the imposition of water-use limitations. When a vote was taken
on Commissioner Norviel's proposal to proceed with reclamation based
on each state's expanded acreage estimates, it became apparent to Hoover
that the commission was divided and deadlocked. The vote was 4–3; four
upper basin states against three lower basin states.

Hoover was discouraged. "We have not been able to get to any agreement on a general single idea of a compact," he said. "Therefore, this session has no result except to define differences. The question arises, is it
worthwhile to have another session? Or shall we make the declaration now
that we are so hopelessly far apart that there is no use in proceeding?"[89]

Some of the commissioners agreed failure was imminent. Others
pointed to progress in getting to know each other and hearing each other's
point of view. All agreed the data was too limited. They needed better facts
and they needed time to consult with their respective constituencies.

Carpenter had been jarred by the open antagonism to his proposal. He believed the conflict he had generated was partly a result of his inability to discuss these views with commissioners prior to the meeting. He had no doubts about the principles involved and he definitely opposed termination of the CRCC. "Hasty treatment would be unwarranted," he stated. "We are here with a pretty sacred trust and it should not be treated lightly. I really believe that in the months and weeks to come many small matters of difference can be argued out. I would say frankly that I would be open to severe censure if I should go home saying that I signed anything without the fullest and most frank understanding with the officials and the government of my state. . . . I think it would be the height of crime to the people who sent us here to adjourn permanently now."[90]

In general agreement with Carpenter, the CRCC voted unanimously to adjourn only temporarily and to meet again "somewhere in the Southwest" around the middle of March, "possibly Phoenix, at which time an opportunity [would] be given for public hearings."[91] Hoover hoped that Carpenter, whom he now saw as a major obstacle to any compact, would soften his attitude at these hearings.[92] But as new elements were injected into the controversy, the Coloradan began to play an even more forceful role in guiding the CRCC to a compact that incorporated the needs of both basins.

CHAPTER 5

The Colorado River Compact: Phase II

This is just by way of mentioning again the admiration and appreciation I have for the way you have built up the whole conception of the compact from its start and for the ingenuity and flexibility of mind which you have brought to bear upon it.

—HOOVER TO CARPENTER, NOVEMBER 27, 1922

When Carpenter returned to Colorado from Washington, Hoover and the other commissioners understood that the Coloradan was agreeable in principle to dam construction on the lower Colorado River. It would be accompanied by water rights for the three lower basin states, even though the sovereign states of origin, in Carpenter's view, could rightfully claim ownership of this water by virtue of geography. Carpenter insisted on signing a compact first, however, and this requirement caused Hoover to conclude that Carpenter's inflexibility could undermine any chance of success the Colorado River Compact Commission (CRCC) might have. He asked New Mexican Stephen Davis to speak with Carpenter, but the resulting contact accomplished nothing.[1]

Carpenter's approach to the lower basin evolved logically from his experience with the Rio Grande and Mexico. More than twenty-five years earlier, the United States as the country of origin had told Mexico that it owned all the water in the Rio Grande by virtue of its geographical location at the headwaters. However, in expectation of amicable relations, or comity, with Mexico, the United States agreed to forgo its absolute right in favor of an equitable solution. Carpenter was not trying to be difficult with the CRCC. No one wanted accord more than he. But his perception of international law as precedent to interstate compact negotiation, and his view of what the Colorado legislature would ratify, persuaded him to take a position that sounded somewhat haughty and inflexible to Hoover and the other commissioners. He also wanted discussions to proceed slowly. Discovering the proper hydrological data, points of law, and economic development issues required time. No matter how desperately California wanted flood control, rushing to an agreement would simply lay groundwork for future litigation.

Although Carpenter appeared to be obsessed with having his own way, experience had taught him that success in negotiation was based on full disclosure, trust among participants, courteous and continuous debate in a private setting, presentation of accurate data, and, above all, time. "The only fear I have," he wrote Clarence Stetson, executive secretary of the CRCC, "is that the desire for speed may cloud or encumber the real progress to be made. Big things require patience and I am going to try to be the most patient member of the commission."[2] The forthcoming public hearings, he believed, were a step in this direction. They offered an opportunity for listening to a variety of views from interested parties. Carpenter urged Hoover to conduct the meetings in a deliberate manner, aiming at a "thorough understanding of the actual physical conditions in much the same way as courts proceed with the taking of testimony before arriving at a judgment or formulating a decree." In this way, Carpenter concluded, "minor points of divergence [would] sink into insignificance in view of the greater objective."[3]

Carpenter was focused as much on the method of negotiation as on its goals. He had a driven personality and often seemed moody, distant, and unbending to colleagues and associates who did not know him. The neuritis of which he complained frequently in his diary caused acute fatigue and pain, resulting in temperament swings. Writing became increasingly difficult due to hand tremors, and the occasional numbness he experienced in other muscles interfered with normal activities. In 1922 he had no idea his suffering was symptomatic of Parkinson's disease.[4] He sought temporary relief with hot Turkish baths at the Metropole Hotel in Denver, but what his body really needed was respite from intellectual and emotional stresses. He longed for a vacation, but a sense of responsibility to the mission at hand, and a nagging fear of financial failure, kept him working at a frenetic pace.

The Crow Creek Ranch continued to drain his resources. With the exception of abundant crops and good prices in 1918 and 1919, farming and ranching operations had not proved remunerative for anyone in agriculture following World War I. Carpenter was better off than most with an ample state salary of fifty dollars a day in 1921, not to exceed $10,000 a year, for interstate water work.[5] But his apparent lack of money management skills and the almost obsessive commitment to his job as interstate streams commissioner for Colorado made him feel that things financial were always getting away from him. Then, too, the four children, Michaela (born in 1902), Donald (1907), Sarah (1909), and Martha Patricia (1914) were beginning to have greater needs.

Carpenter was very dedicated to his family. Although his work took him away from Greeley for long periods of time, he wanted to be a good provider and role model, especially for son Donald. In her eighties, Sarah still remembered her father's constant travels, but she also remembered trips with him in the family car, visits to the stock show, Sunday outings at Crow Creek Ranch, and "fatherly" advice on proper comportment when she and sister Michaela began teaching in the public school system.[6]

"Be careful," Carpenter wrote his daughters. "We are judged by our conduct and associates. . . . [C]ivilization has taught that certain lines of conduct are necessary for the self-preservation of both men and women." There are rules of behavior for men and women, but they are "more strict as regards young womanhood, because they are necessary and imperative to their protection." If one makes up one's own rules, Carpenter warned, the chance of being misunderstood, of being talked about by others is very great. "Your success is our pride," Carpenter admonished. "[Your mother and I] live for you more than for ourselves. We would like to have you stand out as leaders among the finer people of our communities. The more 'correct' you are, the safer you are and we know it. Every time you deliberately take big chances, you not only endanger your own safety but put us on the brink of despair. Your disgrace would be to us a slow death."[7]

Carpenter loved and protected his girls, but Donald was his traveling companion, occasional amanuensis, and his "living hope fulfilled." He was "Honey Boy" on whom Carpenter showered affection and lessons on how

life's battles should be fought. Donald was instructed in self-control, compassion, loyalty to his country, courage, respect for honest work, and the
strength of manhood to "make you love to move mountains and turn rivers
in manhood's fight."[8] These were the values taught to him by *his* parents,
Leroy and Martha Carpenter, and the lessons were repeated when
Carpenter had time to spend with his own children. He took Donald to
sessions of the Colorado senate when his son was only five. On Sundays,
they searched for arrowheads at the ranch, branded and sorted calves,
hunted, fished, and camped together. By age ten, Donald accompanied
his father on trips related to litigation of the Laramie and South Platte
rivers. At seventeen, when Donald was on his way to the New Mexico
Military Institute, Carpenter asked the senior military officer to "consider
him under your special care and protection."[9] As they did with all their children, Carpenter and wife Dot wanted Donald to be successful and if favors
were asked for their offspring, much was expected in return from them.

Dot provided uncommon nurture to her husband when he was ill or
under pressure, and he responded with outbursts of poetic affection. "In
the castle of my heart," he wrote her, "there's a chamber where the colors
of morn blend into the joy of day and twilight fades into the gloaming light
of the hearth. It is yours. . . . When cruel treachery wounds me; when
duplicity fills me with dread; when human coldness benumbs me . . . you
come and dwell in your chamber and with you come peace and repose."[10]

Dot provided the energy and contagious joy for life her occasionally
depressed husband needed. She was active in the Episcopal Church, organized the Centennial Chapter of the Daughters of the American Revolution, and gave time to the Women's Relief Corps during World War I.
She had a vibrant sense of humor, loved and taught music, attended classes
at Greeley Normal School, now the University of Northern Colorado, and
volunteered her services to charitable causes whenever possible.[11] To celebrate their tenth anniversary, Carpenter composed a mock court decree
titled "In the Matter of the Union of Hearts, 'Michaela [Dot] and
Delpho.'" It concluded with the statement that "Michaela and Delpho are
forever lovers [and] that [neither] time nor eternity shall part them. . . ."
Entered into the "Court of the Omnipotant [*sic*] Cupid," this document
revealed Carpenter's sense of humor and his total devotion to Dot.[12] Before
sickness made him so totally dependent on his wife, Carpenter felt free to
express his love for her in poetry and emphasize how important it was not

Dot Hogarty Carpenter.

to take for granted a wife's affection and loyalty. In 1922, he wrote the following untitled verse:

> If with pleasure you are viewing any work that she is doing
> If you like her, if you love her, tell her now,
> Don't withhold your approbation, 'til the parson makes oration
> As she lies with snowy lilies o'er her brow.
> For no matter how you show it, she won't really care about it
> She won't know how many teardrops you have shed.
> If you think some praise is due her, now's the time to slip it to her
> For she cannot read her tombstone when she's dead.
> More than fame and more than money is the comment bright and
>   sunny
> Showing hearty, warm approval to a friend
> For it gives to life a savor and it makes us strong and braver
> Giving heart and soul and spirit to the end.
> If she earns your praise bestow it, if you love her let her know it
> Let the words of true encouragement be said.
> Do not wait 'til life is over and she's underneath the clover
> For she cannot read her tombstone when she's dead.[13]

Delph needed Dot. He entered the CRCC hearings already feeling a kind of war weariness caused by the many legal battles in which he was simultaneously engaged.[14] But when he joined the commissioners for the first hearings in Phoenix, his enthusiasm for the task at hand overcame his diminished physical stamina. With unequivocal support from home, he sensed that an important piece of western history was in the making over which he would have some control. History fascinated him. It helped explain his own values and offered him a challenge to improve upon the world he had inherited.

As secretary-treasurer of the Union Colony, Colorado's interstate-streams attorney, and an active Republican dedicated to Jeffersonian federalism, Carpenter had already begun to define himself historically by 1922. His conservatism emerged in outspoken criticism of the League of Nations, national forests, and labor unions.[15] Although he no longer held political office, he prided himself on continued successes with a Democratic state legislature, where his advice was frequently sought and where he learned how to achieve consensus among men as diverse as those he would face on the CRCC. Though he saw himself as a "boy from the country," somewhat handicapped by a rural Colorado upbringing,[16] Carpenter's experience as a hands-on water attorney with a farming background served him well in negotiations. The experience enabled him to evaluate pragmatically the plans for water appropriation and storage addressed by less informed individuals. He also knew that water could have a very disruptive power when mountain snows melted rapidly or when the works of man to capture it underestimated that water's diligence in seeking escape from entrapment. His self-confidence in matters pertaining to control and distribution of water was buttressed by an intimate connection to water's many mysteries in the western landscape. His study of water took into account the violence of western weather, the sharp terrain, the semiarid climate, and the rapid movement from drought to flood.

Carpenter paid special attention to entire river basins when he was negotiating agreements on interstate streams. He studied rivers from the source in order to understand the extent of their developmental potential. As part of his investigation in *Wyoming v. Colorado*, he and water commissioner Robert E. Moan from Water District No. 48 in Colorado explored the headwaters of the Laramie River in the southern reaches of the Medicine Bow Range. It was business and pleasure. The men climbed several peaks in the Laramie River valley near Glendevy, Colorado, proceeding to the headwaters of McIntyre and Rawah creeks and on to the summit of the nearby mountains. Carpenter wanted precise information on the Laramie River's origins, but he also enjoyed the adventure of planting the first American flag on these unnamed peaks. Having deposited a record of their ascent in a Prince Albert tobacco can at the summit, Carpenter later asked the U.S. Geological Survey to recognize these mountains henceforth as the Carpenter Peaks. "I claim no great credit . . . that the ascent of the peaks was anything out of the ordinary," he wrote. Anyone might have done the same thing. But he wanted his name attached to the peaks, because "the region is a favorite place of recreation with me and one which I frequently visit and have pretty thoroughly explored, especially in connection with the litigation which I have mentioned."[17]

Carpenter hoped that his trip to the headwaters of the Laramie River might result in a landmark named for the Carpenter family. The Geological Survey ignored his request, but the attempt to place his imprint at the source of a freely flowing stream was not unusual for a man who still believed in the pioneering spirit. Land features and waterworks on the

Delph Carpenter wrote that a "six-foot United States flag, attached by a one-fourth-inch rope to a ten-foot peeled spruce pole, was erected on the central peak of the group." Based on a review of other photographs in this collection, as well as recent pictures taken by Dyce Gayton of the Roosevelt National Forest, the flag most probably was located between North Rawah Peak and South Rawah Peak, at an elevtion of 12,484 feet, overlooking Lake No. 4 in the Rawah Wilderness Area.

West's principal streams were frequently named after individuals, and Carpenter believed that men with the foresight and vision to explore and build should be appropriately acknowledged for the risks they took. The dams that controlled running water presented special challenges to their builders and to people who lived around them. Flooding from heavy winter snowpack was diminished by dams and the reservoirs they created, but the fear of dam failure and possible loss of life from inundated farms and cities caused populations to be ever watchful. Memories of the 1889 Johnstown, Pennsylvania, flood that killed more than two thousand people were always present during and after the construction of western dams.*

Carpenter was reminded of this ever-present concern in the spring of 1920 when he was informed that water was leaking from Milton Reservoir near La Salle, Colorado. The three-inch stream of water, gradually increasing in volume from the dam site, alerted nearby residents that a dam break was imminent. The farming towns of Kersey, Evans, and Kuner were endangered. Carpenter and two engineers responded to the threat. They crawled on hands and knees for two hundred feet under the dam through a forty-eight-inch steel outlet pipe half-filled with water, carrying with them lead wool and tinfoil to locate and seal cracks that were the probable source of leakage. They were guided only by the sound of rushing water and a battery-powered light taken from a motorcycle. At the end of their journey, and under thirty-seven feet of reservoir water, they found three places where joints connecting the outlet pipes had spread. They plugged the joints, returned to safety, and hired a group of coal miners to sink a shaft through the earthen core of the dam so that the fissures could be properly repaired from the outside of the pipe.[18]

In his diary, Carpenter simply noted, "Went into tubes for one hour," a rather nonchalant comment on personal heroics. This incident, however, along with his Carpenter Peaks adventure, travels up and down the South Platte, Republican, and La Plata rivers, and numerous hands-on experiences with irrigation, provided him with a pragmatic view of man's struggle to dominate western water. Better than most engineers and attorneys,

---

* Johnstown was a steel town of thirty thousand built on the flood plain at the fork of two rivers. Fourteen miles upstream from the town on the Little Conemaugh River was a 450-foot-high dam that held water in a three-mile-long lake. The dam was poorly maintained. On May 31, 1889, after a night of heavy rains, the dam broke, sending twenty million tons of water crashing down through a narrow valley into Johnstown. The 60-foot-high wall of water bore down on Johnstown at forty miles per hour. Many residents became helplessly tangled in miles of barbed wire from the destroyed wire works. Hundreds of lives were lost, and the town took five years to recover. Although no lawsuits were ever filed, many people blamed the South Fork Fishing and Hunting Club. Composed of wealthy Pittsburgh steel and coal industrialists, including Andrew Carnegie and Andrew Mellon, the club had purchased the reservoir, initiated some repairs on the dam, raised the lake level, and built cottages and a clubhouse for their members. Their failure to properly maintain the aging structure was a major cause of the Johnstown flood.

he understood both the difficulty of containing rushing water in mountainous states with limited irrigable lands, and the storage requirements of agriculturally productive lower basin states that needed reservoirs for irrigation and flood control. These experiences made him a significant player in the six public hearings hosted by the CRCC between March 15 and April 2, 1922.[19]

The purpose of these hearings was to learn the views of people in the seven Colorado River basin states who had a stake in development of the area but were not participants in the Washington meetings. While many new voices were heard, the commissioners also benefited from further interaction with each other as well as from the opportunity to test their own biases in different state venues. During the meetings held in the spring of 1922, five topics, some of them new and controversial, dominated discussion. First was Reclamation director A. P. Davis's idea of dividing the Colorado River states into two basins, designating the San Juan River as a separation point. Carpenter made a note of this suggestion and later used it as a basis for his own draft compact. Some commissioners were reluctant to abandon the idea of appropriating water from the river according to their state's estimate of future irrigable acreage. But eventually, the two-basin plan won acceptance.

A second issue of note concerned the potential for hydroelectric power production. Arizona's state engineer argued that the Colorado River project was a power project and not a reclamation matter at all. California's William Mulholland made a similar statement. Los Angeles, he said, had no interest in Colorado River water but wanted power, a sentiment echoed by Nevada's governor, Emmet D. Boyle.[20] Somehow, the benefits of power generation would have to be included in any water distribution plan. The Federal Power Commission (FPC) was watching the outcome of CRCC negotiations very closely, refusing to issue construction permits to private companies until some agreement was forthcoming on the relationship between power ownership and water storage. Carpenter knew that ownership and distribution of hydroelectric power would have to be tied to any compact agreement. Although commissioners concurred that agricultural interests should have greater consideration than power production, they were divided over what to do about James P. Girand's application to the FPC for a hydroelectric plant at the mouth of Diamond Creek, upriver from Boulder Canyon. Nine months prior to the Phoenix hearing,

Girand had been awarded a preliminary permit, but the FPC had delayed issuance of the final license. A national debate on the merits of public versus private power, and concern that Girand might produce electricity in competition with generators at a Boulder Canyon dam, required commissioners to consider the interrelated aspects of power production and water distribution. Questions were raised about (1) the upper basin's obligation to guarantee enough water to a Boulder Dam site and (2) whether the cost of a federally constructed dam could be returned to the taxpayers through power generation if Girand captured the existing market.[21] The discussion provoked related questions about the upper basin's apparent refusal to limit its use of the Colorado River in any way whatsoever.

A third vexation dominating the hearings was reflected in an undertone of intrastate disunity. Some commissioners faced persistent criticism in their own states from powerful constituencies vying for attention. California Commissioner McClure found himself in dispute with the Imperial Valley's Mark Rose. Arizona's W. S. Norviel, appointed by Governor Thomas Campbell, was censured by George H. Maxwell, one of the sponsors of the Newlands Act, and by Campbell's successor, George W. P. Hunt, for considering a compact that failed to include a Highline Canal from the Colorado River to the mining region of central Arizona. In Colorado, Carpenter had to deal with West Slope residents who were already angry with East Slope advocates of increased transmountain diversion through the Continental Divide.

Diversions out of the Colorado River basin were a fourth concern, expressed most forcefully by representatives of the southern river states. For Professor G. E. P. Smith, University of Arizona irrigation engineer, this was the biggest question before the CRCC. Without specific limitation, the upper basin could cut back the flow of the river so as to reduce significantly the production of hydroelectric power and generation of revenue coveted by the lower basin states. Lucius Chase, representing the Los Angeles Chamber of Commerce, expressed his fears and the fears of others that advancing technology would soon enable the mountain states to construct longer tunnels, allowing them to take greater volumes of water at lower elevations to more distant points.[22]

The fears were realistic. They resulted in relentless challenges to the upper basin to accept limitations on Colorado River water use. A. P. Davis urged the four states of origin to consider limiting the amount of transmountain

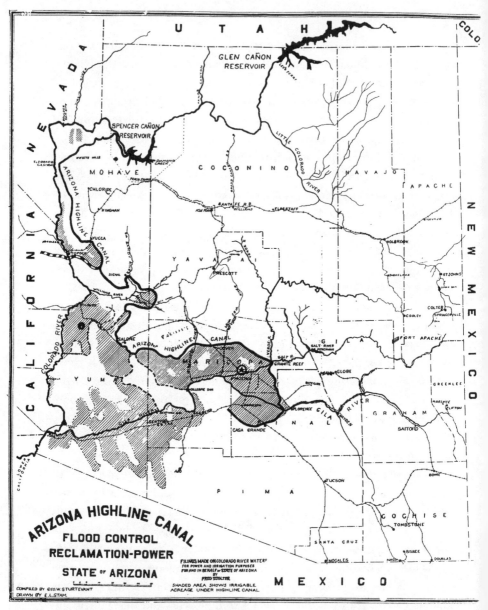

The shaded section on map is land proposed to be irrigated.
Map of Arizona Highline Canal, Glen Canon Dam, Spencer Canon Dam and Water filed on for the State of Arizona, by Fred T. Colter.

Map of Arizona, showing planned location of Highline Canal. (Record Group 115, Bureau of Reclamation, National Archives and Records Administration–Rocky Mountain Region, Denver, Colo.)

diversion to a total of 500,000 acre-feet. Colorado engineers R. I. Meeker and George M. Bull estimated that Denver and Colorado's Front Range farms could use a maximum of 500,000 acre-feet—an estimate very close to present-day diversions—for agriculture and for Denver's postwar population explosion.[23] They also indicated that Colorado would ultimately require a total of 4 million acre-feet from the Colorado River to fully develop irrigable lands. Carpenter's assertion that restrictions on Colorado were already imposed by nature simply did not satisfy lower basin views of equity. Speaking for others, Commissioner McClure asked why Colorado was so reluctant to impose any use limitations on itself if California was willing to lead by example.[24]

This question of equity, more specifically the fairness of imposed restrictions on the upper basin states, was the fifth and perhaps most visceral new issue at the public hearings. Upper basin commissioners were extremely sensitive to embargoes imposed in the past by the federal government on the North Platte and Rio Grande. Such limitations had revealed the negative impact of river controls on growth. Pathfinder and Elephant Butte dams symbolized the injustice of federal water projects constructed without prior agreement on appropriations among the states. Speaking for the upper basin in general, Wyoming Commissioner Emerson objected to any suggestion of use limitations on states of origin. He wanted to avoid a repetition of the same delays in development experienced on the North Platte when Pathfinder Dam was constructed.[25]

In Carpenter's mind, this was a lesson the lower basin had to understand. As of 1922, economic growth in Colorado on the upper Rio Grande was still prohibited by a Department of Interior embargo. For Colorado, and to a lesser extent for Utah, Wyoming, and New Mexico, proposed restrictions on transmountain diversion, limitations on new irrigated acreage, or a requirement to guarantee specified quantities of water to the lower basin were obligations that contained the risk of diminishing future growth. Commissioners from the northern states, therefore, along with their invited spokesmen, resisted such suggestions in the public hearings. Moreover, they lectured spokesmen of the lower basin on the need for time to develop their own economies, the desirability of a storage dam in each basin, and the benefits that Arizona and California would receive from return flows if unconstrained development were allowed in the upper basin.

Carpenter did not intentionally orchestrate a division between the two basins, but he encouraged the presentation of evidence and points of view that corroborated his thinking. Advocates of immediate dam construction on the lower river, including Hoover, became increasingly frustrated with his rigidity. One hundred years, Carpenter asserted, were needed for the upper basin to develop to the point at which the four states could utilize the Colorado River to capacity.[26] A. P. Davis sympathized, but he could only defend the need for a fifty-year period. His estimate was based on the probable development of 50,000 new acres per year, up to approximately 250 million additional irrigable acres in the Colorado River basin. During this period, Davis argued, the lower basin should not be allowed to make priority claims against the upper basin.[27]

But Carpenter wanted even better protection. Bottling up water behind a dam at Boulder Canyon, he opined, would create a priority by virtue of beneficial use. Furthermore, he and others were beginning to have doubts about A. P. Davis's flow data. There might be enough water in the Colorado River for both basins, but if the estimates were wrong and if the upper basin began to develop earlier than expected, competition for federal funds between the two basins could delay construction of flood-control projects in the lower part of the river.[28] However, Carpenter speculated, if a second storage reservoir could be built at the Glen Canyon location on the Utah-Arizona line, it might be possible to agree to a compact that allowed the lower basin to have 50 percent of the river. He made no commitments, preferring to emphasize how rivers improve when irrigation is developed near the headwaters, but by raising the possibility of a compact dividing the water evenly between the two basins, he indicated the course of his own thinking and the ultimate direction of formal compact negotiations in Santa Fe.[29]

Hoover remained skeptical. The CRCC chairman made a statement in Grand Junction obliquely describing the Coloradan as an obstructionist who failed to comprehend the "crux of the situation" and the urgency of conditions on the lower river. Carpenter's states' rights posturing, Hoover claimed, was not conducive to a compromise agreement and, without an agreement, the lower basin states might as well build their dam so they could put the stored water to beneficial use.[30] "Sane men and women," Hoover noted, were required "to put down all extremists and prepare to cooperate."[31] Nevada Governor Emmett Boyle agreed. He suggested that

Colorado was "afraid to spit for fear they [might] sacrifice some of their individual riparian rights." This group of commissioners as a whole, he warned, would have to "cast off the robe of advocate and assume that of judge."[32] If every man was, in fact, participating only for himself and his state, a rapid modification in attitude was necessary.

Carpenter learned a great deal from these hearings. Although Hoover complained that the CRCC was without a leader, Carpenter was gradually assuming this position. Although his sometimes aggressive defense of the upper basin irritated other commissioners, his courtesy, patience, and willingness to solicit conflicting points of view were recognized and appreciated. He made a special effort to defend Commissioner Norviel from unwarranted criticism at the Phoenix meeting. The kindness proved invaluable later on. He also engaged his old opponent, Wyoming attorney Nellis Corthell, in a disagreement over the potential impact of a Supreme Court decision in *Wyoming v. Colorado* if that decision were to come during CRCC negotiations. Corthell believed that a ruling would "lighten the burden of this commission," and Carpenter replied that, win or lose, the Court's opinion would be entitled to "great respect," but would have no bearing on CRCC negotiations.[33] It was a friendly disagreement.

What he wanted, Carpenter stated after the Cheyenne hearing, was an atmosphere of total honesty and trust (comity) in which commissioners might state their fears and disagreements. For Colorado, he insisted on an "open door" for all future development. He would refuse to fix acreage limitations and would continue to defend his premise that topography, climate, and altitude would forever prevent Colorado from using more than an equitable part of "the water arising within our boundaries."[34] Although Hoover might have lacked confidence in the Colorado commissioner, even referring to him as "impossible" at one point,[35] Carpenter was certain Hoover understood the necessity of giving ample freedom to the upper basin for development "as to quantity and time." In sum, Carpenter believed the hearings were a valuable exposition of ideas, that Hoover had been "eminently fair, open minded and possessed of remarkable ability," and that he was "without question of Presidential timber."[36]

Ultimately, Carpenter emerged as the leader Hoover needed to pull the CRCC together. At the penultimate hearing in Denver, the CRCC passed a resolution urging commissioners to submit their suggested form of compact "for the disposition and the apportionment of the waters of the

Colorado River and its tributaries" to CRCC executive secretary Clarence Stetson before the next closed meeting "at some point in the Southwest."[37] Most commissioners assumed this task would rightly fall to Carpenter, who later acknowledged Hoover's wish by drawing up a compact based on a fifty-fifty division of the river.[38] Commissioner McClure encouraged him, stating he would be pleased if the Coloradan would "frame a compact agreeable to the commissioners of all the states."[39] And L. Ward Bannister, attorney for the Denver Chamber of Commerce, a man who frequently criticized Carpenter, observed that the Colorado commissioner seemed to be following "the wisest course which could be taken" in dividing the river. He urged others to back Carpenter and to assist him in educating public opinion in the state.[40]

But time for this important task was hard to find. As the hearings ended, Carpenter was immediately caught up in a whirlwind of accumulated responsibilities involving the South Platte, Arkansas, La Plata and Republican rivers. To further complicate his life, the Supreme Court announced its ruling in the *Wyoming v. Colorado* case on June 5, 1922.

Carpenter was stunned. The Court recognized the legality of interstate priority, but more important to Carpenter was that part of the decision which validated the doctrine of equitable apportionment through recognition of Colorado's right to divert some water from the Laramie River into the Cache la Poudre River. This was good news, but almost immediately, Carpenter noticed, attorneys from Kansas, New Mexico, Wyoming, and Nebraska were announcing intentions to litigate their alleged priority rights against neighboring states. Twisted newspaper interpretations of the meaning of the Court's decision added fuel to the idea that priority would now rule absolutely on all interstate streams. Carpenter felt an increased urgency to settle the Colorado River matter by compact as soon as possible. "We simply must use every endeavor," he wrote Commissioner Emerson, "to bring about the conclusion of a compact at the next meeting at Santa Fe; otherwise, we are badly exposed and we may never again have a like opportunity."[41]

At Hoover's suggestion, New Mexico's Governor Merritt Mechem selected Bishop's Lodge in Santa Fe for the next CRCC meeting.[42] It was a tourist attraction because of the nearby chapel and garden of New Mexico's first Roman Catholic archbishop, Jean Baptiste Lamy. It was also geographically isolated and difficult to get to. Although Stetson feared that the lodge's intimate southwestern atmosphere might actually distract the commissioners from the job at hand, Hoover wanted the CRCC and their advisors to meet in "small, practically executive sessions."[43]

The reunion was scheduled for September, but one postponement followed another as the secretary of commerce attended to strikes in the railroad and coal industries. In the interim, Carpenter reflected further on the *Wyoming v. Colorado* decision and its impact on the upcoming meetings in Santa Fe. Writing Utah's Commissioner Caldwell, he pointed out that "Colorado won completely on the principal contention raised by Wyoming . . . that Colorado could not take the water of the Laramie [River] through the tunnel for use upon lands in the Cache la Poudre [Valley]." But the right of states to protect the first use of water, the priority issue, within their own boundaries had been damaged by the High Court's decision. Angrily, he noted that "Wyoming suicided and incidentally half murdered all the other states of origin. It is unfortunate that a Wyoming judge [Associate Supreme Court Justice Willis Van Devanter][44] brought about such a disaster and the pity of it all lies in the fact that he did not need to have done so in order to have afforded Wyoming ample protection."[45] Accompanying the letter was Carpenter's first draft of a Colorado River Compact. An introductory statement noted "[t]he recent decision of the Supreme Court . . . while probably detrimental to many of the irrigation states and subject to considerable criticism, nevertheless is probably of considerable value to the upper states of the Colorado River in the pending deliberations [at Santa Fe]."[46]

Relating the Laramie River decision to the Colorado River situation, Carpenter pointed to the High Court's endorsement of transmountain diversion and its allocation of a fixed quantity of water between the two states. "Applying this principle to the Colorado River," he concluded, "it would appear that the decision of the Court gives ample justification for a division of the water supply between the states."[47] In other words, for the seven states of the Colorado River basin, the time had come to work out an allocation by compact or have the Supreme Court do it for them. Carpenter put a positive twist on this development, and in a letter to Commissioner Caldwell he outlined general themes for a Colorado River Compact based on data provided by Meeker and Bull. First, he stated, the river divides itself naturally between upper and lower basins with a funnel —the Grand Canyon—between them. Second, irrigation at the upper end of the river will result in return flows at the lower end, so that even if the upper basin were to divert the entire flow of the river, one-half of that water would return to the lower basin. Third, the uses of the lower states, "if economically made," will never demand more than one-half the quantity of water represented by the average natural annual flow of the river.[48]

Using these assumptions as guidelines, Carpenter then suggested what the commissioners needed to address in order to draw up a compact dividing the Colorado River equally between the two basins.

1. Determination of the average annual flow at Lee's Ferry, the upper end of the funnel, and at Yuma, the last gauging station on the river, followed by a mathematical analysis showing what percentage of the larger Yuma flow passed Lee's Ferry. With this information, the upper basin states would be in a better position to know what amount of water had to be guaranteed to the lower end of the river where the Imperial Irrigation District diverted for irrigation.

2. Agreement among all seven states that the upper basin would be allowed to divert *without limitation* (author's emphasis) as future conditions might dictate, except that the upper states would assure the lower states that the river's flow would never fall below one-half the average annual natural flow at Lee's Ferry calculated over a ten-year period.[49]

3. Although the matter of out-of-basin transfers would be moot, if requirements in Number 2 above were agreed to by both basins, the upper basin, to ease the fears of the lower basin, would agree to limit transmountain diversions out of the Colorado River basin to 600,000 acre-feet, an amount representing 5 percent of the flow of the Colorado River as it crossed the state line into Utah.[50]

In his final comments to Caldwell, Carpenter mentioned a few loose ends that required attention. He reminded the Utah commissioner that Colorado could never use even one-half of the "average annual flow of the Grand"[51] or the Yampa rivers, and that Wyoming could not possibly consume one-half of the Green River. Regarding the lower basin, he stressed the importance of including the Gila River as "the first stream that should take care of the Imperial Valley" through water returned to the Colorado River basin after first being utilized in Arizona. On the Colorado River itself, navigation rights that were subject to federal control under the Constitution's commerce clause would be subordinated to other uses more readily controlled by the states: domestic (drinking water), irrigation, and hydroelectric power. Finally, if the needs of Mexico were to be considered, "[s]ome small additional percentage might be allowed," if it were charged as much "against the lower states as is demanded of the upper states so as to keep a 50:50 balance." Both basins, he believed, should share equally in what would come to be known as the Mexican burden.

Carpenter shared these same thoughts with New Mexico Commissioner S.B. Davis, "who look[ed] with favor upon the plan because of its simplicity." Carpenter told Davis that he also expected to speak to Wyoming Commissioner Emerson within the week in order to establish unanimity amongst the upper basin commissioners prior to the Santa Fe meeting. He hoped to avoid publicity if the four of them decided to get together. The possibility existed, Carpenter warned, that "some parties living in the lower states might look with suspicion and misunderstanding upon any such meeting."[52] He wanted to begin the Santa Fe meeting in a spirit of trust, harmony, and good will. Speculation about the supposed effects of the *Wyoming v. Colorado* decision was already rampant, and Carpenter wanted the CRCC to understand that he viewed the ruling as a blessing in disguise. It "makes my work much easier," he wrote Commissioner McClure, because "the extreme views expressed by the representatives of the states in both portions of the Colorado River basin are more or less modified."[53] At the same time, he believed, if the upper basin states were not unified, the lower basin might proceed on its own with dam construction. California, Arizona, and Nevada appeared far more willing to accept the Supreme Court's probable imposition of water allocations for each state as it had done for Colorado and Wyoming in the Laramie River case.

In order to achieve a compact, Carpenter reasoned the seven Colorado River basin states were going to have to abandon some aspects of state sovereignty. Property rights protected by state boundaries were no longer absolute or inviolate where interstate streams existed. Upper states would have to use "every means within their power to prevent the construction of any enormous works upon the lower Colorado River until the right of the upper states to use such water as they need[ed] in the future ha[d] been assured to them by interstate treaty."[54] The lower states would have to find ways to modify their demands for immediate federal assistance in order to achieve a permanent solution to conflicting demands on the Colorado River.

Carpenter had been committed to the general tenure of this plan since talks began in Washington, but his increased edginess in the summer and fall of 1922 was partly a result of the action of California Congressman Philip D. Swing and his colleague, California's senior senator, Hiram Johnson. Swing had been legal counsel for the Imperial Irrigation District. He was elected to Congress in 1920 where he continued lobbying for an All-American Canal and a storage dam on the Colorado River. Swing entered Congress believing California's best chance for a dam was an alliance with the private power companies or a cost-sharing agreement with Los Angeles and other southern California municipalities.[55] But when the Fall-Davis Report became public, he was encouraged to seek a partnership with the Reclamation Service. With this objective in mind, he prepared legislation "to implement its recommendations," receiving assurances that Senator Johnson would sponsor the bill when it came to the Senate.[56] The first of many Swing-Johnson bills was introduced on April 25, 1922. It called for construction of an All-American Canal from the Colorado River to the Imperial Valley and a dam at or near Boulder Canyon for flood control and generation of hydroelectric power.

Reaction from the upper basin states was as expected. Legislation authorizing dam construction while the CRCC was still in negotiation was clearly in conflict with the spirit of cooperation implicit in the legislation authorizing compact negotiations. No matter how urgent conditions were on the lower Colorado River, the singular purpose of the CRCC was to establish rights on the river *before* dams were built. Agreeing to a major dam and reservoir so that California and Arizona could put large quantities of Colorado River water to beneficial use made no sense at all to Carpenter, especially in light of the Supreme Court's recent recognition of interstate priority in *Wyoming v. Colorado*.

Swing disagreed. When he appeared before the House Committee on Irrigation of Arid Lands, he argued that the needs of the Imperial Valley could not wait "an indeterminate length of time." A. P. Davis and Hoover concurred and advocated forward progress on the legislation, causing Carpenter's frustration to boil to the surface.[57] What Swing and Johnson were recommending, he told Utah Congressman Elmer O. Leatherwood, was

"not only untimely but quite discourteous. . . . [T]he present situation is quite similar to that which would obtain in a case where several

nations had agreed to attempt to arrive at an international understanding respecting the waters of a river common to the several nations
and where those nations had appointed their plenipotentiaries who
were then engaged in actual consideration of the subject matter. For
one nation to prematurely proceed with legislation involving . . . the
subject matter under consideration by an international commission,
would not only be considered deliberately discourteous but might well
merit the charge of being deliberately unfriendly and proposed for
the very purpose of embarrassing the deliberations of the international
commission."[58]

Leatherwood sat on the House committee hearing the Swing-Johnson
bill. Carpenter made it clear to him that Colorado's delegates would not dig-
nify the bill by giving testimony, for "[t]his legislation proposes the building
of a structure which may become an interstate menace and provoke interstate controversy." He urged Leatherwood to use his office to discourage
any further hearings and similar measures.[59] To proceed with construction
before the rights of each state and of the United States were definitely and
permanently settled would lay the groundwork for endless litigation. "The
future growth and welfare of the seven states," he advised Leatherwood, "and
incidentally of that portion of the United States, is dependent upon an
orderly development of the use of the stream upon a fixed legal basis . . .
duly ratified and approved by the legislatures and by Congress."[60]

Carpenter was unrelenting, impassioned, and stubborn on this issue. "I
prefer to believe," he wrote Commissioner Caldwell on the same day, "that
you and I are both still looked upon as of the 'long-eared' species. Sometimes those of us who believe in the soundness of the principles we advocate are classed as too unyielding. Possibly, we deserve the criticism, but
an adherence to such position is conducive to peaceful slumber."[61] Ten
days later Carpenter sent a draft compact to Commissioner Emerson. The
cover letter contained additions to the plan he had sent Commissioner
Caldwell six weeks earlier. It argued that consumptive diversions "out of
the watershed or into the Salton Sea" should be "made and cared for at
the expense of the division in which they occur." Evaporation losses from a
flood-control dam built in the upper basin (he was thinking of Glen
Canyon) were to be "charged to the Lower Division," because the benefits
of such a dam would accrue to the lower basin. He suggested a joint commission made up of state engineers, whose task would be to measure

Colorado River flow at Lee's Ferry. Data gathered, Carpenter hoped, would result in assurances to the lower basin of an equitable amount of water based on Colorado River hydrology. Additionally, Carpenter emphasized the importance of both basins sharing equally any obligation to Mexico.[62]

Carpenter recognized that his draft compact was "subject to those infirmities characteristic of the treatment of any given subject matter by a single mind." It would be improved by the thorough and painstaking consideration of the commissioners. He had no "pride of expression" and would be most pleased to receive direct criticism. All he asked was that "the whole matter be kept confidential" and that the "three Upper states [plus Colorado] come to a common understanding before consulting with the remainder of the commission."[63]

The time had now arrived to share his ideas with Hoover, but before sending his draft compact to the secretary of commerce, Carpenter had to attend to a nagging financial matter. He reported to Colorado Governor Oliver H. Shoup that Attorney General Victor E. Keyes was withholding salary promised him by both men on May 9, 1921. As proof, Carpenter cited his diary for that date. It stated that he was to receive fifty dollars a day, up to a grand total of $10,000, for the biennial period.[64] The attorney general, he told Shoup, was limiting him to $5,000 and advising him that any additional hours worked as interstate streams commissioner for Colorado would be uncompensated by the state.[65] Carpenter admitted to feeling humiliated. By concentrating almost exclusively on Colorado River matters, he had been forced to put aside other remunerative business. In 1921 he had worked almost two months without pay and he thought it unfair of the attorney general to ask him to give additional services to the state free of charge. "There is yet much work to be done," he argued, "and financial annoyance will not be conducive to best results."[66] Ultimately, Keyes recognized the validity of his protest. He agreed that Carpenter's compensation could reach almost $10,000, but he would receive no additional salary for services rendered during the remaining four months of 1922.[67] It was a compromise, but it allowed Carpenter to focus on his work as commissioner.

On August 25, 1922, Carpenter wrote to Hoover. "Pursuant to your suggestion," he said, "I am taking the liberty of enclosing for your personal and confidential consideration a copy of a preliminary draft of a compact providing for the permanent and equitable distribution of the Colorado River upon a fifty-fifty basis."[68]

Carpenter's fifty-fifty plan was unique because, instead of focusing on an equitable allocation of water to each state, it divided the states into two groups: the four upper states had to accept the burden of providing water to the three lower states. The three lower states would have to obligate themselves to an equitable division of the water they received from the upper basin. In this scenario, each state was giving up some of its sovereignty to achieve collectively the desired goal of a dam and reservoir on the lower river. Because Carpenter, as Colorado's representative, had fought just as hard as the other state commissioners for an allocation that would meet all of Colorado's present and future needs, his fifty-fifty plan reflects a major shift in thinking. It emerged from an extensive study of the Constitution, the land surrounding the Colorado River, the urgency of California's need for protection, and the political exigencies of compact negotiation.

Carpenter's five-page cover letter to Hoover repeated much of what he had shared with Caldwell and Emerson, but he noted for Hoover's benefit that the simplicity and equity inherent in the plan would allow both basins to move forward without engaging in a "contest of speed giving rise to foolhardy rivalry to result in disaster and financial disappointment." He had tried out his plan on the *Denver Post* and was pleased to report that the reaction was very favorable. "Even the most radical with whom I have conversed," he noted, "are reconciled to such an adjustment. They believe that sufficient latitude is afforded to recommend the plan."

It is the letter's last paragraph, however, that says most about Carpenter's view of himself and the work he had undertaken. It reveals how Colorado River compact negotiations defined him as a person and how he hoped for Hoover's understanding as he searched for a solution acceptable to all seven states and the federal government. He wrote:

> I wish that I might confer with you in person at more length . . . but I fear that I must forego that pleasure. As I stated at the outset I am forwarding this to you confidentially and purely as a personal matter, and I take the liberty of stating that I am prompted so to do out of a feeling of the deepest personal regard. I am keenly appreciative of that underlying spirit of broad-minded fairplay which you have exhibited. The sphere of my personal endeavors during the past fifteen years has frequently provoked a feeling of extreme loneliness which at

times has been almost overwhelming, and as our hearings have proceeded your presence has prompted within me a sense of comrade-
ship which now impels me to forward you the enclosed draft in the
hope that you may give it your most rigid scrutiny, mature thought,
and unstinted criticism.[69]

For Carpenter and the Colorado River Compact, this was an incompa-
rable moment. Carpenter had completed the basic draft that would be
revised, modified, and finally approved in discussions at Santa Fe. To
Hoover's delight, a leader had finally emerged among the commissioners.
Although his busy schedule did not allow a response for almost two months,
Hoover found Carpenter's letter and compact to be of "great interest." He
intended to give both documents "most careful consideration" and encouraged the Coloradan to discuss his ideas broadly with the hope of settling
some differences among commissioners before the Santa Fe meeting.[70]

Carpenter complied. He mailed copies of his draft compact to the commissioners and other interested parties. Commissioner McClure was "very
pleased" and calculated that the fifty-fifty plan was feasible.[71] Congressman
Swing also expressed enthusiasm for the fifty-fifty basis on which the plan
rested.[72] A. P. Davis liked Carpenter's ideas and humbly congratulated him
on developing the fifty-fifty concept. "Some modification may be necessary," Davis suggested, "but this proposition seems to me to contain more
promise of agreement than any I have yet seen."[73]

Favorable responses arrived from most of the other commissioners.
With new hydrology data on Colorado River flows furnished by state engineers and by the United States Geological Survey, Carpenter was soon able
to suggest a specific amount of water that upper states might guarantee to
the lower basin. He based his recommendation on the fifty-fifty principle
of equity. Because the flow of the Colorado River at Yuma averaged 17.4
million acre-feet between 1902 and 1921, and because 2.4 million acre–
feet (14 percent) entered the river between Lee's Ferry and Yuma, the
upper basin would be willing to guarantee 36 percent of the Yuma flow
delivered at Lee's Ferry, so that the lower basin would be assured 50 percent of the entire river. Over any period of ten consecutive years, Carpenter
explained, the Yuma gauging station would measure a minimum average
annual flow of 50 percent of 17.4 million acre-feet: 2.5 million acre-feet

(14 percent) to be contributed by the Gila and Little Colorado rivers and 6.2 million acre-feet (36 percent) delivered by the upper basin at Lee's Ferry, making a total of 8.7 million acre-feet.[74]

As noted above, Carpenter likened the challenge faced by the seven Colorado River basin states to comparable international situations. At one of the CRCC meetings in Washington, Representative Samuel S. Arentz of Nevada called Carpenter's attention to the state of affairs on the Nile River. Arentz recalled certain comments by Egypt's chief engineer on the Aswan Dam when the two men were traveling together on the Southern Pacific Railroad through the Imperial Valley and across the Colorado River. Were he a young man, the engineer told Arentz, "it would be my ambition to have even a small interest in the development of the Colorado River, for in many ways it represents the same difficulties I overcame on the Nile and possesses the same great possibilities of development."[75] Following the Washington meetings, Carpenter learned of a report prepared by H. T. Cory, United States representative to an international commission charged with assisting Egypt and Sudan in drawing up a Nile River treaty. Cory was given the task of recommending an equitable distribution of the river to both nations. His report was published on December 30, 1920.[76]

Carpenter located Cory in Los Angeles and interviewed him about what he had written.[77] The report stated that an international river had to be considered a single entity. In an arid area, the use, conservation, and development of river water must be viewed as a "public trust" with due regard to the eventual rights of generations unborn." Accepting this principle, Cory wrote, "It follows that . . . the arable lands, unwatered but irrigable, belonging to different proprietors . . . enjoy an equitable right to an adequate share of the unappropriated water of the stream."[78]

It can not be determined precisely how this report reinforced Carpenter's thinking about the Colorado River Compact. The Coloradan was no advocate of the "public trust" doctrine as it is known today.[79] But he spent several days studying Cory's work and presumably found further justification for the strategy articulated in the first draft of the compact. The rights of upper basin states, or nations, to develop agricultural land at their own pace, and the benefits of a negotiated compact that aimed at permanent solutions of river matters for the benefit of subsequent generations—these were principles that Carpenter intended to fight for at all cost.

D.E. Carpenter

Plan for 50-50 division of water

Average annual flow, Yuma =
(1902-1921) 17.4 MAF

Average annual flow, Lee Ferry =
-14.9 MAF
LBS Contribution = 2.5 MAF

2.5 MAF = 14% river
UBS guarntee 36% to equal 50%
17.4
.36
6.2 MAF =
UBS obligation to LBS

Delph Carpenter's initial plan for a fifty-fifty sharing of Colorado River water between upper basin states (UBS) and lower basin states (LBS). Prepared by the author.

On November 7, 1922, he boarded a train for Santa Fe with Meeker, Commissioner Caldwell, attorney L. Ward Bannister from Denver, A. P. Davis, and others. At La Junta, Colorado, they were joined by Hoover and Stetson. Carpenter left the train in Las Vegas, New Mexico, and drove to Santa Fe with Commissioner Davis. Their destination was Bishop's Lodge, a few miles north of Santa Fe. The approach to the lodge, as described by Arnold Kruckman, secretary of the League of the Southwest, was "over a convolution of roads that dizzily swoop up and down like a switch-back roller coaster and hang so precariously to the steep sides of the desolate landscape that the passage of a vehicle makes you think of a fly crawling over an eyebrow."[80] Isolation was what Hoover desired, but he arrived to discover that the manager of the lodge had overbooked. In some cases four people were assigned to a room set up for two guests. Hoover wanted executive sessions, not public hearings. He was willing to allow each commissioner a legal and engineering advisor and he welcomed the governors and governors-elect who arrived from all the basin states.[81] But he put his foot down at the size of the California delegation and ordered Stetson to have the manager remove seven of them from the lodge.[82] They protested Hoover's heavy-handed tactics, but Hoover was adamant. Four of the Californians departed for home. The other three decided to commute over the "switchback roller coaster" on a daily basis.

The first session of the CRCC was supposed to begin on November 9, but commissioners Emerson, Scrugham, and McClure were late in arriving. Carpenter took advantage of their absence to visit the little town of Alcalde, where he was shown an old *acequia* (irrigation canal) that had been in operation for three hundred years.[83] He also visited the Indian pueblos around Española and witnessed Native American dances. On November 11, the first of seventeen grueling executive sessions began.

Hoover asked if other commissioners had prepared a written plan for division of Colorado River water. Commissioner Norviel circulated a document calling for early construction of a dam, state control of hydroelectric power revenues, appropriation of water by states, limitation of transfers out of basin, and equitable apportionment among the seven states during times of scarcity. Commissioner Caldwell also presented a brief draft that emphasized a two-basin appropriation system, storage in the upper basin, and unrestricted use of water in the upper basin.

Bishop's Lodge, Santa Fe, N. Mex., in the 1920s.

Colorado River Compact Commission at Bishop's Lodge.

But it was Carpenter's draft that became the focus of CRCC discussions. It was more thorough and responsive to what commissioners had learned in Washington and at the public hearings. Much of what Carpenter had discussed since the hearings was included in the document that became the basis for deliberations: division of the water between basins, not states; an equitable fifty-fifty split of the Colorado River between basins;[84] division of the river at Lee's Ferry; ten-year averaging of minimum-flow guarantees between the basins; equal responsibility by the basins in any future delivery to Mexico; and the designation of navigation and power as subservient to agricultural and domestic uses of the river.[85] As discussions commenced, Carpenter tried to nudge the commissioners away from parochial interests toward broader concerns of the entire basin. He asked his colleagues to consider how much water the upper basin would have to guarantee to the lower basin over a ten-year period; how Mexico should be dealt with; whether or not the compact should say anything about dam construction; and how federal interests in the Colorado River would be considered. With Arizona Commissioner Norviel speaking out stridently for the lower basin and chairman Hoover acting as mediator, Carpenter championed the interests of the upper basin and responded to challenges from all corners with attempts at compromise. He was a tough bargainer, but his patience and courtesy toward adversaries and his determination to produce agreement among the seven commissioners produced results. Those who sparred with Carpenter at Bishop's Lodge credited him later with perseverance, candor, and clarity of thought. Whether one views the final document with admiration or disdain, it is abundantly clear that the Colorado commissioner had a great deal to do with its final form.

This is not to say that the other commissioners allowed Carpenter to lead by default. To a man, they accepted their own responsibilities with gravity. They were sensitive to the way various proposals would be received by their own state legislatures. The political environment of each state was distinct, and each commissioner calculated the response he would encounter when he returned home with a signed compact. No one had more pressure on him than the commissioner from Arizona.

Norviel was a gentleman and a student of water law. Well-dressed and dignified, the only commissioner sporting a moustache, he gave the appearance of a prosperous banker.[86] He may not have been Carpenter's equal in matters of law, but his active questioning of every proposal revealed a profound interest in the Colorado River and an acute awareness of the polarized politics in his own state. Powerful forces in Arizona were opposed to any plan that would abandon Arizona's hopes for a Highline Canal. George H. Maxwell, the principal advocate of the canal, fought against the Boulder Canyon dam because he believed it would contribute to the development of an Asiatic state at the head of the Gulf of California. Cheap labor, he argued, and a railroad connecting Mexican lands to Calexico in the United States would undermine industry and agriculture on the Arizona side of the Colorado River basin.[87] What he favored was a Colorado River dam located upstream in the Diamond Creek area where the water collected in the dam's reservoir could be pumped hundreds of miles through a Highline Canal to Phoenix, Tucson, and the 2.5 million acres of potentially arable land in the central part of the state. He was backed by newly elected Governor George P. Hunt, who had replaced Governor Thomas Campbell just before the Santa Fe meetings began. Campbell favored a compact, but he was a lame duck. Norviel's challenge was to fulfill the mission given him by Campbell in such a way that the final agreement would be acceptable to the incoming governor. In retrospect, it is clear he had no chance of success.

California's "Roman Senator" from Sacramento was state engineer W. F. McClure. A tall, gentlemanly, dignified Scotsman who enjoyed quoting the Bible, McClure was the quietest member of the CRCC. He expressed himself infrequently, mostly when Chairman Hoover brought him into the discussions. He had no lack of interest in the matters at hand, but some said he knew little about the Colorado River and preferred reflecting on the comments of others whose preparation and experience were more extensive. Californians from the Imperial Irrigation District wanted a commissioner who would fight for immediate dam construction and a canal from the river that never entered Mexican soil. But they were stuck with McClure and all they could do was complain when he seemed to be apathetic to their interests.

Representing Nevada, the third lower basin state, was J. G. Scrugham, former state engineer and governor-elect during the Santa Fe meetings. Referred to as "the colonel," Scrugham was, perhaps, the most relaxed of the seven commissioners, possibly because of Nevada's relatively small interest in the Colorado River. Nevertheless, Scrugham had a strong stake in discussions involving hydroelectric power generation. The Boulder Canyon dam site bordered on his state's southern boundary, and he viewed the potential for revenue generation as a benefit Nevada was entitled to if a hydroelectric plant was included in the dam.

Of the upper basin commissioners, R. E. Caldwell, Utah state engineer, was most outspoken. Most of the time, he agreed with Carpenter on matters of principle. Along with his proprietary defense of Utah's sovereignty, especially Utah's rights on the Virgin River, Caldwell occasionally brought levity to the somber discussions. Considered "the salt of the earth," he was also a serious thinker whose critical comments reflected an appreciation for the work at hand and a deep respect for the arguments brought forward by delegates from the lower basin.

Frank Emerson, state engineer from Wyoming was the "boy commissioner." Youngest of the group, he arrived in Santa Fe without advisors and determined to avoid the kinds of difficulties Wyoming had experienced previously on interstate streams. Emerson was emboldened by the *Wyoming v. Colorado* decision, but he realized the principle of interstate priority won on the Laramie River could work against Wyoming on the Colorado River. He and Carpenter were not without disagreements, but respect for one another, a result of having participated as adversaries in the Laramie River litigation, combined with mutual interests as headwater states' representatives, resulted in the two men agreeing on most issues most of the time.

New Mexico's S. B. Davis, the only other attorney in the CRCC, was sometimes critical of Carpenter's leadership. Although New Mexico belonged to the upper basin group, the state also had issues in common with Arizona. Judge Davis was an independent thinker. Recently defeated for the United States Senate and suffering occasional attacks of neuralgia, he gave the appearance of being cantankerous and uncooperative. He respected Carpenter because of compact work they had almost completed on the La Plata River, and as the meetings progressed, Davis fell in line with the other upper basin representatives.

Of the seven commissioners, Carpenter was the most active and energetic when they gathered in the bridal suite at Bishop's Lodge to begin their discussions. Hoover asked him to explain why the two-basin approach to water allocation made more sense than a distribution based on potentially irrigable acreage in the respective states. A state-based system, Carpenter replied, would encourage a growth race. To oversee distribution of water to each state, a super-government agency would be required. If court challenges occurred, legal decisions would be based on proof of interstate priority. Carpenter had consistently characterized the intervention of a federal agency as a violation of states' rights, and he viewed any contest of speed between the states as a guarantee of temporary and unstable economies, to say nothing of the potential for increased interstate conflict.

To avoid potential conflict, he told commissioners, "the very future of our states, as well as of our Nation, depends upon . . . development . . . follow[ing] its natural course as economic and human conditions warrant." The legal basis for his two-basin proposal was framed in consideration of "the method that the [High] Court might or might not accept when forced to the extremity in trying to arrive at some adjustment of conditions after the causes have come into being."[88] What he meant was that the *Wyoming v. Colorado* decision was still very much on his mind. He did not want the Supreme Court appropriating water from the Colorado River to the state, and he believed the CRCC was perfectly capable of writing a compact minimizing the Supreme Court's possible involvement in river administration. "[O]ur jurisdiction is broad," he said, "and our powers are full to proceed irrespective of the technical, legal feature."[89]

But progress on the compact would require unanimous agreement by the commissioners, and Norviel was suspicious of the two-basin approach. He characterized the fifty-fifty plan of water distribution between basins as "infeasible . . . impossible" and "abhorrent."[90] Carpenter tried to explain that his idea was based on the physical facts of nature as well as a somewhat arbitrary estimate that such a division by basins would ultimately assure equity to individual states. Because of evaporation, irregular flow of tributaries, and unknown precipitation cycles, it would be difficult to determine exactly what a fifty-fifty division should be. But comity had to be an important pillar of the compact, and if Norviel could be persuaded that the upper basin's intentions were well-meaning, he might be willing to give up Arizona's demand for a finite and unalterable appropriation. The more the states trusted each other, the better chance they would have to work out interstate problems in the future. "We are now proceeding," Carpenter stated, "upon the big problem of building up comity. The minute we get into matters of refinement and detail, we are getting into trouble. As comity is established, this great proof of a result of comity will grow and be encouraged in specific localities as between two or more states."[91]

Norviel continued to insist, however, that the discussions address precise quantities: How much water would his state be guaranteed on an annual basis? How much would the lower basin be obligated to Mexico? How long would the compact be in effect before a revision was possible? What agency would oversee the delivery of water guaranteed from the upper to the lower basin? When could a hydroelectric dam be built on the Colorado River? They were all good questions, and they emanated logically from Arizona's suspicion that there was not enough water in the Colorado River for the needs of all seven states, that too little data was available to show how much land could be irrigated in Arizona after the copper mining played out, and that California would appropriate the water to which Arizona had a legal right.[92] Norviel wanted protection for Arizona as much as Carpenter wanted protection for the upper basin.

Recognizing the psychological benefits of a sensitive response to Norviel's fears, Carpenter began showing more empathy for Arizona's concerns. "I think there is not a man in the upper states," he said, "and who understands the situation in the lower country, who is not hoping to see a reservoir on the lower river."

"I am glad the heart strings have been touched at last," Norviel replied.

"They always have been," Carpenter concluded.[93]

But such an expression of compassion did not mean the Coloradan was willing to abandon the essence of his compact scheme. Having studied A. P. Davis's data on river flows since 1902, Carpenter still urged a division of water between basins based on a running ten-year average. After consultation with the other upper basin commissioners, he was prepared to guarantee 65 million acre-feet to the lower states at Lee's Ferry over a period of ten years.

Norviel was unimpressed. The ten-year period was too long. Upper basin states might hoard water during "famine" times, delivering the contracted amount in one or two years. The lower states could not count on a minimum annual flow. Because Carpenter was effectively opposing a stated commitment to reservoir construction in the compact, Norviel worried that the lower basin would not have enough storage to hold the water during a drought. He also worried about Governor Hunt's reaction and the possibility that Arizona would receive none of the water promised in a two-basin compact because of California's political aggressiveness. Congressman Phil Swing's bill to authorize construction of a dam at Boulder Canyon had been introduced in Congress seven months before the Santa Fe meetings began.

Carpenter wanted Norviel to understand the reason why ten-year averaging made sense. He felt that Norviel had difficulty seeing that future droughts would visit both basins with equal punishment. Shortages along the lower river, Carpenter pointed out, would be the natural result of aridity at the source. The alternative plan of a guaranteed minimum annual flow might be considered, but Carpenter had difficulty coming up with an appropriate amount the upper states could promise to the lower states during the next cycle of drought. This was why ten-year averaging made more sense. Furthermore, the ten-year averaging plan took into consideration the worst river flows of the past twenty years, as recorded in the Fall-Davis Report. Nevertheless, Norviel still favored a minimum annual flow to meet the minimum domestic and agricultural needs of the lower states.

As tension rose, Carpenter challenged the Arizonan's logic. "[I]sn't it always your disposition," he asked, "to get assurance for your dry deserts below and ask us to bear the brunt of that visitation of drouth [sic], which paralyzes us just as much as or more than the lower country? If I am in error that that is your frame of mind, well and good, I beg your pardon."

"You are forgiven for all your sins up to date as far as I am concerned," Norviel replied, "but as I said before . . . . [t]he assurance we ask is no more than our legal rights any other section to the contrary notwithstanding. We ask no more from you than we ask from New Mexico or California or Nevada. We only want what is ours."

"You want the Gila River because it rises in your territory." Carpenter countered. "Supposing we include the Gila so we know where the water supply is. Don't the people of the upper states have as much right to demand that you let the Gila flow in the Imperial Valley as you have to ask that we do something?"

"You have as much right to ask for as much as you can use under the Gila," Norviel retorted. "If you have any chance to appropriate any water out of the Gila, it is yours. Whatever appropriation you have made out of the Gila is yours and whatever appropriation we can make out of the Colorado is ours."[94]

Stalemate! By the seventeenth meeting, the two basins appeared to be growing farther apart. Norviel wanted a guarantee of 82 million acre-feet over a ten-year period. The upper states' offer of 65 million acre-feet, he argued, would not meet the minimum needs of the lower basin. But Carpenter was reluctant to be too generous, given the limited hydrological information available. He was determined not to bind the upper states to an agreement they could not fulfill in dry years. Consequently, the two basins remained deadlocked, 17 million acre-feet apart.[95]

Hoover, director of debate and master of compromise, was hopeful some basis for agreement was still possible. He first asked representatives of the upper basin if there was any chance of their considering responsibility for the entire Mexican burden. When Carpenter replied with a resounding, "None at all," he made a second proposal. "[T]he business of the chair," he announced, "is to find a medial ground, so I am wondering if the northern states will make it seven million five hundred thousand?"[96] Over ten years, the guarantee would be 75 million acre-feet.

Norviel grumbled once again about ten-year averaging, but Carpenter agreed to take up Hoover's proposal with other members of the upper basin. He encouraged Norviel to do the same. "There is no need," he reminded Norviel, "of injecting cumbersome machinery [into the compact]. In the final analysis, when time has passed, the river will automatically take care of itself, in the matter of supply and demand. There is no desire [on the part of the upper basin] to see how much we may reduce you. The spirit of the whole meeting has been to provide a compact which we can fulfill."[97]

Perhaps Carpenter was naive, but he was sincere. The stakes were so high for Norviel that it was hard to imagine consenting to a compact on the basis of good will and friendship. Norviel wanted the critics back home to believe he was a tough bargainer, and he was convinced the people of Arizona would stand behind a compact based on true equitable apportionment. He and Carpenter were gentlemen. They respected each other's intellectual integrity. When the commissioners renewed discussions at the eighteenth meeting, Norviel agreed to accept the Hoover amendment.

It is doubtful he was seduced by Carpenter's lectures on comity, but if he had been unable to trust the Coloradan, the vote might have been different. In later years, Norviel teasingly blamed Carpenter for his role in getting him into "an awful fix, and purposely, I guess,"[98] but Norviel's willingness to compromise was, in fact, proof that Carpenter had prepared the groundwork for an honest relationship with him since the spring of 1922. "Many of us are accused of untrue motives and untrue objectives," Carpenter wrote the Arizonan, "but I want you to understand, friend Norviel, that you are at liberty to ask me at any time and at any place such personal questions as you wish in order to verify what I have said. . . . Let's not let anybody rush us off our feet. Time, thought, patience and honest personal intercourse, I believe, will solve the whole problem, because in the end it will be found that there are no real 'issues' or points of difficulty between us."[99] Trust between the two men emerged gradually, but it played a significant role in achieving consensus on the CRCC.

On the morning of November 16, Hoover presented a memorandum listing those principles upon which all had supposedly agreed. Paragraph five stated that each basin could divert up to 7.5 million acre-feet of water per year with an equality of right. It was accepted unanimously after very little discussion.[100] The memorandum was to serve as a basis for drafting the final compact. It included the following principles: (1) a description of the Colorado River basin; (2) a division of the Colorado River basin into two parts, with a demarcation line just below the mouth of the Pariah River; (3) the length of time the compact would be in force and how it would be revised in the future (commissioners agreed on a time frame somewhere between forty and fifty years and charged the drafting committee to decide on an exact period); (4) priority of beneficial use to be agricultural, domestic, hydroelectric power, and navigation; (5) division of water between the two basins to be 7.5 million acre-feet guaranteed to each; (6) circumstances under which all rights to beneficial uses would vest; (7) ten-year obligation of the upper basin to deliver 75 million acre-feet and a minimum annual flow of 4 million acre-feet; (8) responsibility divided equally between basins to provide water to Mexico; (9) creation of a commission to collect data on water flow and consumption; and (10) recognition of the right to divert water out of the basin and the right to store water in one basin for use in another.[101]

Following modification and approval of these points, the commissioners tried to agree on a period of time the compact would be allowed to stand prior to revision. An intense discussion ensued in which members of the upper basin pushed for fifty years. Norviel said he could not even think past forty years. Extremely frustrated, he began to feel he had made too many compromises. "I think we have conceded on every point up to date," he lamented. "I feel we have been borne down at every stage of the game to a minimum and I don't think we should be asked to concede anything more. If we do, we are very liable to go to a point where I myself could not go before my legislature and say I am satisfied with this pact."[102]

But things got worse for Norviel before they got better. He discovered that Hoover's suggested 75 million acre-feet did not include Arizona's alleged rights to the Gila and Little Colorado rivers. Frustration turned to anger. At no other time during the two weeks of hard negotiations did the CRCC come closer to breaking apart. Norviel had every reason to believe that Hoover's compromise suggestion was linked to previous discussions. Neither the chairman nor the commissioners had ever stated, or even implied, that the offer of 75 million acre-feet was based on limitations or conditions that were any different than those assumed to be operative by both sides in previous exchanges. Norviel had accepted the compromise, believing that the flow of the Gila and Salt rivers was exclusive to Arizona and did not figure in the 75 million acre-feet apportioned to the lower basin. He felt isolated and deceived, especially because commissioners McClure and Scrugham, supposedly his allies in matters pertaining to the lower basin, had pretty much kept to themselves up to this point.

In his diary, Carpenter mentioned the "blow-up by Arizona."[103] When Norviel asked for revision of certain portions of the compromise, Carpenter was troubled. Commissioners were tiring. They were becoming restless and impatient at having to start over again with the division of water between basins. Norviel had refused to commit his views to writing, preferring to parry the offerings of the upper states. Hoover sensed they were at loggerheads. He suggested representatives of both basins meet in separate caucuses to present some form of compromise plan to the chair.

The tactic worked. To this point in the negotiations, Hoover had shown little preference for either basin, but he chose the moment to lecture the upper basin on "the crux of the anxiety of the people of the lower river," demonstrating in the process a genuine sympathy for the crisis building on the lower river.[104] Norviel responded especially well to Hoover's timely expression of empathy for the lower basin. He agreed to a new draft of Article III of the compact that included 75 million acre-feet of water from the "Colorado River System" to the lower basin, plus the "right [of the lower basin] to increase its beneficial consumptive use of such waters by one million acre-feet per annum."[105] The crisis passed. Norviel viewed the additional wording as recognition of Arizona's absolute right to the Gila and Salt rivers, even though that was not understood by all the other commissioners. At the last meeting, therefore, when the guarantee of 4 million acre-feet annual minimum flow to the lower basin was removed from Article III, only a murmur slipped past the lips of the Arizona commissioner.

Hoover's leadership was largely responsible for saving the day. The chairman inspired the very trust Carpenter had hoped to build. Additionally, Hoover's determination to make the compact understandable to laymen resulted in a compact containing enough generalities for future generations to interpret. The chairman's tactics endeared him to all commissioners, especially Norviel, who anticipated severe criticism from Governor Hunt and George Maxwell. Respect for Hoover had increased exponentially during the discussions, as the chairman sought opinions from all commissioners, not just those who were outspoken. He found ways to keep discussions moving forward, and he used his analytical skills to rise above the details of each paragraph so commissioners could comprehend the totality of the river basin environment in the evolving document they were producing.

As discussions came to an end, Hoover noted that the compact was no longer a fifty-fifty division of water between the two basins. The CRCC was actually allocating percentages of water subject to revision at a later date. He also observed that the allocation of water in the compact was essentially a use right, not a private property right to the water itself. He schooled commissioners on how Congress would react to the document, particularly how that body would respond to the loss of navigation rights on the Colorado River, and he advised the commissioners to prepare the final agreement in such a way that it would be acceptable to the states and to the United States. To this end, he suggested new language. He trimmed certain phrases to achieve that goal, boasting on one occasion with a twinkle in his eye that he had managed to save "42 words on Carpenter by taking out courts, equities, rights, by-laws and so forth."[106]

Carpenter accepted the teasing in good grace. His primary concern was how the compact read as a whole, but his training and experience mandated from him a legal and constitutional phraseology sometimes objectionable to the others. Commissioners appreciated his precision but deplored the conceptual complexity of such language. As one of four draftsman of the final compact,[107] Carpenter's legal expertise was much in demand, but he had to make concessions where clarity called for compromise. He lost some battles and refused to allow publication of his own version of the compact due to revisions by the drafting committee.[108] But the core of the final document was still his. Steadfastly, he refused to abandon the essential principles of equitable apportionment,[109] comity between the states, preservation of state sovereignty, and resistance to inclusion of dam construction in any form as a prerequisite for compact ratification. He was willing to sign a resolution, however, separate from the compact itself, stating unequivocally the support of the upper basin for a dam at some point on the Colorado River, but he did not want to specify a location. Such a commitment might bring about a jealous response from the basin left out, thus delaying ratification interminably. "I am willing to recognize broadly the necessity for flood control on the whole river," he stated. "I am willing to yield in resolution, but not by compact, immediate construction of reservoirs above in order to facilitate the construction of reservoirs below. [B]ut if it has to come as a matter in the compact, then I must insist that the matter of reservoir construction be distributed over the entire basin, because when it becomes a matter of compact, it must go back to the legislatures of these several states for ratification."[110]

His argument was persuasive. A resolution on the dam accepted by all commissioners read as follows: "The Colorado River Commission earnestly recommends and urges the immediate construction by the government of the United States of a dam or dams on the Colorado River of sufficient size to impound at least the average annual flow of the river, to control the floods and permanently avoid the menace, such construction to be made subject to the Colorado River Compact."[111] The most important principle undergirding successful interstate water negotiations, Carpenter believed, was the idea that future development of any kind on the Colorado River could only proceed subject to the rules of a compact. This principle extended equally to power projects.

When Norviel asked commissioners for a show of good will to be expressed in support of James P. Girand's application for a license to build a power plant on the Colorado River, Carpenter said nothing. He did not have to. Hoover echoed what the Coloradan had been preaching all along: that the Federal Power Commission (FPC) should issue permits that explicitly recognized terms of the Colorado River Compact. Norviel appealed eloquently to the commissioners to make an exception in the case of Girand. Approval of the Girand project, he pointed out, would go a long way in persuading the Arizona legislature to ratify the compact. But Hoover spoke for all the commissioners when he stated that Norviel's request was out of order. The chairman suggested a letter to the FPC, urging that agency to issue all future licenses "subject to this compact."[112] It would be Carpenter's job to continue this fight with the FPC during the six-year struggle for ratification by the states.

Carpenter also insisted that the interests of other departments of the federal government must remain subservient to the compact as written, but Hoover urged caution. He worried that some language in the document might appear to emasculate the government's frequently expressed rights on navigable and unappropriated waters of the West. In fact, during the Santa Fe meetings, the most vocal defense of federal rights on the Colorado River came from solicitor Ottamar Hamele of the Reclamation Service. Hamele argued that United States ownership of Colorado River water was protected under the commerce clause of the Constitution because the Colorado had been, and still was, a navigable river.[113] Prior to the Supreme Court's decision in *Wyoming v. Colorado*, Hamele also defended the principle of interstate priority on western streams, and in the fall of 1922, after the High Court's decision had been rendered, he insisted that interstate priority was the most equitable way to divide the waters of the Colorado River. With a federally appointed board to execute appropriations to the states, the government, he believed, would preserve its control of the river and the states would benefit by protection under one system of laws.[114] In his view, Carpenter's compact went against both the *Wyoming* decision and the legislation that authorized compact negotiations. In neither of those acts, he concluded, did the federal government abandon any water rights, and the FPC and Bureau of Indian Affairs, which held supervisory roles on many western lands, could never lose constitutionally preserved water rights to the states by virtue of a ratified Colorado River Compact. What Hoover should do, Hamele stated, was to include a recommendation in his report that Congress qualify its approval of the compact with a statement that "the United States is the owner of all unappropriated water of the Colorado River system."[115]

Hoover refused. The two men were quartered close to each other in the South Lodge of the hotel and had numerous opportunities to exchange views. Hamele reported to Morris Bien, acting director of the Reclamation Service, that Hoover often dropped by to do his share of "discussing and cussing" over the CRCC's seemingly endless wrangling. But Hoover only reluctantly agreed to share the solicitor's views on federal water rights with the commission. Hamele was clearly unhappy in Santa Fe and he told Bien that he would be glad to get away. He also mentioned to Hoover that the act of July 26, 1866, which the states claimed as proof that Congress wanted western water under state control, should be repealed insofar as it extended to the Colorado River basin.[116]

Carpenter was not alone in rejecting Hamele's criticism of the compact. Director A. P. Davis was pleased that the compact divided Colorado River states into two basins, because the interests of each were so different. He was also contented by the mistaken assumption that approximately 4 million acre-feet of surplus water in the river had been reserved for future distribution by the seven states. In a letter to Commissioner Emerson, he noted that the work of the CRCC was most commendable. He was not always in agreement with Reclamation Service attorneys, but he hoped the compact would bring the federal government's theory and practice into conformity with state laws. He was confident the compact would obviate litigation, and he praised Hoover for accomplishing so much in such a short time. "It is not too much to say," Davis commented in the *Congressional Record*, "that the adoption of this compact constitutes an important step in the progress of civilization. It is a triumph of those qualities and impulses which distinguish civilized man from the savage."[117]

All agreed that nothing in the compact should "be construed as affecting the obligations of the United States of America to Indian tribes." Likewise, the compact was not intended to give Mexico any idea of the amount of water it might expect in future dealings with the United States. At Hoover's suggestion, all references to Mexico were expunged from the final minutes. He did not want to preempt the terms of any treaty the State Department might make with Mexico in the future. The free flowing comments in the record about Mexico's use of the Colorado River might easily imply approval of Mexican rights when the time came to negotiate an international agreement.

In the final hour of deliberations, Carpenter addressed the group around him with considerable passion. "We have about completed the task assigned to this commission," he said, "which is the first exemplification

Colorado River Commission at the signing of the Colorado River Compact, November 24, 1922, Palace of the Governors, Santa Fe, N. Mex.

Signed picture of Herbert Hoover, inscribed to Delph Carpenter.

of interstate diplomacy in the history of the United States on so large a scale." He credited each commissioner with contributing to the final plan, and directed his most fervent appreciation to Hoover. "Our chairman," he said, "is due the great measure of credit for making possible this successful conclusion. [A]s we are about to enter upon the concluding chapter, I am designated by the other members of the commission to express to you not only our admiration, but our love and esteem."

Hoover was grateful for these words. From experiences gained as head of the American Relief Administration that had attempted to rebuild a war-ravaged Europe, Hoover understood how difficult it was to achieve consensus among men with different passions and objectives. "The days of romance in the West are gone," he noted, "and the job of western men is one of construction. . . . [W]e have possibly made here . . . one of the most constructive steps that has been taken in the West. It will take time to prove it, but it is possible that this [compact] will stand out as one of the landmarks of western development."[118]

As their last act at Bishop's Lodge, the commissioners unanimously adopted the Colorado River Compact and agreed to a formal signing at 6:30 that evening, November 24, 1922, in Santa Fe's historic Palace of the Governors. A milestone in western water law had been reached.

On November 27, Hoover wrote a letter of thanks to Carpenter in which he mentioned the "admiration and appreciation I have for the way you have built up the whole conception of the compact from its start and for the ingenuity and flexibility of mind you have brought to bear upon it."[119] The letter was accompanied by a signed picture. In response, Carpenter was equally complimentary and expressed appreciation for Hoover's kind remarks. "Your good offices," he wrote the secretary, "made possible the conclusion of the compact and the privilege of working and being associated with you will always stand out as a bright light in the field of my memory. I shall consider it an honor to be of service to you upon any occasion."[120]

This moment was very possibly the high point of Carpenter's career.

The Struggle for Compact Ratification

"I am not so much interested in my worries as I am in expressing to you the feeling I have over the consummation of the Colorado River Compact. That compact was your conception and your creation and it was due to your tenacity and intelligence that it has succeeded. Sometime I want to be able to say this and say it emphatically to the people of the West".
— PRESIDENT HERBERT HOOVER TO CARPENTER, JUNE 29, 1929

When he left the Palace of the Governors on the evening of November 24, 1922, Carpenter was at the apogee of his professional life. He was forty-five years old, politically connected, admired for his intellectual integrity, and pleased that CRCC negotiations had ended in a compact. His skills as negotiator and compact expert were in demand in several western states. On November 27, he and New Mexican Stephen B. Davis signed the La Plata River Compact. In the next six months Carpenter began or renewed similar discussions with other states, hoping to draw up compacts on the Arkansas, North Platte, South Platte rivers and the Rio Grande. He was optimistic that the Colorado River Compact would be ratified by the seven state legislatures, and he believed Congress would authorize funding for dam construction on the Colorado River once state ratifications were official. Optimism was in the air.

While his life seemed to be going well professionally, Carpenter was exhausted by the Santa Fe meetings. The strain of negotiations became manifest in increased illnesses, more severe hand tremors, longer periods of fatigue, and speech problems. Symptoms of Parkinson's disease brought on more frequent pains in various parts of his body and worrisome constrictions in his throat. A general feeling of malaise sapped his physical energy. His sense of accomplishment was tempered by all these debilities. He longed for rest and heat treatments, but unexpected difficulties with compact ratification, problems with the Federal Power Commission (FPC), and his personal and proprietary connection to the Colorado River Compact caused him to work continuously, sometimes at a frenetic and unhealthy pace.

In the decade following the Santa Fe signing, Carpenter was the West's compact ambassador with portfolio. He traveled to many western states and to Washington, cajoling, testifying, interpreting the Colorado River Compact, and rallying support for what the seven commissioners had accomplished. His neuritis immobilized him at times when he wished to travel, but Carpenter was never far removed from the controversies that swirled around state ratification. The congressional legislation passed in 1921 that authorized the seven Colorado River basin states to proceed with compact negotiations also stipulated that no agreement would be binding until each of the seven state legislatures and Congress had expressed approval.[1] Carpenter was the author of this legislation, and he knew full well that the achievement celebrated in Santa Fe would be meaningless unless the compact received a favorable reception by lawmakers. He was unprepared for the struggle that lay ahead, but his determination to achieve ratification was so great that he threw himself into the political battles with whatever vigor he could muster.

Dot continued to be his best companion and amanuensis. She took dictation, transcribed and signed many of his letters, cared for him when he complained of flu symptoms, and occasionally accompanied him on trips. But even Dot could not eradicate Carpenter's greatest fear that Congress would simply vote to build a dam, acceding to pressure from California Congressman Phil Swing and Senator Hiram Johnson. Both men introduced legislation to authorize immediate construction of Hoover Dam prior to ratification of the Colorado River Compact.[2] They assumed Arizona would fail to ratify the compact before serious flooding erupted again on the lower river. If Swing and Johnson were successful, everything Carpenter had fought for in Santa Fe would be nullified. In one sense, therefore, the ratification struggle was his biggest battle, one he had to fight in a weakened condition.

Under the leadership of George Maxwell and Democratic Governor George W. P. Hunt, the Arizona legislature defeated ratification by one vote in 1923. The powerful mining, agricultural, and power interests had considerable influence on the Arizona legislature, insisting the compact left Arizona with too much uncertainty. In the opinion of writer Dean Mann, elected officials of the ten-year-old state "did not wish to take precipitate action they might later regret. They did not believe the river could be developed without the consent of Arizona and [concluded] that Arizona's only bargaining power lay in refusing to ratify the compact."[3]

Additional reasons existed for Arizona's negative votes on ratification. State representatives felt isolated and vulnerable to California's whims. The inability of California, Arizona, and Nevada to agree to a three-state compact dividing up the lower basin's allotment of water indicated the depth of interstate discord. Southern California wanted water and power for its growing communities, while rumors circulated that some Californians wanted the water to colonize Mexican lands with Asians. Already suspicious of California's tendency to play the role of bully, Arizonans were easily convinced that Swing and Johnson were seeking legislation for dam construction without any limitations on California's future use of the lower basin's 8.5 million acre-feet authorized in the Colorado River Compact. Nevada was of less concern to Arizona, because that state's primary interest was in revenue from the future sale of hydroelectric power generated at Hoover Dam. But the lack of unity among the three states resulted in failure of lower basin deputies to agree on terms of a three-state compact, and this circumstance left Arizona feeling unprotected.

The situation in Arizona exacerbated ratification difficulties in the other states and handicapped progress of the Swing-Johnson bill in a Congress that refused to do anything until all the Colorado River basin states officially agreed on what they wanted. Any possible accord was further undermined by Los Angeles' surprise plan to build the Colorado River Aqueduct to the metropolitan area.[4] Such a project threatened Arizona's inchoate design for a Highline Canal and added to concerns that the Gila River, which Arizonans viewed as their own, was coveted by California proponents of Imperial Valley development. Denied the right to tax power that would be generated at Hoover Dam, and concerned about a future treaty with Mexico that might award additional water across the border, Arizonans felt fully justified in opposing the Colorado River Compact until they could assure themselves adequate protection from California.

By March 1923, the other river basin states had ratified the Colorado River Compact, but Congress refused to enact construction legislation so long as Arizona remained uncommitted. Various forms of persuasion were attempted by a host of individuals, but Arizona resisted them all. In 1924, Carpenter suggested a way out of the dilemma. If the ratifying states would amend their ratifications to approve a six-state compact that allowed Arizona to join at a suitable time, Congress would be encouraged to pass the appropriate legislation funding dam construction.

Over the next four years, Swing and Johnson submitted various bills in Congress, some of them incorporating this six-state plan, but as time passed unexpected complications arose from several corners. After accepting the six-state plan, Utah repealed its ratification. A new legislative majority viewed approval of the Colorado River Compact as an abandonment of Utah's sovereignty, especially its ownership rights to the bed of the Colorado River for possible oil exploration in the future. In California, a division developed between those who favored cooperation with Arizona and those determined to support a Swing-Johnson bill regardless of the Santa Fe agreement. In Colorado, L. Ward Bannister, attorney for the Denver Chamber of Commerce, launched a campaign to pressure Arizona to sign the compact through litigation. Meanwhile, Nevadans objected to the six-state plan because the issue of hydroelectric power revenue distribution remained unsettled. Even in the upper basin, unity was threatened. New Mexico and Wyoming favored the six-state plan in contrast to groups in Colorado and Utah that continued to hold out for seven-state ratification.

These were the ever-changing and multifarious concerns Carpenter dealt with as the compact's principal proponent. As the ratification struggle wore on, tired him out, and made him bitter, he felt justified in changing his mind about what would be best for the West. Holding out for seven-state ratification seemed to be the only way to protect fully Colorado's future development. Bannister accused him of being a "bitter-ender,"[5] and it appears the criticism was somewhat justified. But between 1922 and 1928, when the Boulder Canyon Project Act (Hoover Dam legislation) was finally passed, Carpenter spent so much time reiterating his theories on states'

rights and local control of water that he came to view a seven-state compact as his raison d'être. The more he battled his health during these years,
and the more he engaged in extensive correspondence and discussions
on the compact, the more he personalized the accomplishments achieved
in Santa Fe. Although his activities between 1922 and 1928 did little to
shape the Hoover Dam legislation, they contributed in a significant way to
a wide-spread agreement that Carpenter was, indeed, the "Father of the
Colorado River Compact."[6]

The most consistent praise for Carpenter came from those who concurred with him on states' rights. In Santa Fe he had warned the Colorado
River Compact Commission (CRCC), and anyone else who would listen,
that the Department of Interior was determined to exercise ownership of
all unclaimed waters in the West unless the states reclaimed their sovereignty. Interior's intentions, as seen through the actions of its attorneys,
represented an "insidious and well organized assault on the [states'] right
to the waters in their own rivers."[7] The national government, he believed,
had every right to oversee navigation and international obligations. But
"inherent sovereignty [was] in the states and the states own[ed] the water
of their streams (as they do the game of their fields) in virtue of their inherent sovereignty."[8] The United States, Carpenter argued, based its erroneous and "shocking doctrine" on the "lame" theory of private property
law, which ignored not only the fundamental law of state sovereignty but
also "the fact that every claim [of a] right to [the] use of water by the abut-
ting or other land owners derives its authority from, vests under and is
ever subject to the law of the state in which the diversion is made."[9] It would
be easy for the seven states to abandon their sovereign responsibility of
managing the river to the federal government, but in the long run, Carpenter maintained, the states would regret giving up this power to the
ever-changing whims of a national bureaucracy. An interstate compact, by
contrast, guaranteed "permanent allocations" of water that would allow
for present and future appropriations without fear of servitudes to a federal entity claiming authority and priority.[10] It was the expectation of permanence, as well as a reduction in litigation, that drove Carpenter to fight
so hard for seven-state ratification of the compact.

But Carpenter also cautioned against haste and pressure tactics during
ratification. He had compassion for Arizona's fear of a more powerful and
developed California. That situation, he believed, was not unlike the rela-

tionship between upper basin and lower basin states, in which demands for protection by the former sprang from the reality of California's economic and demographic head start. Coercion of Arizona, he believed, would only breed bitterness and would undermine the interstate comity so essential to an enduring compact. Referring frequently to the psychology of compact negotiation, Carpenter advocated giving Arizona time to heal. "Her greatest need," he told Secretary of the Interior Ray Lyman Wilbur, "is time and opportunity for reflection free from annoying suggestion." Arizona should be left to her own devices. If the human situation changed materially, he concluded, ratification of the compact would occur for the right reasons at the right time.[11]

Determined to leave a legacy on the Colorado River in which both water rights and power development were subject to the compact, Carpenter became especially sensitive when he felt the commissioners' accomplishments were under attack. It was hard for him to accept the criticism, particularly from those who appeared to have a political agenda. Compacts were his signature achievement, and when he defended the Colorado River Compact as "the permanent law of the river" even before it became law,[12] he was indicating both his opinion regarding the compact's eventual legal standing and a personal passion of his own for some kind of public recognition. Resentment toward him came from adversaries who disregarded or misunderstood the legal, political, and geographical framework on which he believed any international or interstate treaty should be based. Between 1922 and 1928, therefore, he tried to be the teacher, and as teachers frequently discover, some of his students were slow learners.

The burden of Carpenter's illness, and the restrictions it caused in travel, contributed to a mild form of paranoia that surfaced from time to time in correspondence. He imagined the government conspiring to undermine interstate compacts all over the West. He feared that California was destined to have its way in Congress or that Arizona would be allowed to ratify the compact with unthinkable reservations. At the same time, he believed a certain amount of luck was responsible for the commissioners' success at Santa Fe. The seven states had taken advantage of a moment in history that would never again appear. The Colorado River Compact, he insisted, should not be reopened, amended, or revised in any way. It should stand as written. It was a simple document. It assured equity to the states involved and it adhered closely to the natural conditions in the basin.

Responding to questions about what the compact's articles actually meant required Carpenter to articulate repeatedly the premises upon which compact theory depended. In discussing its meaning and intent, he was at his best, and what he wrote constitutes some of his most enduring contributions to western water law. The misunderstandings in Colorado, for example, caused Carpenter to consult Secretary Hoover for corroboration of his own opinions. Coincidentally, while Carpenter was facing a "heavy battery fire of opposition" from Colorado's West Slope,[13] he was fine-tuning his own thinking in correspondence with Hoover. This juxtaposition of events brought out Carpenter's first extensive analysis of the meaning and intent of the Colorado River Compact.

What Carpenter needed to know, he telegraphed Hoover, was how the secretary interpreted Article VIII.[14] Critics in Durango, Colorado, worried that this article gave the lower basin an unlimited right to expand on the amount of water they could take from the river. If this interpretation was accurate, the lower basin's thirst would bankrupt the West Slope. But Carpenter was of the opinion that the lower basin was clearly limited by the compact. In Article III (b), he told Hoover, the commissioners intended "that the lower basin may increase its annual beneficial consumptive use of water one million acre-feet and no more .... Article VIII is not intended to authorize, constitute or result in any apportionment of water to the lower basin beyond that made in paragraphs (a) and (b) of Article III."[15]

Hoover concurred and stated that he would "so advise Congress in his report. Nothing in the compact, Hoover stated, prevents either basin from using more water than the amount apportioned in Article III, "but such use would be subject to the further apportionment provided in paragraph (f)[16] of Article III and would vest no rights under the present compact."[17]

So far the two men were in agreement. Compact opponents from the West Slope accepted the Hoover-Carpenter interpretation and dropped their opposition to ratification. Even California's deputy attorney general, R. T. McKissick, whose opinion Carpenter had sought, concurred.[18] But Hoover's answers to other questions were more problematic for Carpenter.

The federal act authorizing the Colorado River Compact Commission required Hoover to make a report to Congress. Senator Hayden, a supporter of ratification, sensed a level of ignorance in Washington regarding specific aspects of the compact, so early in January 1923, he addressed twenty-six questions to Hoover, A. P. Davis, Ottamar Hamele, solicitor of the Bureau of Reclamation, and Philip S. Smith, acting director of the United States Geological Survey. Hoover responded on January 27.[19]

Question 10 asked for clarification of the "undivided surplus of the annual flow of the Colorado River." Hayden wanted to know if Mexico would be able to use the surplus water for forty years (1923 to 1963) and if that nation would then be able to make a claim to the surplus by virtue of prior beneficial use?[20] Hoover responded that there were approximately 5 million acre-feet of surplus water in the river. If each basin reached the limit of its allotment before 1963 "and there should still be water unapportioned, in my opinion such water could be taken and used in either basin under the ordinary rules governing appropriations, *and such appropriations would doubtless receive formal recognition by the commission at the end of the 40-year period* (author's emphasis)."[21] The compact, he stated, made no mention of any Mexican rights and Mexico could only establish rights by treaty with the United States.

"Your answer to question ten," Carpenter bluntly pointed out, "is wrong." If the lower basin could use surplus water and expect to receive formal appropriative rights at the end of forty years for what they use, Article III (f) of the compact is "misleading and ineffective." Under the "spirit of the compact," Carpenter insisted, one basin can not appropriate unapportioned waters. "If the interpretation suggested by you is correct," he admonished, "reservation of rights for [the] upper basin in accordance with [the] spirit of the compact would need to be imposed upon any reservoir construction allowed."[22] In other words, water in the reservoir created by Hoover Dam would have to belong in part to the upper basin.

Carpenter believed Hoover had made at least three additional errors in his response to Hayden's twenty-six questions. Although Hoover's secretary, Clarence Stetson, initially tried to suggest that Carpenter had misunderstood Hoover's answers, it is clear from the secretary of commerce's report to Congress that Carpenter's interpretation of Article III was eventually adopted by the secretary.[23]

Carpenter learned from the experience with Hoover and clarified his own thinking on the compact in the process. In his "Supplemental Report" to the Colorado Assembly, he developed collateral interpretations for the Colorado River Compact that were incorporated by him and by other commissioners as models in preparation of other compacts on interstate streams. He argued that individual articles should not be taken out of context. "The

intent of the compact," he noted, "is to be ascertained from a consideration of the entire instrument," each clause being studied in connection with
the other clauses.[24] As with the Colorado River basin itself, every piece of
the compact was connected, just as the tributaries, main stem, and future
works of the Colorado River were connected. Because permanence was an
objective of compact negotiations, the extra 1 million acre-feet permitted
to the lower basin "was recognized in order that any further apportionment
of surplus waters might be altogether avoided or at least delayed to a very
remote period."[25] Carpenter believed the Colorado River contained approximately 4 million acre-feet of surplus water, over and above the 16 million
acre-feet assigned to upper and lower basins by the compact. He did not
view the extra 1 million acre-feet allocated to the lower basin as a "final
apportionment," believing instead that parties for both basins should have
an equal chance to make their case for additional water after the passage
of forty years. When taken as a whole, Carpenter concluded, the compact
perpetually set apart for Colorado "a preferred right to utilize the waters
of the river to the extent of [the state's] present and future necessities." It
also protected Colorado's development from adverse claims resulting from
a reservoir on the lower river. It eliminated any chance of an embargo being
placed on future development, and it left the state free to develop its territory "in the manner and at the times our necessities may require."[26]

The "Supplemental Report" was prepared by Carpenter to reassure
Colorado legislators who were about to vote on ratification. His written
comments responded to concerns most frequently raised by compact critics, especially those of the Colorado attorney general, Russell Fleming.[27]
Fleming opposed ratification because Colorado was being asked to abandon its sovereign control over waters produced within state boundaries.
Additionally, Fleming saw no protection in the compact against priority
rights established by the Imperial Valley's potential to use the entire flow
of the Colorado River during droughts or warmer periods of the year.
Lower basin power development was also problematic for Fleming, because
demands for water to drive the turbines year around could require the upper
basin to deliver water, thus hindering upstream economic development.

Carpenter addressed these concerns directly. He pointed out that any
claims the Imperial Valley might have against upper basin states would be
"cut off" when reservoir storage was provided behind the dam on the
Colorado River. A reading of Article III and Article VIII made this very

clear. Similarly, a proper understanding of lower basin power rights could be determined by reading Article III (e) and IV (b) together. "[T]he compact means," Carpenter wrote, "that power claims by the Lower Basin cannot compel the Upper Basin to turn down any water which cannot reasonably be applied to domestic and agricultural uses in the Lower Basin. . . . All power uses in both Basins are made 'subservient to the use and consumption of such water for agricultural and domestic purposes and shall not interfere with or prevent use for such dominant purposes.' "[28] Furthermore, he assured the legislature, Colorado's constitution and laws would continue to control appropriation and distribution of water within the state after compact ratification. "The compact does not attempt to invade such matters of local concern . . . . When approved, the compact will be the law of the river as between the states. It deals wholly with interstate relations. . . . No law of any state can have extra-territorial effect or interfere with the operation of the compact as between states."[29] In his conclusion, Carpenter reasoned, the Colorado River had more water than had been apportioned in the compact, and this single fact meant that "the States of the Upper Basin may safely guarantee 75 million acre-feet aggregate delivery at Lee Ferry during each ten-year period."[30] Seventy-five years later it became clear that the Colorado River's annual flow approximates 13 million acre-feet, but in 1923 it was generally believed that the volume was closer to 20 million acre-feet.

Some Colorado legislators wanted a preamble to interpret the compact and put it in some kind of broader context, but the "Supplemental Report" and Hoover's corroboration of Carpenter's views made an interpretive preamble unnecessary. As a result, unanimous legislative approval came from the Colorado legislature in March 1923. Newly elected Governor William E. Sweet signed the bill ratifying the Colorado River Compact on April 2, 1923. Carpenter passed on the good news to Hoover by telegram, and the secretary responded in kind. "This is real congratulation on a fine battle effectually won under your leadership," Hoover replied.[31] Sweet agreed with Hoover. Carpenter's patience and attention to detail had disarmed the opposition. From this point on, Sweet told Carpenter, water matters could be handled by the interstate streams commissioner without the need to seek signatures from the governor's office.[32]

Accolades also came from California Commissioner W. F. McClure, who addressed Carpenter: "I am now quite convinced that any attempt to

hasten matters beyond the rate of speed at which we proceeded would
have been dangerous and perhaps disastrous. My compliments to you for
your unfailing courtesy and my expression of appreciation for the ability
with which you met the issues."[33]

Carpenter was pleased, but he still worried about conditions in Arizona.
He and Commissioner Norviel had become good friends, and though
Arizona's opposition to the compact was deepening, Carpenter believed
that a strong minority led by Senator Hayden would eventually prevail.
The state as a whole needed time, but Norviel had been told his office
would be merged into another department. He expected to be "scraped
off, like a man going through under a low bridge on the top of a freight
car."[34] However, vocal support from the much-respected Hayden and
Dwight Heard, owner of the powerful *Arizona Republican*, indicated that
the Maxwell-Hunt opposition might be meeting its match.

For a brief period after the Santa Fe conference, therefore, Carpenter
was pleased with the flow of events and optimistic that ratification by all
seven states was about to happen. When University of Colorado officials
decided to honor him with a distinguished service medal, he felt great satisfaction. It was especially meaningful to be recognized by University of
Colorado President George Norlin, who singled out the originality demonstrated by Carpenter's application of the treaty powers of the states to the
solution of interstate river problems. Dot relayed the good news to her
husband in the San Luis Valley, where he had begun work on a Rio Grande
compact. He was deeply touched. "Words utterly fail to express my surprise
and deep appreciation," he replied to Norlin. "Your letter comes like a
bright light to illuminate the lonely clouds of long years of solitary effort
among the unsympathetic crowd. . . . It will afford me great pleasure to be
present on June the eleventh [1923]." Dean John Fleming of the Law
School made the special presentation. Feeling the effects of another bout
of neuritis, Carpenter asked daughter Michaela to accompany him to the
ceremony. It was a powerful experience for the entire family, prompting
Michaela to ask for a copy of Fleming's address. After hearing it again, her
father responded warmly in a letter to Dean Fleming: "The letter and the
medal will always be my dearest treasures."[35] Four years later, the University
of Colorado bestowed on him the degree of Doctor of Laws.

Carpenter's feelings of loneliness and sacrifice as an attorney special-
izing in water, emotions he had previously expressed to Hoover, were exac-

erbated by a barrage of criticism he began to receive from Denver attorney L. Ward Bannister. Although the two men learned to respect one another at the conclusion of many years of compact ratification, they contended for the governor's ear in a struggle to determine who would direct Colorado water policies and under what conditions the upper basin states would support legislation to build Hoover Dam. Bannister was angry with Carpenter for his apparent unwillingness to cooperate with Swing and Johnson. Believing Carpenter was too ill to continue as interstate water commissioner, Bannister decided to speak for Colorado in sometimes delicate conferences and discussions with officials of other states. Outspoken and rarely deferential to the state's appointed leaders, Bannister engaged in these unrestrained actions in Washington and throughout the West at a time when Carpenter had become increasingly preoccupied with his illness. The Denver attorney's actions engendered in Carpenter a stubbornness that resulted in his threatening to fight for seven-state ratification of the compact at any cost.

Bannister was a decent person and a respected attorney, but he tended to think a bit too much of himself. Carpenter viewed him as an impractical academic. He had matriculated with Hoover at Stanford and received a law degree from Harvard. Compared to Carpenter's pioneer rural upbringing and hands-on water experience, Bannister's background was urban and privileged. He was a bookish intellectual who liked to boast of his association with the writer Hamlin Garland.[36]

Carpenter was proud of his own credentials. He interpreted Bannister's unwelcome interference as an attempt to assert superiority over a farm boy who had worked his way through the University of Denver. Bannister belonged to the Denver Country Club, was on the board of the Denver Art Museum, and traveled internationally. He hobnobbed with the Denver elite and aggressively represented the City of Denver during compact and ratification debates. He believed California was about to establish itself with a prior claim to waters of the Colorado River, thus depriving Denver of any chance at transmountain diversion from the Colorado River. Carpenter, the self-made man, resented Bannister's interference, which he encountered at every turn. His tendency to personalize the compact, and his self-image as a pioneer in the field of water law, accentuated conflict between the two men. The resulting unpleasantness was unfortunate, but the heated exchanges that characterized their relationship in the

1920s served to further define a number of major issues related to compact ratification.

Bannister was no fool. He was well read in the principles of western water law, and much of what he believed was consistent with Carpenter's own views. He defended state's rights, equitable apportionment, and the compact method of interstate water allocation. Though he often acted unofficially, Bannister justified his actions because he believed that the best interests of Denver were no longer protected by the Colorado commissioner.

The two men began their careers as water attorneys about the same time, but their paths did not cross in any significant way until 1922. At that time the Colorado Bar Association asked Governor Oliver Shoup to appoint a committee to assist the Colorado River Compact Commission "in effecting an equitable and fair distribution of waters having origin in Colorado and flowing into neighboring states."[37] Bannister was chosen to head the ten-man committee. In this capacity he went to Santa Fe as an observer of compact discussions. Although Bannister subsequently reported to Shoup that Carpenter was the "best informed" of all the commissioners,[38] Carpenter felt that his authority and responsibility were being undermined by Bannister's presence. As soon as the compact was signed, therefore, he warned Shoup that Bannister might be giving public interviews which he regarded as "very dangerous to [the] interests of [the] upper states unless properly guarded and expressed."[39]

The two men collaborated on a speech to the State Historical and Natural History Society of Colorado a week before Christmas of 1922. Carpenter described the background of the compact and how it was a product of lessons learned on the Rio Grande and North Platte, Arkansas, and Laramie rivers. He noted how development in Denver and the East Slope of Colorado would be limited without the right to construct tunnels for transport of water from the Colorado River to the Front Range. He encouraged ratification of the compact at every opportunity. Bannister spoke about the meaning and intent of the compact.[40] Both men, while admitting to fatigue, seemed to agree on the importance of what had been accomplished in Santa Fe one month earlier. But Bannister's approach to ratification was inclined to be more aggressive than Carpenter's. He was less patient, and his independent actions were sometimes seen by Carpenter as a blatant attempt to usurp duly constituted authority.

Potential for conflict between the two men was realized early in 1923 when Arnold Kruckman, secretary of the California based League of the Southwest, telegraphed Colorado's newly elected Governor Sweet, urging attendance at a meeting of the League of the Southwest in Santa Barbara for the purpose of "formulating another Colorado River Compact."[41] Sweet replied that he would not attend the League meeting and would not send a Colorado delegation. He told Kruckman that the meeting was "unwise and untimely," especially in view of the fact that six of the seven Colorado River basin states had already ratified the compact. Arizona, he said, was entitled time for deliberation and Colorado would not participate in any discussions that might appear coercive.[42]

But Bannister wanted to attend. He feared that, without representation from the upper basin states, conference attendees might rally in support of Arizona's opposition to the compact. Carpenter emphasized that Bannister should make an appearance to counteract talk of organizing a new compact commission whose alleged objective was to attain federal control of the Colorado River based on the federal right to regulate navigable streams and to protect citizens from floods.[43] Bannister went to Santa Barbara as a private citizen, but he spoke as a representative of the upper basin. He assured Sweet that his address had been primarily for Arizona's consumption, that the anticompact sentiment in California was defunct, that no resolutions were passed against the Colorado River Compact, and that for all intents and purposes, the League of the Southwest was little more than a forum for discussion.[44]

Carpenter was still suspicious. He brooded over how Arizona would react when that state's officials learned about the Santa Barbara meeting. Bannister "has always injected himself into the Colorado River matters without invitation," he wrote Commissioner Norviel. He had no authority to speak for Colorado either officially or unofficially, and "I fear," Carpenter apologized, "that he may have been indiscreet in his remarks and may have damaged the good work done by yourself and others by putting Colorado in a false position with respect to her attitude toward Arizona." Carpenter had urged Bannister not to speak in Santa Barbara, even if he did attend, "but of course," Carpenter added, "Bannister is one of those academic gentlemen who is not prone to take advice."[45] He was impulsive, and he was jeopardizing the unity among upper basin states.

Carpenter wanted Arizona to debate the merits of the compact without outside interference and with ample time for intrastate deliberation. He was convinced that if any individual, state, or group of states applied pressure on Arizona to ratify, the chasm between opponents and supporters of the compact would widen. In Carpenter's thinking, Bannister represented the worst possible threat to seven-state ratification. He was interfering with Arizona's sovereign right to make up its own mind about the compact, and he was sowing discord among other states of the Colorado River basin that were growing impatient with the slow speed of ratification. For these reasons, Carpenter wanted Norviel and Senator Hayden to understand that he, Carpenter, was still in charge as commissioner for Colorado, that Bannister was not "the leading factor in the drafting and conclusion of the compact." He was not Carpenter's legal advisor, and he was not Governor Sweet's unofficial representative in the arena of interstate water policy.[46]

Governor Sweet was in Carpenter's corner. He chastised Bannister for proceeding along a "radically different line from that which is characteristic of Mr. Carpenter." And when Bannister revealed a plan to bring Arizona to its knees, Sweet made clear the importance of first seeking Carpenter's opinion.[47] But Bannister marched to his own drummer, and he was immune to Carpenter's view of him as a "meddler" and "rank outsider" with no apparent sensitivity to local state affairs. He was constantly "butting in" where he was not wanted.[48] When Arizona appeared unable to make progress toward ratification, Bannister supported the suggestion of a lawsuit against Arizona under a plan conceived by Fred S. Caldwell, Colorado's assistant attorney general.

Carpenter was appalled and immediately vented his anger to Hoover. "Caldwell," he said, is "much of the crusader type . . . who is never satisfied unless he is contesting or quarreling with someone and who has made a failure of everything he ever undertook."[49] Caldwell's scheme was to institute a suit in the U.S. Supreme Court in which the six ratifying states would be plaintiffs against Arizona. The Court would be asked to determine whether the compact was equitable to Arizona "and[,] if not[,] to determine what would be Arizona's equitable part of the waters of the stream."[50] The principal object of the compact, however, was to avoid litigation. Arizona had not acted either for or against the agreement and needed time to determine its attitude. A lawsuit, Carpenter complained to Hoover, "would destroy the whole compact plan. . . . [I]t was unwarranted, untimely and even if brought, the proceedings would be so prolonged that no favorable results could be expected."[51]

But Caldwell persuaded Sweet the suit had merit, and Sweet referred him to Bannister because he thought Carpenter was out of town. Eventually, the governor asked Carpenter to determine the legal feasibility of suing Arizona, but he wanted the "comity between the six states that had ratified [the compact] *preserved at all costs* and . . . nothing . . . said or done which [would] provoke a feeling of hostility or resentment in Arizona."[52] Carpenter disagreed with Sweet's decision to explore the possibility of litigation, but he complied. He told Caldwell to prepare a legal brief and bill of complaint and assigned to Bannister the task of determining attitudes in the other ratifying states. Both men were instructed to use delicacy, to avoid publicity, and not to represent themselves in any official capacity for the State of Colorado.[53]

Because Caldwell believed that Colorado's "only recourse" was a lawsuit, he performed his duties quickly and collected the retainer Bannister had arranged for him. Carpenter suspected he did little research to earn his fee. Bannister, on the other hand, made extensive inquiries of the other states' governors and attorneys general. In a report to Carpenter, he endorsed the theory of "equitable division" as a basis for the suit, arguing that the Supreme Court's ruling in *Kansas v. Colorado* had established this interstate principle. It followed, Bannister reasoned, that the High Court should be able to enforce parts of the Colorado River Compact by judicial decree. Furthermore, with the High Court engaged in hearing the suit, the Federal Power Commission would have to suspend the granting of licenses to power companies, and Congress would be obligated to table discussion of the Swing-Johnson bill until the High Court handed down a ruling. Bannister concluded that Caldwell's bill of complaint and brief of support were sound and that the suit was worth pursuing "if Arizona, after having been given every encouragement, failed to ratify the compact."[54]

The suit died aborning. Clarence J. Morley replaced Sweet as governor in 1925 and chose a new attorney general. Both officials opposed the litigation, preferring to explore Carpenter's latest suggestion of a six-state compact. If approved by Congress, a six-state compact would lead to legislation authorizing works on the Colorado River. Bannister had "stirred up the animals in Arizona"[55] during his visits to other states, and ratification

was most certainly delayed by his actions. But the idea of a six-state compact had merit. It was a novel approach to the existing stalemate, and it
seemed to offer a way around Arizona's opposition. If Congress accepted
the six-state plan and passed the appropriate construction legislation,
California would have its dam, reservoir, flood control, and water supply
regardless of Arizona's stand on ratification. Arizona was still free to approve
the compact at a future date, and the upper basin states would have the
protection of a compact in place prior to federally funded construction on
the river.

In preparing the six-state plan just before Christmas, 1924, Carpenter
was assisted by New Mexico's Stephen B. Davis, as well as Wyoming's S. G.
Hopkins and Frank Emerson. These men, representing three of the four
upper basin states, developed the framework of the idea in Washington
with Hoover's blessing. Recent elections convinced Carpenter that Arizona
would continue opposition to the compact for at least an additional two
years. He still preferred a seven-state compact, but as an acceptable alternative for the time being, he wrote California's deputy attorney general
R. T. McKissick, "If . . . the compact were agreed to as binding upon the
United States and the six states which have already ratified, it would in
large measure serve the desired purposes, particularly in view of the fact
that the entire canon [sic] in Arizona is one great Federal Power Reserve
and the river forms the boundary between Arizona, California and
Nevada."[56] Attached to the letter was a draft copy of a suggested amendment to the legislation that each of the six states had already passed to ratify the compact.

McKissick was ill and unable to respond to Carpenter's letter, but California Governor Friend Richardson and Commissioner McClure stated
their approval of the six-state plan. Resistance came from the Imperial Valley, where concern was expressed about the impact of drought and the
inadequacy of the Colorado River Compact as a tool to force the upper
states to deliver water past Lee's Ferry. Some California officials favored a
suit against the upper basin states, and others opposed the six-state plan
entirely in retaliation for a perception that Colorado had been the principal obstructionist against the Swing-Johnson bill. Carpenter was not
eager to interfere in southern California politics, but he urged Governor
Richardson to obtain prompt action in that part of the state in hopes of
securing general approval of the six-state plan.[57]

Officials from New Mexico, Utah, and Wyoming found a variety of ways to endorse Carpenter's plan. Only Nevada's Governor Scrugham failed to give initial approval to the six-state compact. He preferred a conference with Governor Hunt to discuss a two-state agreement on the disposition of hydroelectric power, hoping that such a discussion would inspire Hunt to support seven-state ratification. When Carpenter met with him, Scrugham asked for a memorandum of advice that would guide his meeting with Hunt. Carpenter provided the advice, but he also urged Scrugham to stipulate to Hunt unqualified approval of the Colorado River Compact as a prerequisite to consideration of a two-state power agreement. Scrugham was pleased with Carpenter's memorandum, but after meeting with Hunt, he realized that winning over Arizona to the compact would take more time than he thought. Confidentially, he told Carpenter, he would put over the six-state program with the Nevada legislature before it recessed.[58]

All six states had now expressed interest of some degree in proceeding with Carpenter's six-state plan. Hoover agreed it was the only way to move forward. "This [approach] does no harm to Arizona," he telegraphed Carpenter, "and gives California and Nevada the ability to enjoy the benefits of government undertaking the necessary construction works."[59] For the next ten months, Carpenter was a whirlwind of activity in spite of his debilitated physical condition. He communicated constantly with governors, river commissioners, and congressional delegations of the upper basin, hoping to preserve their unity against California's pressure for immediate construction of a Colorado River dam. He met with A. P. Davis on several occasions in California, seeking his advice on a possible Rio Grande compact, the peculiarities of California politics, and on the altered state of affairs at the United States Reclamation Service.

Interior Secretary Hubert Work had removed A. P. Davis as director of the Reclamation Service in 1923. Since passage of the Reclamation Act in 1902, all of Reclamation's directors had been engineers, but Work wanted leadership that placed more emphasis on the economic and social needs of existing reclamation projects. He appointed David W. Davis, a politician and businessman, to head the Reclamation Service and then announced formation of a committee to study the problems of federal reclamation. Elwood Mead was the "guiding light" of what came to be known as the Fact Finders' Commission. He inspired most of the formal report that Congress passed into law in December 1924. By then, David Davis had resigned. He was replaced by Mead, already sixty-six years old, who remained director of what came to be known as the Bureau of Reclamation until his death by stroke in 1936.[60]

Although Mead had cut his teeth on irrigation in Colorado and Wyoming, Carpenter was uncomfortable with him as director of the Bureau. Mead wanted to reform reclamation. He believed that projects should pay their own way, and that settlers selected for reclamation communities should be screened for financial solvency. He did not want farmers to become wards of the state. True to ideals of the 1920s, Mead wanted Bureau policies to be more scientific so as to benefit the average settler. He believed in the family farm as the foundation of society, and he promoted greater cooperation between the federal government and the states. At the same time, he recognized that social and economic conditions had changed in the arid areas served by the Bureau. Settlers were no longer willing to undergo the hardships of pioneer life. Although Congress had passed legislation, extending the length of time settlers had to pay for irrigation projects, the problems of making a living as a farmer on a reclamation project had increased as a result of higher taxes, higher interest rates on borrowed money, and higher costs for irrigation water. A long-range plan for reclamation was overdue. Because state laws on water differed in the fifteen states served by the Bureau, and because the U.S. Department of Justice was faced with thirty-one pending lawsuits from these states, the Bureau desired a comprehensive plan that would clarify the role of the federal government "in the interest of comity" between the states and the United States.[61]

What most irritated Carpenter was Mead's advocacy of federal commissions to control interstate rivers. In 1911, when Carpenter was a state senator, he had criticized Mead for wanting "Boards of Control" on interstate streams. Such agencies, Carpenter believed, would expand the role of the federal government and would encourage water users to litigate.[62] In 1926, when the Justice Department was trying to respond to various lawsuits to determine federal rights on western rivers, Carpenter remained convinced that the ultimate objective of the federal government was ownership of all surplus waters in western streams. Mead steadfastly maintained his respect for the theory that western states controlled their own water, and he pointed to his authorship of the water rights provision in the Wyoming constitution as an example of his views on decentralization and local control of water supplies. Nevertheless, he was unable to state unequivocally that each state owned all the water within its boundaries, because such a policy would favor the states of origin and would complicate ownership of water rights on interstate streams.[63]

Even though Carpenter had much in common with the Bureau of Reclamation's director, Mead personified the government's long-standing interest in the nationalization of water rights.[64] Because that interest was so frequently articulated by Morris Bien, the Bureau's chief legal officer, Mead and the Bureau came to represent everything Carpenter disliked about the federal government. What made Mead appear even more heinous was his criticism of the compact process, his advocacy of the Swing-Johnson bill, his promotion of power development on the Colorado River, and his California connection at the University of California, Berkeley.[65]

Mead's leadership of the Bureau, however, did not deter Carpenter from continuing to advocate the compact process on western rivers. Despite considerable pain and fatigue, he traveled to Nebraska to begin discussions of a North Platte River treaty. When time permitted, he worked on new articles defining an Arkansas River compact, about which he was much less sanguine. In California he conferred with Southern California Edison officials in Los Angeles over the potential for power production at the future Hoover Dam, after which he met with officials of the Coachella Valley in El Centro, where the United States Senate committee on irrigation and reclamation was seeking information on the proposed All-American Canal. On his way back to Colorado, Carpenter toured Roosevelt Dam on the Salt River in Arizona and visited the Grand Canyon. He inspected the Black Canyon dam site, took a boat trip with Governor Hunt on the Colorado River, and visited Lee's Ferry. He encouraged Hunt to work on an agreement with California as soon as possible and was pleased that Hunt seemed receptive to his advice. Before leaving Arizona, he spoke with Dwight Heard, who had barely lost to Hunt in the 1924 gubernatorial election. It was an uncomfortable meeting, and it reflected the extent to which ratification issues had increased interstate tensions. Heard, for some unexplained reason, demanded the upper states guarantee 200,000 acre-feet of additional water at Lee's Ferry. Following what Carpenter referred to in his diary as additional insults, the Colorado commissioner told Heard to "go to Hell" and refused an invitation to dine.[66]

In December 1925, Carpenter returned to Washington to testify before the Senate committee on irrigation and reclamation. He was tired, tense from traveling, and generally worn down by the exertion of parrying the adversarial views of many different factions. But testimony before this committee was a command performance. Congress needed upper basin commentary on a new version of the Swing-Johnson bill, and Carpenter did not want Bannister representing these four states. Additionally, he was eager to review the background of the Colorado River Compact and to explain once again why the upper basin was so committed to compact ratification prior to construction of a Colorado River dam. The La Plata River Compact had been signed into law by President Calvin Coolidge in January 1925. State ratification of the South Platte River Compact was completed in February and signed into law by Coolidge in March 1926. Carpenter's confidence in the efficacy of compacts was at an all-time high.[67] Because California was continuing to urge passage of the Swing-Johnson bill before compact ratification, it was a good time for him to make the strongest case possible for protecting the water rights of Colorado, Utah, New Mexico, and Wyoming.

Carpenter testified for three days. He brought with him a copy of a resolution signed at Denver by the four governors of the upper basin states on August 29, 1925. Article IV stated, "We can not and will not cooperate with the lower basin States until protection is afforded our States by compact between the States interested. . . . [C]onsiderations of self-preservation compel us to oppose the construction of any works for flood control, power development, or any other uses, and we call upon the Senators and Representatives in Congress of the States of Colorado, Nevada, New Mexico, Utah and Wyoming, and the other public officials of said States, to use every legitimate means to protect the rights of our States as set forth herein."[68]

Following an explanation of Colorado River hydrology, Colorado River Compact history, and the principle of equitable apportionment to which the upper basin was willing to adhere, Carpenter painted a picture of potential strife and litigation in the Colorado River basin resulting from probable machinations of the federal government. "[T]he idea of conflict between State and Federal jurisdiction is not chimerical," he stated. "It is an actual, tangible, present existing institution, backed by all the power of the Federal Government and carelessly ignored by the people of the States even involved, who, perhaps, can not conceive that a Federal Government would go to such extremes in attempting to encroach upon State prerogatives." He cited once again the government's embargoes on the North

Platte and Rio Grande and compared the Colorado River Compact to a quiet title procedure in which the ownership of land is established prior to building structures.[69]

Carpenter emphasized the importance of local control of water projects. "Irrigation," he lectured the solons, "is not a theory; it is a hard, practical, living science. The conditions vary so on each stream . . . that the ordinary rules of law are usually a misfit. . . . [C]onditions obtaining in one State will call for the shading of any given rule of law in order to fit the local situation. . . . The whole problem is one of practical operation in the hands of the States. It means the lifeblood of communities. . . . Powerful States can not be subjected to the servitude and dictation of mere private citizens [he was referring to federal officials] claiming control of the State's most vital resource."[70] For this reason, Carpenter continued, the Colorado River Compact was drawn up in consideration of the natural topography, to provide storage and flood control, and to award each basin with approximately 50 percent of the river. "[T]he point I wish to press to your attention," he said, "is that not one right, whatever it may or might be, of the Imperial Valley is injured by this compact. [Southern California] is fully protected by the specific provisions of Article 8. These lower river rights are left without impairment and we of the north are left exposed to attack until the reservoir has been provided."[71] Any statement that the compact "gave away certain rights that the lower country had is evidently based upon a misconstruction of the terms and provisions of the very compact under discussion."[72]

In regard to Arizona, Carpenter said, that state was fully justified in taking whatever time it needed to investigate its potentialities and to be fully advised before proceeding. The effect, however, was to delay the pressing demand for flood control. In consideration of this need, the upper states proposed a six-state compact. California demurred, insisting that Congress should first authorize dam and reservoir construction on the lower river. This inaction, Carpenter concluded, "has shrouded the [six-state] plan in doubt. . . . [T]he destiny of the States should not rest upon doubt. . . . Pardon me for being so direct," he pleaded, ". . . but we respectfully insist . . . that no major construction . . . on this river system, either above or below, which might disturb the present status or affect any State, or the rights of any of them, should proceed until this question of title is settled [by interstate compact]."[73]

California had now become Carpenter's bête noir. Because several of that state's political leaders, including former Colorado River Compact commissioner W. F. McClure, were voicing serious objections to the compact, California legislators rejected Hoover's advice and attached reservations to their six-state ratification. Whether ratification was by six or seven states, they said, the compact would not be binding on California until Congress (1) authorized a dam on the lower Colorado River large enough to create a reservoir of at least 20 million acre-feet of storage and (2) exercised the power and jurisdiction of the United States to enforce the terms of the compact.[74] In response, and at Hoover's suggestion, Carpenter called for a conference of governors from the states of origin, at which time a resolution of solidarity passed, referred to in his opening testimony before the Senate committee. California then withdrew its reservations and supported the six-state compact. He would do everything in his power, Carpenter told the senators, to convert the existing Swing-Johnson bill into law, but he wanted to make one more attempt to obtain seven-state ratification. If he failed, Carpenter said, he would favor a six-state compact that Arizona could ratify at a later date.[75] Congress, of course, would have to approve the six-state compact, but in Carpenter's view, no Colorado River Compact would succeed without California ratification. The upper states would continue in their resistance to the Swing-Johnson bill until California sanctioned the six-state plan unconditionally.

Four months later Carpenter submitted a statement to the House committee on irrigation and reclamation. He covered some of the same ground, but what he said was more accusatory. He criticized the Bureau of Reclamation for violating the National Reclamation Act (1902) and for seeking "to place control of water supplies in the keeping of appointees of distant federal courts or of persons responsive only to federal authority . . . contrary to the decision of the Supreme Court (*Kansas v. Colorado*). . . . The breach of this pledge has been the root of great evil."[76] Diabolical schemes to garner control of western rivers were in the making, Carpenter noted. They took the form of adverse legal theories prepared for interstate litigation, denial of the authority of state courts, administration of western rivers by federal bailiffs, and the preparation of quasi-legal reports justifying these actions. In an article published in the *Grand Junction Daily Sentinel*, Carpenter was quoted as denouncing the Bureau for secretly sending investigators into the various capitals of the upper basin states. Without announcing their purpose, these men did research on state water rights and then followed up with a "series of typewritten reports bound in four volumes . . . since kept in the confidential files of the Bureau of Reclamation at Washington and Denver." The "plot" outlined therein stated that the Bureau "was to become and continue to be the repository of all knowledge on the subject of water supply, reclamation, and other like matters in the Colorado River drainage, [and] that the control of the river must ultimately come into the hands of the [Bureau] and be taken away from the states."[77] What the Bureau wanted, Carpenter surmised, was for two or more states in any river basin to bring suit in federal courts. The United States would intervene, appoint a master, produce a "gigantic final decree," and then appoint the Bureau of Reclamation, "the repository of all knowledge," to be the "perpetual administrator" of such a decree. It was a conspiracy against state sovereignty and it was all based on an "unrighteous doctrine" that the federal government owned all of the nonappropriated waters of the West.[78]

After reading the article, the Bureau's acting commissioner, P. W. Dent responded in a memorandum to Secretary of Interior Hubert Work. None of the Bureau's reports, Work stated, contained the information to which Carpenter alluded. In his view, Carpenter had failed to appreciate the Bureau's policy of proceeding in harmony with "the laws of the states in which works and lands to be irrigated are located." In fact, Dent pointed out, Commissioner Mead would never sanction the "inaccurate, intemperate, and overdrawn" statements proposed by Carpenter."[79]

Given Carpenter's previous experience, however, it is not surprising he placed so much emphasis on the perceived evils of federal intervention. He was convinced the Bureau hungered for power and would not hesitate to implement on the Colorado River the same dictatorial policies it had employed on the Rio Grande and North Platte. Such a development would be equivalent to a death sentence for the upper basin states. Whenever the federal government curtailed development on the upper reaches of a river in order to benefit downstream entities, the threat of adverse claims against the upper basin tended to "discourage the investment of private capital in irrigation works and [would] divert investment into other channels."[80] The Swing-Johnson bill also seemed insensitive to concerns of the upper basin states that had agreed to underwrite the hazard of Arizona's failure to ratify the compact by offering to make it effective among the other six states.

They had done everything to solve the underlying legal problems involved in the construction of flood control works, but they would not "permit their territory to be burdened and their people to be harassed with any such conditions as have prevailed on the Rio Grande, North Platte and other rivers." In necessary self-defense, Carpenter concluded for the benefit of the House committee, "[the upper basin would have to] resist the construction of any reservoir upon the lower river until their rights [were] settled by compact."[81] To this end, he urged the House to postpone action on the Swing-Johnson bill.

Swing was irritated with Carpenter's testimony. Such recommendations to Congress caused the Californian "worry and uneasiness," and Swing surmised that Carpenter's actions resulted from his owing some favors to Arizona. Swing reminded the Coloradan:

> Last spring, when we had adopted each and every one of the amendments you suggested, you wired the committee that you had withdrawn your protest against the passage of the bill. . . . [Y]ou should not put any further obstacles in our way. . . . [Y]ou should assist us in getting this bill through, as it is the only way you are ever going to get your Colorado River Compact ratified. . . . We want to reach an agreement with Arizona just as much as you want us to, but we will reach that agreement quicker if you assist us in bringing about a situation where Arizona will be more reasonable in her demands. That situation can only be brought about by the prompt passage of the Swing-Johnson bill. Speaking frankly, [your] attitude . . . simply insures Arizona continuing to assume the attitude of the cock of the walk or the dog in the manger—an unreasonable attitude which has prevented and is preventing an agreement."[82]

Bannister also expressed impatience with Carpenter. He wanted to support in "affirmative and vigorous fashion" the version of the Swing-Johnson bill Carpenter opposed. That opposition, Bannister conjectured, rested on Carpenter's twisted version of political reality. Carpenter strongly believed law makers would not agree immediately to a Swing-Johnson bill, preferring instead to delay commencement of construction until California ratified the six-state compact without reservations.[83] Bannister appeared to be undermining upper basin unity by his outspoken endorsement of the Swing-Johnson bill. Such behavior was tantamount to treason. Bannister was an embarrassment to the upper basin. He attended upper basin meetings as a representative of the Denver Water Board, wrote to Governor Hunt with his own interpretation of such proceedings, and appeared as a witness before congressional committees in Washington without authority from upper basin officials.

This behavior, along with Swing's self-serving criticism, was increasingly offensive to Carpenter. Bannister was undermining everything Carpenter had been struggling to achieve, while Swing appeared incorrigible, fixated on a single issue (the dam) and insensitive to the needs of upper basin states.

At this point, Carpenter began to rethink the advisability of a six-state compact. Bannister's mind, Carpenter wrote, "while bright, is academic, his retainer is by one community with very 'political' influences and his affiliations with the California interests give him but one side of the question and that side is very dangerous to us." Carpenter concluded, "The more I view the field, the more I am convinced that the four upper states must firmly assert that they must have a seven-state compact ratified before or concurrently with any Congressional action and that no Act pass Congress until the states have ratified. We cannot tolerate Congressional action conditioned upon future state action. So to do is to trust the future of our states to the mercy of a repealable promise."[84]

Viewed from Bannister's perspective, however, Carpenter was becoming increasingly inflexible, resistant to compromise, and hostile to any legislation that failed to include seven-state ratification. Bannister agreed seven-state ratification was preferable, "but if it cannot be had," he told Governor Hunt, "[Denver] will want at this session [of Congress] Boulder Canyon legislation on a basis of fewer states."[85] The City of Denver, Bannister explained, recognized that California had "a bunch of water priorities out of the main river antedating 1900." Arizona also had senior rights, although the volume of water was approximately one-third less than that allotted to California. When the Colorado River was in low stage, there was insufficient water to satisfy both these lower basin rights as well as the existing rights of the upper basin, especially "if the doctrine of priority regardless of state lines is the law of the Colorado River." Because "Denver's water rights in the Western slope [only] go back as far as 1914," the city's rights would be subject to claims by Arizona and California if the priority doctrine were to be strictly applied. Stored water behind a dam on the Colorado River would prevent the need to call down water from the upper basin. "California," Bannister pointed out, "was Denver's greatest enemy upon the river, because her draught from the main stream is over three times the draught of Arizona. For the reason that she is our greatest enemy, it also is true that she is the one with whom it is most important for Denver to make peace by Interstate Agreement."[86]

Bannister wanted Arizona, California, and Nevada to agree to a tristate compact in which each state would be assured the water and power interests it coveted. But if they failed, Bannister argued, Denver could not continue to jeopardize its own safety by attempting too long to assist Arizona. "As I see it," he stated, "that period of safety expires within the next few weeks, for by that time a reasonable period allowed for negotiations will have passed, and we have no advance assurance that the provisional embargo upon the Federal Power Commission will be extended."[87] If a seven-state compact was not forthcoming, he concluded, "Denver must uphold . . . the Boulder Canyon bill predicated on less than Seven State action."[88]

Aside from his concern for Denver's future, Bannister continued to believe that a more aggressive behavior on his part was required due to Carpenter's poor health. Francis C. Wilson, New Mexico's recently appointed interstate rivers commissioner, encouraged Bannister to fill the leadership vacuum. Even if Carpenter could travel to Washington, he wrote, "we could not hope to get any real assistance from him."[89] Wilson respected Carpenter, but he believed that the Coloradan had already enjoyed his moment in the limelight. Henceforth, Denver and the state of Colorado "would have to look to [Bannister] for new leadership."[90]

Bannister was more than ready. He had been feuding with Carpenter for some time without giving vent to his feelings publicly. Now that officials in New Mexico and Wyoming also questioned Carpenter's ability to continue as leader of the upper basin, he was willing to take the offensive. Carpenter had burned his bridges with California, was resistant to anything but seven-state ratification as a prerequisite to congressional legislation, and had failed to represent accurately the interests of Colorado and the City of Denver. From a legal standpoint, the Colorado commissioner had made egregious mistakes. "If . . . Commissioner Carpenter should try again to undermine me in the way he did," Bannister warned, "by seeking my recall; if he should be responsible for sending out statements in Col-

orado purporting to emanate from our state officials, criticizing the City
of Denver, or me, for being active in Colorado River affairs . . . he simply
will compel me to fire a broadside I should rather hold back. . . . In saying
this I am not unmindful of the credit side of his account, and shall always
acknowledge it."[91]

Without doubt, Bannister was correct when he recognized that the
problems with Carpenter were to some extent a consequence of the latter's
health problems. From 1925 through 1928, Carpenter's diary contains
many entries describing the unpleasant symptoms of his malady. He tried
to take a three-week vacation in Thermopolis, Wyoming, but rest proved
impossible due to conferences with Commissioner Mead and Secretary of
the Interior Hubert Work regarding Rio Grande compact developments.
He took sun baths and slept more, but the neuritis spread to his tongue
and throat. At times he was entirely unable to speak. His doctor put him
in the hospital for rest and lung treatments and recommended a trip to
Hot Springs, Arkansas, to meet with a specialist.

A 1926 medical report from a Hot Springs doctor noted a severe tremor
in his right hand that spread to his entire arm when he moved. His voice
was "husky" and "slightly tremulous." His mouth sagged slightly on the
right side and he favored his right leg when he walked. From all appearances, however, Carpenter enjoyed relatively good health. Although he
was a bit overweight and somewhat restless, his attention, memory, and
orientation were excellent. Excitement or stress, the doctor remarked,
"made all the symptoms more apparent . . . [and the] patient [is] especially disturbed by [the] uncertainty of vocal activity and by increasing tendency to emotional 'weakness.' Mr. Carpenter has lived a very active life,
apparently not recognizing the fact that there is a limit to the amount of
high-tension work (largely sustained mental endeavor aggravated by acute
responsibilities and added financial worries) any man may do, and yet
retain coordinate muscular responses; and especially is this true when one
considers the character of the work extending over inordinately long periods of time, and without vacation or respite from extreme fatigue of body
and mind." The medical evidence indicated Carpenter was suffering from
"a natural 'fatigue syndrome' in which the 'Parkinsonian symptoms' developed only after an attack of influenza in 1918."[92] Carpenter had a good
chance of improving his physical condition if he omitted "all exciting
recreation and unduly fatiguing work, both mental and physical." He would

need eight to ten hours of sleep every night, moderate exercise, massage, hot baths, as much sunshine as possible, a diet rich in fruits and vegetables, and a new attitude that enabled him to "just let things work out for themselves with [the] least attention possible."[93]

It was good advice, and Carpenter made an honest attempt to follow it, but Secretary Work frequently sought his counsel even at Hot Springs. Returning to Greeley, he tried to spend more days at Crow Creek Ranch. He persuaded Donald to sign on as his secretary on a trip to Washington, but work was still his passion. When he journeyed to Ojo Caliente in New Mexico to enjoy the natural hot springs, his itinerary included meetings with Francis Wilson to discuss the La Plata Compact and the pending Rio Grande and Colorado River compacts. Even when he returned home, there were problems to address and decisions to be made. Dot suffered a severe attack of appendicitis in the late fall of 1926. The operation was successful, but Carpenter knew it was time to draw up wills for both of them. Father-in-law Captain Hogarty died in 1925 and Leroy, his own father, was becoming feeble. Carpenter decided to sell the home ranch when Leroy passed away in November 1927. By 1928 Donald was available only infrequently to help his father, having departed for Washington University in the fall of 1926 with a paternal admonition to complete his studies in three years to save money.

The greatest source of professional worry to Carpenter continued to be the potential break-up of the Colorado River Compact states. There was nothing he could do about Arizona, but California's arrogance frustrated him. When the Utah legislature indicated it might renege on six-state ratification, Carpenter became alarmed. As the doctors predicted, his health deteriorated immediately. "[I] feel that my going to Utah might be misconstrued by members [of the] Utah legislature," he wired Governor Dern, "and [I am] not feeling very well, but if my presence there [is] imperative to save [the] main compact and my coming will be agreeable to leading legislators, I will make a short trip upon your request to Governor William H. Adams . . . [but] I can make no speeches or address no committees as my throat still bothers me."[94]

Utah was experiencing a states' rights crisis. Because of recent discoveries of oil in the channel of the Colorado River near Moab and increased transportation of machinery and commodities traveling downstream from

Green River, a significant faction of a very Republican Utah legislature wanted to remove the state from the compact. Article IV of the compact stated that the Colorado River was no longer navigable for commerce. Republicans feared that Utah's participation in the compact would endorse this statement, thus denying the state its sovereign ownership of the streambed. The federal government would then intervene with works on several dam sites with the result that Utah's development would be impeded.

Democratic Governor Dern and his interstate streams commissioner William R. Wallace were powerless to stem Utah's retreat from the compact.[95] In mid-January 1927, the Republican legislature voted to remove the state from the compact and followed this act with legislation claiming the state's right to the bed of the Colorado River.[96] Ironically, as Carpenter had pointed out to Dern, Utah might have undermined the very sovereignty it sought to protect because the government could easily use the navigability issue as "an excuse to 'claim the whole river.'"[97]

More importantly, Utah's actions in regard to the compact constituted a major blow to Carpenter. His respect for Dern, however, and his belief that Utah acted "in good faith and with serious intent" encouraged him to blame California for this "tragedy." By ratifying the six-state compact with reservations, California had set a bad example. That state's attitude was "coercive" toward the upper basin. California had proceeded under the mistaken belief that the upper basin was so desperate for a compact that it would accept any terms dictated by California. But now, Carpenter noted, "California . . . finds herself in a position of trying to drive her measure through Congress in the face of her own folly." Utah's decision reflected its own view of the future and even if its interpretation of Article IV was erroneous,[98] California was now faced with another reminder that diplomacy and cooperation were essential to passage of the Swing-Johnson bill. From Carpenter's point of view, any talk of a five-state compact was "ridiculous." Utah needed time to reconsider its actions and to return ultimately as participant in either a six- or seven-state compact.[99]

Bannister was much less charitable when he learned what had happened. Utah's actions were a disappointment, especially because that state was now holding out for seven-state ratification that Bannister thought unrealistic. He attended two conferences called by upper basin states for the purpose of uniting around a new strategy. Representatives of all four states agreed their best plan was to redouble efforts to bring Arizona into the fold. On December 19, 1927, therefore, each representative signed a resolution in Denver stating "that no legislation proposing construction of any project upon the Colorado River should be enacted by Congress, or otherwise authorized by any Federal Agency, before the negotiations *now in progress* (author's emphasis) have been completed and every reasonable effort exhausted to reach such agreement between the seven states."[100]

Bannister signed the resolution. Three weeks later he was in Washington urging legislators in the House of Representatives to pass the Swing-Johnson bill as soon as possible. Dern was also there. He was appalled. Bannister seemed to have forgotten the terms of the resolution he had just signed in Denver. Dern telegraphed his grave concern to Colorado Governor William H. Adams. Bannister told the House committee that "passage of [the] Swing-Johnson bill [was] essential to [the] upper basin and that we will derive practically as much benefit from it as California." Such a statement, repudiating the upper basin governors and "by inference" discrediting the whole Denver conference, "is fatal to us," Dern wrote. "Unless you can secure his recall immediately, he will doubtless repeat his performance before [the] Senate committee next week and spoil everything we have done."[101]

Carpenter was equally shocked. He, too, telegraphed Governor Adams, commending Dern on a "masterly presentation [of the] case for the upper states." He added, "Unfortunately, Bannister without previous notice or consultation with us made [a] two-hour plea for [the] Swing-Johnson bill and criticized and opposed in detail statements made by Dern and ignored [the] policy agreed on at [the] Denver meeting [of] December nineteenth." Carpenter went on to say that he and Dern were "deeply humiliated." They had extended apologies on the governor's behalf "as well as our own, but apologies do not erase the unfortunate Bannister speech from the records."[102] Adams was surprised. He contacted Denver Mayor Ben Stapleton and was assured that Bannister would be told to work in harmony with the upper basin states.[103]

But Bannister refused to let the matter drop. He was angry that the Dern and Carpenter telegrams had been published and that Adams had appeared through his remarks in the press to accept their version of events in Washington. He felt both his motives and his words before the House committee had been twisted. He made clear to Adams the Denver resolution he had supposedly violated referred only to negotiations "in progress." In other words, if seven-state agreement proved unattainable in discussions presently under way, a second stage of negotiation would bring the upper basin to an endorsement of a six-state compact.

Dern and Carpenter, he said, had gone beyond the Denver resolution to tell Congress that under no circumstances, and at no time, would the upper basin back anything less than a seven-state compact. They showed "excessive zeal," he said, and they condemned the Swing bill "savagely" as unconstitutional. Instead, Bannister noted, as representative of the City of Denver, he had every right to defend the constitutionality of the Swing bill "if based upon the improvement of navigation," and his testimony simply asserted its worth to Denver and the upper basin if passed into law.[104]

The Dern-Carpenter telegrams and Bannister's response exposed an upper basin leadership crisis nine months before Congress passed the Boulder Canyon Project Act in 1928. Bannister, Wyoming Governor Emerson, and New Mexico Commissioner Wilson were ideologically opposed to the seven-states-or-nothing approach of Carpenter and Governor Dern. For all his elitist faults, Bannister's anger on this occasion was warranted to some extent, but there was another reason for his embarrassment. "Those telegrams," he wrote Emerson, "were the most injustifiable [*sic*] and dastardly attack on me that any human being ever made, but I never have said that to the public, because in the interest of maintaining as much cooperation as possible, I did not want to see the breach widened."[105] Bannister also might have confessed to Adams that his actions in Washington were to a great extent attributable to his respect for the political power of Frederick Bonfils, owner and editor of the *Denver Post*. Bonfils was at war with Colorado Senator Lawrence Phipps, chairman of the House committee on irrigation and reclamation. Bannister was so awed by Bonfils' power, he was sure Phipps would eventually be destroyed by the *Post*. Hoping to preserve intact his own political aspirations, Bannister was careful not to do or say anything that would associate him with the senator. Phipps wanted Congress to accept a substitute for the Swing-Johnson bill that more closely reflected Carpenter's interests. He failed. Bannister's strong support for the existing Swing-Johnson bill was partially responsible. What no one knew was that Bannister's enthusiasm for Swing-Johnson was as much an expression of his deference to Bonfils as it was a commitment to Boulder Canyon Dam legislation and a six-state compact.[106]

The antagonism between Carpenter and Bannister continued several months longer, but their confrontation over Bannister's testimony in Congress was the nadir of the relationship. Bannister recognized the great respect Carpenter commanded in different circles. He praised Carpenter's efforts to produce a Rio Grande compact, used his own political connections to assure the Colorado interstate streams commissioner a continuous salary, and nominated Carpenter for a seat on the Colorado World Court Committee.[107] Shortly after President Coolidge signed the Boulder Canyon Project Act in December 1928, Bannister told the Denver Chamber of Commerce that Carpenter had "devised the idea of the Colorado River Compact." He hoped that "legislators present would continue providing funds for [him]. . . . We are going to see the Colorado River Compact made the law of the Colorado River basin," he concluded. "Death to all resistance!"[108]

Carpenter appreciated the kudos, but he needed more time to forgive and forget. He was still irritated that Bannister seemed unwilling to follow his lead, and he was weary of the ongoing burden of having to preserve upper basin unity. There were times, he wrote Clarence Stetson, when he could scarcely walk or talk "and felt and *was* 498 years old. To all appearances, I am affected with paralysis agitans although experts tell me that I merely have a case of flu poisoning. At any rate, I am barely able to stagger around, can talk but little and with difficulty."

His future appeared gloomy, he confessed to Stetson. Neither Michaela nor Sarah was married; both daughters were teachers and "very available." Carpenter wanted "a son-in-law with sufficient means to provide a pension. . . . I would not require much," he mused, "ten or fifteen cents per month plus tobacco and orange juice."[109] Facetious, perhaps, but Carpenter never ceased worrying about his financial security.

Despite the expression of woe, Carpenter was still in charge of upper basin affairs. Nevada state engineer George W. Malone noted that Carpenter was, indeed, in "very bad shape" and barely able to sign his name. Nevertheless, he was still the "guiding hand of Utah, Wyoming, as well as Colorado."[110] Anticipating congressional action on the Swing-Johnson bill in the spring of 1928, Carpenter sent amendments he favored to Senator Phipps. They stated a now familiar theme, that no works could be built on the Colorado River until the compact was ratified by the seven states. If, however, the seven states failed to ratify in the year following enactment of the legislation by Congress, a six-state compact could be proclaimed in force by the president, provided one of the six states was California. A third provision mandated that California limit its diversion to a total of no more than 4.6 million acre-feet annually from the Colorado River.[111]

Carpenter was pessimistic about California's willingness to accept these amendments, but he worried needlessly. No form of the Swing-Johnson bill appeared before any legislators during the first session of 1928. Rumors that Arizona, California, and Nevada might yet agree on a three-state compact continued to circulate. In addition, some senators and representatives were worried about their own chances in fall elections. They were nervous about appropriating money to finance the reclamation of 1.5 million acres of new land when agricultural prices were so depressed. And they feared going on record in favor of a bill to authorize a large power project without first determining how the power would be disposed.[112]

Although the Bureau of Reclamation was not expected to enter the power debate in Congress, Director Mead continued to back passage of the Swing-Johnson bill. He offered assistance to the commissioners trying to reach agreement on the most appropriate version. He expected power contracts to be awarded to both public and private agencies, and he fully endorsed compensation to the states of Arizona and Nevada on whose soil a dam would be built. True to his deepest convictions, Mead favored an All-American Canal to provide water for irrigation in the Imperial Valley, but he insisted that repayment costs should be assigned to owners of lands that benefited. The entire project had been sold to the country as self-supporting. He did not expect general taxpayers to assume the financial burden.[113]

Carpenter was especially interested in how and when the power contracts would be written. He was afraid reservoirs built for power generation would enable lower basin water users to establish priority claims to the Colorado River; but he was as acutely interested in the principles of equity and states' rights that had guided him through compact negotiations. He continued to see California as a bully. Nevada and Arizona, he believed, should each receive at least one-third of the power generated at Hoover Dam, the other one-third going to California. Because the dam was to be built on the borders of Arizona and Nevada, these states were entitled to a significant amount of hydroelectric power, even if they had no immediate use for it. When the Federal Power Commission indicated an interest in issuing power permits on the Colorado River over the objections of the upper basin states in 1924, Carpenter had been inspired to come up with the idea of a six-state compact.[114] At the time, it seemed to be the only way to deter the FPC from complicating the already difficult ratification process.

But the FPC wanted the works built and believed that Arizona's unwillingness to ratify meant that the compact would ultimately fail. Since its inception in 1920, the FPC had done little more than act as a clearinghouse for power permits. Its members, including the secretaries of the Interior, War, and Labor department, were too busy to address the potential conflict inherent in an expanded and centralized power distribution system. Definition of the roles of local, state, and federal governments was still in a formative stage.[115] Hoover favored dam construction, and he expected to use power production revenue to pay for it. He was outspokenly positive regarding his interest in some form of "giant power development" if it would lead to reduction in waste, industrial efficiency, and the kind of centralized planning that also respected states' rights. He favored leasing hydroelectric power to private power companies, "which in their charges to the consuming public [would be] regulated by local authorities." For Hoover, the test of any such project was its "social usefulness."[116]

Carpenter was concerned as always about states' rights. He told Hoover an equitable distribution of power implied a balanced distribution among the three lower basin states. Just as he felt about water distribution, so Carpenter believed the allocation of power should take into account fairness to future generations and the growth that would occur eventually in states that now had less industry and population. He opposed the 1930 contract that officially awarded 64 percent of Hoover Dam power to California, a state, he pointed out, that provided neither land nor water for the project. To Wyoming's state engineer, he wrote that the government had acted with "ruthless disregard of the rights of other states" and ignored the wishes of the upper basin. "But why comment?" Delph asked rhetorically. When Hoover the Californian became president, he had appointed another Californian, Ray Lyman Wilbur, to be his secretary of interior. "The king can do no wrong," Carpenter concluded.[117] An equitable distribution of power would encourage seven-state ratification of the Colorado River Compact. "Your solicitude for preserving the equal opportunity for allocation of power among the three states," he wrote Secretary Wilbur, "will do more than any other factor to open the way to settlement of interstate difficulties. When the people of Arizona and Nevada realize that you are going to insure equal justice and will protect the weak states as against aggression by the strong, hostility will gradually disappear and settlement be made possible." The "human element" was the controlling factor, Carpenter stated. "People who labor under a sense of injury or injustice do not readily compose their differences with those whom they believe to be the beneficiaries of the injustice."[118] Comity, once again!

This philosophy applied as much to his relations with Bannister as it did to the states. By the end of 1928 their feud was over. The two men had found agreement over the need to incorporate special language in FPC licenses. Even if the Boulder Canyon Project Act provided statutory recognition of the compact, Arizona might feel threatened enough to challenge the statute in court and the court might invalidate the legislation.[119] In fact, Carpenter argued, the upper basin needed more protection. He wanted the FPC to refrain from issuing permits until both upper and lower states had consummated compacts among themselves, allocating finite amounts of water to individual states in their own basin. But Secretary Wilbur was impatient to get on with project development on the Colorado River, where more than two dozen applications were pending. To bring these applicants under control of the Colorado River Compact, Carpenter drew up an article to be included in future FPC licenses on the Colorado River and its tributaries. In consideration of receiving a fifty-year license to develop a power site, permittees would agree that their use of water would at all times be "subject to and controlled by the Colorado River Compact."[120] Bannister traveled to Washington to persuade Wilbur that Carpenter's draft article was a logical and equitable method of assuring the upper basin that a federal power permit remained subject to the states' right to utilize water for agricultural and domestic purposes. Wilbur accepted the article and assured Carpenter that it would be inserted in all future permits.

Most of the obstacles to passage of the Swing-Johnson bill had now been removed. In a paper he prepared for the American Water Works Association, Carpenter reviewed some of those obstacles and the underlying philosophy of good compact negotiation. He pressed his claim to state control of water within state boundaries. Individuals, businesses, and government entities could hold titles to the water, he noted, but these titles were usufructuary, "subject always to the dominant will of the state" and varying in accordance with the laws of each state. Water rights could not be absolute because interstate compacts had the effect of modifying vested interests in irrigation, domestic water supply, or power generation.[121] River treaties, Carpenter explained, while imperfect, helped secure titles to property and thus made investment in such property more secure. They were not a panacea, but if properly prepared with patience, ample time for deliberation, proper investigation of pertinent data, and competent commissioners, they could anticipate the needs of future generations and avoid the litigation that tears governments apart. Sitting back and allowing federal agencies the right to allocate and supervise the distribution of interstate waters would constitute a death knell to the federal system. "[Nationalization of] our streams," Carpenter noted, "would tend to destroy our nation, for . . . the states would be deprived of control of that natural element [water] essential or imperative to their very existence. The agency which controls the element will control the states."[122]

Bannister agreed with Carpenter's comments. He endorsed the states' rights framework upon which Carpenter based so much of his thinking, and he used the 1928 election to speak out for both of them. The Democratic candidate, Al Smith, was his target. Because Carpenter was serving as interstate streams commissioner under a Democratic governor, he was reluctant to comment on Smith's stated plan to scrap the compact and the Swing-Johnson bill in favor of a control organization similar to the New York Port Authority.[123] In response to Smith, Bannister delivered a radio address in which he revealed his philosophical accord with Carpenter in matters of state and federal authority on the Colorado River.

Smith favored organization of a public interstate corporation, chartered by all seven Colorado River basin states, with authority to administer water and power on the river. The Colorado legislature would not embrace such a concept, Bannister said. It would not delegate to such an authority the power to divide the water in the river. But representatives of the upper basin felt even more strongly about the suggestion by Smith that the government should build a dam whether or not the river basin states ratified the compact. "No! No!" Bannister fumed. "We are not going to discard the principle of interstate agreement. . . . We cannot procure interstate agreement without the dam and we are not going to allow the dam to be built without interstate agreement among all, or at least nearly all, of the states."[124]

By November 1928, one month before the Swing-Johnson bill was enacted into law as the Boulder Canyon Project Act, Carpenter was able to state that he and Bannister were "working in full accord."[125] Overcoming petty jealousies and recognizing common interests, the two men began to show intermittent signs of cordiality. Progressing to formal expressions of admiration, they succeeded in developing a genuine friendship. Carpenter urged Bannister to participate with him in shaping an upper basin states compact, and Bannister used his political connections to urge retention of Carpenter as interstate streams commissioner during the onset of the Depression.

Hoover's election gave them another common bond. Carpenter had forecast the results a year earlier,[126] but knew he would lose contact with his friend if, in fact, his prediction came true. Congressional enactment of the Swing-Johnson bill on December 18, 1928, setting aside a waiting period of six months for either six-state or seven-state ratification of the compact, meant that Hoover would be the one to activate Hoover Dam construction. This was poetic justice. But before that moment arrived on June 25, 1929, both Utah and California would have to ratify the six-state compact. Within two days of each other they got the job done. When power contracts were agreed to the following year, work began on Hoover Dam.

Carpenter worried about the impact of the economic downturn on the new president. He wrote Hoover's secretary, Lawrence Richie, expressing concern about a newspaper article that described the president as tense, overworked, and lacking his usual sense of humor. Carpenter was worried that his good friend might work himself to death.[127] But Hoover replied that present worries were of less importance to him than the consummation of the Colorado River Compact. Carpenter's "tenacity and intelligence" were responsible for that accomplishment, and someday he would say this "emphatically to the people of the West."[128]

The appropriate moment for Hoover to express these views would have been at the dedication of Hoover Dam in 1935, but it was a new day and a Democratic administration under Franklin D. Roosevelt was in charge. Secretary of the Interior Harold Ickes did not even invite Hoover to the celebration. The mayor of Boulder City was so embarrassed, he took it

Hoover Dam. U.S. Bureau of Reclamation, *Reclamation Project Data*, 1961.

upon himself to invite Hoover, but Hoover declined. He had hoped to be a bystander at these ceremonies, but Ickes's insult persuaded him to stay home to avoid being "so public an exhibit of vindictiveness."[129] Although everyone involved with the compact and the Swing-Johnson bill had referred to "Boulder Canyon Dam," Secretary Ray Lyman Wilbur specifically named "Hoover Dam" in a speech of September 17, 1930, inaugurating construction. Dams had already been named after presidents Woodrow Wilson and Theodore Roosevelt, so Wilbur's decision was not unprecedented. Unfortunately, however, Ickes engaged in the worst sort of petty politics. He launched a campaign to change the name back to Boulder Dam. Although the Harry Truman administration formally reestablished Hoover Dam as the official name, confusion has endured to the present.

Such was the political angst generated by Hoover's presidency during the Great Depression. Carpenter's contribution to the compact and the ratification process, about which Hoover felt very deeply, suffered by association. Except for his name on a commissioners' plaque at the dam, nothing educates the public about the Coloradan's part in making the dam possible. Fewer people understand the synergy, created by Carpenter's close working relationship with Hoover, that carried the compact through nearly ten years of ratification struggles to legislative recognition in the Boulder Canyon Project Act.

CHAPTER 7

Last Years as Interstate Streams Commissioner

"I am busily engaged in the performance of a great undertaking in the nature of a public trust . . . and I will not forsake that trust until my duty is performed. . . . I would rather my name would go down to posterity as one successful in my present undertaking than I would . . . have it said that I was President of the Republic. My line of duty is plain and I expect to follow it."
—CARPENTER TO CHARLES W. WATERMAN, JUNE 19, 1924.

As work began on Hoover Dam, Carpenter turned his attention to the unfinished business of interstate compacts on the Arkansas, Rio Grande, North Platte, and other rivers. Simultaneously, he initiated compact discussions for the Colorado River's upper basin in order that the four states could divide equitably their 7.5 million acre-feet of water. The lingering embarrassment of his neuritis was muted by a keen sense of duty to Colorado and the West. He believed the West's future was at a crossroads, that failure to maintain momentum on interstate river compacts would encourage a larger federal presence in the West.

Finding the strength to continue interstate river negotiations was problematic. His illness had begun to affect the muscles of his diaphragm, chest, and certain spots along his spine. "I am unable to walk a great deal and

[I] talk with difficulty," he wrote an old friend. "The most unpleasant part of my affliction is that my thinking machinery works better than ever, but I cannot walk or talk and you well know how much I like to talk. . . . I sympathize with [Charles] Darwin, who was able to dictate only during twenty minute intervals. [I have the satisfaction of knowing that] 'me and Darwin' both belong to the cripple class."[1]

Carpenter kept his sense of humor as he pursued suggestions of innovative drugs and physical treatments. On his return to Colorado from the last visit to Hot Springs, Arkansas, he reported to Dr. George Eckel that his situation had worsened following an attack of influenza. Eckel had hoped that his palsy would disappear, but when advised of the influenza experience, he warned Carpenter that the flu virus could be "devastating" to a person with Parkinson's disease. "Surely," Eckel wrote, "I do wish I could tell you of something new in the way of treatment. . . . [T]he truth is we have not made a great deal of progress in the treatment of the disorder from which you suffer." He recommended administration of collip parathyroid hormone with calcium (Collip's Extract), plus cortin (Eschatin) for energy, and starmonium leaves to stem excessive salivation and bring about relaxation.[2] But he was clearly out of new ideas. Carpenter correctly sensed he was pretty much on his own.

A fellow Coloradan and future governor, Ralph Carr, urged him to try Christian Science. Carpenter, the devout Methodist, responded with alacrity. He wrote W. Stuart Booth, a healer in Denver, asking if he might be treated for his neuritis. "The tremendous pressure of my official work," he noted, "with all its cross currents of human elements coupled with the crushing strain and worry incident to financial depression following the slump in agriculture in 1922, have doubled me up."[3] Booth urged him to keep his focus on God and Divine Law. "As one expresses the qualities of Divine Mind [with] humility, gratitude, unselfishness and the desire for spiritual understanding," Booth assured him, "one is healed."[4] But relief was elusive. "I have been gaining but very slowly," Carpenter wrote Booth. "For some reason which I am unable to ascertain, I do not 'tune in' as I should, but I will come out all right in the end."[5]

Carpenter was an optimist and a scrapper, but he was also a pragmatist. His interest in Christian Science continued through the 1930s, but experiencing few results, Carpenter resigned himself to the disease and to the dependable care Dot provided. She picked up his spirits when he became depressed and attended to his physical and emotional needs.[6] She spoke on the telephone when acquaintances called seeking compact advice, and she took dictation from him, lowering her head to hear the whispered thoughts that flowed from his still active mind. She made it possible for him to remain connected to the world of water long after Carpenter was restricted to his bed. She was Florence Nightingale, amanuensis!

Dot was no ordinary caretaker. She fed her husband, traveled with him, and even wrote out the legal briefs Carpenter dictated. Her own spiritual strength, love of life, and kittenish demeanor made her the perfect companion under trying circumstances. Colorado state engineer M. C. Hinderlider recognized her extraordinary sacrifice and gave her highest praise. "I know of no woman," he marveled to Carpenter, "who is more deserving of the acclaim of not only the members of her sex, but of the public at large for her contribution through you to the welfare of our State and its citizens."[7] Journalist Alva A. Swain agreed. A Denver resident whose newspaper column frequently expressed admiration for Carpenter, Swain wrote Dot that her attention and devotion resulted in "doing a great service for a great man."[8] Carpenter also acknowledged Dot's contributions. Her aid made possible the continuation of work to which he was so dedicated. He rested his hopes of recovery on her "constant care."[9]

Even before Carpenter's infirmities caused him to be so dependent on Dot, he struggled to put compacts in place on all of Colorado's interstate streams. It was stressful work, and he gained only partial success.

Working out a settlement with Kansas on the Arkansas River, for example, had consumed a major portion of Carpenter's time since 1921, but he never had all the parties together or the social and economic environment under sufficient control to effect a compact. To Governor Oliver Shoup he admitted that "conditions confronting the commissioners for this river are the most difficult of any of the interstate streams under my jurisdiction."[10] Serious negotiations commenced in 1921, following a devastating June flood that caused $19 million in damages in Pueblo and the loss of more than a hundred lives. Officials of both states recognized the need for a storage reservoir to control the river. They also had grown tired of the litigation that characterized their relations since 1901.[11] With knowledgeable commissioners who respected each other, promises of a settlement seemed encouraging in the early stages of discussion. Carpenter dealt with the Arkansas River issues, using many of the same tactics and arguments he employed on other interstate streams. His leadership was respected by the Kansas commissioners with whom he negotiated.

Kansan C. A. Schneider was his first official contact. As litigation between Colorado and Kansas ditch companies simmered in federal district court in Denver, the two men joined forces to reconnoiter the Arkansas River, its tributaries and the irrigated lands in both states. In addition to hydrographic and geographic data, Carpenter determined to learn the history of prior litigation between the two states, especially the active case brought by the Finney County Water Users Association of Garden City, Kansas, against certain Colorado appropriators in the Arkansas Valley. He interviewed Kansas' attorney general and state water commissioner and inspected damage resulting from the June flood.[12] In his opinion, repeated on other occasions when negotiating compacts on interstate streams, ample water existed in the Arkansas River for both states. However, a storage reservoir was needed if Colorado were to guarantee a minimum annual flow to its downstream neighbor. He advised Shoup, that an interstate compact needed to be worked out prior to reservoir construction. He also urged the governor to fund an extensive study of return flows, to investigate a potential dam site on the Purgatory River in Colorado, and to assign additional engineers to the project. He advocated confidentiality and avoidance of publicity in order to develop trust with the Kansans.

Regrettably, the good intentions of 1921 were never realized. Ongoing problems, not the least of which was Carpenter's own distraction with the early phases of Colorado River Compact negotiation, made it difficult to sustain momentum. Once that work entered the level of serious negotiations, he was for all intents and purposes unavailable to Schneider and his replacement, George S. Knapp. After the Colorado River Compact was signed, he had to devote his energies to ratification by the states, amendment of the Swing-Johnson bill in Congress, and the challenges presented to him on other interstate rivers affecting Colorado. Limited monies in Colorado's Water Defense Fund, Colorado's concerns about guaranteeing water to Kansas in a dry year, and "radical elements" in Kansas detoured what might have been productive compact talks.[13] Carpenter succeeded in drawing up a draft compact in 1924, and Knapp agreed to have it published in the Kansas state engineer's annual report. But it was never printed in Colorado and it lacked finalization by representatives of both states.[14]

Even if it had been published for further discussion, the real obstacle to a speedy agreement on the Arkansas River was the June 1922 decision of the U.S. Supreme Court in *Wyoming v. Colorado*. Once justices decided that priority of use was a legitimate basis for equitable apportionment in interstate water cases, Kansans were more inclined to press their alleged advantage in the courts. Carpenter admitted that "the trend of decisions, including that in the Republican River case [decided at the same time as the *Wyoming* case],are all toward recognition of a preferred status for all prior appropriations upon interstate streams regardless of the state lines."[15] He believed, however, that many lawyers and judges misinterpreted the *Wyoming* decision. The general perception was that interstate priority ruled, encouraging entities in both Kansas and Colorado to claim senior rights. Among Colorado irrigators in the Arkansas Valley, defiance of Kansas in the courts had become a custom,[16] while in Kansas, as much as Knapp wanted a compact, he had to admit in 1927 that interested parties in his state were losing faith in the idea of an interstate agreement.[17] Although compact talks failed, Carpenter's early efforts at brokering an interstate accord helped pave the way for a compact in 1948.[18]

On the Rio Grande, where New Mexico, Colorado, and Texas had significant claims, his endeavors paid off more quickly. Carpenter wanted a compact, but he soon learned that many of the same issues that had caused delays on the Arkansas, Colorado, South Platte, and La Plata rivers were barriers to agreement on the Rio Grande. Additionally, the international nature of the Rio Grande, and the federal government's active interest in the river, complicated compact negotiations. As previously mentioned, Carpenter was peeved that in 1907 the secretary of interior had approved recommendations from the State Department and Department of Justice to deny applications for rights of way on public lands for irrigation in Colorado's San Luis Valley. This area, located upstream in Colorado from what would later become Elephant Butte Reservoir on the Rio Grande, was essentially frozen to development by the government's embargo until 1925. The embargo's stated purpose was to protect the water supply of the Rio Grande project as a whole and to preserve the prior rights claimed by the Reclamation Service and Mexico.[19]

Farmers in Colorado's San Luis Valley were gravely affected by the government's actions. To all intents and purposes, agricultural development was shut down. Reclamation Service director A. P. Davis favored lifting the embargo, and because more than 500,000 acres of irrigable land in Colorado and northern New Mexico were at stake, he recommended to Secretary Albert B. Fall in 1922 that a storage reservoir be built in Colorado and certain waterlogged lands drained, so that vested rights in all parts of the Rio Grande basin would be protected.[20]

But the embargo continued. To Carpenter, it represented a total disregard of the Supreme Court's ruling in *Kansas v. Colorado.* It was a violation of the principle of equitable apportionment enunciated in that case, and it allowed the federal government to strengthen its claim to ownership of all unappropriated waters in the West and its right to initiate projects without seeking approval of the states. In Colorado, this reprehensible attitude forced the conclusion that the government had engaged in "an arbitrary and unwarranted assumption of power,"[21] a behavior Carpenter described as "despotic."[22] To preserve comity among the states and to realize the court's goal of equitable apportionment of water on the Rio Grande, immediate organization of a compact commission was essential. It would function in a manner similar to that of the Colorado River Compact Commission (CRCC) with representatives from each of the three states and the federal government. Its objective would be to apportion the water equitably after consideration of the needs of the entire river basin.

As he had done for the CRCC, Carpenter drew up the bill forming the Rio Grande Compact Commission (RGCC).[23] He knew the success of any compact commission would depend to a great extent on securing a federal representative who was not a bureaucrat and who placed interstate compact-making on the same level as negotiating international treaties. Quite logically, Carpenter asked recently appointed Interior Secretary Hubert Work to name Herbert Hoover. New Mexico commissioner J. O. Seth agreed that Hoover was a man of broad vision without biases. "Can you not persuade Mr. Hoover to act on this river as he did on the Colorado?" Carpenter asked Work. The United States "[has] taken the attitude that they have appropriated the whole river and that no further development can proceed in either Colorado or New Mexico."[24]

Hoover was, indeed, an advocate of states' rights, but he was already overcommitted as chair of the St. Lawrence Waterway Commission. Carpenter promised the secretary that, if he would accept the job, he would be protected from the "annoying features that developed in the protracted hearings before the Colorado River [Compact] Commission."[25] Appropriate data would be presented completely and in written form, Hoover's time would not be wasted, and negotiation sessions would be limited to small groups of duly appointed officials.

Hoover accepted when President Calvin Coolidge asked him to be the federal representative to the RGCC, but when his other duties escalated, Hoover asked Secretary Work if he could resign. Carpenter was so eager to have Hoover's participation, he traveled to Washington to appeal to his friend personally and delayed scheduling the first meeting, partly to placate Hoover and partly to allow more time to collect the important hydrologic and geographic data he had promised. Hoover acceded to Carpenter's petition. The first meeting of the RGCC was held on October 26, 1924. Carpenter met the Hoovers on the train at Julesburg, Colorado, and rode with them to Denver, where Hoover was scheduled to give a radio talk. The next day, Carpenter drove them to Colorado Springs for the meeting of the RGCC at the elegant and historic Broadmoor Hotel.[26]

As chairman of the RGCC, Hoover welcomed Richard F. Burges of Texas to the meeting. Burges represented Texas in Pecos River negotiations with New Mexico. He was not an official representative to the RGCC, but Hoover recognized his presence as "a relief from the old problem of litigation in water rights. . . . [T]he whole question of organizing the work of the Commission depends on a thorough understanding of what the position of Texas is and what steps we should take in that [direction]."[27] In other words, Hoover agreed with Carpenter that a successful compact would have to include the comments and concerns of all three states.

Burges pointed out he was hopeful of an official appointment to the RGCC from the Texas state legislature. In the meantime, he wanted to state that Texas viewed the Rio Grande as two distinct rivers. The northern part, from its source to Fort Quitman, Texas, approximately sixty miles south of El Paso, raised issues of a related nature concerning the three states and Mexico. South of Fort Quitman, the river flowed for six hundred miles to the Del Rio Valley, winding its way through a canyon from which irrigation would be difficult at best. In the Del Rio Valley, farmers used the Pecos and Devils rivers for their needs while the Rio Grande journeyed another six hundred miles to the Gulf of Mexico.

As he had done during negotiations on the South Platte, La Plata, and Colorado rivers, Carpenter focused on the constitutionality of the compact process. He appreciated Burges's presence, especially the fact that

Burges was an experienced negotiator on the Pecos River. He was less concerned by Burges's unofficial status, which he compared to that of Secretary Hoover. Hoover had been appointed to the RGCC by the president without congressional approval. Although the chairman might not carry the same degree of authority as he did on the CRCC, his official role, Carpenter believed, made it possible for the RGCC to begin discussions. More importantly, Carpenter argued, Burges's presence made possible the exchange of ideas dealing with the entire river basin. Like New Mexico and Colorado, Texas deserved its "place in the sun." Progress could be made by negotiators without formal legislative authority and state governments had nothing to fear because a safety net was built into the process: if and when the RGCC agreed on a compact, it could only go into effect after ratification by the state legislatures.

Seth and Hoover disagreed somewhat with Carpenter. They stressed the importance of public opinion. If negotiations were commenced by representatives appointed by duly elected legislators, the ignorance, prejudice, and lack of education of the general public would be defused. Ratification, the ultimate goal, would stand a better chance if the three states were represented by officials holding statutory mandates.

Carpenter accepted the validity of their contention. He knew it would be better if Texas sent an official member to the RGCC, but as Colorado representative, he also sensed restlessness among his constituents. The seventeen-year embargo had been a millstone around the neck of those wanting agricultural development in southwestern Colorado. Many of these same people suspected that New Mexico and Texas wanted to continue the stranglehold on the upper country. "[P]ersonally," Carpenter concluded, "I am impatient to proceed, because I probably have given more time and individual effort to this work than the other members, and naturally, being ready myself, I am probably a little bit too insistent."

He might have added that he, too, was suspicious, believing that delays in Texas were an outgrowth of the "stubborn desire of . . . Reclamation Service subordinates to block any further progress by the Commission. We are lead to believe," Carpenter confided to his friend Albert Moses, "that they have been deliberately omitting all of the Texas portion of the Elephant Butte project in the conduct of the studies which they were forced to undertake by orders from headquarters." Secretary Work, Director Mead, and Secretary Hoover had been advised of Reclamation's supposed bias , but no demonstrable changes had appeared in government policy. Consequently, Carpenter persisted in believing that "the attitude of [Reclamation] subordinates [was] such that Texas will not join us in the hope that the delay will work to the benefit of her territory."[28] Carpenter was accusing the Reclamation Service of deliberately sabotaging Rio Grande compact talks, and when the first RGCC meeting adjourned, participants agreed not to convene again until Texas formally designated a representative. Soon thereafter, Burges wrote Carpenter from home, saying he would "get the machinery in motion to secure the necessary legislation in Texas to authorize the state's representation upon the Commission."[29]

Surprisingly, by the summer of 1925, problems developed not with Texas but between New Mexico and Colorado. The Rio Grande embargo was declared illegal in May of that year, and almost immediately, private parties in Colorado asked for and were given permission to construct the Vega Silvestre Dam along the Rio Grande in the San Luis Valley. New Mexico withdrew from the RGCC and announced its intention of suing Colorado in the fall. Carpenter could readily see that, as with Kansas, the 1922 Wyoming decision encouraged states to litigate rather than negotiate, especially if they were confident of the seniority of their water diversions. New Mexico Governor A. T. Hannett telegraphed Colorado Governor Clarence J. Morley:"The lifting of the embargo by Secretary Work and granting the right for construction of Vega Silvester [sic] Dam and other permits, in our judgment gravely threatens New Mexico's priorities in waters of [the] Rio Grande. We cannot sit idly by while Colorado interests appropriate water."[30]

Although Carpenter had already expressed his regrets to Commissioner Seth regarding the dam permit, assuring the New Mexican that the Vega Silvestre grantees had agreed to abide by the terms of any Rio Grande compact, Hannett was adamant regarding New Mexico's rights. New Mexico had established "vested rights to [the] waters of the Rio Grande centuries before there was any substantial development in Colorado," he wrote, "and we propose to protect such interests by every lawful means within our power."[31]

New Mexico's fear of water-dependent development in Colorado was similar to what Colorado feared vis-à-vis California during Colorado River Compact discussions and the ongoing ratification process. Any state planning to construct storage facilities before negotiating an interstate compact agreement threatened the future economic security of its neighbors.

New Mexican officials seemed convinced the Supreme Court's 1922 *Wyoming* decision had given the state carte blanche to claim unlimited water use by virtue of ancient Hispanic irrigation projects.

Carpenter did not accept this interpretation, and neither did his friend R. I. Meeker or state engineer M. C. Hinderlider. The fact that the court had awarded Colorado an absolute decree to water from the Laramie River in the *Wyoming* case enabled Carpenter to conclude that compact negotiation, based on the doctrine of equitable apportionment without High Court intervention, was the preferred solution to interstate conflict. Still, when a neighboring state threatened litigation based on the assumption that interstate priority and vested state water rights were one and the same, defendant states like Colorado had to respond, either in court or through appeals for renewed compact negotiation.

Events in New Mexico favored renewal of discussions. During the summer of 1926, Rio Grande water levels dropped alarmingly. New Mexicans assumed that Colorado was diverting excessive amounts of water, but the real culprit was a periodic drought. Simultaneously, a federal judge enjoined New Mexico from using certain funds for the purpose of litigating the Colorado suit. Following the fall elections, outgoing officials left the incoming administration with the choice of appealing the court's decision or settling the interstate dispute by negotiation.[32] When Seth resigned and Francis C. Wilson was appointed interstate rivers commissioner in his place, New Mexico informed Carpenter that a resumption of talks was the preferred course.

Wilson was as hostile to litigation as Carpenter. Furthermore, and of no small importance, he was a gentleman. In Wilson, Carpenter saw a man who believed in fair play, disdained underhanded methods, and was interested in doing the right thing at all times. "He is entitled to our wholesome respect and very courteous treatment," Carpenter wrote to Colorado Lieutenant Governor and Alamosa attorney George Corlett.[33] Although Wilson was getting pressure from several New Mexican groups who wanted immediate action, he recognized the importance of entering into discussions, and asked Carpenter to draw up a draft compact. New Mexico was of the opinion that with the passage of time, Colorado would be establishing increasingly larger claims to water from the Rio Grande. A compact would set finite limits.

Carpenter was pleased to oblige. He outlined a course of events leading to an acceptable compact, although he was troubled by the fact that

Hoover, who had been nominated for the presidency in 1928, would have to be replaced as federal representative on the RGCC. "A Charles E. Hughes could bring about a three-state compact," Carpenter noted,[34] but as of yet no one had a legitimate candidate of his stature in mind to replace the secretary of commerce.[35] Additionally, Carpenter wanted public hearings involving the State Department, the International Boundary Commission, and the Bureau of Reclamation, along with semiexecutive and executive sessions of the RGCC. Carpenter advised Wilson that this process would take time, and that all the different angles and points of view of the three states needed deliberate consideration if a compact was to succeed.

Commissioners and their advisers met in Santa Fe on December 19, 1928, with the new federal representative, Colonel William J. Donovan, to renew discussions. Donovan was assistant to the United States attorney general and a decorated World War I veteran. In the negotiations that extended through January, a temporary compact was agreed upon and signed on February 12, 1929. Colorado's legislature approved the temporary compact in April. New Mexico and Texas, both waiting to see what Colorado would do, followed suit shortly thereafter. Federal approval was secured in 1930 when President Hoover signed a congressional act ratifying a permanent settlement.[36]

Carpenter managed to persevere through the strenuous debates, unwilling to succumb to fatigue until after the compact was signed. With each controversy, he assured Texas and New Mexico commissioners that "Colorado would listen to every suggestion offered until the crack of doom."[37] Reassured by the atmosphere of trust Carpenter had created, Texas and New Mexico agreed to make compromises on issues related to water delivery across state lines, a storage reservoir in Colorado, and drainage of lands in the San Luis Valley. L. Ward Bannister was impressed with Carpenter's success. Speaking for himself and the Denver Chamber of Commerce, Bannister told Carpenter that he was pleased to acknowledge the indebtedness the Chamber and people of Colorado felt in light of his accomplishment.[38] But in Carpenter's eyes, the kudos belonged to two engineers: R. I. Meeker and Royce Tipton. They had provided reliable data, acceptable to all parties, which served as the basis for profitable discussions. Because there was little dispute over their figures, the three states reached agreement in a relatively short amount of time.

But Congress rejected the Rio Grande Compact, because it was temporary, and because government officials believed they would have to incur considerable costs to build a dam and drainage system. Carpenter blamed the agreement's ambiguity and the speed with which it was negotiated,[39] but he also suspected the Department of Interior recommended rejection, because Colonel Donovan had been selected federal representative over a bureaucrat from Interior. In Carpenter's eyes, this was another example of the federal government's interest in usurping states' rights. It motivated him to fight for unequivocal congressional approval.

In a written defense of the compact, Carpenter argued that the federal government was under no obligation to build any of the works mentioned in the compact until and unless Congress authorized such construction in separate legislation. Additionally, the temporary nature of the compact was perfectly justified, especially since the amount of water in Colorado's Closed Basin (the San Luis Valley) was yet unquantified. Until that basin was set up for draining by pumps, no one would know for certain how much water would be added to the Rio Grande for the benefit of downstream diverters. "Prudence and good policy," Carpenter stated, "indicate the wisdom of temporarily suspending permanent 'settlement of the Rio Grande water question' for a few years" until the amount of water available for permanent apportionment could be accurately determined. As written, the Rio Grande Compact would bring order out of confusion, "cooperation out of turbulent and discordant conditions," and would establish "a working basis which [would] lead to permanent settlement. It is satisfactory to the three states which have been on the verge of litigation for many years."[40] So, why, Carpenter wondered, was it unacceptable to the federal government?

Congress finally approved the temporary compact,[41] but ten years passed before the three states signed a permanent compact. During that time, Carpenter's physical condition kept him from attending meetings. He vowed to "sit on the sidelines, advise with the associate commissioner, draft compacts, phrase articles, and, above all, refuse to sign an unsatisfactory compact."[42] But for all intents and purposes, his active participation ended in 1934 when he was restricted to his home and his bed for extended periods.

Many friends lamented his absence at RGCC meetings. They missed Carpenter's knowledge of constitutional law, his unequivocal endorsement of states' rights, and his exemplary leadership. Carpenter had set the stage, and he knew the importance of preserving small victories in an atmosphere of comity and good will. When time came for Colorado to sign the permanent compact, Colorado Governor Ralph Carr gave him credit for establishing the "armistice" between the states in 1929 that led to the final agreement.[43] T. H. McGregor, the official Texas representative on the RGCC, summed up the feelings of many in 1934 when he asked the RGCC to thank Carpenter for starting the compact process. "I have been close to, and in, public life practically all of my life," McGregor noted, "and I have never met a man that I thought was more devoted to his duties and to the sense of duty, more loyal to his state, than Delph Carpenter." Carpenter was deeply touched. "Knowing and loving you all," he replied, "I have unbounded confidence in your satisfactory permanent adjustment of Rio Grande problems. My services are at your command."[44] His confidence in the negotiating team was well founded. Following additional conferences and political maneuvering in Washington, Congress approved a very complex, permanent compact in 1939.[45]

Unfortunately, Carpenter's work on the North Platte River did not lead to a compact, but he entered into negotiations with the same determination, optimistic that men of reason could find ways to resolve daunting conflicts of interest on interstate streams. His goal was to achieve a compact before the federal government built more dams on the North Platte River, but he failed to find the right combination of motivated individuals in Nebraska and Wyoming with whom to exercise his negotiation skills. Ironically, that very failure led him to recommend to East Slope Coloradans that they dig a tunnel to the "Last Water Hole in the West": the Colorado River.[46] What came to be known as the Colorado–Big Thompson Project, authorized in 1937, was Carpenter's idea. It was the direct result of his inability to get agreement on a tristate compact for the North Platte River. In the eyes of many, it has proved to be one of the most successful transmountain diversion projects in the world.

The failure of compact negotiations on the North Platte River stemmed from a variety of unique circumstances. Carpenter's keen interest in that river was attributable to the federal government's construction of Pathfinder Reservoir. When the Department of Justice decided to sue the states of Wyoming and Nebraska for adjudication of water rights on the North Platte, Carpenter visited Wyoming Governor William B. Ross to suggest formation of an interstate compact commission to avoid litigation. The governor was enthusiastic. He appointed Seldon G. Hopkins of Cheyenne to represent Wyoming. Colorado Governor William E. Sweet named Carpenter and Nebraska Governor Charles Wayland Brown designated Robert H. Willis, Carpenter's friend from South Platte Compact negotiations, to fill out the tristate commission. Carpenter was delighted to be working again with Willis. "I anticipate many pleasant hours on the North Platte problem," he said. "If I should at any time leave the impression that I am irritable, impatient, or otherwise out of kilter, when talking over some of our problems, just remember that I am a poor, crippled-up old man and that it is not intended to be personal."[47] He was forty-seven.

Interior Secretary Hubert Work was equally eager to avoid litigation. He conferred with Carpenter in Washington and endorsed the Coloradan's goal of helping Wyoming and Nebraska bring about an adjustment of their differences. He also suggested to President Coolidge that another of Carpenter's friends, Stephen B. Davis of New Mexico, represent the United States. Davis was then serving as solicitor general for the Department of Commerce. He had proven himself in CRCC negotiations and was most acceptable to Carpenter as a representative of the federal government.

The first meeting of the North Platte River Commission (NPRC) took place in Washington on March 20, 1924. It was followed by six public hearings in the small towns along the North Platte River in Nebraska, Wyoming, and Colorado, a strategy reminiscent of CRCC discussions. Carpenter could soon see that a gap existed between the skeptical conservatism of Nebraska farmers, who demanded defense of their priority rights, and the confidence of Willis that upstream irrigation in Wyoming and Colorado would actually stabilize the river on which these farmers depended. It was also apparent to Carpenter that since the resignation of Reclamation director A. P. Davis in 1924, the Bureau of Reclamation seemed to have adopted a more open policy of hostility toward interstate river compacts. Davis's departure was viewed by many as a loss for the West. He was an "honest, upright man of great ability," Carpenter noted, and even though he had been Davis's "avowed enemy for years," he came to appreciate the man's "merit and ability." Director Davis "built up the Service from its beginning and [was] the best informed of its problems of any man in America." Unfortunately, Carpenter lamented, his replacement, Elwood Mead, allowed his employees to place obstacles in the way of duly authorized interstate compact commissioners.[48] Reclamation employees were told, Carpenter complained, that "they are expected to aid in consummating a compact, but evidently, under the advice of the Legal Department, [they] have been given to understand that the Bureau of Reclamation does not want a compact and that without a compact, the United States will always administer the river, thereby furnishing jobs in perpetuity."[49]

For Carpenter, whose suspicion of the federal government had reached conspiratorial proportions, the Bureau's actions under Mead were in violation of the 1902 Newlands Act. That act, he believed, guaranteed the Reclamation Service would not usurp and override the powers and jurisdiction of the states. Another danger Carpenter saw was that compact-making looked far too easy to inexperienced engineers, businessmen, and demagogues. A bad compact would bring years of costly litigation to the states involved. In the absence of strong state leadership, federal bureaus were "prone to assume authority to conclude such compacts and congressmen and senators [got] the idea that they should do the formulating." The bureaucrats, Carpenter pointed out, were inherently incapable of dealing with such matters fairly and without being influenced by "federalistic and preconceived notions and theories. The task is one for free men," he contended, "and not for those bound by higher authority or those imbued with fear, servility or bigotry."[50]

No matter how frequently and vociferously Carpenter complained, Reclamation officials continued to argue that rights to unappropriated western water were acquired from France, Spain, Mexico, and the Republic of Texas.* Within this legal framework, they claimed, proprietary rights to water passed to the United States and not to the states.[51] Additionally, Carpenter noted, the government manifested a condescending attitude from the "so-called conservationist types . . . who [felt] called . . . to protect the West from itself. . . . We are tired of having said to us," Carpenter stated in the first meeting of the NPRC, "'leave it to the government and it will be all right.' Every time we have left anything to the government, we have been left behind."[52]

The breakdown in compact negotiations between Colorado, Wyoming, and Nebraska was as attributable to parochialism and greed as it was to the Bureau's desire to build an empire out of the West's rivers. Unquestion-

---

* When the federal government argued that it owned all the land and water in the West by virtue of the nation's legal acquisition from prior sovereigns, it was denying the efficacy of the Constitution, as well as the legitimacy of laws of the nineteenth century identified in the Introduction to this book. So the claim had a legal-historical basis, but it was made moot by the nature of a developing federal republic.

ably, the Bureau hoped to establish a strong priority right on the North Platte by increasing power production at Guernsey Dam.[53] However, Nebraska's blind fear of irrigation development in Wyoming and Colorado, exacerbated by Wyoming's desire for a government-financed Casper-Alcova project, weakened the probability of successful tristate compact negotiations. Colorado could do little to pacify the Nebraskans, but Carpenter thought he had a chance for a quid pro quo with Wyoming: Colorado support in Congress for Casper- Alcova in return for a bilateral agreement that would guarantee Colorado's right to a certain quantity of North Platte River water.

By 1927, heads of two of the leading irrigation projects in Nebraska were threatening opposition to a Colorado-Wyoming compact. They were dead set against any agreement that would drain off part of the North Platte River into Colorado. Consequently, Wyoming became tentative in its dealings with Colorado. Once again, Carpenter explained, there was ample water in the river for the needs of each state. Nebraska's claims of interstate priority were unnecessary and counterproductive. He also told Wyoming commissioner John A. Whiting that Colorado could not support the Casper-Alcova project in Congress unless and until an acceptable compact was signed between their two states. Compact first, then construction! This principle of interstate stream negotiations, to which he had adhered throughout discussions on other rivers, was the sine qua non of Carpenter's compact philosophy. Once works were built on the North Platte, he feared "the rights which would be acquired by the Casper-Alcova project would be perpetual in their nature and would not depend upon, and could not be limited by, assurances between state officials."[54] Without first achieving agreement on an appropriation formula, the existence of appropriative water rights based on priority had the potential to create significant legal problems throughout the West.

For this reason, Carpenter continued to encourage a tristate agreement over the course of the next five years, but he felt increasingly out of touch with the negotiations. His illness restricted travel. Political maneuvering in Washington by Wyoming and Nebraska officials, depression woes, and drought in the West combined to undermine any spirit of comity between the states. He drew up several compact drafts for Wyoming and Nebraska, but by the spring of 1932, it was apparent that he was making little headway. He wrote Commissioner Whiting: "I have been a bleacher witness at long distance to the interchange of pleasantries at Washington among representatives of the three States and am moved to suggest that the only true way of arriving at a settlement . . . is not by many voices but by the efforts of the Commissioners in executive sessions until a draft of compact has been agreed to."[55] He still believed in his ability to hammer out a one-on-one agreement with commissioners Whiting and Willis, but he was not overly sanguine regarding their ability to convince their constituencies in Nebraska and Wyoming that river sharing would ultimately benefit each of the three states far more than a litigated settlement based on prior appropriation claims.

Carpenter had learned from experience that no state should be coerced during the compact process. To him had fallen the responsibility of drawing up the compact drafts, but he did not blame Whiting and Willis for the lack of progress. Over the eight years since the first NPRC meeting, commissioners had changed, state governments had been reconstituted, new data had been introduced on river flow, and the nation's economy had suffered a near-mortal blow. Although the delays were frustrating, Carpenter was still willing to give Wyoming and Nebraska the time they needed to work out an agreement they could take back to Cheyenne and Lincoln with reasonable assurance of approval.

Colorado Congressman Ed Taylor was annoyed with Carpenter for what seemed endless delays. He felt he had been made the congressional goat as a result of his consistent opposition to Casper-Alcova during committee discussions. When Carpenter finally recognized that Wyoming Senator John B. Kendrick had forsaken the compact approach altogether and was doing everything possible to persuade Congress to authorize construction of the Casper-Alcova dam, Carpenter, too, lost his patience. He urged Taylor to oppose the "adverse legislation" until Colorado was protected by a compact.[56]

At the same time, Carpenter prepared a separate bill for Congress, calling for a tunnel from the North Platte River into the Cache la Poudre Valley. This plan, he explained to Senator Edward P. Costigan, was for the purpose of providing *supplemental* water to farmers using "existing completed canals . . . and not for reclamation of new lands as is proposed by the Casper-Alcova Project in Wyoming. The Colorado project is much less expensive than is the Wyoming project and will be supported financially by the exceptionally fertile cultivated lands of the Cache la Poudre Valley . . . a region of greatest economy in use of water with unusual productivity."[57]

Wyoming's response to this bill was to boycott Colorado products. In principle, transmountain diversion was acceptable to Wyoming, but Colorado was asking for one-fifth of the water in the North Platte, all of which would be permanently removed from the basin.[58] Wyoming would agree to only 30,000 acre-feet (about one-third what Colorado wanted). The Kendrick bill seemed to be moving through Congress, and Wyoming's interest in negotiating a compact declined proportionately.

Carpenter was upset with this turn of events. Colorado was out of money to continue negotiations and newly elected Governor Edwin C. Johnson was opposed to replenishing the depleted Water Defense Fund because of the state's financial problems. Backed against a wall, Carpenter resorted to the very arguments he had opposed during previous compact negotiations on interstate streams. The only recourse remaining to the state, he telegraphed Senator Costigan, was to insist that Wyoming recognize "the prior, preferred and exclusive use in perpetuity of the waters of the North Platte in Colorado." Such claims were necessary "to protect against senior claims of appropriation of [the] entire river by Casper-Alcova and [the] huge Seminoe Reservoir."[59] Costigan would have to oppose the Kendrick bill in Washington until some form of interstate settlement could be successfully concluded.

The policy was a retreat to the very principles he had abandoned at the beginning of negotiations on the Colorado River. It was diametrically opposed to what he believed was best for the future of the western states, but he had simply run out of options. He was tired, frustrated by the unreasonableness of myopic officials and, cornered, he decided to fight for North Platte River water with the same weapons used by his opponents. In resorting to the old methods of conflict resolution, he revealed his vulnerability, his humanness, and his exhaustion. It was not a pretty way to end his career, but achieving a North Platte River compact when the nation was trying to climb out of a deep economic depression was not a viable course to pursue. As Carpenter gradually retreated from active negotiations, state engineer M. C. Hinderlider assumed leadership of North Platte affairs. He continued to consult Carpenter, agreeing with him that the three states had reached an impasse. The only remedy Carpenter could suggest was to

amend the Kendrick bill to make construction of Casper-Alcova dependent on the unconditional acceptance of a compact by Congress and the
signatory states.[60]

But a new mood in Washington arrived with the election of Franklin D.
Roosevelt. The president's top priority was to get the country back to work.
In July 1933, Interior secretary Harold Ickes announced that Casper-
Alcova construction had been approved as a Public Works Administration (PWA) project. No water had been reserved for either Colorado or
Nebraska, he noted, because the government had no interest in providing
solutions to interstate water problems.[61] Governor Johnson was appalled.
He asked the president to intervene, and Roosevelt directed the PWA to
reconsider its decision. But Ickes was so intent on initiating public works
projects, especially those which promised hydroelectric power, that he
directed Casper-Alcova to proceed as planned.

Hoping to accomplish some form of agreement before construction
began, Hinderlider resumed talks with Wyoming. He asked for a guaranteed appropriation for Colorado from the North Platte River. By December 1933, however, the New Deal's incredible momentum, combined with
the resistance of local groups to out-of-basin diversion, effectively terminated North Platte discussions. Wyoming reveled in the assurance of
Casper-Alcova, but northern Colorado would have to take Carpenter's
advice and look to the Colorado River for supplemental water.[62]

Carpenter never dwelled on the North Platte situation as a defeat. He
knew that success in interstate treaty negotiations depended on commitment from all parties, consistent political and financial support by the
states, cooperation from the federal government, patience without coercion, and stability in regional and national affairs. The intervention of
drought, national elections, economic depression, or crises over which
commissioners had no control could result in failed negotiations. Compact making was tricky business, but he never questioned the efficacy of
interstate river agreements; the only alternatives to compacts were federal
administration or litigation. A compact offered a far greater possibility for
stability on interstate rivers than either alternative imposed by disinter-
ested bureaucrats unfamiliar with local issues.

These convictions were part of his thinking when he volunteered to
draw up the first draft compact for the upper basin states of the Colorado
River. The Boulder Canyon Project Act of 1928 stipulated that the seven

states should consider supplemental compacts with each other in conformity with the Colorado River Compact. Subsidiary agreements, Carpenter observed, would aid in the comprehensive development of the Colorado River, "providing for the storage, diversion and use of the waters of said river."[63] Although a final agreement was not signed until 1948,[64] Carpenter launched the process that led to the Upper Colorado River Basin Compact. Without this agreement to share the 7.5 million acre-feet of water allocated under the Colorado River Compact, Congress would have been unwilling to provide funding for the 1956 Colorado River Storage Project.[65]

On July 15, 1929, Carpenter wrote letters to Commissioner Whiting of Wyoming and Commissioner Wilson of New Mexico suggesting that work begin on an upper basin compact. Both letters stressed the importance of not having a big preliminary conference with speeches containing "loud and extravagant claims by the champions of each state." Far better, Carpenter said, would be a meeting of the four commissioners, who, with a representative of the United States appointed by the president, would outline a course of action including public hearings. This would be followed by executive sessions dealing with a draft compact. "I am conceited enough to believe," Carpenter commented to both men in a postscript, "that I can prepare a compact which will be acceptable to everybody concerned, without the formality of a meeting."[66]

What he had in mind was a short, simple agreement recognizing the limitations on the upper Colorado River imposed by nature. In Article I of an August 1929 draft, Carpenter wrote, "Topography and natural conditions will permit each State to use the waters available within its borders without limitation and without claim of appropriation as against any other State."[67] Division of water on the basis of acreage, or allocation of a specific quantity, he noted, would encourage states to make exaggerated claims. If such claims were to be pared down in negotiation, bitterness would result. What he hoped for in this, as in other interstate agreements, was a feeling of comity, arising from agreement on a basic document that allowed each state to develop without "artificial limitations [and] without undue injury to others."[68]

This was the same argument he used in Colorado River Compact negotiations. In 1922 it had infuriated commissioners from Arizona and California who felt they were being asked to limit their own needs while Colorado demanded the privilege of unfettered development over an

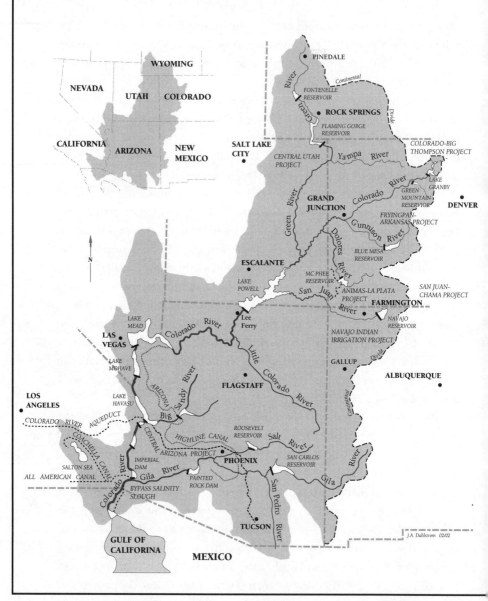

Colorado River Basin, showing 1956 Colorado River Storage Project. (U.S. Bureau of Reclamation, *Reclamation Project Data*, 1961)

undetermined period of time. But Carpenter's motives involved more than the defense of water originating in Colorado. He was an expert on charters, constitutions, and treaties. He believed that a locally formatted agreement, couched in general terms, would allow problems to be solved by local entities having the most to gain or lose. "I am convinced," he wrote Utah Governor George Dern, "that [the four-state compact] must be extremely simple and direct in its terms and if we attempt to make it complicated, or to go into detail, we are lost."[69]

By the first meeting of the Upper Colorado River Commission (UCRC) in Denver on December 3, 1929, Carpenter had recognized that an upper Colorado River compact based on unlimited use of water by each of the four states would be a difficult challenge.[70] Downstream states would always feel unprotected unless some restrictions were placed on upstream diversions. Nevertheless, he held to the principle that most potential problems among the four states had already been resolved by "topography, natural conditions and controls, geographic location of the states and the Colorado River Compact."[71]

The greatest potential for future problems, beyond the control of nature, was transmountain diversion. By 1930, both Colorado and Utah were engaged in out-of-basin transfers. Without having specific plans to review, the UCRC was troubled that such diversions might cause "deficiencies" under the Colorado River Compact, requiring that *all* (author's emphasis) upper basin states give up water to fulfill obligations to the lower basin.[72] Additionally, while UCRC agenda and information presented for discussion were well managed by federal representative William J. Donovan, river data introduced by the states proved unacceptable to Utah, which asked for delays in order to permit federal officials time to gather additional information at government expense.[73] By the spring of 1931, UCRC negotiations had reached a stalemate. Utah was waiting for its data; Donovan was distracted by attempts to get a supplemental agreement from the lower basin states;[74] and all seven Colorado River states anxiously awaited a Supreme Court ruling on Arizona's 1930 suit against California and the United States.

This suit, introduced on October 6, 1930, was the first of four attempts by Arizona to have the Colorado River Compact and the Boulder Canyon Project Act nullified, or, failing this, to have the High Court stipulate Arizona's rightful share of the 8.5 million acre-feet awarded to the lower basin states. In the words of Stanford Professor Charles Meyer, Arizona "sued the Secretary of the Interior and all six of the other Colorado River Basin states to enjoin the building of Hoover Dam and the All-American Canal, to stop the formation and performance of contracts for delivery of water from the projected reservoir, and to declare the Colorado River Compact and the Project Act unconstitutional."[75] Arizona claimed that these official acts would deprive the state of its sovereign jurisdiction over water, that favoritism to the Imperial and Coachella valleys in California discriminated against Arizona, and that its right to store and sell water, or to tax power-generating facilities, was unjustly and unconstitutionally denied.[76]

The defendant states filed a motion to dismiss. They argued that the Supreme Court lacked jurisdiction, that there was no controversy and therefore no basis for a lawsuit.[77] But they also recognized the potential for significant damage to Colorado River development plans if the Supreme Court found in favor of Arizona. If evidence and briefs needed to be filed, Carpenter was the upper basin's attorney of choice. But the Coloradan declined to participate. In addition to his work on the upper basin compact, Carpenter was still working on compacts for the Rio Grande, the Arkansas, the Little Snake, the North Platte, and other rivers. These responsibilities, however, did not prevent him from formulating a theoretical defense. In a speech prepared for a conference of attorneys general and interstate river commissioners, Carpenter urged defendant states to maintain unity.[78] Given each state's unique motive for agreeing to the compact and dam construction, and the fact that California's riparian and prior appropriation doctrines differed from the strict priority doctrine in other states, a potential existed for disagreement on how the suit should be answered. If disunity prevailed, there might be a tendency among the six states to let federal government bureaucrats establish the basis on which the states defended themselves.

Such a result, Carpenter believed, "would be extremely hazardous and might prove suicidal."[79] The government would probably develop the same line of reasoning used in *Kansas v. Colorado* and *Wyoming v. Colorado*. It would argue that the United States owned and had the right to dispose of unappropriated waters in western streams, without regard to the will or consent of the states. What Congress had already approved in the form of flood control and other works on the Colorado River was totally consistent with this principle. It was clear, Carpenter reasoned, "[t]he States cannot afford to sacrifice a great underlying and fundamental principle of government necessary to the very existence of statehood." States' rights!

A good defense, therefore, would also make the following points: international peace depended on adherence to the compact and the Colorado River Project Act; the federal government was charged by the Constitution with the improvement of navigation through flood control; the planned reservoir and hydroelectric plants would have to be located on territory belonging to the United States; reclamation of lands in the Imperial Valley came under the dictates of the Newlands Act; and the Colorado River Compact eliminated the probability of chaotic development in the Colorado River basin.

As to the litigants, Carpenter had always been far more sympathetic to Arizona than to California. During attempted arbitration of a supplemental compact for the three lower basin states, his hostility to California had increased. But his total commitment to the Colorado River Compact as a model for future interstate treaties appealed more to the constitutional lawyer in him than to the long-standing emotional connection he had with Arizona. He was delighted when the Supreme Court announced on May 18, 1931, that it was dismissing the suit. The Court decided that the Boulder Canyon Project Act was a legitimate exercise of congressional power under the commerce clause of the Constitution. Arizona would be able to bring suit again at a later date if operation of Hoover Dam interfered with its rights, but for the moment, the Court had no evidence indicating that such was the case.[80]

Carpenter suspected Arizona would eventually find some way to obtain justice. The state's officials were angry and itching for a fight. "The feeling of oppression and hostility," Carpenter wrote Secretary of the Interior Ray Lyman Wilbur, "has been growing with the years and the recent decision fanned the flame."[81] He warned Colorado to be prepared, but he had no idea Arizona might resort to physical force to keep California from building its aqueduct to the Metropolitan Water District.[82] He was just hoping the Court's decision had cleared the way to consummate a compact for the upper basin states.[83]

Unfortunately, momentum had been lost to a variety of factors over which he had no control. He continued to urge patience and the gathering of acceptable data. He warned against the negative consequences attached to premature meetings and inadequate information. He urged

Commissioner Wilson to have him appointed a committee of one to draft a compact so that his work would not be viewed as pure volunteerism.[84] And even when he was restricted to his home in Greeley in later years, Carpenter expressed a desire to continue this work to fruition.[85]

Meanwhile, he carried on negotiations with Wyoming on the North Platte and Little Snake, with New Mexico on the San Juan, and with Kansas on the Arkansas. This was his duty, his job, and his passion. But these responsibilities ended officially, and not unexpectedly, when newly elected Democratic Governor Johnson eliminated the office of interstate streams commissioner in January 1933.

Carpenter saw it coming. The Roosevelt landslide was not kind to Republicans in official roles. Although Johnson did not consider himself a New Deal Democrat, Carpenter had been closely associated with Hoover, and Hoover was seen as the cause of the nation's economic debacle. Carpenter offered to reduce his annual salary. He wanted to keep his job and was proud that his appointment as interstate streams commissioner had never been subject to the whims of politics. "It has required constant vigilance so to do," he wrote his friend Albert Moses, "but the results attained proved the wisdom of the policy."[86]

He was also aware that rumors of his failing health worked against him. Shortly after the election, he admitted his limitations to an attorney friend in San Francisco. "I am confined to my house with my pet neuritis, cannot write and talk in a whisper except when swearing. I still dictate river compacts to Mrs. C. and she stands for dictation which is more than you can say for your wife."[87] Nevertheless, he believed that he alone had the necessary experience to protect Colorado and the West in compact negotiations. He wanted to continue as interstate streams commissioner.

Others agreed. They appealed to Johnson to rethink his decision. Moses, a Democrat, wrote the new attorney general, Paul Prosser. " [I]t would be a very serious mistake," he said, "to allow the fact of Senator Carpenter being a [R]epublican to mitigate at all against continuing him in this position as Interstate Water Commissioner for Colorado. I am convinced that no man possesses the knowledge of the situation that he does, nor is more capable, notwithstanding his physical disability, of rendering valuable assistance to the state."[88]

But Prosser was new to Colorado and ignorant of the history of interstate streams controversies. He told Johnson that "there ought to be some end" to the interminable negotiations and warned that so long as they continued, the Water Defense Fund would require hard-to-find appropriations.[89] Johnson was looking for ways to reduce expenses. On January 24, 1933, he assigned to state engineer Hinderlider the duties of commissioner to represent Colorado in interstate compact negotiations. Carpenter was out of a job and without a pension.

Bannister spoke to Johnson to see what he could do. He asked the governor to consider some form of retainer in return for Carpenter's services as consultant to the state. He received no encouragement. "The economy axe is falling on everything," he told Carpenter.[90] Ralph Carr was equally discouraged. "It would seem that your work on behalf of the people should be repaid in a different fashion," he told his friend. "There are only a few who know and understand the efforts you have made and the good you have brought to Colorado and the rest of the irrigated West."[91] Ditch company spokesmen, the Colorado State Water Users Protective Association, acquaintances of Carpenter, and the state engineer spoke out against Johnson's decision, but the governor's mind was made up.

For Carpenter, the dismissal was undeniably hurtful, but he attributed Johnson's decision to the governor's inability to comprehend how interstate river compacts were connected to security and economic growth in western states. "The fact that I am 'abolished' from serving as commissioner," he commented to Senator Edward P. Costigan, "does not prevent expression of opinion regarding matters now pending before Congress, and I trust that you will permit me to be of service whenever you desire. My interest in the welfare of our state is uneffected [sic] and my services are at your command."[92] Given the fact he had been an outspoken supporter of Hoover, he would take his "suspension" in stride. "This need not cause us to lose our interest in interstate river matters," he wrote Bannister, "nor [should it] diminish our zeal in protecting the most vital interests of our beloved state."[93]

It was a matter of pride to Carpenter, but it also involved his sense of duty. Although he deeply believed his work had "saved an empire for Colorado [and that] in so doing he [had] sacrificed his health and fortune," Carpenter was not vindictive.[94] He would continue in interstate water matters for as long as he and Dot could respond productively to the many questions they received about local, regional, and national water matters.

CHAPTER 8

Vindication

Dear Mr. Hoover: The Supreme Court has approved without dissent the compact method of equitably apportioning the waters of interstate rivers, in the recent case of Hinderlider v. La Plata River [and Cherry Creek Ditch Co.], *involving the La Plata River Compact between Colorado and New Mexico.* We were right *(author's emphasis).*

—CARPENTER TO HOOVER, MAY 5, 1938

In the spring of 1934, eighty men gathered under the leadership of Charles Hansen, publisher and editor of the *Greeley Tribune*, to endorse the Grand Lake Project. This enterprise, renamed the Colorado–Big Thompson Project, proposed delivery of water from the Colorado River to supplement existing sources used for agriculture along the South Platte River and its tributaries. Construction would include a thirteen-mile tunnel under the Continental Divide in Rocky Mountain National Park and a reservoir collection system located in the park at the source of the Colorado River. As part of the meeting, state engineer M. C. Hinderlider offered a resolution of appreciation to Delph E. Carpenter, "who worked for years to preserve Colorado rights in interstate streams so that the Grand Lake Project and similar plans [would be] possible of carrying out."[1] The Grand Lake Committee passed the resolution unanimously and then began four years of negotiations with representatives of Colorado's West Slope to work out the details of a very complex transmountain diversion project.

Carpenter later recalled that a Grand Lake Project had been considered "very feasible and meritorious" during Colorado River Compact discussions in 1922. Article II (b) and (f) and Article III of the compact anticipated exportation of water from the natural basin of the Colorado River to Colorado's East Slope, but the Grand Lake Project was not debated openly by the commissioners for fear of delaying compact ratification by California and Arizona.[2] More importantly, construction of a tunnel under the Continental Divide by any entity other than the Bureau of Reclamation could not begin unless special legislation was passed by Congress, providing Colorado with a proper right-of-way through federal lands.

As of 1927, Colorado had not yet ceded exclusive jurisdiction of Rocky Mountain National Park land to the United States. Carpenter believed the loss of such a large amount of land in a major watershed to the federal government might impede the state's future development. In a letter to Colorado Senator Lawrence E. Phipps, he listed four options Colorado lawmakers might consider. First, the state could refuse to cede the park and encourage Congress to abandon it altogether. Second, Colorado could insist that the act of cession be conditioned upon the state's right "to construct tunnels, canals and other works as may be necessary." Third, a paragraph in the act of cession could request Congress to provide for a right-of-way. Fourth, the state could cede the area unconditionally to the United States, "allowing ourselves and future generations to be at the mercy of Congress."[3]

The park had been created by Congress in 1915 with a promise from the Colorado delegation in Washington that the state would eventually cede police power over the land to the United States. Although a retraction of that promise might be justified, Carpenter reasoned, "[i]t would be a thousand times better to abandon the Park altogether than to lose the right to build this tunnel and such other tunnels, reservoirs and irrigation works as future necessities may dictate." The 1915 congressional statute authorized the Reclamation Service to "enter upon and utilize for flowage or other purposes any area within said Park which may be necessary for the development and maintenance of a Government reclamation project."[4] But the reclamation plans of state and private parties were unprotected in the original act.

Carpenter favored the second option he had suggested in his letter to Phipps. It would require a clause in Colorado's act of cession, stipulating that the state and its water users "should always have the right to build such tunnels, canals and other works, over and across the lands within the Park as may be necessary for domestic and irrigation purposes." If the state had to go to Congress every time it wanted to build a ditch, canal, or reservoir, he told Phipps, it would lose certain rights generally agreed upon by all parties when the park was first created. An appropriate clause in the state's act of cession, therefore, was the "only safe procedure." It would not violate the understanding between Colorado and the United States, and it would guarantee the state's "free and uninterrupted development of its water resources in that region."[5] The only question remaining was whether Congress would accept such a clause. The answer to that question, Carpenter speculated, would be determined by the behavior of the Department of Interior.

In reality, however, it was the Colorado legislature that determined whether Carpenter's recommendation would be approved. When the state assembly finally passed the act of cession in 1929, Carpenter's suggested clause was omitted. No right-of-way was included for a new water project and only "vested, appropriated and existing water rights and rights-of-way connected therewith" were protected.[6] Carpenter blamed "skillful lobbying by transportation interests,"[7] but he also recognized the Park Service's vigorous opposition to any construction that would change the "natural conditions" within the park. "It is their idea and purpose to preserve nature in the raw," he stated "and they are prone to view those who construct works to supply fields and cities as trespassers and even as vandals, because such construction violates the ideals of the National Park administration."[8] It followed, therefore, that when Weld County engineer L. L. Stimson tried to run the first survey line for the Grand Lake Project tunnel, officials at Rocky Mountain National Park did not allow him on the ceded land. He had to accomplish his work through triangulation, using peaks located outside the park as his points of reference. Not until Congress formally contracted the Grand Lake Project in 1938 were engineers representing the Bureau of Reclamation allowed inside the park.

Carpenter had assumed that Colorado would control the Grand Lake Project and that either state or private capital would provide funding. He concluded, albeit erroneously, that the federal government would not allow Coloradans the right to develop water for beneficial use in and around the park. He foresaw the state being forced to abandon its sovereign right to unappropriated waters within its boundaries.[9] As noted in previous chapters, state sovereignty was Carpenter's cause célèbre. It was an obsession, resulting from a lifetime of study on how best to preserve the health of the American federal system. Although his constitutional logic was, for the most part, impeccable, the efficacy and power of his state sovereignty argument was diminished by the federal government's growth during and after World War I. The industrialization and electrification of America, along with the growing social and economic interdependence of distinct regions, demanded partnerships and more creative solutions to interstate water problems. Writing in the *Yale Law Journal* in 1925, Justice Felix Frankfurter expressed his own concerns about overly simplistic labeling when he cautioned against the use of rigid categories to define state and federal interaction in the United States. "[T]he false antithesis embodied in the shibboleths: 'States-Rights' and 'National Supremacy,'" he wrote, were inappropriate in a nation that had been so dramatically changed by war and industrialization.[10]

But Carpenter had trouble understanding how federal and state interests had merged. He failed to consider fully the new direction of American federalism since the end of World War I and the onset of the Great Depression. The election of Franklin D. Roosevelt, he told Hoover in the fall of 1933, left him confused. The "orgy of spending" was reprehensible. It doomed future generations to "unbearable collars of servitude." He disdained the multiplication of political jobs and the "wholesale exchange of patronage for legislative 'cooperation'" as a sign of "moral disintegration."[11] The "chaos" he witnessed included the lamentable proliferation of federal agencies whose power, he believed, would "eventually . . . usurp and encroach upon the rights and jurisdiction of the states."[12] Unhappy with Democrats in government, he fervently hoped that the records of the Colorado River Compact negotiations would not fall into the "vandal hands" of the New Deal.[13]

Carpenter believed that the election of Roosevelt was a monumental mistake. If the nation had to be ill with an economic depression, he wrote Hoover, it would be better to have it run its natural course than to create programs and policies that obscured the real causes.[14] As his way of ignoring the New Deal, Carpenter decided to focus his attention on Hoover's

1929 suggestion that surface water rights on public lands be ceded to the states, and if the public lands could be ceded to the states, so much the better.

Hoover's plan resonated well with Carpenter's strong bias against the growth of federal power, but Hoover was primarily focused on conserving the health of the nation's grazing lands. Dust Bowl conditions in the West had resulted from drought and overgrazing in the 1920s. Hoover felt the states would know how to preserve their natural resources, but he also believed in cooperative relations between states and the federal government to achieve best results. In a speech written for delivery at the Western Governors' Conference in 1929, he expressed enthusiasm for plans that would "retard the expansion of the federal bureaucracy" so that communities would be in control of their own destinies. He recommended that "the surface rights of the remaining, unappropriated, unreserved public lands should, subject to certain details for protection of homesteaders and the smaller stockmen, be transferred to the State Governments for public school purposes and thus be placed under state administration." He opposed transfer of any "forest, park, Indian and other existing reservations" to the states because of their national and local importance, and he urged modification of the existing reclamation policy so that "states would have the entire management of all new reclamation projects and would themselves deal with the irrigation land questions and land settlements."[15]

Carpenter endorsed Hoover's proposition, viewed it as a watershed event, and provided his own interpretation of what it meant. In a statement published in the *Weld County News*, he described the plan as one "of the utmost importance to the entire West and . . . the most forward step for preservation of state autonomy since the admission of the western states into the Union." If accepted by the states, Carpenter remarked, there would be an end to federal agencies meddling with the inherent rights of the states in their waters and the control and use and disposition thereof except for purposes of navigation which the states granted to the federal government by the Constitution. It would mean an "end to the scheme of national control of waters of all the western states."[16] Carpenter hoped it would also mean the end of a government policy that replaced local control of western waters with administrative and legal control by federal courts and Washington bureaus. Additionally, Carpenter noted, there was a "deeper reason" for the states to acquire title to public lands within their boundaries. *"Fee simple"* acquisition of federal lands, he told a fellow Coloradan, would "give the western states the same *dominion* over their territory as that possessed by the original thirteen. . . . It is of first importance that we come into our full equality guaranteed by the Constitution and this may best be accomplished by acquiring control of the public lands at the earliest date. I am certain that this was the underlying motive of the President [Hoover] in recommending cession of these lands to the States."[17] Carpenter resented the establishment of forest reserves (national forests) and Indian reservations because they severely eroded the taxing power of western states. Hoover's plan, he argued, was a way to restore balance in the federal system—equal footing—by returning control of natural resources to the states.

The public lands committee recommended by Hoover and appointed by Congress in 1930 deliberated Hoover's ideas for a year. The committee was composed of twenty members who represented eastern and western states equally, secretaries of interior and agriculture (Ray L. Wilbur and Arthur M. Hyde), and James R. Garfield, Theodore Roosevelt's secretary of interior, who served as chairman. Encountering conflicting points of view, the committee discovered that federal agencies not only had great interest in maintaining control of public lands, but each had a different outcome and plan of management. Among the states, some wanted immediate access to public lands, while others were content to leave administration to the government. In its report to the president, the committee could only urge "responsible administration and regulation for the conservation and beneficial use" of the resources of the public domain. Congress was encouraged to pass legislation granting unreserved and unappropriated lands to the public lands states, to consolidate and coordinate executive and administrative bureaus interested in the public domain, to encourage state control, appropriation, and distribution of water and to support settlement of interstate matters by agreement and compact "and not by Federal intervention."[18]

The work of the committee eventually produced results, reflecting some of what Hoover had suggested and some of what Carpenter had been advocating for more than ten years. The response of Congress to overgrazing and competition between stockmen on the open range was the 1934 Taylor Grazing Act. Millions of acres came under federal administration, but the permit system developed by Coloradan Farrington R. Carpenter (no relation) featured the establishment of grazing districts governed by local boards of control. F. R. Carpenter's plan to award permits based on a first-in-time-first-in-right system reflected the cultural influence of the priority doctrine that, until then, had been restricted to intrastate water disputes. The administration of these 179 million acres under the Bureau of Land Management (BLM) represented a combination of Delph Carpenter's insistence on local control of natural resources and the New Deal's determination to centralize power over the national landscape.

Creation of another federal agency to govern the West disappointed Carpenter. His tirades against federal courts and the expansion of federal agencies continued without respite. Ironically, one of his greatest victories came from the Supreme Court he was so prone to criticize for its lack of understanding of the arid West and its domination by easterners, whom he criticized for marginalizing western lands and resources. Carpenter had to watch events playing out in the courts from the sidelines, but the satisfaction he eventually experienced at the outcome was an emotional vindication of what he had been fighting for during his career as Colorado's interstate streams commissioner.

At stake was the La Plata River Compact, signed by New Mexico and Colorado in 1922 and by President Calvin Coolidge in 1925. New Mexico continued to be nervous about Colorado taking too much water from the La Plata River in dry years, but Carpenter had designed the compact so that both states would enjoy maximum beneficial use of the stream flow on a rotational basis. This interstate water-sharing agreement was similar to ancient Hispanic and Indian compromises on streams and *acequias* of the Southwest, where the potential for conflict was always present because of unreliable and wildly variable climatic conditions. But Colorado water users, especially the La Plata and Cherry Creek Ditch Company, continued to believe that their water rights, as recognized by the state of Colorado, were superior to any interstate agreement approved in the 1922 compact. Colorado state engineer M. C. Hinderlider, they argued, had no right to shut down their head gate in order to satisfy Colorado's obligation to New Mexico. Their "vested rights," claimed the ditch company, were a legitimate property right and could not be taken without compensation. An interstate compact, in their view, could not be used to deprive individuals or corporations of a bona fide property right. To do so was to violate due process of law. Claiming that the actions of the state engineer were unconstitutional and void, the ditch company asked for an injunction against Hinderlider's actions.

The case opened in June 1928. A district court ruled against the ditch company, but the Colorado Supreme Court reversed the decision on appeal, calling the compact "a mere compromise of presumably conflicting claims, a trading therein, in which the property of citizens is bordered, without notice or hearing and with no regard to vested rights."[19] The state engineer appealed the case to the U.S. Supreme Court. It was dismissed and returned to the district court, where it was retried and a decree entered in favor of the ditch company. The Colorado Supreme Court affirmed the lower court's ruling, at which time Hinderlider appealed again to the U.S. Supreme Court.

Ralph L. Carr, an unabashed admirer of Carpenter, first argued the case in support of the La Plata Compact in the state courts. Making his home in Antonito, Colorado, Carr was experienced in Hispanic land and water law and was known for his community service, public speaking, and outspoken defense of civil rights. When the Colorado Supreme Court rejected his argument in defense of the La Plata Compact, he wrote Carpenter to apologize, stating that he had done his "darndest to convey [to the court] the reasons why the La Plata Compact should not in any manner be modified."[20] If the decision could not be overturned, Carr believed, "all compacts are useless."[21] Carpenter was surprised by the state court's decision. He commended Justice Charles C. Butler on his dissenting opinion, correctly predicting it would "long outlive the majority opinion and [would be] a great contribution to the orderly settlement of interstate river controversies. The welfare and autonomy of the Western States," Carpenter asserted, "call for rehearing of the case."[22]

In a significant turn of events, the U.S. Supreme Court unanimously overturned the Colorado court decision. The justices agreed the La Plata Compact represented an equitable apportionment of interstate water in conformity with the Court's rulings in *Kansas v. Colorado* and *Wyoming v. Colorado*, and that Colorado and New Mexico as "quasi-sovereign entities [could] adjust and apportion interstate waters."[23] Unless states were unable to agree upon the terms of a compact, or Congress refused its consent, said the High Court, the compact method of conflict resolution was both legal and historical. It "adapts to our Union of sovereign states the age-old treaty-making power of independent nations."[24] Because Colorado's right to water from the La Plata River was equitably determined by the terms of the compact, the apportionment made by the compact "can not have taken from the Ditch Company any vested right."[25]

In terms of western water law and the future of compacts on interstate streams, this was a landmark decision. Attorney, engineer, and water referee George Vranesh has stated the importance of the *Hinderlider* decision in *Colorado Water Law*. "There can be no doubt today," Vranesh wrote, "that the holders of . . . decreed rights have no claim that their rights are superior to [a] compact. Any such hope was put to rest in *Hinderlider v. La Plata River and Cherry Creek Ditch Co.*"[26]

For Carpenter, the High Court's decision of April 5, 1938, was the best news he had received in a long time. "I feel that this is a personal tribute," Hinderlider wrote him, "to your vision and clear understanding of the fundamental right of a state to adjust its differences with a sister state, in the interest of the people as a whole as against the asserted rights of an individual."[27] "This was the "sweet news" Carpenter had wanted to hear.[28] From Ralph Carr, who wrote immediately following his presentation before the Supreme Court, came words of praise: "You should have been here to say it yourself—but since you were not—Jean [Breitenstein] and I have tried to justify your splendid theory and to defend your monumental works."[29] Francis Wilson referred to the decision as "a splendid consummation of [Carpenter's] life's work." Having noted that his name was also on the bronze plaque at Hoover Dam, Wilson went even further, stating that the "great structure and mighty project" on the Colorado River would forever be "a lasting memorial to you and your good work."[30]

Not until February 24, 1944, when Arizona finally ratified the Colorado River Compact, did Carpenter experience total victory. That must be "sweet music to your ears," Meeker wrote him.[31] Since 1937 Carpenter had been trying to persuade Senator Carl Hayden to let him draw up a resolution that would allow Arizona's legislature to ratify the compact with the upper basin states. "Such [a] procedure," he telegraphed the senator, "would result in [an] offensive and defensive alliance between Arizona and [the] upper states."[32] But Arizona ratified unconditionally on its own when it became clear the United States had signed a Colorado River treaty with Mexico three weeks earlier.[33]

As satisfying as this moment in 1944 must have been for Carpenter, his legal and constitutional proclivities were rewarded most by the Supreme

Court's decision in the *Hinderlider* case. He had little control over Arizona politics, but he felt personally responsible for the theories argued in the U. S. Supreme Court regarding the law of interstate water compacts. Small wonder, then, that Carpenter wrote Hoover in 1938 with understated pride to say that—after all the litigation, the criticism and doubts about the compact method of resolving interstate water disputes—in the final analysis, "We were right."[34]

But being right in the eyes of history would require more than one man's sense of personal satisfaction. If Carpenter's compact theory applied to interstate water conflicts precluded costly litigation, as he believed it would, and if the development of western states proceeded with minimal conflict because of the security and confidence gained from interstate compacts, historians would have to conclude that his contribution to the West has been overlooked. Providing a framework for resolution of water disputes in which states were able to preserve their sovereignty, while the Bureau of Reclamation contributed the expertise, funding, and construction of major water distribution projects, would have to be seen as a stroke of genius. But Carpenter was not clairvoyant or omniscient, and after eighty years of living with interstate water compacts, critics have joined Carpenter's strongest boosters in speaking out about the impact of his work on the American West.

CHAPTER 9

Carpenter and the Compact Legacy

We are deeply grieved by the passing of Delph Carpenter, our old friend and associate and the greatest figure in western water law. The Colorado River Compact and the respect and affection of all who knew him are his monuments. Our sympathy to you and the other members of his family.

—TELEGRAM, SIMS AND NORTHCUTT ELY TO
DONALD A. CARPENTER, FEBRUARY 28, 1951

Carpenter died at the Island Grove Park hospital on February 27, 1951, three months short of his seventy-fourth birthday. He was survived by his wife, Dot; son Donald, a Weld County judge; daughters Michaela, Sarah, and Patricia; his two brothers, Fred and Alfred; and seven grandchildren.

Since taking to his bed in 1934, Carpenter had been dependent on his wife to maintain contact with others who continued to be engaged in interstate water compacts. Dot made this possible. She was, in effect, his caregiver for nearly twenty years. After her husband's death, her sense of humor, joie de vivre, and strong religious faith enabled her to continue an active and productive life. She saw no point in crusading to keep alive her husband's public memory, but a continued interest in music, literature, and church activities allowed her to circulate widely in the Greeley community. In 1966 she entered a nursing home. Ten years later, at the age of ninety-eight, she was interviewed by a reporter from the *Greeley Tribune*, who found her as lively and playful as ever. She died on May 19, 1980, at the age of 101.

Although newspaper obituaries covered Carpenter's career in less depth than some might have desired, measurement of his achievements was generally positive, focusing on what interstate water compacts had accomplished for Colorado. The *Denver Post* columnist Roscoe Fleming wrote that Carpenter was "Colorado's most valuable citizen of all time . . . that more than any other person, he saved our water for Colorado's development." Had he been a politician, Fleming mused, or "one of those persons who looted the hills of their treasure and then fled east to spend his winnings," he might have been better known. Instead, he was "an acute and far-seeing pioneer water lawyer who laid down and fought for principles that have enabled us to save at least some of Colorado's water for Colorado."[1] But Fleming and other Colorado writers found it difficult to evaluate the impact of interstate water compacts on western development. It was too early to measure the extent of the victory Carpenter had celebrated fifteen years earlier when the Supreme Court handed down its decision in the *Hinderlider* case. Additionally, writers did not know much about Carpenter's life after he was removed from his job as interstate streams commissioner in 1933. How could they? His illness forced him to remain at home for nearly two decades.

In retrospect, Carpenter's active life was consumed by work. He took too little time to enjoy Crow Creek Ranch and the Shorthorn herd he had built from scratch. By 1929, with the agricultural economy suffering a decade of decline, he had become "tired of the burden," selling most of his cattle and wishing that he could sell the ranch as well.[2] A few years later, Carpenter found himself heavily in debt. He was forced to consider the sale of his two Greeley farms and the rest of the Shorthorn cattle to the Greeley Investment Company.[3] Outstanding loans from the Greeley National Bank and the Federal Land Bank accentuated his indebtedness. He requested delays in making interest payments and reminded creditors that he had taken considerable risks in reclaiming the ranch from unbroken sod. In addition, he noted, he had personally surveyed a fourteen-mile extension ditch that made possible irrigated agriculture in the lower Crow Creek Valley.[4]

But the financial institutions had difficulty being charitable. They were as hard-pressed as the farmers to whom they made loans during many years of better agricultural prices. Like other second-generation residents of Weld County, Carpenter was land rich and cash poor. He had lost his job as interstate streams commissioner and was without a pension. Worse still, son Donald, the best hope for a family income, had been told by the State of Colorado that he was ineligible to take the bar exams. In an ironic twist of fate, Donald's willingness to save his father money by obtaining a law degree at National University in the shortest possible time had backfired. To be eligible for bar exams, the state required three years of liberal arts courses. Donald did not meet this requirement and his father claimed insufficient funds to send Donald back to school.[5] Although he had received an adequate salary of $5,000 annually between 1929 and 1932 from Colorado's Water Defense Fund, Carpenter was broke and broken-hearted.[6] He asked Supreme Court Justice John T. Adams if his son might be "admitted [to the bar] on motion. [I am] in an extreme situation," he told Adams. If Donald could practice in Colorado, he could "undertake [his father's] burden."[7] When the court failed to respond, Carpenter tried to find a position for his son in California, but friends in that state reported jobs were as hard to find there as in Colorado. Eventually, Donald found employment in Colorado.

At this stage of his career, Carpenter should have been enjoying the fruits of his labors. Instead, he felt destitute. He failed to make payments on insurance policies and stopped sending membership dues to the Colorado Bar Association. To old friend Clarence Stetson, he noted in 1928 that both Michaela and Sarah were still unmarried. Both were teachers, he wrote, and both were available. He hoped they would find satisfactory mates and that, in turn, he would acquire at least one rich son-in-law.[8]

The following year, Michaela met Ewell Slade, her husband-to-be, in Flagstaff, where she was teaching. The son of a New York doctor, Slade was raised in Japan, where he worked as assistant to the general manager of an exporting firm. Carpenter worried that the marriage might not be recognized in the United States, but he was pleased when his daughter tied the knot in Yokohama in 1930. Sarah started teaching in Greeley at nineteen years of age "because of my father's condition," she explained.[9] Her pay was only ninety dollars a month, but it helped the family considerably. She married O. B. "Tommy" Thomson a few years later. Martha Patricia married Donald Peterson of Greeley.

Judge Donald Carpenter.

Carpenter survived the years of agricultural depression. Difficult times sharpened his sense of history and reinforced the pioneer work ethic articulated by founders of the Union Colony. He was shocked to learn from the Colorado Department of State that the colony's corporate charter had been declared defunct in 1928 due to a failure to pay taxes or file annual reports since 1924.[10] As secretary-treasurer, with the colony's books at his office, Carpenter took the necessary steps to reinstate the corporation by sending a bill to the state legislature. He was determined to preserve the organization whose leaders he recognized as pioneers in western reclamation. He was also motivated by President Franklin D. Roosevelt's apparent inclination "to turn everything wet" and he hoped his bill, in addition to reinstating the Union Colony as a corporation, would "enforce the liquor clause" in the original certificate of organization.[11]

Onset of the New Deal in 1932 also prompted Carpenter's suggestion to Hoover that certain aspects of Colorado River Compact negotiations needed clarification by the original participants, many of whom were dead or getting very old. He did not want compact history left in the hands of New Deal Democrats, whom he saw as drunk with power and presiding over a sick nation. The American people had sufficient "recuperative powers" to emerge from the chaos, he predicted, but Carpenter wanted the story told by the people who made the history.[12]

Hoover replied positively from his office at Stanford University in Palo Alto, California. "A friend of ours," he informed Carpenter, was "devoting his odd time to writing on the development of the Colorado River." Hoover mentioned to this friend (Stanford Professor Charles A. Dobbel) that Carpenter had played an important role in completing the compact. Would Carpenter be interested, Hoover queried, in composing an essay on the origins of the Colorado River Compact Commission, the meetings of 1921 and 1922, and the efforts made by the seven states to secure ratification?[13]

Carpenter's answer was delayed by the emotional turmoil he experienced following his removal as interstate streams commissioner. He thanked Hoover for the invitation and promised a "sketch" of the compact's origins if he could be given a little more preparation time.[14] Hoover agreed to the request and Carpenter began dictating his recollections. The resulting sketch, which in Charles Dobbel's hands became a foreword to part two of his book on Colorado River development, was delivered to Hoover in 1934. Two years later Carpenter inquired if the book had been published. "Regrettably," Hoover responded, "Professor Dobbel failed to find a publisher."[15]

In fact, Dobbel's complete manuscript had been submitted to McGraw Hill with the title "A History of the Hoover Dam." Hoover recommended it to the publishers as "the only reliable book on the subject [that] nails the facts in an engineer's fashion."[16] Unfortunately, McGraw Hill's reader was unimpressed. He panned the manuscript, questioned the accuracy of some statements, and picked apart Carpenter's introduction as little more than "a general criticism of the Bureau of Reclamation's attitude toward state control of water."[17]

This was a shallow and parochial censuring of Carpenter's historical recollections. The sketch is illuminating and accurate for the most part. It does contain Carpenter's bias against federal control over non-navigable western streams, but a wealth of additional information is provided from memory and most of it coincides with other credible sources. To an eastern publishing company, trying to exist economically during the height of the New Deal, Carpenter's criticism of the federal government may have appeared to be heresy. Dobbel's book was never published, but Carpenter's forty-five page introduction in manuscript form is a valuable source for anyone interested in the origins of the Colorado River Compact.[18]

Carpenter also had a disagreement with Reuel Leslie Olson, a Harvard student whose doctoral thesis, self-published as *The Colorado River Compact*,[19] seemed inaccurate to him and in violation of the confidentiality under which minutes of the Colorado River Compact Commission were supposedly protected. Olson was a fourth-year law student in the fall of 1922, taking a class on administrative law at Harvard. He wrote to the Colorado legislature to request information on relevant laws, the authority given commissioners, and steps Colorado planned to take after the compact was signed in Santa Fe. His inquiry was referred to Carpenter.

For the next four years, Carpenter answered Olson's questions patiently and availed himself of the opportunity to teach what he had learned as interstate streams commissioner. He described the evils of litigation and warned Olson that fifteen years might pass before the seven Colorado River states ratified the compact. The "bringing of suits" to force ratification, he lectured Olson, was "commercial and unsatisfactory, if not foolish."[20] Colorado was "not in the business of bringing suits and does not intend to start at this time. . . . [A lawsuit] would take not less than a quarter century to conclude. . . . and no one would be capable of enforcing the [resulting court] decree."[21]

When Olson was about to publish his thesis in 1926, Carpenter's criticism of Olson became virulent. He telegraphed Harvard President Lawrence Lowell, complaining that Olson had included in both text and notes "copious quotations from rough drafts of minutes of [the] Colorado River [Compact] Commission." Carpenter insisted that these minutes were privileged and confidential and were deliberately protected from circulation prior to compact ratification so they would not be used for political purposes. In Carpenter's judgment, the Colorado River Compact Commission had engaged in open and honest discourse of very sensitive political issues, believing their goal of comity among states could only be achieved through total honesty. If the minutes were published prematurely, at a time when the commissioners' careers were still developing, foes might easily exploit comments made in Santa Fe for the purpose of achieving competitive advantage. In Carpenter's view, the real danger was the possibility that future interstate commissioners might be unwilling to enter into the give-and-take debate required to make compromises leading to settlement of complex water conflicts. "Other members of the commission," he admonished Lowell, "join with me in expressing our surprise and shock and in earnestly protesting, both personally and officially, against the publication of the thesis until after the manuscript has first been edited and approved by the commission or Secretary Hoover. We are unable to believe that such an act of transgression will be permitted by Harvard University or that it will directly or indirectly approve conduct by its students which may disturb the peace and involve the welfare of seven states, the nation and international relations."[22]

Carpenter's fit of pique was exacerbated by Olson's California connection and by his matriculation at an elite eastern university, but he was irritated more by the possibility that the first real interpretation of the compact would be published by someone who had not participated in the proceedings. When Harvard's dean of the graduate school of arts and sciences replied that Olson had received permission to publish from acting Secretary of Commerce Stephen B. Davis and the executive secretary of the Federal Power Commission, Oliver C. Merrill, Carpenter had to retreat.[23] But he continued to view Olson's writing with disdain, insisting that it bristled with "inaccuracies and false assumptions."[24] Except for his argument that commissioners expected the minutes to be withheld from the public until compact ratification, Carpenter's charges reflect the extent to which he had personalized the compact. He never specified Olson's errors and at a later date he openly recognized Olson's analytical skills in correspondence regarding the 1930 *Arizona v. California* case.

The *Colorado River Compact* is, in fact, quite useful. It provides preliminary analysis of compact articles, a discussion of engineering and economic considerations, and a review of constitutional and political issues addressed by the commissioners. It is also a good reference for primary source materials. More than half of the 527 pages are documents relating to compact negotiation and ratification. If one is aware of Olson's limited practical experience, a reading of his book can be a useful introduction to the Colorado River Compact.

The spat with Olson underscores Carpenter's sensitivity when challenged by those he viewed as elitists, dilettantes, or others who had not paid their dues in the world of interstate water work. His reaction to Olson follows the same pattern developed early on with L. Ward Bannister, another Harvardian. In the long run, Carpenter recognized the potential of both men, but he was so close to his work and so passionately invested in the inalienable nature of his theories, that he sometimes showed intolerance for those who questioned his reasoning. These jealousies, petty quarrels, and occasional outbursts of temper were sometimes seen as arrogance by Carpenter's critics.

Because the legal and constitutional aspects of interstate water agreements were so complicated, Carpenter's ideas were initially accepted by default. When it later became clear to critics that he was a savvy advocate for his own state, that his "principles" could actually be abandoned because Colorado's future seemed to be at stake, he appeared human, vulnerable, and prone to the same weaknesses and temptations experienced by everyone in the public eye. He was not an easy person to deal with, especially when he felt poorly, and he had more than his share of vanity and self-interest. But even with the occasional clash that transpired with Hoover, Bannister, A. P. Davis, Olson, and a few others, he was, for the most part, admired by the men with whom he worked. The legacy he left to succeeding generations acknowledges the fact that he was an attorney in an unfamiliar field of water law at a time when powerful individuals and organizations, public and private, resisted change.

No one articulated this legacy with greater sincerity than Ralph Carr, admittedly one of Carpenter's closest friends and admirers. Carr had much in common with Carpenter. Ten years younger, he was raised in Cripple Creek, received a law degree from the University of Colorado, and specialized in water law both in private practice and as Conejos County attorney. Politically, he was a rock-ribbed Republican and was as outspoken as Carpenter on the importance of states' rights. He was Carpenter's greatest cheerleader in La Plata and Rio Grande compact negotiations, and when Carpenter was unable to represent Colorado in the *Hinderlider* case before the U.S. Supreme Court, Carr presented his friend's arguments and won the victory that guaranteed legal supremacy of interstate compacts over previously vested individual and corporate water rights.

Carr was also a Christian Scientist and a courageous humanitarian. A two-term governor in Colorado from 1939 to 1943, he provided state land for Japanese-Americans exiled from California during World War II. This was a time when anti-Japanese phobia was at its peak, and some believe that Carr lost the 1942 senate race to Democrat Edwin Johnson because voters were angry at his decision to bring so many Asians into the state in that same year.

On October 29, 1943, at the annual banquet of the National Reclamation Association (NRA) held at the Shirley-Savoy Hotel in Denver, Carr offered a "Salute to Delph Carpenter." A fine orator, Carr spoke to a sympathetic and appreciative audience. He recounted his friend's pioneering solution to the challenge of preserving the intrastate doctrine of prior appropriation while adhering to the Supreme Court's evolving doctrine of equitable apportionment among interstate water users. He lauded Carpenter's study of the Constitution, his understanding of how the federal republic operated, and his commitment to state sovereignty. He described Carpenter as one who looked for solutions acceptable to future generations, inexhaustibly patient in defending his beliefs because he "knew he was right." Carpenter's conviction that "any river question could be settled by any group of men with all the facts in their possession, who were honestly bent on reaching an agreement, was proved true," Carr stated. The arguments of "the man with 'the piercing blue eyes, the twinkling blue eyes, the understanding blue eyes,' finally got the job done." The Colorado Compact, Carr concluded, was his most fitting memorial.[25]

One can only imagine the enthusiasm evoked by Carr's speech among NRA delegates. Representatives of the seventeen member states responded by signing a "testimonial of appreciation," in which they referred to Carpenter as the "Counsellor of all who till the soil; Crusader for better irrigation theories . . . who went forward patiently and unselfishly, when illness and physical suffering dictated rest and relaxation; Father of Interstate River Compacts; Dreamer who visioned the West's potential greatness; Westerner . . . Diplomat . . . and Statesman who sought the ultimate good of this Nation through fair adjustments among the sovereign States of our Great Republic."[26]

It was heady stuff, but from his sick bed, Carpenter was most grateful. Although Carr had ended his remarks with a prediction that Carpenter's name would "live as long as our civilization persists,"[27] recognition of his work, both then and now, has been limited generally to those whose special interest is western water. But Herbert Hoover understood the meaning of the moment for Carpenter. From his suite at the Waldorf-Astoria Hotel in New York, Hoover congratulated Carpenter on the NRA award. "I just want you to know," he wrote, "that I would like to have been there and to have joined in that declaration."[28]

Even before Carr's speech, praise for Carpenter's compact work arrived sporadically at his home, continuing on through the years of illness and past his death. Letters and memorials from dozens of well-wishers thanked him for his good judgment, for his seemingly endless patience in negotiations, and for his integrity, courtesy, and honesty. They called him wise in many ways; sage of Greeley, generalissimo of the upper states, father of the Colorado River Compact, ambassador of liquid gold, the salvation of Colorado, and a fighter for plans and programs that would have repercussions far beyond Colorado's borders. In the opinion of Sims Ely, who had first known Carpenter as Arizona's representative to the League of the Southwest, Carpenter had the ability to be broad-visioned, to see the future in terms of the needs of all the people, and to be in his own right something of a prophet.[29] Ely believed that Carpenter's perception of the law was that it should provide equity for as many people as possible, that blind legal precedents were inadequate building blocks for interstate harmony. At times, Ely reasoned, Carpenter appeared willing to challenge the established thinking of politicians and jurists alike in order to create new relationships and institutions that would better respond to the West's arid conditions.

Carpenter also left the impression that he was deeply concerned about the West's future. Application of the treaty powers of the states to the making of interstate stream compacts rested on his conviction that only compacts would provide the security needed by the states for sustained economic growth. Likewise, his anticipation of transmountain diversion in the upper Colorado River basin provided flexibility and the promise of gradual development in the upper basin states. His determination to preserve states' rights against encroachment by the federal government recognized the evolving tensions of American federalism as they played out in the West. Likewise, his fear that rapid growth in southern California could have a permanent and detrimental effect on states located at the source of the Colorado River revealed an understanding of the dilemma faced by mountain states with fewer opportunities for economic growth.

In the words of Colorado district judge George H. Bradfield, what the apex doctrine was to mining and the appropriation doctrine was to irrigation, the compact system was to interstate comity.[30] When Carpenter found a way for states, institutions, and individuals to trust each other, negotiating a solution to any water conflict was possible. He set an example by being, for the most part, discreet and respectful of adversaries. He was fair with those whose ideas he opposed, and was a master of detail in negotiations. He knew how to keep small group discussions on track, how to make progress toward a goal, and when to break off talks to allow ungovernable emotions time to simmer down. As H. S. McCluskey, secretary to Arizona Governor George W. P. Hunt, noted, Carpenter always appeared to be optimistic.[31] For this, he earned the regard of those with whom he disagreed.

The example he set as a public servant and statesman was also noteworthy. No greater duty called, Carpenter believed, than that of public service. One of Colorado's "greatest benefactors" and "a patriotic son of the centennial state," in the words of Congressman Ed Taylor,[32] Carpenter epitomized the selfless public servant. He possessed a keen sense of place and worked to better the city, county, state, and region his family had inherited from earlier pioneers. In this sense, he proved himself a statesman, disdaining partisan politics to concentrate on goals that had the potential to improve the world in which he lived. His hard work and persistence sometimes irritated others, but when men learned they could no longer count on his presence at interstate conferences, they appreciated the high standards he had set, and they expressed the loss of his wry sense of humor, his ingenuity, his unfailing good manners, his sincerity, and, above all, his courage. Almost always cheerful when colleagues thought he should be under a doctor's care, Carpenter earned admiration for his willingness to place duty above the aches, pains, and embarrassments of a very debilitating disease.

That admiration was frequently expressed with affection. Both during and after his life, acquaintances recognized what Carpenter had accomplished and how he should be remembered. Some recalled him as a second generation pioneer, one who articulated a workable water policy for the western states. Most agreed he was the "brains of the Colorado River Compact," although students of that covenant also recognize the invaluable leadership of Hoover and the thoughtful contributions of each commissioner present in Santa Fe.[33] Unquestionably, he was a fine lawyer, a citizen with a strong sense of stewardship for his state and region, a consummate negotiator, and a political appointee who tried to keep politics out of compact making.

The best-known aspect of Carpenter's legacy will always be the Colorado River Compact. It is the accomplishment for which he is best known, visibly expressed in Hoover Dam, which could not have been built without the compact. The success of that compact from Carpenter's perspective was that each of the two segments of the Colorado River basin—the four upper states and three lower states—received equitable treatment in the division of water on a permanent basis. The allocation of 7.5 million acre-feet to the upper basin and 8.5 million acre-feet to the lower basin was crafted to allow the more slowly developing upper basin to grow at its own pace. Under the terms of this compact, 7.5 million acre-feet of Colorado River water are available for beneficial use *whenever* (author's emphasis) the states of Utah, Wyoming, Colorado, and New Mexico are able to use it. The compact was a trade-off: long-term protection for the states at the upper end of the river in return for immediate political support in Congress for a dam to provide flood control, power, and storage water for California, Arizona, and Nevada. Believing that avoidance of future litigation was a worthy goal, Carpenter committed himself to persuading others that federally constructed works on interstate streams must be delayed until involved states first agreed to a plan of apportionment. The Colorado River Compact met these objectives and has proved remarkably durable, considering the economic, demographic, and political changes the basin has witnessed in the past eighty years. But the Colorado River Compact, like any interstate compact, must have the capacity to respond to society's changing values and requirements if litigation, as Carpenter hoped, is to be avoided in the future.

At conception, the Colorado River Compact represented an extraordinary compromise that diminished upper basin fears, allowed California to continue its growth, and enabled a nation to regain self-confidence through the construction of Hoover Dam. But with the passage of time, the flaws in the agreement have appeared increasingly problematic. The most obvious problem stems from miscalculations of river flow in 1922. Compact commissioners and Reclamation Service officials lacked access to a sufficiently lengthy hydrological history. Consequently, negotiators accepted statements that the river flowed at an annual rate of at least 20 million acre-feet. When the seven states agreed to divide the water equally between the two basins, they believed that after signing the compact at Santa Fe, a time would come when the surplus could be allocated. With a river that now appears to have a mean annual flow of 13 million acre-feet, the upper basin states find themselves committed by compact to delivering 8.5 million acre-feet to the lower basin, far more than the 50 percent (plus 1 million acre-feet) Carpenter thought he had negotiated in Santa Fe in 1922.

Another problem, possibly unavoidable, was the failure of the Colorado River Compact Commission to insist that the lower basin states consummate a tristate compact dividing up their own share of the river before the dam was built. The upper basin got this job done fairly easily, making possible the works of the Colorado River Storage Project.[34] But Arizona and California could not agree on how their share should be divided. They ended up in court four times, litigating issues that Carpenter hoped the compact had resolved. When the final case ended in 1963, the Court had given Congress authority to allocate water on the Colorado River, precisely what the compact was designed to avoid. But California was still unwilling to limit itself to the 4.4 million acre-feet it had agreed to in 1929. Seventy years later it was still diverting far more water than what was authorized by the secretary of the interior, designated watermaster by Congress for the lower basin. Not until four days before the end of President William Jefferson Clinton's administration in January 2001 did California agree to a "Record of Decision" (ROD) that weans the state to 4.4 million acre-feet over a fifteen-year period.[35] Carpenter's prediction that the faster growing states in the lower basin would never give up water to which they could establish a prescriptive right proved to be an accurate, although, hopefully, not a permanent condition if the ROD works out.

Carpenter's solution to the Colorado River crisis was appropriate for the times. It was executed in the face of skeptics who continued to advocate litigation. States whose water needs have increased gradually in the past eighty years see his accomplishment as extraordinary, because their rights have been negotiated in perpetuity through a compact recognized as legal by both Congress and the Supreme Court. Their gratitude toward Carpenter is even stronger today as the courts appear to be increasingly reluctant to overturn or amend duly negotiated compacts between states.[36]

Nevertheless, critics of water allocation compacts, especially those who find fault with the Colorado River Compact, point out significant difficulties the states may face as they attempt to adhere to agreements made many years ago. Ever since the early fifties, observers have pointed out how compacts hinder water marketing by failing to allow exchanges and lease rights for more than a short period of time.[37] Nevada, for example, has limited options to provide water for fast-growing Las Vegas. Colorado, on the other hand, is unable to use all the water to which it is entitled under the Upper Basin Compact. A temporary arrangement by which Nevada would use Colorado's excess water might benefit both states, but Coloradans fear that Nevada could obtain a permanent legal claim to this water if it was applied to beneficial use in Nevada over a long enough period of time. The same scenario applies in more general terms to excess water flowing from all states of the upper basin and California's shortages resulting from drought and population growth. By and large, upper basin states shun suggestions of water marketing, preferring instead to adhere strictly to the compact as the best guarantee of adequate water in the future.

Others critics have noted that compacts encourage wastage in areas where excessive use of water has contributed to salt and salinity buildup in western rivers. But compacts written prior to World War II were not negotiated with environmental issues in mind, and the framers of these agreements looked upon the construction of dams, reservoirs, and aqueducts as the most logical use of federal funds to spread water around the arid West. Over time, these works have severely impacted the native flora and fauna of the river basins they were intended to ameliorate.

SILVER FOX OF THE ROCKIES

The entire Colorado River Storage Project was designed to provide the upper basin with a bank account of water that could be used to meet Colorado River Compact obligations in dry years. But the dams associated with this Project have had a negative impact on downstream riparian areas by eliminating floods. Attempts by the Bureau of Reclamation to flush the natural channels of the river have had only limited success. Sand bars have disappeared and fish and wildlife have been severely impacted by cold water and irregular flows that result from demands for irrigation water, recreation, and power downstream. Furthermore, although Carpenter and many others in state and federal government envisioned agricultural benefits to western farmers from federally constructed irrigation projects, some areas, especially in western Colorado, have proved to be the principal source of heavy loads of salt entering the Colorado River. In other words, the early western compacts resolved conflicts that were known to negotiators at the time, but from the vantage point of the environmentally conscious twenty-first century, it becomes clear that these agreements also play a role in the degradation of riparian areas.

Compact critics also decry the alleged undemocratic character of interstate compacts. They complain that compacts are difficult to amend, because participating states and Congress, if the compact has been approved by statute, have to agree on the changes.[38] By their very nature, compacts are designed for long periods of time. The commissions or administrative agencies designed to administer them are not especially responsive to changing social values, with the result that there is an ongoing tension between the hoped-for longevity of a compact and the people's need for participatory democracy. Only when interstate water allocation compacts are entered into for geographical, economic, and regional reasons is the demand for review and revision lessened. But in the opinion of Jill Elaine Hasday, democracy is challenged most in compacts where administrative agencies are established as part of the compact, or when compacts are entered into for the purpose of avoiding federal action. In general, she notes, it is the "permanency" of compacts that threatens the democratic process, a conclusion with which Donald Worster appears to align himself in his 1987 *Rivers of Empire*.[39]

Other compact critics comment on the amount and cost of interstate litigation that continues in spite of Carpenter's most fervent expectations to the contrary. Although this study of Carpenter's life does not evaluate this aspect of extant interstate river compacts in the West, it is true that, for Colorado alone, legal expenses related to just the Arkansas, South Platte, and Republican rivers have already reached a total of $15 million, and this figure fails to include a recent penalty of $23 million placed on Colorado by the Supreme Court for violation of the Arkansas River Compact.[40] One must remember that a compact is a contract, and contracts are based on principles of law that change over the years. If the parties in contract are locked into an unreasonable agreement, or if the agreement is vague or imprecise, litigation is one method the states use to seek redress.[41] States may also decide to litigate if Congress imposes its own meaning on a compact after an interstate agreement has already been ratified. Although litigation has not resulted from congressional action regarding the Colorado River Compact, such a threat will persist until all three of the lower basin states are content with the actual division of water.

Proponents of interstate compacts who have analyzed these covenants since 1922 argue that they represent a state's best chance to exercise stewardship for generations to come. In a previously quoted article authored by Felix Frankfurter and James M. Landis in 1925, the writers trace the history of interstate compacts from the colonial period to the twentieth century. Frankfurter was a defender of states' rights, and he also had a keen sense of history. He recognized the United States had entered a period after World War I in which the industrialization and electrification of America would establish regions with unique needs. Congressional action could not properly address these needs.[42] In the semi arid West, Frankfurter and Landis wrote, competing demands for a limited water supply presented "one of the most permeating aspects of the conservation problem." While it remained an "ever-present concern in the daily lives of the people of one region . . . it hardly touches the imagination, let alone the lives, of millions of people in other parts of the country." Citing the Court's decision in *Kansas v. Colorado*, Frankfurter concluded that "no one State can control the power to feed or to starve, possessed by a river flowing through several States."[43] Compacts offered flexibility and usurped none of the power delegated to Congress in the Constitution.

In 1971 Jerome C. Muys observed two new developments since the Frankfurter-Landis article appeared: (1) the authority of the federal government to regulate navigable and non-navigable streams was no longer in doubt; and (2) few questions remained concerning the usefulness of interstate water compacts in the management of water resources.[44] The compact method had been used to resolve water allocation, pollution, and river basin problems. It was also involved in addressing interstate questions of education, crime, energy control, radioactive waste distribution, taxation, Native American gambling, and a host of other interests.[45] Muys concluded that the Colorado River Compact had provided a model for interstate agreements reached after 1922. Of the sixteen water allocation compacts negotiated and approved between 1922 and 1971, all but three followed a similar pattern developed by Carpenter of negotiation by commissioners, participation of a federal representative, and approval by Congress.[46] Compacts worked, Muys stated, because they could provide comprehensive river basin plans, a realistic hope of avoiding litigation, an opportunity for local interests to be recognized, and overall efficiency.

Muys was aware that taking a position on compacts in the abstract could produce as much applause from one quarter as condemnation from another; that designing a compact was less of a challenge than making it work.[47] That said, he argued that compacts represented democracy at work. Public participation, he opined, was essential to the success of the compact process. Negotiators were obligated to consider their problems against the background of the needs of the entire river basin, and, most importantly, men "with a vision and determination to solve . . . water problems" were the key to success.[48] He could have added that compacts now have a long tradition in American law; they are enforceable by suit in federal court, and they take precedence over ordinary state statutes. They also represent a form of sustainability, not the ecological sustainability so important to the environment movement but a sustainability of relations between states and the federal government at a time when state governments have become more obsolescent and less efficient as a result of a strong centralized national government.[49] Compacts also represent a kind of sustainability in regard to long-term water supply as well as sustainability of the Constitution and laws of the states.[50]

Without mentioning him by name, Muys believed that Carpenter had pioneered the techniques of compact negotiation. A highly charismatic, motivated, and determined leader during South Platte, La Plata, Colorado, Republican, Rio Grande, Arkansas, Laramie, North Platte and other compact negotiations, Carpenter had a modus operandi that inspired confidence. The "I Will" philosophy, perfected during his tenure in the Colorado

Senate, was contagious. He would have been anguished by recent criticism, suggesting that the compact process was undemocratic,[51] inflexible, insensitive to grass roots interests, and resistant to amendment. Given the chance, he would have agreed with compact protagonists of today who argue that the twenty-five water allocation compacts in existence at the end of the twentieth century represent cooperation among the states and their citizens, implementation of needed change, political accountability, and what amounts to a sensible compromise of issues.[52] But when all is said and done, the future of interstate water allocation compacts will depend to a great extent on the men and women who understand the importance of nonparochial, selfless, and patient leadership required to avoid the kind of polarization usually followed by litigation.

A few months before his death in 1999, *Cadillac Desert* author Marc Reisner commented to an audience at Colorado State University that what the West really needs today is leadership: "[l]eadership willing to take this country where it wants to go, not where entrenched power, money and habit insist it stay. Serious leadership," Reisner concluded, "more than anything, is, in my view, what is missing in America today."[53]

Although Reisner's gospel of "the greatest good for the greatest number," and his affection for rather extensive social engineering in the West overlook past successes effected under the laws of prior appropriation and equitable apportionment, his appeal for a new generation of leaders resonates with all those who have struggled to avoid legal conflict. Solutions to future water problems will require a more extensive breadth of debate than what has been brought to the table in the past, because there are now so many additional interests involved in the water allocation process. The generally accepted view that a minimum quantity of water should remain in a river for environmental health reasons (instream flows) is but one example of the many new concerns requiring consideration by federal, state, and local water authorities. As competent and knowledgeable as the legal establishment may be, the best solutions to conflict on interstate streams will come from compromise agreements reached by representatives with a stake in a reasonable and enduring settlement.

Carpenter commented on the parochialism of his own profession to Judge Charles C. Butler when he learned the *Hinderlider* case had been struck down by the Colorado Supreme Court. "We lawyers are very local minded," he wrote. "We live and practice in an atmosphere of purely local law and are seldom called to seriously consider interstate or international relations or the principles involved. We are narrow in our prejudices and opinions and are prone to close our minds to all but our local views. Election to the Court works no miraculous changes and we carry our prejudices with us."[54]

Real leadership, Carpenter believed, required expanding traditional thought processes beyond the confines of local squabbles. Such extended thinking in his own mind produced the fifty-fifty solution to allocation of Colorado River water, six-state endorsement of the Colorado River Compact, equal appropriation rights for reservoirs and ditches, transmountain diversion to bring water to growing populations, and other adjustments in the system of water allocation designed to provide for generations yet unborn. His intellectual compass occasionally failed. He resisted the initiative and referendum and opposed almost any form of government control of natural resources. But for the most part, he had a clear view of what the future would bring and the leadership required to persuade people to look ahead instead of at their feet.

In order to accomplish anything, Carpenter had to be a consensus builder. He fully understood the requirements of successful negotiation, although for reasons of personal health, the exigencies of interstate politics, or his own vulnerable personality, he was unable always to practice what he understood as fundamental truths. During almost twenty years of litigation and compact negotiations, he had learned that lasting agreements require patience, and patience is fundamental to productive negotiations. When he reflected on the dynamics of good negotiations, Carpenter showed extraordinary insight. "Take time, take time and above all take time," he advised a friend in 1929.

> Time is such a wonderful solvent. It permits wounds to heal and turbid waters to settle. Hold court strenuously for a short time, then adjourn to meet again and repeat the program. Deliberation and meditation are imperative to the solution of great problems.... Most great religions and philosophies have been evolved in solitaire [sic] places. The human machine is like water: it picks up its load while in action and sorts it when quiet. Let the trumpets sound and the mob howl, then take thought in quiet and solitude. Give the other fellow credit for constructive ideas and suggestions even though they origi-

nated with you and he voiced them at your suggestion. Feed the radical with private appreciative discussion of his ideas, neither agreeing with nor opposing, but bringing him out into the open where he will be kindly disposed toward the other fellows and be ready to accept a middle ground. Treat the hide-bound conservative in the same way. There is nothing more valuable than kindly, private conversation.[55]

Negotiating compacts required an element of formality and solemnity, but Carpenter also believed in the essential good nature of his fellow humans. He preferred tranquil discussions to litigation because he felt that more could be accomplished if adversarial conflict could be avoided. Confidentiality was important. It meant keeping each confidence "to the last ditch," respecting all players and betraying none. Good leadership required insistence on fair play, being certain that every man had his day. The secret, Carpenter opined, was to keep the "human equasion [*sic*]" in mind. Every problem is ultimately a "human problem which must be solved to suit opinion both for today and for tomorrow.

Because the proliferation of opposing views has the potential for discord, the longer discussion continued and the more freely ideas could be presented, the better the chance that give-and-take would "drift toward a center of solution in which all must and can agree." Although he preferred compacts that avoided detailed and specific terms, he was committed to presentation of all relative data, no matter how much the discussions were extended, and he made it his business to contract advisors known for their grasp of consequential facts. The idea is to "[b]e in at the finish," Carpenter reasoned. "You build to this position step by step as you convince the other members of your fairness, ability, kindness and wisdom." And don't forget to "[s]ustain the chairman. You may disagree with him, but if he is wrong, time will reveal the error to him without your assistance." And in respect to him, you must "[w]ork, work, incessantly work, with the ultimate solution of your problems as the final objective. . . ."

Nothing Carpenter wrote came closer to summarizing his own experience in negotiations. He looked for the best in a man's character and was convinced that trust among negotiators would produce acceptable compromises. If the data were accurate and negotiators were sufficiently prepared to spend time doing on-site surveillance, interstate water problems could be resolved in a manner beneficial to future generations.

It is this focus on the future that seems most appropriate in summing up Carpenter's legacy. The environmental concerns of today were beyond his visionary capability, and the legislative response to these problems was out of reach of his most fertile and creative moments. Today, we discuss how best to proceed in the West so that future generations can enjoy the natural resources that have been this region's most spectacular attribute. From John Wesley Powell to modern-day scholars of the western landscape, suggestions have been made about how man can sustain a harmonious relationship with the land in this semi-arid region. Powell recommended changes in the political system so that populations would be identified by river basin, rather than by states established under a range-township-section survey system. He also urged modification of land laws to reflect the fact that 13 percent of the West is desert and most of the rest of it is arid.

In the spring of 2000, Colorado University Law School professor Charles F. Wilkinson described sustainability as operating on two levels: (1) as a symbol of what the American people believe, "a philosophical and moral force of fairness to future generations;" and (2) as a program to moderate economic exploitation of the land while sustaining the life of diverse species and maintaining the purity of the water systems.[56] In other words, Wilkinson noted, the challenge is to discover how one generation can meet its needs without causing subsequent generations to suffer loss.

In his own way, yet with his feet still rooted in a pioneer past, Carpenter was committed to an inchoate form of sustainability. He would have abhorred giving power to the public to overturn decisions made by duly appointed water commissioners, but he believed that lasting interstate agreements required public commentary at some point if they were to endure. He also believed in the importance of local decision-making and was committed to his own version of Aldo Leopold's land ethic: commitment to long-term land and water health.[57] It is Carpenter's view of nature that most suggests this primitive yearning for sustainability. Agreements affecting the future of the West, he believed, would have to acknowledge nature's power, especially in the area of flowing water. He was in love with the unspoiled outdoors. It was his heritage, what gave him pleasure as a rancher and Colorado resident. He believed in harnessing nature's power to expand agricultural possibilities for the West's farmers and ranchers, but he knew the canyons, deserts, floods, droughts, and variable terrain of the West would exert limitations on man's desire to dominate the landscape. In the last analysis, Carpenter believed, nature would have to have a place at the negotiating table. He would not be surprised that today the seven Colorado River basin states struggle with how best to preserve the endangered Colorado River fishes while allowing full compact use by all participants.

In this sense, perhaps, Carpenter was ahead of his time. Somewhat in contrast to the real silver foxes in the Rocky Mountains, he had difficulty adapting as the political and economic environment around him changed, but the principles and policies to which he committed were sufficiently revolutionary at the time of introduction to cause a significant impact on the western landscape. If survival for Carpenter included a stubborn adherence to a pioneer upbringing, it can still be said to his credit that the Silver Fox of the Rockies was a crafty, intelligent, and creative innovator whose qualities might be profitably emulated by future leaders interested in limiting interstate conflict and furthering development of the American West.[58]

Notes

INTRODUCTION

1. Donald J. Pisani, "Enterprise and Equity," 22, 23.

2. On 3 March 1877, Congress enacted "An act to provide for the sale of desert lands in certain States and Territories," *U.S. Statutes at Large*, 19: 377. On 26 July 1866, Congress passed "An Act granting the Right of way to Ditch and Canal Owners over the Public Lands, and for other Purposes," *Statutes at Large* 14: 251–53; and on 9 July 1870, Congress approved "An Act to amend 'An Act granting the Right of Way to Ditch and Canal Owners over the Public Lands, and for other Purposes,'" Statutes at Large 16: 217, 218. The 1866 act stated that the water rights of entrymen on the public domain would be "maintained and protected" if they were recognized by "the local customs, laws and decisions of the courts." See also Donald J. Pisani, "State vs. Nation": 266–67, and Robert G. Dunbar, *Forging New Rights*, 46–47, 76–77.

3. Act of 17 June 1902, ch. 1093, 32 Stat. 388.

4. Pisani, "State vs. Nation": 268–76. Pisani concludes that by 1905, "federal authority was as cloudy as it had been in the nineteenth century."

5. This is a reference to *Kansas v. Colorado*, 206 US 46 (1907), in which the United States Supreme Court decided that Kansas had not proved injury regarding Colorado's diversion of waters of the Arkansas River. If in the future, the Court stated, Kansas could prove that the equitable apportionment of benefits between the two states resulting from the flow of the river was favoring Colorado, the Court would entertain new proceedings. More importantly, the Court dismissed an intervening petition by the United States, stating in its decision that it was up to the states to choose their own water rights. In 1922 the Court made a more definitive ruling regarding interstate streams when it endorsed the principle of interstate priority in *Wyoming v. Colorado*, 259 US 419 (1922). Carpenter's interstate compact plan was perfected during the fifteen years between these two cases.

6. Donald Worster, *A River Running West*, 359. Worster's comments occur in the context of John Wesley Powell's *Report on the Lands of the Arid Region of the United States*, 354–60.

7. The ten rivers include the Laramie, North Platte, South Platte, Republican, Arkansas, Rio Grande, Animas, La Plata, Colorado, and the Yampa-White system.

8. As quoted in Ira G. Clark, *Water in New Mexico*, 214. Clark cites 51st Cong., 1st sess., S. Rep. No. 928, IV, 63 and 112 in "Views of the Minority."

9. See Gregory J. Hobbs, Jr., "Colorado Water Law: An Historical Overview," University of Denver *Water Law Review*, 1 (Fall 1997): 2, 3. Colorado Supreme Court Justice Hobbs states that "Western prior appropriation water law is a property rights-based allocation and administration system, which promotes multiple use of a finite resource. The fundamental characteristics of this system guarantee security, assure reliability, and cultivate flexibility." Senior water rights are oldest by date of diversion and will be filled prior to more junior rights if there is insufficient water in the stream. By contrast, the riparian system of water law, evolved from English common law, states that running water is the property of the public and a riparian landowner may only own the banks of the stream and not the water itself. Any water that is used for milling and domestic purposes must be returned to the stream "without substantial alteration to either its quality or quantity." Because of the nature of water courses in arid areas and the need to divert water away from the stream for irrigation, the prior appropriation doctrine is more suitable in the West.

10. The riparian system, born of English common law in a humid environment, required that streams be unaltered, that they continue to flow undiminished in an unobstructed water course, and that owners of land adjacent to the water course return to the stream the same quantity and quality of water used on their lands. The doctrine of prior appropriation, first used to define the rights of conflicting mining claims in California, was based on a principle of squatters' rights: the first settler had the first and best right to the land. In most of the West, this first-in-time-first-in-right doctrine became part of the states' water code. An excellent study of the origins of the prior appropriation doctrine is Donald J. Pisani, "Enterprise and Equity," 1987. See also Dunbar, *Forging New Rights*, 60–61.

11. This is a claim westerners have made throughout the twentieth century. It means different things to different people, but in the broadest terms, the West was asking for the same rights accorded to other states in the Union. As Michael McCarthy has noted, "Neither the phrase nor the concept of equal footing appears in the Constitution, and without constitutional roots it has no force of law." See Richard D. Lamm and Michael McCarthy, *The Angry West*, 311, 312. Nevertheless, the concept of equal footing has a strong taproot in the West, where feelings of second-class citizenship and colonization by the federal government have percolated for a hundred years.

12. Art. I, sec. 10. "No State shall enter into any treaty, alliance or confederation. . . . No State shall, without the consent of Congress . . . enter into any agreement or compact with another State, or with a foreign power. . . ."

13. Art VI, clause 2. "No two or more States shall enter into any treaty, confederation, or alliance whatever between them, without the consent of the United States, in Congress assembled."

14. Joseph L. Sax, Robert H. Abrams, and Barton H. Thompson, Jr., *Legal Control of Water Resources*, 733. Constitutional scholars note that very little information is available on the origins of the compact clause, but most agree with Sax and his co-authors that the Framers were following "the long-held principle of international law that sovereign states should have means to resolve joint matters of mutual concern administratively, without engaging the full government." They were aware that "the state system was not altogether compatible with centralized government and that some states might sometime make some kind of formal interstate agreement which would endanger the Union as a whole." See Marian E. Ridgeway, *Interstate Compacts*, vii–viii.

15. *Kansas v. Colorado*, 206 US 46 (1907) is the Supreme Court's first application of equitable apportionment to an interstate water dispute. Because the two states were operating under different systems of water law, and because Kansas failed to prove sufficient injury from Colorado's diversions from the Arkansas River, the Court decided not to side with either plaintiff or defendant. In this case equitable apportionment meant balancing the benefits accruing to Colorado against the alleged injury to Kansas. In the next equitable apportionment case, *Wyoming v. Colorado*, 259 US 419 (1922), the Court used priority as the basis for equitable apportionment. Both states honored this system of water law. Given the amount of water Wyoming would need to irrigate lands settled before Colorado planned to divert part of the Laramie River into the Cache la Poudre River basin, the Court decided that equity required protection of Wyoming's needs while Colorado would have to be content with the quantity of water remaining after Wyoming received its share. The doctrine of equitable apportionment has become increasingly sophisticated over the years as the Court has applied a multifactored approach to these cases. (See Richard A. Simms and Jennifer Davis, "Water Transfers across State Systems," p. 12, in which the authors list nine factors considered by the Court in an equitable apportionment decision.) Carpenter's view of equitable apportionment incorporated his deep respect for state sovereignty, the realities of river hydrology in the semiarid West, and the principle that each state had an equal right to economic development without the pressure of competition from other states.

16. Carpenter's concept of equitable apportionment was based on political, economic, and environmental circumstances. Although he recognized that all states sharing the same watercourse should do so in an equitable fashion, he frequently called attention to hydrological and geographical limits imposed by nature and geography. River gorges, soil conditions, altitude, and return flows to the river were as important to him as states' rights and the extent to which negotiating parties could prove beneficial use of water. One is reminded of the manner in which Hispanic water disputes were adjudicated

NOTES TO PAGES 10–13

in the American Southwest prior to United States' sovereignty. Spanish and

NOTES TO PAGES 10–13

in the American Southwest prior to United States' sovereignty. Spanish and Mexican judge-administrators used a panoply of measures, including just title, need, beneficial use, priority, the public good, intent, and injury to a third party to determine how all parties in conflict would receive an equitable amount of the water in question. See Michael C. Meyer, *Water in the Hispanic Southwest*, 148–62.

17. G. Michael McCarthy, *Hour of Trial*, 77. McCarthy cites J. Leonard Bates, "Fulfilling American Democracy," 38, and Samuel Hays, *Conservation and the Gospel of Efficiency*, 2.

18. Gilbert C. Fite and Norman Graebner, *Recent United States History*, 26.

19. McCarthy, *Hour of Trial*, 87. McCarthy's quote is from Elmo R. Richardson, *Politics of Conservation*, 25.

20. Richardson, *Politics of Conservation*, 122.

21. Samuel P. Hays, *Conservation and the Gospel of Efficiency*, 91, 266.

22. McCarthy, *Hour of Trial*, 88, 89.

23. Karen R. Merrill, "In Search of the 'Federal Presence' in the American West": 457. In her stimulating essay, Merrill argues that historians and political scientists need to do a lot more research before we really understand the meaning of "federal presence" in the West.

24. Ibid., 469.

25. Susan J. Buck, Gregory W. Gleason, and Mitchel S. Jofuku, "'The Institutional Imperative': Resolving Transboundary Water Conflict in Arid Agricultural Regions: 595–628. In note 9, 598, the authors state that "[a]t least ninety-one treaties governing international rivers have been documented." They also note that the term *equitable apportionment* was too imprecise for international usage because it suggested allocating a quantity of water. Because of the reality of the hydrologic cycle, *equitable apportionment* has been modified over time to *equitable utilization*, implying the right to use, not own, an equitable amount of water. See p. 600.

26. The United States' claim to "absolute jurisdiction" over its territory, including water originating therein, was enunciated by U.S. Attorney General Judson Harmon in 1895. The Harmon Doctrine was the expression of a proprietary view of sovereignty on the international level similar to what Coloradans were articulating on the interstate level. In a 1906 treaty with Mexico, the United States recognized the need for comity and guaranteed sixty thousand acre-feet a year to Mexico. Carpenter argued in 1921 that the Harmon Doctrine was still a principle of international law and that neither nation nor state needed to relinquish water to a downstream neighbor "until such time as the upper nation shall see fit to make some concession by treaty as a matter of politics and not of international law." See Delph E. Carpenter, "Application of the Reserve Treaty Powers of the States to Interstate Water Controversies": 124.

27. Minutes, Sixth Meeting, Colorado River Compact Commission, Washington, D.C., box 7, Carpenter Papers, Northern Colorado Water Conservancy

District (NCWCD), Loveland, Col. Hereinafter cited as Carpenter Papers, NCWCD. These papers are temporarily on loan to the NCWCD, Loveland, Colorado, pending final distribution by the Carpenter family. References to folders and box numbers may change when the papers are eventually moved from the NCWCD to a university, historical society, museum, or public archive.

28. William Kevin Voit and Gary Nitting, "Interstate Compacts and Agencies, 1998," 118–33. Because it is difficult to know the extent to which interstate compacts continue to be operative, the number twenty-five should be considered a rough approximation. More recently, George William Sherk counts twenty-seven water allocation compacts in force. See *Dividing the Waters*, 30, n. 6. Jill Elaine Hasday estimated that as of 1997 there were about 165 interstate compacts of all kinds in effect: 36 signed between 1783 and 1925; 65 between 1931 and 1955; 47 in the 1960s and less than 20 in the 1970s. See "Interstate Compacts in a Democratic Society," n. 18, 4.

29. A discussion of the status of existing interstate water compacts is more fully addressed in the last chapter.

30. I am in debt to Professor Donald J. Pisani for this observation.

31. Art. XVI, sec. 5: "The water of every natural stream, not heretofore appropriated, within the state of Colorado, is hereby declared to be the property of the public, and the same is dedicated to the use of the people of the state, subject to appropriation as hereinafter provided." Sec. 6: "The right to divert the unappropriated waters of any natural stream to beneficial uses shall never be denied. Priority of appropriation shall give the better right as between those using the water for the same purpose; but when the waters of any natural stream are not sufficient for the service of all those desiring the use of the same, those using the water for domestic purposes shall have the preference over those claiming for any other purpose, and those using the water for agricultural purposes shall have preference over those using the same for manufacturing purposes." As Robert Dunbar points out, the first version of this paragraph stated that "the stream waters of the state were 'the property of the people,' but the phrase was altered . . . to read 'property of the public.'" See Dunbar, *Forging New Rights in Western Waters*, 79.

32. Dunbar, "Water Conflicts and Controls in Colorado": 180–86.

33. McCarthy, *Hour of Trial*, 21, 22. McCarthy cites Henry Nash Smith, *Virgin Land*, 138. Readers will enjoy a more recent study by Mark Fiege, *Irrigated Eden: The Making of an Agricultural Landscape in the American West*, which describes how pioneers in the Snake River Valley of Idaho found their romanticized dreams of an ideal society destroyed by the realities of irrigated agriculture.

34. Delph Carpenter, draft copy of a speech presented on the senate floor at the third reading of the initiative and referendum bill, box 84, folder 2, Carpenter Papers, NCWCD.

35. The vote was on one sentence (the Parrish Amendment) in Section Four (4) of Senate Bill No. 134, Laws of 1911. It was held on 5 November

1911 and resulted in a 2:1 victory for the opponents of the amendment. See *Digest of Initiated and Referred Constitutional Amendments and Laws . . . 1912 to 1968,* 1912, 2, sent to me courtesy of Colorado Supreme Court Justice Gregory J. Hobbs.

36. 259 US 419 (1922).

37. The Colorado River Compact of 1922 included upper basin headwaters states (Colorado, Wyoming, Utah, and New Mexico) and lower basin states (California, Arizona, and Nevada).

38. At the same time, he spoke with officials of the Reclamation Service about the possibility of their completing the Greeley-Poudre Project when work was stalled because of the lawsuit.

39. Michael C. Robinson, *Water for the West,* 19.

40. Robinson, *Water for the West,* 26, 27.

41. Ibid., 29. In his semiofficial history of the Bureau of Reclamation, William E. Warne notes that the Reclamation Service had been interested in the benefits of hydroelectric power ever since Arthur P. Davis became Frederick H. Newell's principal assistant at the Bureau of Reclamation. See Warne, *Bureau of Reclamation,* 86.

42. Robinson, *Water for the West,* 53. Robinson specifically states that the three-fold increase took place between 1913 and 1928.

43. Ibid., 43. See also Donald J. Pisani, "The Many Faces of Conservation: Natural Resources and the American State, 1900–1940," 123–25, 155.

44. Robinson, *Water for the West,* 39–41.

45. James E. Sherow, *Watering the Valley,* 110, 111, 114.

46. Ibid., 117. Sherow cites *Kansas v. Colorado,* 206 US, 653–67.

47. Pisani, "State vs. Nation": 279, 280.

48. This statement reflects the views of Professor Donald Pisani presented in his thoughtful criticism of this manuscript.

49. Gerald D. Nash, *American West in the Twentieth Century,* 22, 23, 63.

50. Worster, *Rivers of Empire,* 200, 201.

51. Ibid., 208.

52. Ibid., 26, 34.

53. Harry N. Scheiber, "The Condition of American Federalism: An Historian's View," 69. Scheiber's views were first published in an article, "Federalism and Legal Process: Historical and Contemporary Analysis of the American System," *Law and Society Review* 14 (Spring, 1980): 679–81.

54. Ibid.: 51.

55. Gerald D. Nash, *The Federal Landscape,* 18.

56. Joseph F. Zimmerman, *Interstate Relations,* 34.

57. *Hinderlider v. La Plata River and Cherry Creek Ditch Co.,* 304 US 92 (1938), reversing 101 Colo. 73, 70 P.2d 849 (1937).

58. George Vranesh, *Colorado Water Law,* vol. 3, 1763. Vranesh cites 93 Colo. 128, 25 P.2d 187 (1933). The Vranesh work is available in a revised edi-

tion edited by James N. Corbridge, Jr., and Teresa A. Rice, *Vranesh's Colorado Water Law* (Boulder: University of Colorado Press, 1999).

59. Ibid., vol. 3, 1764. Vranesh cites 304 US at 106.

60. Ralph I. Meeker to Delph Carpenter, 26 April 1938, box 84, folder 7, Carpenter Papers, NCWCD.

61. See Jill Elaine Hasday, "Interstate Compacts in a Democratic Society": 4, n. 18. Hasday states that sixty-five compacts were negotiated between 1931 and 1955.

62. See David Alderton, *Foxes, Wolves and Wild Dogs of the World*, 16–19, 24–29, 39–56, 63–65.

63. Carpenter to E. V. Wilcox, 14 August 1920, box 85, folder 21, Carpenter Papers, NCWCD.

64. M. C. Hinderlider to Governor Ralph Carr, 22 May 1942, RCC 27047, Johnson Papers, Colorado State Archives. Hinderlider states that Carpenter had contemplated vacating Room 24 in the Capitol Building, "but later decided he would have to retain the room for some time."

65. This issue is addressed in a paper by Jerome C. Muys, "Beyond Allocation: Equitable Apportionment and Interstate Watershed Protection and Management," presented at the San Diego meeting of the American Bar Association, 15 and 16 February 2001. The author argues that it may very well be incumbent on the courts to insist that compact participants respond to the water related issues addressed in thirty-five years of federal environmental statutes. Muys's paper was sent to me courtesy of Colorado Supreme Court Justice Gregory Hobbs.

66. See Daniel Tyler, *Last Water Hole in the West*.

CHAPTER ONE: LINEAGE AND LOVE LETTERS

Epigraph: From "Never Despair," box 79, brown folder, Carpenter Papers, NCWCD.

1. In a handwritten note attached to a poem entitled "Never Despair," Carpenter wrote that his father could recite the entire poem from memory at the age of eighty-three. Supposedly, the source is an 1864 *McGuffey Reader*, but the author was unable to locate it. See brown folder in box 79, Carpenter Papers, NCWCD.

2. See "'Give-A-Damn' Carpenter, Greeley Exponent of 'I Will' Philosophy, Says Blood and Determination Win," *Denver Daily News*, 13 February 1911.

3. The communication between Leroy S. Carpenter and his future bride, Martha A. Bennett, is taken from letters exchanged during a courtship between December 1870 and April 1872. Leroy wrote from Greeley, Colorado, and Martha responded from Calamus, Tipton, and DeWitt, Iowa. These letters are in box 30 of the Carpenter Papers, NCWCD.

4. Delph Carpenter to Mr. Olson, 20 August 1920, box 34, Carpenter Papers, NCWCD. The letter asked if Olson would "go to my grandfather's old homestead, now owned by Alfred R. Reeder of Tipton, Iowa, and there take such photographs as I wish. . . . My grandfather built a log cabin, during the latter forties, the remains of which will be found in a grove of trees north of the Reeder farm house. When I was there in 1912, the side walls were standing." From an early age, Carpenter preserved a strong interest in his family's history.

5. Interview with Delph Carpenter, published in the *Greeley Republican*, 30 April 1908.

6. Mary P. Carpenter, Reminiscences of My Early Life and Later Experiences as a Western Pioneer, April 1906, copied 1908, provided to the author by Doris M. Carpenter, Greeley, Colorado.

7. Delph Carpenter, *Weld County News*, 4 July 1917, reporting on the published statement of Meeker that first appeared in the *New York Herald Tribune*, 4 December 1869. See also David Boyd, *A History: Greeley and the Union Colony of Colorado*, 34.

8. Remarks by N. C. Meeker at the first anniversary of the location of Union Colony No. 1, *Greeley Tribune*, 12 April 1871. The location committee met on the banks of the Cache la Poudre River on 5 April 1870.

9. *Greeley Tribune*, 9 August 1871.

10. Of Daniel's twelve surviving children, those who left Iowa with him and his second wife, Nancy, on 5 April 1871 were Sarah, Leroy, Silas, and Mattie. Peter was already in Colorado. Cyrus had died in infancy. Others came to Colorado later.

11. Leroy Carpenter, Tipton, Iowa, to Martha Bennett, Calamus Station, Iowa, 11 December 1870, box 30, Carpenter Papers, NCWCD. This is one of approximately seventy-five letters that the two exchanged during a correspondence courtship lasting until their marriage on the old Bennett homestead in Iowa on 25 April 1872.

12. Box 30, Carpenter Papers, NCWCD.

13. Martha Bennett to Leroy Carpenter, 12 January 1871, ibid.

14. Leroy Carpenter to Martha Bennett, 15 April 1871, ibid.

15. *Greeley Tribune*, 12 April 1871.

16. The legal description of this land is: W½ of the SE¼ of section 30-6-65. In recent times, the farm was referred to as the old Sargent place. The Carpenters lived in Greeley while they built a house on this property, moving in during October 1871.

17. Delph Carpenter, "The Union Colony of Greeley," *Weld County News*, 4 July 1917. The colony originally intended to construct four canals. No. 1 was never built. It was supposed to divert water from the mouth of the Poudre Canyon, extending eastward to serve farmlands north and west of Greeley. The Larimer and Weld Canal, subsequently built by Governor Ben Eaton with English money, followed this route. When completed in 1878, Canal No. 2,

engineered by E. S. Nettleton, extended thirty-six miles from the Poudre River, eventually reaching a point east of Crow Creek. Construction began with colony money, but farmers had to pay an additional assessment when colony money ran out. (See Robert G. Dunbar, *Forging New Rights*, 22, 23.) Canal No. 3 was constructed to water the town of Greeley as well as farmlands and garden tracts south and east of the town. No. 4 was supposed to divert water from the Big Thompson River, but it was never built.

18. Leroy Carpenter to Martha Bennett, 28 May 1871, box 30 Carpenter Papers, NCWCD. Among loose papers included in this box is a note in Leroy's hand dated 5 December 1871 in which he lists the properties purchased and the amounts paid.

19. *Greeley Tribune*, 11 June, 1910.

20. *Greeley Tribune*, 14 May 1871.

21. Ibid.

22. By the fall of 1871, Union Colony officials had decided that Canal No. 2 should be six feet wider. They estimated the cost at $300 per mile, a total of $8,000 for the planned twenty-seven miles of canal. Unable to borrow the money at less than 15 percent, Union Colony officials decided to assess farmers .25 per acre for each acre planted, with the farmers doing the work themselves. When completed, Canal No. 2 would be fifteen feet wide and four feet deep. See *Greeley Tribune*, 6 September and 8 November 1871.

23. Leroy Carpenter to Martha Bennett, 7 July 1871, box 30, Carpenter Papers, NCWCD.

24. Martha Bennett to Leroy Carpenter, 17 June 1871 and 2 October 1871, ibid.

25. Leroy Carpenter to Martha Bennett, 14 January 1872, ibid.

26. Martha Bennett to Leroy Carpenter, 12 May 1871, ibid.

27. Leroy Carpenter to Martha Bennett, 10 June 1871, 23 June 1871, ibid.

28. Leroy Carpenter to Martha Bennett, 23 June 1871, ibid.

29. Leroy Carpenter to Martha Bennett, 14 January 1872, ibid.

30. Martha Bennett to Leroy Carpenter, 23 January 1872, ibid.

31. "Dangers stand thick through all the ground; To push us to the tomb; And fierce diseases wait around; To hurry mortals home." As quoted in Leroy Carpenter to Martha Bennett, 12 March 1872, ibid.

32. Martha Bennett to Leroy Carpenter, 19 March 1872, ibid.

33. Leroy Carpenter to Martha Bennett, 18 April 1872, ibid.

34. Leroy Carpenter to Martha Bennett, 7 July 71, ibid. It is not clear why Leroy mentioned the need to "make the homestead good," because his father had purchased both of the eighty-acre sections from private parties.

35. Leroy Carpenter to Martha Bennett, 10 November 1871, ibid.

36. Leroy Carpenter to Martha Bennett, 25 September 1871 and 12 March 1872, ibid.

37. *Greeley Tribune*, 20 December 1871. This is the first newspaper reference to the Carpenters. Neighbors were not plentiful on the north side of the river, but according to the paper, they expected to establish a school district and have "occasional preaching."

38. Leroy Carpenter to Martha Bennett, 27 October 1871, box 30, Carpenter Papers, NCWCD.

39. Martha Bennett to Leroy Carpenter, 18 January 1872, ibid.

40. *Horizons*, 1978, box 77, Carpenter Papers, NCWCD. *Horizons* was an insert in the *Greeley Tribune*.

41. *Greeley Tribune*, 21 February 1872, ibid.

42. David Boyd, *A History*, 410.

43. This information comes from an interview between Delph Carpenter and his Uncle Silas on 20 August 1919, located in box 78, Carpenter Papers, NCWCD, and from the Carpenter Family Genealogy prepared by Fred G. Carpenter, Delph's brother, on 27 August 1960. There are some differences in dates between the two sources, but the information is consistent for the most part with the obituary of Leroy S. Carpenter published in the *Greeley Daily Tribune*, 21 November 1927. The Fred G. Carpenter genealogy was provided to the author courtesy of Doris A. Carpenter.

44. Leroy Carpenter to Martha Carpenter, 4 December 1871 and 9 January 1872, box 30, Carpenter Papers, NCWCD. See also *Greeley Tribune*, 17 January and 14 February 1872.

45. Leroy Carpenter to Martha Bennett, 26 December 1871, ibid.

46. Martha Bennett to Leroy Carpenter, 7 January 1872, ibid.

47. Leroy Carpenter to Martha Bennett, 14 January 1872, ibid.

48. *Greeley Tribune*, 28 June 1871.

49. Ibid., 6 and 13 December 1871. The newspaper concluded that if women turned out to vote they would make a difference in the outcome of publicly contested offices.

50. Martha Bennett to Leroy Carpenter, 3 February 1872, box 30, Carpenter Papers, NCWCD.

51. Martha Bennett to Leroy Carpenter, n.d., ibid.

52. Martha Bennett to Leroy Carpenter, 10 February 1871, ibid.

53. Martha Bennett to Leroy Carpenter, 16 February 1872, ibid.

54. Obituary, Leroy S. Carpenter, *Greeley Daily Tribune*, 21 November 1927.

55. Leroy Carpenter to Martha Bennett, 2 May 1871, box 30, Carpenter Papers, NCWCD.

56. L. S. Carpenter, "Little Things," an essay written 14 February 1866 in Iowa City, while he was attending the university, ibid.

57. Leroy Carpenter to Martha Bennett, 12 March 1872, ibid.

58. Martha Bennett to Leroy Carpenter, 19 March 1872, ibid.

59. Martha Bennett to Leroy Carpenter, 4 November 1871, ibid. The melodeon was a small reed organ worked by treadles. Martha told Leroy that she would be bringing this instrument to Colorado with her.

60. Leroy Carpenter to Martha Bennett, 12 and 15 February 1872, ibid.

61. Martha Bennett to Leroy Carpenter, 16 February 1872 and 19 March 1872, ibid.

62. Martha Bennett to Leroy Carpenter, 28 May 1871, ibid.

63. Martha Bennett to Leroy Carpenter, 2 October 1871 and 7 March 1872, ibid.

64. Leroy Carpenter to Martha Bennett, 14 October 1871, ibid.

65. Leroy Carpenter to Martha Bennett, 9 January 1872, ibid.

66. Martha Bennett to Leroy Carpenter, 18 January 1872, ibid.

67. Leroy Carpenter to Martha Bennett, 31 January 1872 and Martha Bennett to Leroy Carpenter, 1 February 1872, ibid.

68. Leroy Carpenter to Martha Bennett, 12 February, 1872, ibid.

69. Martha Bennett to Leroy Carpenter, 16 February 1872, ibid.

70. Leroy Carpenter to Martha Bennett, 18 April 1872, ibid.

71. Martha Bennett to Leroy Carpenter, 3 February 1872, ibid.

72. Martha Bennett to Leroy Carpenter, 20 March 1872, and Leroy Carpenter to Martha Bennett 21 November 1871, ibid.

73. Leroy Carpenter to Martha Bennett, 2 January 1872, ibid.

74. Leroy Carpenter to Martha Bennett, 18 April 1872, ibid.

75. Leroy Carpenter to Martha Bennett, 26 March 1872, ibid.

76. Interview with Sarah Thompson, Delph's daughter, 11 February 1994, Sacramento, Calif.

77. L. S. Carpenter, "Energy," an essay written at some point during his education, box 30, Carpenter Papers, NCWCD.

78. Obituary, L. S. Carpenter, *Greeley Tribune*, 21 November 1927.

79. L. S. Carpenter, "Little Things," box 30, Carpenter Papers, NCWCD.

80. Leroy Carpenter to Martha Bennett, 27 October 1871, and Martha Bennett to Leroy Carpenter, 4 November 1871, ibid.

81. Delph Carpenter, as quoted in *Pueblo Chieftain*, 13 March 1925.

82. Delph Carpenter to E. V. Wilcox, Washington, D.C., 14 August 1920, box 85, Carpenter Papers. Wilcox wrote a story on Carpenter that appeared in *Country Gentleman*, 9 October 1920.

CHAPTER 2: EDUCATION AND THE BEGINNINGS OF A CAREER

Epigraph: Delph Carpenter, 1897 diary, box 4, Carpenter Papers, NCWCD.

1. Boyd, *A History*, 174.

2. *Wyoming v. Colorado* 259 US 419 (1922).

3. Boyd, *A History*, 161, 164.

4. Robert G. Dunbar, "Water Conflicts and Controls," ch. 18 in Carl Ubbelohde et al., *A Colorado Reader*, 222. This same article was published in *Agricultural History*, xxii (July 1948): 180–86.

5. *Greeley Tribune*, 8 July 1874. Quoted in Dunbar, "Water Conflicts," 223.

6. See the section titled "Blueprint for a Dryland Democracy" in Wallace Stegner, *Beyond the Hundredth Meridian*, 202–42. Most probably, Meeker and Powell had no contact, but it is interesting to note that Powell's plan to establish political administration in the West along lines of entire river basins was earlier suggested in part by Nathan C. Meeker.

7. Ibid.

8. Boyd, *A History*, 120.

9. Article XVI, sec. 5: "*Water of Streams Public Property.* The water of every natural stream, not heretofore appropriated, within the state of Colorado, is hereby declared to be the property of the public, and the same is dedicated to the use of the people of the state, subject to appropriation as hereinafter provided. Sec. 6: *Diverting Unappropriated Water—Priority Preferred Uses.* The right to divert the unappropriated waters of any natural stream to beneficial uses shall never be denied. Priority of appropriation shall give the better right as between those using the water for the same purpose; but when the waters of any natural stream are not sufficient for the service of all those desiring the use of the same, those using the water for domestic purposes shall have the preference over those claiming for any other purpose, and those using the water for agricultural purposes shall have preference over those using the same for manufacturing purposes."

10. The best discussion of the origins of the doctrine of prior appropriation is Pisani, "Enterprise and Equity": 15–37.

11. Robert G. Dunbar, "Water Conflicts": 220.

12. 1879 *Colorado Session Laws* 94, as cited in George Vranesh, *Colorado Water Law*, 1: 470.

13. Ibid., at 99, sec. 18. See also *Colorado Water Law*, 1: 471.

14. 1881 *Colo. Sess. Laws* 119, secs. 1–6, as cited in *Colorado Water Law*, 1: 471.

15. 1887 *Colo. Sess. Laws* 295, secs. 1 and 2, *Colorado Water Law*, 1: 472.

16. Unpublished essay by Peggy Ford, Greeley Museum, titled, Historic Background [of] Greeley, Colorado: Agricultural Mecca of the West, 1996, 14.

17. Boyd, *A History*, 165. Boyd refers to an article written in the *Greeley Tribune*, "Is Niagara Before Us?"

18. Boyd, *A History*, 249, 254.

19. Letters between Leroy and Martha Carpenter, April–June 1880, box 30, Carpenter Papers, NCWCD.

20. Box 48, folder 9, Carpenter Papers, NCWCD.

21. Ibid., box 18, folder 1.

22. Ibid. See also the black-bound book in box 26.

23. Ibid. "The Fatal Gate" can be found in box 79, brown folder.

24. As reported in the *Greeley Tribune*, 4 June 1896.

25. The author is not trying to suggest that Delph Carpenter was in any way a stereotypical middle child, but the research done by Kevin Leman and

published in his *New Birth Order Book* (1998) is reasonably consistent with the behavior patterns Carpenter developed in his career.

26. Author's interview with Sarah Thompson, Delph Carpenter's daughter, 11 February 1994, Sacramento, Calif.

27. Carpenter to Lawton W. Luther of the *Weld County News*, 17 June 1929. See also the ledger book of senior class meetings, box 26, and a 20 May 1899 essay by Delph Carpenter in box 18, folder 1—both in Carpenter Papers, NCWCD.

28. *Greeley Tribune*, 15 June 1899.

29. Delph Carpenter, "A Freshman and Only a Freshie," essay written in 1897, published in *Greeley Tribune*, June 1899. This clipping can be found in box 31, folder 3, Carpenter Papers, NCWCD.

30. "Great Men," ibid.

31. Carpenter, "The Sunnyside Kid," and "Of Life and Happiness," in diary, box 4, Carpenter Papers, NCWCD.

32. *Greeley Tribune*, 15 June 1899.

33. Exceptions filed in Weld County Court to the Executor's Report filed 21 February 1899, by Henry Currier and his attorney Charles D. Todd. The exceptions include rents, interest, and income from farm produce in the amount of $2896, which the plaintiffs alleged should have been distributed to the heirs of the estate. See Probate Case no. 381, Colorado State Archives, Denver, Colo..

34. See Delph Carpenter's brief autobiography written in about 1918, box 78, clippings envelope, Carpenter Papers, NCWCD. Delph's obituary also mentions that he participated briefly in the Currier estate case and then turned to general litigation. See the *Greeley Tribune*, 27 February 1951.

35. Phrenology Exam, box 21, Carpenter Papers, NCWCD. The folder is labeled "Private Reading DEC" in Delph Carpenter's handwriting.

36. This Hogarty family genealogy was made available to the author courtesy of Doris Carpenter. It is taken from materials collected by historian M. Wallingford at the Soldiers and Sailors Historical and Benevolent Society, Washington, D.C., and compiled in a handwritten report dated 30 December 1908.

37. Captain Hogarty tried in vain to persuade Congress to promote him to brigadier general. In 1909 he wrote Colorado Senator Simon Guggenheim, providing details of his military service. Guggenheim introduced a bill in the Senate and Representative Edward Taylor introduced a similar bill in the House, but neither achieved the desired result. See M. J. Hogarty to Senator Simon Guggenheim, 22 March 1909 in box 53, folder 1, Carpenter Papers, NCWCD.

38. *Greeley Tribune*, 26 July 1976.

39. Newspaper clipping, February 1901, in box 31, folder 3, Carpenter Papers, NCWCD. See also *Denver Times*, 5 June 1901.

40. *Greeley Tribune*, 14 August 1902.

41. Receipt from the General Land Office, 1 February 1909. This receipt recognizes the purchase of 152.4 acres for $1 per acre, described as the east ½ of the northwest ¼ of section 30, township 6N, range 63W, 6th meridian. See box 18, folder 1, Carpenter Papers, NCWCD.

42. Delph Carpenter to W. R. Wood, Ottawa, Kansas, 13 April 1906, box 25, Carpenter Papers, NCWCD.

43. Delph Carpenter, diary, 1904, box 78, Carpenter Papers, NCWCD. An unidentified newspaper clipping in the 1905 diary notes that Delph always brought fine quality steers to the Denver market, where they were sold to packers for $4.20 to $4.25/hdrwt. The steers averaged 1200 pounds.

44. Delph Carpenter, essay on stockraising published in the *Greeley Tribune*, 14 August 1902, as part of a twenty-seven-page insert on Weld County farming and livestock raising.

45. Delph Carpenter, "The Colorado Wolf Hunt," unpublished essay sent to *Cosmopolitan* magazine sometime after March 30, 1903, box 21, Carpenter Papers, NCWCD.

46. Delph Carpenter to the Windsor Mercantile Co., 27 September 1906, ibid.

47. Delph Carpenter to A. H. Stevens, Trinidad, Colo., 26 May 1906, ibid.

48. *Denver Post*, 26 August 1907.

49. *Weld County Republican*, 12 September 1907.

50. Ibid., 5 December 1907; see also "The People of the State of Colorado against Charles Simonsen," Weld County District Court, no. 311. Some of the testimony can be found in box 27, Carpenter Papers, NCWCD.

51. Michael J. Hogarty, National City, Calif. to Delph Carpenter, 7 December 1907, box 27, ibid.

52. Delph Carpenter to M. J. Hogarty, 4 April 1908, ibid.

53. *Greeley Sun*, 11 September 1906.

54. *Greeley Daily Pioneer*, 31 October 1908.

55. *Kansas v. Colorado*, 206 US 46 (1907).

56. As quoted in Ubbelohde et al., *A Colorado History*, 265.

57. Newspaper clipping, unidentified source, Carpenter Papers, NCWCD.

58. Colorado, Senate Report of the Committee on Irrigation Investigations of the Senate, by Authority of S. R. no. 16 of the Seventeenth General Assembly (Senate Journal, 1909, 1092), 16 pp., submitted by Delph E. Carpenter, J. H. Crowley, and Geo. E. West. Delph's concerns about the Reclamation Service were rooted in its decision to embargo water development in the San Luis Valley, pending construction of Elephant Butte Dam on the Rio Grande. He was concerned, as well, about the aggressive actions of Department of the Interior solicitors in *Kansas v. Colorado* (1907).

59. In the spirit of other voluntary associations that became permanent, the National Irrigation Congresses met from 1891 to the end of World War I.

Their objective was to unite the various western interests and influence the government in its formation of a national irrigation policy. See Pisani, *To Reclaim a Divided West*, 239.

60. Delph Carpenter to Charles D. Hayt, 26 June 1911, box 47, folder 2, Carpenter Papers, NCWCD. Elwood Mead was commissioner of reclamation from 1924 to 1936. In addition to devising Wyoming's water code, Mead directed construction at Hoover, Grand Coulee and Owyhee dams. Something of a crusader who believed in establishing strong federal support for irrigated communities, Mead represented a philosophical threat to Carpenter's concept of states' rights.

61. *Denver Republican*, 22 April 1911.

62. Delph Carpenter to M. J. Hogarty, 4 February 1911, box 47, folder 2, Carpenter Papers, NCWCD.

63. See "The Greeley-Poudre Irrigation District, Weld County, Colorado," n.d., printed in Greeley, Colorado by the District. L. G. Carpenter's Report on the Greeley-Poudre Irrigation District, printed by Farson, Son and Co., Chicago, for prospective bond buyers is also valuable. Both may be found in box 27, brown folder, Carpenter Papers, NCWCD.

64. *Wyoming v. Colorado*, 259 US 419 (1922).

65. I am indebted to Donald Pisani, University of Oklahoma, for sharing his insights on this subject with me. Both his letter of 9 June 1998 and his draft chapter, "Hydroelectric Power and the New West," in a forthcoming book on the Bureau of Reclamation, have proved helpful.

66. *Denver Republican*, 18 March 1909.

67. Delph Carpenter to Senator Knute Nelson, Washington, D.C., 8 March 1910, box 86, folder 21, Carpenter Papers, NCWCD.

68. Delph Carpenter to John E. Law, 1 November 1910, box 47, folder 2, ibid.

69. *Colorado Session Laws*, 1899–1901, Chapter 85, 193, law of 13 April 1901, "An Act in Relation to Irrigation; Prescribing Penalties in Relation thereto and Defining Certain Duties of the State Engineer and Superintendents of Irrigation." Colorado, Senate Bill no. 134,. Sec. 4. The act states that "The owners or possessors of reservoirs shall not have the right to impound any water whatever in such reservoirs during the time such water is required in ditches for direct irrigation or for reservoirs holding senior rights." If applied literally by water officials and the courts, this sentence would have required a perpetual subordination of reservoirs to all ditch rights, regardless of priority, because the 1901 law did not contain the word *senior* in front of *ditches*.

70. *Denver Republican*, 28 March 1911.

71. Delph Carpenter to M. C. Hinderlider, Colorado state engineer, 14 January 1932, courtesy of W. D. Farr, Greeley, Colorado.

72. *Denver Republican*, 1 April 1911.

73. *Greeley Republican,* 20 July 1911; *Fort Collins Courier,* 15 July 1911.

74. *Greeley Tribune,* 10 September 1911.

75. Ibid.

76. Delph Carpenter, draft of speech against the initiative and referendum, 1910, box 86, folder 21, Carpenter Papers, NCWCD.

77. Colorado Senate, S.B. 134, "A Bill for an act to amend an act entitled, 'An Act in Relation to Irrigation; Prescribing Penalties in Relation thereto and defining Certain Duties of the State Engineer and Superintendents of Irrigation,' approved April 13, 1901." The Parrish Amendment would have correctly stated that reservoirs with junior priorities would be subject to the exercise of senior ditch and reservoir rights. After defeat of the Parrish Amendment by the voters, the 1901 sentence that Carpenter proposed to delete was dropped by the reviser of statutes. The rest of Carpenter's legislation remained intact.

78. Delph Carpenter to Ray Regester, Greeley, 5 November 1912, box 48, folder 6, Carpenter Papers, NCWCD.

79. Delph Carpenter to M. C. Hinderlider, 14 January 1932, courtesy of W. D. Farr, Greeley, Colorado.

80. Campaign literature, box 85, folder 23, Carpenter Papers, NCWCD.

81. Delph Carpenter to D. E. Gray, 14 June 1912, box 86, folder 2, ibid.

82. Ibid., 15 June 1912.

83. Delph Carpenter to D. E. Gray, 28 July 1912, and Delph Carpenter to Hubert Reynolds 13 August 1912, box 86, folders 2 and 4, ibid.

84. Delph Carpenter to Senator William H. Adams and to Matt N. Lions, 11 November 1912, box 85, folder 21, ibid.

85. Delph Carpenter, speech, Proceedings of the 40th Anniversary of the Coming of the Union Colony to Greeley, 10 May 1910, box 82, ibid.

86. *Daily News,* 13 February 1911.

CHAPTER 3: THE MAKING OF AN
INTEERSTATE STREAMS COMMISSIONER

Epigraph: Delph to cousin Alfred, 30 October 1914, box 79, brown folder, Carpenter Papers, NCWCD.

1. Delph Carpenter to Alfred G. Carpenter, Cleveland, Ohio, 30 October 1914, box 79, brown folder, Carpenter Papers, NCWCD.

2. Diary of Delph Carpenter, 20 and 22 March 1914, box 78, ibid.

3. The Greeley-Poudre Irrigation District was formally organized in 1909. Each of the 125,000 acres was bonded at forty dollars with the intent of raising five million dollars for the construction of the reservoirs, tunnel, and delivery canals. By the time of the *Wyoming v. Colorado* suit, enough cash had been raised through bond sales to contract the Laramie-Poudre Reservoirs and Irrigation Company for one million dollars to build the tunnel, but sales of bonds to finish the project slowed dramatically when Wyoming filed suit.

4. Delph Carpenter to Governor Elias M. Ammons, 13 January 1913, box 24, Carpenter Papers, NCWCD. Colorado lawmakers attempted to appropriate $50,000 for its defense, but the legislation was found unconstitutional. Wyoming, on the other hand, appropriated $25,000 and quickly began gathering evidence. By 1913, thanks in large part to Delph Carpenter's urging, Colorado established a water defense fund, out of which funds were drawn for litigation on interstate streams.

5. Delph Carpenter to D. C. MacWatters, 14 November 1912, box 24, ibid.

6. Delph Carpenter to C. W. Crouter, Wheatland, Wyoming, 20 July 1911, box 47, folder 2, ibid. Delph believed the case was politically motivated and it had been initiated by two men who planned to turn Laramie River water into Lake Hattie near Woods Landing, Wyoming. Knowing their planned project was "junior" in priority to the Greeley-Poudre Project, they "started a series of agitations around Laramie City to the effect that the Colorado diverters were about to take *all* of the water of the Laramie River in Colorado and divert it to the Cache la Poudre Valley." According to Carpenter, they used this threat to gain votes during the most recent political campaign.

7. Delph Carpenter to Laura E. Hughes, Downers Grove, Illinois, 13 November 1912, box 86, folder 3, ibid.

8. Diary of Delph Carpenter, 20 March 1914, box 78, ibid.

9. Delph Carpenter to Governor E. M. Ammons, 3 January 1913, box 24, ibid.

10. Delph Carpenter to United States Consulate, Paris, 8 December 1913, box 29, folder 9, ibid.

11. Delph Carpenter to the American Minister, Berne, Switzerland, 13 January 1914, ibid.

12. Direct examination of Louis G. Carpenter in the Supreme Court of the United States, *The State of Wyoming Complainant v. The State of Colorado, The Greeley-Poudre Irrigation District, a municipal corporation, The Laramie-Poudre Reservoirs and Irrigation Company, a corporation, Defendants.* No. 8, Original in Equity. Evidence taken on Behalf of the Defendants before Newton C. Garbutt, Commissioner, vol. 1, December 15, 1913, 1422 ff.

13. In the Supreme Court of the United States, October Term, 1916, No. 7, Original in Equity. *The State of Wyoming, Complainant, v. The State of Colorado, The Greeley-Poudre Irrigation District, and the Laramie-Poudre Reservoirs and Irrigation Company, Defendants,* Brief for Defendants, vol. II, 36.

14. Delph Carpenter to E. F. Shellaberger, Dekalb, Ill., 23 January 1913, box 24, Carpenter Papers, NCWCD. See also Delph Carpenter's brief, October term, 1916, No. 7, Part II, Prior Appropriation, in which he states, "Prior appropriation ("Colorado Doctrine") does not apply to the use and distribution of water between the states," 130.

15. In the Supreme Court of the United States, October term, 1917. Re *The State of Wyoming, Complainant vs. The State of Colorado, The Greeley-Poudre*

Irrigation District, and the Laramie-Poudre Reservoirs and Irrigation Company, Defendants. Supplemental Brief on Behalf of the Defendants. Vol. I. The Law. Conclusions, 364–66. In this instance, Carpenter's discussion of priority related to diversion dates and not to alleged sovereignty rights of headwaters states.

16. From all the data available, estimates of normal flow in the Laramie River ranged from 188,000 acre-feet to 300,000 acre-feet. No matter what figure was used, the Greeley-Poudre Project would have taken between one-third and one-half of the total flow.

17. In March 1916, the Court asked both sides to consider (1) whether the rights of states are to be determined by state boundaries; (2) whether priority of appropriation is to be determined by state lines; (3) the extent to which each state has used Laramie River water since the lawsuit was filed and the amount of work done on their respective projects up to the filing of the suit; (4) whether the United States should have a right to intervene in the case because of Reclamation projects in affected districts. See *Weld County News,* 16 March 1916.

18. Diary of Delph Carpenter, 2 December 1916 to 8 December 1916, box 78, Carpenter Papers, NCWCD.

19. *The Poudre Valley,* 14 December 1916.

20. Diary of Delph Carpenter, 10 April 1914, box 78, Carpenter Papers, NCWCD.

21. A. P. Davis to Delph Carpenter, 19 February 1915, and Delph Carpenter to A. P. Davis, 23 February 1915, box 86, folder 1, ibid. The essence of the Ballinger-Pinchot controversy is that Pinchot, a crusader for conservation of natural resources, Theodore Roosevelt's friend and chief forester, accused Richard A. Ballinger, President Taft's secretary of the interior, of corruptly alienating public domain lands by giving them to a Morgan-Guggenheim syndicate. Congress vindicated Ballinger, but in the court of public opinion Pinchot scored his own victory. Carpenter disliked Pinchot's paternalistic approach to the states' natural resources and he was quite supportive of Secretary Ballinger.

22. Diary of Delph Carpenter, 4 March 1914, box 78, ibid.

23. Delph Carpenter to L. R. Temple, Fort Collins, 14 June 1912, box 24, ibid.

24. Delph Carpenter to A. L. Davis & Son, Princeton, Illinois, 12 December 1912, box 24, ibid.

25. Delph Carpenter to H. T. Groom, Groom, Texas, 8 May 1914, box 46, ibid.

26. Delph Carpenter to Benjamin C. Allen, Colorado Springs, 24 June 1914, ibid.

27. Diary of Delph Carpenter, 11 May 1916, box 78, ibid. Carpenter was referring to the Great Western Sugar Company.

28. Delph Carpenter, Report of two trips down the South Platte River in May and June of 1916, box 83, folder 4, ibid.

29. Diary of Delph Carpenter, 17 February 1917, box 78, ibid.

30. Ibid.

31. Ibid., 21 February 1917.

32. Diary of Delph Carpenter, 7 March, 1917, ibid.

33. Delph Carpenter to Alfred W. Craven, Chicago, 1 May 1917, box 86, folder 22, ibid.

34. Diary of Delph Carpenter, 14 March to 22 March 1917, box 78, ibid. See also *Greeley Tribune*, 14 March 1917.

35. Diary of Delph Carpenter, 1 April 1917, box 78, ibid.

36. Ibid., 10 September 1917.

37. Ibid., 13 May 1917.

38. Ibid., 1 January 1918.

39. Michaela "Dot" Carpenter to Delph Carpenter, 6 January 1918, box 85, folder 21., ibid.

40. Diary of Delph Carpenter, 10 January 1918, box 78, ibid.

41. Ibid., 11 January 1918.

42. Ibid., 5 and 11 January 1918.

43. The Court did not ask for additional testimony, but nearly four years passed before Justice Van Devanter's opinion was readied and released on June 5, 1922.

44. Delph Carpenter to Platt Rogers, 3 July 1919, box 86, folder 26, ibid.

45. *Adelbert A. Weiland, as State Engineer of the State of Colorado, et al. v. The Pioneer Irrigation Company*, decided 5 June 1922 and reported in 259 US 498.

46. Vranesh, *Colorado Water Law*, vol. 3, 1744. In note 248, Vranesh cites 151 C.C.A. 455, 238 F. 519 (D. Colo. 1916) as the earlier phase of the case.

47. Diary of Delph Carpenter, 11 November 1918, box 78, ibid.

48. The so-called Spanish flu was misnamed. It began in the United States in the spring of 1918, most probably in Fort Riley, Kansas, where soldiers were training for war. From there it spread to Europe and then back to the eastern United States, where it traveled from Boston down the coast at a rapid rate. In October 1918, the virus killed 195,000 Americans. Doctors were unable to see it in their microscopes. They believed it was a bacteria and were helpless to stop the worst epidemic in American history that ultimately claimed 600,000 American lives. Carpenter might have been infected anywhere, but chances are he was exposed to the disease when pleading a case before the Supreme Court in January 1919.

49. Diary of Delph Carpenter, 1 December 1918, box 78, ibid.

50. Delph Carpenter to W. A. Walker, Racine, Wisconsin, 12 April 1919, box 86, folder 27, ibid.

51. Delph Carpenter to Platt Rogers, 3 July 1919, and to Fred A Sabin, 28 October 1919, box 86, folder 26, ibid.

52. *Wyoming v. Colorado* 259 US 419 (1922); *Weiland v. Pioneer Irrigation Company* 259 US 498 (1922).

53. M. C. Hinderlider to Delph Carpenter, 22 March 1941, box 23, folder 1, Carpenter Papers, NCWCD.

54. As of June 2001, the Republican River Compact is the subject of a lawsuit in the U.S. Supreme Court: *State of Kansas v. State of Nebraska and State of Colorado*, no. 126, original.

55. Article V, The Republican River Compact, signed by commissioners from Colorado, Kansas, and Nebraska on 19 March 1941; ratified by Colorado's State Assembly on 31 December 1942.

56. From his studies of the international law of rivers, Carpenter wrote that "a lower nation may not justify a claim of servitude upon the stream within the upper nation upon the ground of prior appropriation (by the lower nation) of either all or a part of the waters of the stream rising within the territory of the upper nation . . . [or a claim] that a recognition of an international rule of distribution and administration of waters by prior appropriation would amount to a recognition of an international servitude upon the territory of one nation for the benefit of the other and would be entirely inconsistent with the sovereignty of the upper nation over its national domain." See Delph E. Carpenter, "Application of the Reserve Treaty Powers of the States to Interstate Water Controversies," an address published in *Interstate Compacts*, 1: 127.

57. Delph Carpenter to Ralph G. Lindstrom, chair, Executive Committee, The Law Club of Denver, 28, June 1923, box 37, folder 3, Carpenter Papers, NCWCD. See also Tyler, "Delph E. Carpenter: Father of Interstate Water Compacts," *Colorado History*: 85–105. In the foreword to the South Platte River Compact, signed in April 1923, Carpenter wrote, "The study and research necessary to sustain the application of the treaty plan of interstate distribution of the waters of the South Platte laid the foundation for the suggestion and conclusion of the Colorado River Compact and the application of the policy of resort to interstate diplomacy, in lieu of litigation, had its origin with South Platte problems."

58. Diary of Delph Carpenter, 3 November 1917, box 78, Carpenter Papers, NCWCD.

59. Ibid., 25 and 26 June 1918. Among some of the published works Delph studied were Eugene F. Ware, *The Indian War of 1864* (Topeka: Crane and Co., 1911), and George Armstrong Custer, *My Life on the Plains; Or, Personal Experiences with Indians*. (New York: Sheldon and Co., 1876).

60. Delph Carpenter, memorandum, to Governor William E. Sweet, n.d., South Platte River Compact, p. 9, box 87, folder 22, Carpenter Papers, NCWCD.

61. Delph Carpenter to Russell W. Fleming, attorney for the North Poudre Irrigation Company, 10 March 1919, box 86, folder 23, ibid.

62. Delph Carpenter to F. W. Harding, 19 April 1919, box 46, ibid.

63. Carpenter, "Application of the Reserve Treaty Powers," *Interstate Compacts*, 1: 112.

64. Press release, n.d., titled "Governor Shoup—Weld County," describing Delph's role in the 1920 political campaign. See box 85, folder 19, Carpenter Papers, NCWCD.

65. Norris Hundley, Jr., *Water and the West*, 58.

66. *San Diego Union*, 16 November 1917, as cited in Hundley, *Water and the West*, 59, n. 11.

67. *Los Angeles Times*, 17 November 1917, as cited in ibid. 60, n. 13.

68. Hundley, *Water and the West*, 61–64, 73–79.

69. Franklin K. Lane, "Homes for Former Servicemen," *American Legion Weekly*, 1, no. 1 (4 July 1919): 13, 14, 28. See also box 17, RG 115, General Administration and Project Records, 1919–1945, General Files, 1919–1929, National Archives and Records Administration —Rocky Mountain Region. The team of fact-finders working for Powell provided Davis with information later published by Congress as the Fall-Davis Report, or as "Problems of the Imperial Valley and Vicinity," Sen. Doc. 142, 67th Congress, 2d, sess., 2 February 1922.

70. *Annual Reports*, Bureau of Reclamation, 1915–1922, RG 115, ibid.

71. Blue Notebook titled "Colorado River Commission: Commerce Papers A–C," 6, Hoover Library, West Branch, Iowa. This is a finding aid whose "Scope and Content" section includes a reference to the 16 February 1918 agreement by the Interior Department to pay one-third of the cost of an engineering survey. The agreement also created the All-American Canal Board, which recommended that the canal be built by the federal government after the survey was completed.

72. Delph Carpenter to R. P. Teele, United States Department of Agriculture, 11 February 1919, box 81, folder 4, Carpenter Papers, NCWCD. Carpenter had been in contact with Teele, hoping to employ him as a consultant on South Platte River matters, because Teele had done a report on the South Platte in 1904.

73. L. G. Carpenter to A. J. McCune, 16 June 1920, State Engineer Records, RG 0037, CRCC box 2, League Correspondence, 1920–23, Wyoming State Archives, Cheyenne, Wyoming.

74. Delph Carpenter, Historical Sketch of the Colorado River Commission, box 51, brown folder, Carpenter Papers, NCWCD.

75. Delph Carpenter, ms copy of a "Foreword" to part 4 of the never-completed "History of the Colorado River Compact," box 12, Ray Lyman Wilbur Papers, Hoover Presidential Library, West Branch, Iowa. Delph Carpenter's reference is to government embargoes on the Rio Grande and the North Platte River while construction of Elephant Butte and Pathfinder dams was underway. This Foreword was brought to my attention by Professor Donald Pisani, University of Oklahoma.

76. Salt Lake Conference Resolutions, January 21, 1919, Historical Sketch, box 7, Carpenter Papers, NCWCD.

77. *Proceedings of the Third Convention of the League of the Southwest at the Trinity Auditorium in Los Angeles, California, April 1, 2, 3, 1920* (Los Angeles, 1920), 155, copy in the Huntington Library, San Marino, California, as cited in Hundley, *Water in the West*, 86, n. 4.

78. Ibid.

79. Hundley, Water in the West, p. 89.

80. *Proceedings of the Third Convention*, 33, 38, as cited in Hundley, *Water in the West*, 87, 88. Prior to 1921, the Grand River was that part of what is now called the Colorado River from the point above where the Green River enters the Colorado River in Utah to its source in Rocky Mountain National Park in Colorado. Colorado's Representative Edward T. Taylor proposed the name change in 1921 and Congress approved. See "Renaming of the Grand River of Colorado," Hearing before the Committee on Interstate and Foreign Commerce of the House of Representatives, 66th congress, 3rd sess., H. J. Res. 460, February 18, 1921.

81. Hundley, *Water in the West*, 89, 90.

82. Ibid., 51, 101. The 18 May 1920 Kinkaid Act resulted in the Fall-Davis Report of 4 February 1922.

83. Ibid., 16.

84. Ibid., 100, 101.

85. Ibid., 104. In note 39, Hundley cites League of the Southwest, Denver Proceedings, 53–54.

86. A. J. McCune to George Anderson, Los Angeles, 22 July 1920, Shoup Papers, RCC 26796, Colorado State Archives.

87. Hundley, *Water in the West*, 96. In note 23, Hundley cites Proceedings of the League of the Southwest, Denver, Colorado, August 25, 26, 27, 1920, typescript (n.p. [1920]), 5, 28.

88. Ibid., 97. In note 24, Hundley cites League of the Southwest, Denver Proceedings, 14, 28.

89. League of the Southwest, Denver Proceedings, 287, 288. Adjoined to this paragraph were other resolutions that expressed League opposition to any restrictions on development in the upper basin and reaffirmed resolutions adopted in Salt Lake City and Los Angeles.

90. Delph Carpenter, Foreword, "The History of the Colorado River Compact," MS version, 23, box 12, Ray Lyman Wilbur Papers, Hoover Library.

91. Ibid., 23, 25.

92. Hundley, *Water in the West*, p. 108.

93. Delph Carpenter to E. V. Wilcox, 14 August 1920, box 85, folder 21, Carpenter Papers, NCWCD. Wilcox was an unusual man. He truly believed that his eastern readers should understand the peculiarities of western irrigation and to this end he hoped to publish thirty articles on the subject. The first and only article published was "The Water Oracle of Greeley," *Country Gentleman*, 85, no. 41 (October 9, 1920): 6, 7, 26.

94. Ibid.

95. Ibid.

96. *Denver Post,* 3 April 1921.

CHAPTER 4: THE COLORADO RIVER COMPACT: PHASE I

1. Minutes of the Twenty-Seventh Meeting of the Colorado River Commission, 24 November 1922, Santa Fe, New Mexico, Colorado River Commission, Hoover Presidential Library.

2. Meeker to Carpenter, 27 June 1921, RCC 20559, folder 5, Department of Natural Resources, Colorado River Commission, Colorado State Archives.

3. Meeker to Carpenter, 26 April 1938, box 84, folder 7, Carpenter Papers, NCWCD. See also Meeker to Carpenter, 23 December 1944, box 50, letter box, ibid. Delph's nickname was entered in the *Congressional Record,* 6 February 1950, 1559, by Senator Mark Malone of Nevada, who referred to the Coloradan as "the brains of the Colorado River Compact" and "one of the greatest water lawyers who ever lived in the United States of America."

4. Carpenter to Reid Carpenter, Mansfield, Ohio, 15 October 1924, box 84, folder 11, Carpenter Papers, NCWCD.

5. E. V. Wilcox, "The Water Oracle of Greeley": 6, 7, 26.

6. Ibid.

7. Carpenter to Reid Carpenter, Mansfield, Ohio, 15 October 1924, box 84, folder 11, Carpenter Papers, NCWCD.

8. Carpenter to Howard Strange, Greeley, 13 February 1921, box 47, ibid.

9. Carpenter to Edward G. Ingraham, New Raymer, Colorado, 22 December 1920, ibid.

10. As quoted in a brochure announcing a bull sale in 1920, ibid.

11. Alvin T. Steinel, "A Boy's Dream That Came True," 8, 9. Steinel later wrote *History of Agriculture in Colorado,* in which he discusses the few Shorthorn herds in Colorado.

12. Carpenter to D. C. Bascomb, county agent, Larimer County, 27 March 1920, box 47, Carpenter Papers, NCWCD.

13. Carpenter drew on his extensive study of Article I, sec. 10, paragraph 3 of the United States Constitution, which reads that "No State shall, *without the consent of Congress* [author's emphasis], lay any duty of tonnage, keep troops, or ships of war in time of Peace, *enter into any Agreement or Compact* [author's emphasis] with another State, or with a foreign Power, or engage in War, unless actually invaded, or in such imminent Danger as will not admit of delay."

14. Sims Ely, secretary of the Arizona Resources Board, to Governor Oliver Shoup, 25 October 1920, RCC 20559, folder 5, Department of Natural Resources, Colorado River Commission, Colorado State Archives.

15. Press release, "Governor Shoup—Weld County," n.d., box 85, folder 19, Carpenter Papers, NCWCD.

16. Newspaper clippings, n.d., box 31, folder 3, ibid.

17. In a letter to Judge Evan A. Evans, Chicago, 24 January 1921, Carpenter wrote that $2.8 million of $5.1 million bonds were sold as of 1911 when Wyoming sued Colorado. Outstanding bonds had depreciated to approximately 25 percent of their value and lands that were supposed to benefit from this project had depreciated to a "nominal value" due to the fact that the project was only 54 percent complete. Box 86, folder 23, ibid.

18. As quoted in the *Greeley Tribune*, 24 January 1921. The Colorado River Compact was first approved by six states and went into effect in 1928. The seventh state, Arizona, ratified in 1944.

19. *Denver Post*, 3 April 1921. In so doing, Shoup stated that he was in compliance with action taken by the League of the Southwest designed to help avoid interstate water litigation. Carpenter preferred to use the title of commissioner, because he felt that an ambassador dealt more specifically with international matters.

20. Carpenter to Shoup, 20 January 1921, RCC 20559, folder 5, Department of Natural Resources, Colorado River Commission, Colorado State Archives.

21. Carpenter to Shoup, 17 February 1921, ibid.

22. Carpenter, preliminary statement, directed to Governor Oliver Shoup in anticipation of how a meeting of the governors and commissioners of the Colorado River basin should proceed, ibid.

23. Carpenter, "Application of the Reserve Treaty Powers of the States to Interstate Water Controversies," *Colorado Bar Association*, vol. 24 (29 January 1921) and reprinted as Chapter 6 in *Interstate Compacts*, 1: 111–40.

24. Carpenter, Foreword to "The History of the Colorado River Compact," prepared at the request of Herbert Hoover but never published, box 12, folder on Hoover Dam, Ray Lyman Wilbur Papers, Hoover Presidential Library, 28, 29.

25. *Greeley Tribune-Republican*, 13 June 1921.

26. Carpenter, "Sketch of Inducing Events and Causes Leading to Creation of the Colorado River [Compact] Commission," 43. Hereafter cited as "Sketch." Hoover urged Carpenter to develop a sketch of the "prenatal" period of the Colorado River Compact for possibie publication. See container 30, Post-Presidential Papers, Herbert Hoover Presidential Library.

27. *Greeley Tribune-Republican*, 13 June 1921.

28. *Granting the Consent of Congress to Certain Compacts and Agreements between the States of Arizona, California, Colorado, Nevada, New Mexico, Utah and Wyoming*, Hearing before the Committee on the Judiciary, House of Representatives, 67th Congress, 1st sess. on H.R. 6821, serial 6, June 4, 1921, Washington, GPO, 1921.

29. *Congressional Record*, 67th Cong., 1st sess. (1921), 2271, 2773–74, 5864, as cited in Hundley, *Water in the West*, n. 6, 113.

30. Hearing, H.R. 6821, 4 June 1921, 10, 11.

31. Ibid., 10, 12, 13, 17.

32. Ibid., 23–25.

33. Ibid., 31.

34. *Congressional Record*, 67th Cong., 1st sess. (1921), 2771, 2773–74, 5864, and *U.S. Statutes at Large*, 42: 171, as cited in n. 6, p. 113 of Hundley, *Water in the West*. The act is also cited as Public No. 56, 67th Cong. In addition to "providing for equitable division and apportionment . . . of the water supply of the Colorado River and of the streams tributary thereto," it appropriated $10,000 to pay the salary and expenses of a federal representative.

35. Carpenter, diary, 21 to 31 May 1921, box 78, Carpenter Papers, NCWCD.

36. Ibid; see also draft of a memorandum to Governor Shoup, 21 June 1921, titled "Appearance Before President Harding—Colorado River Compact," box 1, brown folder, ibid.

37. Delph Carpenter, "Sketch," ms copy, Ray Lyman Wilbur Papers, box 12, folder labeled "Hoover Dam—Dobbel Material—Colorado River Compact History—Undated," Hoover Library. I am grateful to Professor Donald Pisani for calling this essay to my attention. Various drafts can be found in the Carpenter Papers, NCWCD, where they are referred to either as the "Sketch" or the "Foreword." In 1934, Hoover asked Carpenter to write up the early history of the compact. The material was to be used as a foreword for Part II of a book that Stanford Professor Charles A. Dobel was writing on the compact. McGraw Hill reviewed the manuscript but rejected it, describing Carpenter's contribution as a harangue against the Bureau of Reclamation. The manuscript was then abandoned. See Carpenter to Hoover, 5 January 1934, box 79, Hoover Letters, Carpenter Papers, NCWCD, and V. T. Boughton of McGraw Hill to Hoover, 24 May 1935, Post Presidential Papers, Hoover Association to Hoover Dam, folder on Hoover Dam Correspondence, 1929–1935, Hoover Presidential Library.

38. Carpenter to the Arizonan Thomas Campbell, 14 October 1921, Department of Natural Resources, Colorado River Commission, RCC 20559, folder 7, Colorado State Archives.

39. *Kansas v. Colorado*, 206 US 46 (1907) had ruled basin-of-origin states were required to provide an equitable apportionment of water to their downstream neighbors. This momentous decision had not yet become a rule of law, because the Court determined not to take sides. It also noted that Kansas was a riparian state and Colorado was a prior-appropriation state. The Court stated it could make no determination of Kansas' right until it could be shown the state had suffered injury at the hands of Colorado. The High Court rejected the claim of the United States that the Reclamation Act provided for federal

reservation of western waters, to be developed as the national government saw fit. Observers expected that the status of interstate priority would be clarified when the Court handed down its decision in *Wyoming v. Colorado* (1922).

40. Root-Casasus Treaty, 1906. Delph frequently cited the 1895 ruling of Attorney General Judson Harmon respecting Mexico's claims to Rio Grande water based on that nation's priority of use. Harmon's opinion stated that if Mexico's demand for a definite quantity were allowed, it would place a servitude on the United States which would, in turn, arrest development of the United States. What was appropriate for Mexicans within their own boundaries, Harmon stated, could not extend across international limits, but "from considerations of comity, the question should be decided as one of policy and settled by treaty." Carpenter was citing U.S. Department of Justice, *Official Opinion of the Attorneys General of the U.S.: Advising the President and Heads of Departments, in Relation to Their Official Duties*, vol. 21 (Washington, D.C.: GPO, 1873), 274.

41. Carpenter, memorandum, n.d., box 26, Carpenter Papers, NCWCD.

42. In a letter to Governor Oliver Shoup, 9 September 1921, Carpenter mentioned the possibility of transferring water from the Animas River to the La Plata River, a project that had already been surveyed by Colorado state engineer M. C. Hinderlider. See box 26, ibid.

43. See "Report of Delph E. Carpenter Commissioner for the State of Colorado *in re* La Plata River Compact *with* Copy of the Compact and Brief of the Law Respecting Interstate Compacts Submitted to the Judiciary Committee of the House of Representatives, 67th Cong., 1st sess., at Hearing on June 4, 1921, *in re* H. R. 6821," box 37, brown folder, ibid.

44. See Philip C. Jessup, *Elihu Root*, 2 vols., 1938; Richard W. Leopold, *Elihu Root and the Conservative Tradition*, 1954; and James B. Scott's "Elihu Root," in Samuel F. Bemis, ed., *American Secretaries of State and Their Diplomacy* (New York: Cooper Square Publishers, 1929), 193–282.

45. Carpenter, "Application of the Reserve Treaty Powers of the States to Interstate Water Controversies," *Colorado Bar Association*, vol. 24 (29 January 1921) and reprinted as Chapter 6 in *Interstate Compacts*, 1: 136, 137.

46. Carpenter to Campbell, 18 August 1921, Department of Natural Resources, Colorado River Commission, RCC 20559, folder 6, Colorado State Archives.

47. Carpenter to Scrugham, 20 June 1921, folder 5, ibid.

48. Carpenter to Scrugham, 15 August 1921, folder 6, ibid.

49. Carpenter to Scrugham, 26 November 1921, folder 7, ibid. Carpenter was also interested in meeting Harry Chandler, publisher of the *Los Angeles Times*, who was a partner in 840,000 acres in the Mexicali Valley and whose newspaper had come out forcefully in favor of Colorado River development. See Carpenter to B. W. Ritter of Durango, Colorado, 26 November 1921, in ibid; and Hundley, *Water in the West*, 33, 90, 91.

50. Ely to Carpenter, 17 September 1921, folder 7, ibid. Hundley, in *Water in the West*, pp. 114–17, notes that A. P. Davis issued a preliminary report on July 8, 1921, advocating construction of an All-American Canal and a dam at Boulder Canyon. This report, "Problems of Imperial Valley and Vicinity," was printed in February 1922 as Senate Doc. 142, 67th Congress, 2nd sess., and is popularly known as the Fall-Davis Report. Carpenter agreed to speak for twenty minutes on "Settlement of Inter-State Relations on Rivers by Inter-State Compact." See telegram, Carpenter to Kruckman, 18 November 1921, Department of Natural Resources, Colorado River Commission, RCC 20559, folder 7, Colorado State Archives.

51. Carpenter to Scrugham, 15 September 1921, folder 6, ibid.

52. Carpenter to Campbell, 23 September 1921, folder 7, ibid.

53. Kruckman to Carpenter, 7 November 1921, ibid.

54. Speech by Hoover, Minneapolis, Minn., 26 August 1920, extracted in Ray Lyman Wilbur and Arthur Mastick Hyde, *Hoover Policies*, 254, 255.

55. Ibid., 258.

56. For some Republicans, Hoover was not a team player. A frequent criticism was that he did not get along well with other cabinet members and he was too internationally minded. See Robert K. Murray, "Herbert Hoover and the Harding Cabinet," in Ellis W. Hawley, *Herbert Hoover as Secretary of Commerce*, 19.

57. David Burner, *Herbert Hoover*, 159-161.

58. Murray, "Hoover and the Harding Cabinet," 30.

59. Ibid.

60. Ibid., 31–34.

61. Proceedings of the Conference on Construction of the Boulder Canyon Dam, Held at San Diego, California," in Senate Doc. 142, 67th Congress, 2d sess. (1922), 251, 302, 320, as cited in Hundley, *Water in the West*, 135–137.

62. Telegrams, Hoover to Carpenter, 24 December 1921; Carpenter to Hoover, 27 December 1921; and Carpenter to Scrugham, 27 December 1921, in file of Department of Natural Resources, Colorado River Commission, RCC 20559, folder 8, Colorado State Archives.

63. Caldwell to Carpenter, 29 December 1921, and Scrugham to Carpenter, 27 December 1921, ibid.

64. Scrugham to Carpenter, 28 December 1921, ibid.

65. Hundley, *Water in the West*, 139.

66. Telegram, Carpenter to Norviel, 20 January 1922, in file of Department of Natural Resources, Colorado River Commission, RCC 20559, folder 8, Colorado State Archives.

67. Minutes and Record of the First Meeting of the Colorado River Commission, 26 January 1922, container 36, Colorado River Commission, Hoover Presidential Library, 2,3.

68. Ibid., 15.

69. Ibid., 15-17.

70. Ibid., 18.

71. Ibid., 25.

72. Ibid.

73. Kinkaid Act, May 18, 1920 (41 Stat. 600). The Fall-Davis Report appeared in preliminary form on July 8, 1921. It was submitted to Congress in final form on February 28, 1922, as "Problems of Imperial Valley and Vicinity," Sen. Doc. 142, 67th Cong., 2d sess. (1922).

74. Scrugham to Carpenter, 21 July 1921, RCC 20559, folder 6, Department of Natural Resources, Colorado River Commission, Colorado State Archives.

75. Carpenter to Scrugham, 23 July 1921, J. G. Scrugham Papers, Nevada Historical Society as cited in Hundley, *Water in the West*, n. 9, 115.

76. Comments of Franklin Mondell as reported in the *Congressional Record*, vol. 35, 1902, 6679, in which Mondell points to the acts of 26 July 1866, 9 July 1870, and 3 March 1877 as the definitive congressional recognition of state control over the appropriation and distribution of water.

77. Carpenter presented these views on many occasions, but the best summary came long after the Compact had been signed. See Delph Carpenter, "Conflict of Jurisdiction Respecting Control of Waters in Western States": 162–72.

78. See Gene M. Gressley, *The Twentieth-Century American West: A Potpourri*. One of the six essays is entitled "Reclamation and the West via Arthur Powell Davis," 78–101.

79. Pisani, "Water and the American State, 1902–1933," (tentative title as of May 2000), 31, and Norris Hundley, *The Great Thirst*, 207.

80. Minutes and Record of the First Colorado River Commission, 26 January 1922, container 36, Colorado River Commission, Hoover Presidential Library, 28–38. Final recommendations of the Fall-Davis Report included a recommendation that (1) a canal be built from Laguna Dam to the Imperial Valley with government funds; (2) public lands reclaimed from these works be reserved for ex-servicemen; (3) government funds be used to construct a reservoir at or near Boulder Canyon; (4) any state willing to contribute money to the dam's construction be provided a proportionate share of hydroelectric power at cost; (5) the secretary of interior be empowered to allot power privileges and to allocate cost and benefits of the canal; (6) in every development undertaken on the Colorado River priority or right and use to be given first to river regulation and flood control, then to storage for irrigation and finally to development for power. See "Problems of Imperial Valley and Vicinity," 28 February 1922, Senate Doc. 142, 67th Cong., 2d sess., 21.

81. Table A, "Areas and Water Requirements" (Reclamation Service Data), Minutes, Colorado River Commission, 70. The states contested Davis's

estimate of irrigable acres, but most eventually agreed that the average annual flow at Yuma was about 17.3 million acre-feet.

82. Ibid., 80. It should be noted that Davis's proposal listed the states, but did not include specific numbers for base acreage.

83. Ibid., 95, 96.

84. Ibid., 100.

85. Ibid., 105, 111.

86. Ibid. 110.

87. Ibid., 114, 115.

88. Ibid., 117, 118.

89. Ibid., 141.

90. Ibid., 146, 150.

91. Ibid., 152.

92. Hundley, *Water in the West*, 154.

CHAPTER 5: THE COLORADO RIVER COMPACT: PHASE II

Epigraph: Hoover to Carpenter, 27 November 1922, box 20, folder 8, Carpenter Papers, NCWCD.

1. Norris Hundley, Jr., *Water and the West: The Colorado River Compact*, 153–54.

2. Carpenter to Clarence C. Stetson, executive secretary of the Colorado River Compact Commission, 7 March 1922, box 5, folder 5, Carpenter Papers, NCWCD.

3. Carpenter to Hoover, 7 March 1922, box 5, folder 5, ibid.

4. Carpenter began seeing specialists in 1923, one month after signing the Colorado River Compact. Three years later a specialist in Hot Springs, Arkansas, made a thorough evaluation of his condition, concluding that "we are dealing with a natural 'fatigue syndrome' in which the 'Parkinsonian symptoms' developed only after an attack of influenza in 1918." See the 28 February 1926 report of the Hot Springs Sanatorium, box 78, folder 4, ibid.

5. Diary, Delph Carpenter, 9 May 1921, box 78, ibid.

6. Author's interview with Sarah Thompson, 11 February 1994, Sacramento, Calif.

7. Carpenter to "My Dear Daughters," 12 April 1929, box 86, folder 17, ibid.

8. Carpenter, "Honey Boy," an undated essay found in box 79 of the Carpenter Papers, NCWCD, along with documents related to Carpenter's term in the Colorado Senate. The essay concludes, "The man of you bids me have no fear, the love of you that I have no despair, the smile of you that my mind have joy, the courage of you that out of your life shall come to the world the blessings of work well done and that your shield shall bear no mark of treachery,

debauchery or disloyalty and that when I am gone and you the shield lay by, 'twill have been better that you had lived for your country, your home, your fire side and your God, Honey Boy, mine."

9. Carpenter to Major H. A. Flint, NMMI, 26 August 1924, box 86, folder 17, ibid.

10. Essay, typed and undated, found with a letter from President Calvin Coolidge to Stephen B. Davis, 1924, box 51, folder 2, ibid.

11. Rose Mary Koob, "Descendant of Union Pioneers to be 98 Saturday," *Greeley Tribune*, 26 July 1976.

12. "In the Matter of the Union of Hearts, Michaela and Delpho," n.d., box 50, folder 10, Carpenter Papers, NCWCD.

13. This poem was written in Carpenter's handwriting and found in an invitation to dinner for Herbert Hoover at the Phoenix Country Club, March 16, 1922, box 53, folder 8, Carpenter Papers, NCWCD.

14. Carpenter to Frank G. Carpenter, Washington, D. C., 2 September 1920, box 49, brown folder, Carpenter Papers, NCWCD. Carpenter wrote that he was "getting to feel like an old 'track state' race horse at times," and he hoped to "retire to my ranch and my cattle and avoid for a time at least, the strain of being the buffer between contending commonwealths. The task, he noted was so "strenuous and continuous that one gets war weary."

15. Speech to Gill, Colorado, farmers, as reported in the *Greeley Tribune*, 26 October 1920.

16. Carpenter to George C. Wilson, editor-in-chief, *American Journal of International Law*, 13 May and 10 June 1924, box 86, folder 20, Carpenter Papers, NCWCD. Wilson had asked Carpenter to prepare a ten-thousand-word article for his journal on the legal aspects of negotiating the Colorado River Compact.

17. Carpenter to Engineer E. C. Ecklund, USGS, 23 September 1914, box 78 expanding folder, Carpenter Papers, NCWCD.

18. *Rocky Mountain News* and *Greeley Tribune*, 10 June 1920.

19. Phoenix (15–17 March); Los Angeles (20 March); Salt Lake City (27–28 March); Grand Junction (29 March); Denver (31 March–1 April); Cheyenne (2 April). New Mexico and Nevada were the CRCC states that did not host public meetings.

20. William Mulholland, Colorado River Commission Hearings, Phoenix, 15 March 1922, container 42, Hoover Presidential Library; Emmett Boyle, Colorado River Commission Hearings, Denver, 31 March 1922, Colorado State Archives.

21. D. C. Merrill, executive secretary, Federal Power Commission, to Hoover, 3 March 1922, RCC 20559, folder 1, Department of Natural Resources, Colorado River Commission, Colorado State Archives.

22. Colorado River Commission Hearings, Phoenix, 15 March 1922, container 42, Hoover Presidential Library. Interestingly, Professor Smith expressed

concern about Colorado's potential to remove 310,000 acre-feet of water from the Colorado River to the Front Range, an amount designated ten years later in the 1937 legislation authorizing the Colorado–Big Thompson Project.

23. Ibid., container 46. W. F. R. Mills of the Denver Water Board estimated that the population of Denver had increased from 275,000 to 500,000 in one generation.

24. W. F. McClure, Colorado River Commission Hearings, Denver, 31 March 1922, folder 22, Colorado State Archives.

25. Frank C. Emerson, state engineer and Wyoming's commissioner on the CRCC, Colorado River Commission Hearings, Grand Junction, 29 March 1922, folder 21, Colorado State Archives.

26. Carpenter, Colorado River Commission Hearings, Phoenix, 16 March 1922, container 42, Hoover Presidential Library.

27. A. P. Davis, Colorado River Commission Hearings, Salt Lake City, 27 March 1922, and Los Angeles, 20 March 1922, container 46, Hoover Presidential Library.

28. Carpenter, Colorado Commission Hearings, Los Angeles, 20 March 1922, container 46, Hoover Presidential Library.

29. Carpenter first mentioned the fifty-fifty idea at Salt Lake City. Utah Commissioner Caldwell estimated that each basin would receive 7.5 million acre-feet. Colorado River Commission Hearings, Salt Lake City, 27 March 1922, container 46, Hoover Presidential Library.

30. Hoover, Colorado River Commission Hearings, Grand Junction, 29 March 1922, folder 21, Colorado State Archives.

31. Hoover, Colorado River Commission Hearings, Denver, 1 April 1922, folder 22, Colorado State Archives.

32. Emmett Boyle, Colorado River Commission Hearings, Cheyenne, 2 April 1922, Colorado State Archives.

33. Carpenter reasoned that if the Supreme Court ruling would have to apply, "these states could not enter into an agreement as we are trying to do." See Colorado River Commission Hearings, Cheyenne, 2 April 1922, folder 23, Colorado State Archives. Carpenter asked reporters not to mention discussion of the *Wyoming v. Colorado* case because the attorneys were not supposed to be discussing it.

34. Carpenter to Charles E. Hall, secretary, *The Durango Exchange*, 8 April 1922, box 48, folder 16, Carpenter Papers, NCWCD.

35. Franklin Mondell to Frank C. Emerson, 22 May 1922, January–May Correspondence File, RG 0037, Colorado River Compact Commission, State Engineer Records, Wyoming State Archives, Cheyenne, Wyoming.

36. Newspaper clipping, 6 April 1922, box 31, folder 3, Carpenter Papers, NCWCD.

37. Colorado River Commission Hearings, Denver, 1 April 1922, box 7, Carpenter Papers, NCWCD.

38. Carpenter to Clarence Stetson, 7 July 1922, box 48, folder 13, Carpenter Papers, NCWCD.

39. McClure to Carpenter, 6 May 1922, box 7, Carpenter Papers, NCWCD. McClure wrote this letter upon hearing the Supreme Court's decision in *Wyoming v. Colorado.*

40. L. Ward Bannister to R. I. Meeker, 25 May 1922, RCC 20559, folder 12, Colorado River Commission, Department of Natural Resources, Colorado State Archives.

41. Carpenter to Frank Emerson, 7 September 1922, box 7, Carpenter Papers, NCWCD.

42. Clarence Stetson to Merritt Mechem, 27 May 1922, Colorado River Commission File, Mechem Papers, 1922 letters received, New Mexico State Archives. Mechem responded that if a compact were to be signed, "it might be a good idea to have it signed at the Capital in Santa Fe."

43. Carpenter to Clarence Stetson, 8 August 1922, box 83, Carpenter Papers, NCWCD.

44. Associate Justice Willis Van Devanter wrote the unanimous opinion. Born in Indiana in 1859, he moved to Wyoming as a young adult, was chief justice of the territorial supreme court, and was appointed to the Supreme Court of the United States by President Howard Taft in 1911, serving the Court until 1937. He died in 1941.

45. Carpenter to Commissioner R. E. Caldwell, 5 July 1922, box 7, Carpenter Papers, NCWCD.

46. Ibid.

47. Ibid. Delph wrote: "The Court . . . foxes [*sic*] the rights of the two states by allocating the water supply between them."

48. Ibid.

49. This ten-year averaging is included in the existing Colorado River Compact. Carpenter's computations were based on first determining the flow at Yuma. If that figure was found to be 18,000,000 acre-feet, for example, and the flow at Lee's Ferry was generally 90 percent of the Yuma flow, or 16,200,000 acre-feet, the upper basin would guarantee to the lower basin a ten-year average of 8,100,000 acre-feet per year. This was a running average and did not guarantee the delivery of 8,100,000 acre-feet every year. Over ten years, looking backward, the deliveries would have to average at least 8,100,000 acre-feet.

50. Meeker estimated a total of 13,215,000 acre-feet of Colorado River water flowing across the state line into Utah—12,100,000 of it coming from the Colorado Rockies, the remaining 1,115,000 contributed by Utah and Wyoming.

51. Until 1921, that part of the Colorado River from the mouth of the Green River to its source in Rocky Mountain National Park was named the Grand River. By means of H. J. Res. 460, 66th Cong., 3rd sess., 18 February 1921, the Grand River became the Colorado River.

52. Carpenter to Commissioner R. E. Caldwell, 5 July 1922, box 7, Carpenter Papers, NCWCD.

53. Carpenter to Commissioner W. F. McClure, 11 July 1922, ibid.

54. *Denver Post,* 18 July 1922.

55. Hundley, *Water in the West,* 119, 120.

56. Ibid., 170, 171.

57. Ibid., 172, 173. Hundley cites the House Committee on Irrigation of Arid Lands, *Hearings on Protection and Development of Lower Colorado River Basin,* H.R. 11449, 67th Congress, 2nd sess., (1922), 18, 53, 54.

58. Carpenter to Congressman Elmer O. Leatherwood, 8 August 1922, box 48, folder 16, Carpenter papers, NCWCD.

59. Ibid.

60. Ibid.

61. Carpenter to Commissioner R. E. Caldwell, 8 August 1922, box 7, Carpenter papers, NCWCD.

62. Carpenter to Commissioner Frank C. Emerson, 19 August 1922, State Engineer Office, RG 0037, Colorado River Compact Commission, box 1, June–December 1922, correspondence file, Wyoming State Archives.

63. Ibid. It is not clear why he left out New Mexico Commissioner Davis, representing the fourth upper basin state. He may have felt the principal issues on which he focused required unity on the part of the three basin-of-origin states. New Mexico was interested in the San Juan River, a tributary of the Colorado River, whose source is in Colorado's San Juan Mountains.

64. Diary, Delph Carpenter, 9 May 1921: "Consult gov and atty gen'l in re compensation to me as interstate river commissioner for Colo. Agreed on $50/day and expenses for time actually put in, not to exceed $10,000 for biennial period." See box 78, Carpenter Papers, NCWCD.

65. Carpenter to Shoup, and Carpenter to Keyes, 24 August 1922, State Engineer's Papers, RCC 44816, South Platte River File, Colorado State Archives.

66. Ibid.

67. Ibid. See note attached to Carpenter's 24 August 1922 letter to Keyes.

68. Carpenter to Hoover, 25 August 1922, box 20, folder 8, Carpenter Papers, NCWCD.

69. Ibid.

70. Hoover to Carpenter, 13 October 1922, box 1, folder 17, Carpenter Papers, NCWCD.

71. McClure to Carpenter, 5 October 1922, ibid.

72. As reported by Clarence Stetson in a letter to Carpenter, 12 October 1922, ibid.

73. Davis to Carpenter, 24 October 1922, box 48, folder 16, Carpenter Papers, NCWCD.

74. Compact or Agreement for the Equitable apportionment of the water supply of the Colorado River and the streams Tributary thereto, confidential

preliminary draft, n.d., box 1, folder 1, Carpenter Papers, NCWCD. In a letter to McClure, 28 September 1922, Carpenter stated the upper basin would guarantee to the lower basin an "annual average delivery of one-half the Yuma flow in return for free and unlimited development in the upper basin." It is most likely that he meant one-half the Yuma flow less the amount of water contributed by the Gila and Little Colorado rivers. See Ibid., box 50, brown folder.

75. As quoted by Congressman Samuel S. Arentz, minutes of the second meeting of the Colorado River Compact Commission, Washington, D.C., 27 January 1922, Hoover Presidential Library.

76. H. T. Cory, "The Struggle for the Nile," 30 December 1920, box 1, folder 4, Carpenter Papers, NCWCD. Carpenter copied this report in September 1922.

77. Diary, Delph Carpenter, 29 April 1922, box 78, Carpenter Papers, NCWCD.

78. Cory, "The Struggle for the Nile," 27.

79. As understood in California, this doctrine has emerged in litigation where certain groups have argued that the absolute right associated with prior appropriation works to the disadvantage of the public good.

80. Arnold Kruckman, "Inside Story of River Conference": 5, as quoted in Hundley, *Water in the West*, 188.

81. Along with the seven commissioners and their advisers, Hoover and Stetson, A. P. Davis and chief counsel Ottamar Hamele of the United States Reclamation Service made up the core group. From time to time, invited guests were included in the executive sessions.

82. Hundley, *Water in the West*, 188.

83. Diary, Delph Carpenter, 10 November 1922, box 78, Carpenter Papers, NCWCD.

84. As will be noted, the lower basin eventually won an additional one million acre-feet, but this amount was far less than what the Arizona commissioner fought for and was agreed to by the upper basin as compensation for the fact that Arizona was already diverting most of the Gila River, whose flow was estimated at a little over one million acre-feet per year. In general terms, the division remained at approximately 50 percent for each basin.

85. Carpenter, Compact or Agreement for the Equitable Apportionment of the Water Supply of the Colorado River and of the Streams Tributary Thereto, box 1, folder 1, Carpenter Papers, NCWCD.

86. "A Pen Picture of the Colorado River Commission and Its Work," *Nevada State Journal*, 25 November 1922. Unless otherwise noted, descriptions of the other commissioners are taken from this article.

87. George H. Maxwell to the CRCC, 13 November 1922, received and read to the commissioners at the fourteenth meeting in Santa Fe, 1–5, box 7, Carpenter Papers, NCWCD.

88. Minutes, eleventh meeting of the CRCC, 11 November 1922, 40, box 7, ibid.

89. Ibid.

90. Minutes, thirteenth meeting of the CRCC, 13 November 1922, 3 and twelfth meeting of the CRCC, 12 November 1922, 5, box 7, ibid.

91. Minutes, eighteenth meeting of the CRCC, 16 November 1922, 43, 44, box 7, ibid.

92. Donald R. Van Petten, "Arizona's Stand on the Santa Fe Compact and the Boulder Canyon Dam Project Act": 8–10. Van Petten was a member of the Arizona House of Representatives, 1928–32.

93. Minutes, fifteenth meeting of the CRCC, 14 November 1922, 32, box 7, Carpenter Papers, NCWCD.

94. Ibid., 11–13.

95. Discussions of an annual minimum flow ranged from four milliion acre-feet to six million acre-feet, but Hoover and the commissioners were focused on first attaining agreement on a ten-year average.

96. Minutes, seventeenth meeting of the CRCC, 15 November 1922, 23, box 7, Carpenter Papers, NCWCD.

97. Ibid., 23.

98. Norviel to Carpenter, 21 October 1924, box 48, folder 13, Carpenter Papers, NCWCD.

99. Carpenter to Norviel, 7 March 1922, box 5, folder 5, ibid.

100. Minutes, eighteenth meeting of the CRCC, 16 November 1922, 23, 24, Carpenter Papers, NCWCD.

101. Agreement on this tenth principle proved to be the foundation of northern Colorado's right to divert 310,000 acre-feet of water from the source of the Colorado River, through a tunnel under the Continental Divide, for beneficial use in the South Platte River valley. This is the Colorado–Big Thompson Project, contracted between the Northern Colorado Water User's Association and the U.S. Bureau of Reclamation in 1938.

102. Minutes, eighteenth meeting of the CRCC, 16 November 1922, 55, 56, Carpenter Papers, NCWCD.

103. Diary, Delph Carpenter, 18 November 1922, box 78, Carpenter Papers, NCWCD.

104. Minutes, twenty-first meeting of the CRCC, 20 November 1922, 16–19, Carpenter Papers, NCWCD.

105. Colorado River Compact, draft inserted at the end of the Minutes of the twenty-fourth meeting of the CRCC, 23 November 1922, Carpenter Papers, NCWCD.

106. Minutes, twenty-third meeting of the CRCC, 22 November 1922, 32, Carpenter Papers, NCWCD.

107. The four commissioners assigned by Hoover to draft the compact were Carpenter, Caldwell, McClure, and Davis. Carpenter and Davis were attorneys, Caldwell and McClure were engineers.

108. Telegram, Carpenter to D. H. Stackelbeck, Denver, 17 November 1922, box 1, file 1, Carpenter Papers, NCWCD.

109. See Daniel Tyler, "Delph E. Carpenter and the Principle of Equitable Apportionment," *Western Legal History* 9, no. 1 (Winter-Spring 1996): 34–53.

110. Minutes of the twenty-first meeting of the CRCC, 20 November 1922, 4, Carpenter Papers, NCWCD.

111. Minutes of the twenty-seventh meeting of the CRCC, 5, 24 November 1922, ibid.

112. Ibid.

113. Memorandum, Ottamar Hamele to Clarence Stetson, 20 January 1922, General Administration and Project Records, Entry 7: Colorado River Project, RG 115, box 461, National Archives and Records Administration–Rocky Mountain Region.

114. Ibid. See also the 26 October 1922 commentary by Hamele in a folder titled "Settlement of Water Rights, Colorado River Compact, Mar–Oct, 1922," in ibid.

115. Memorandum, Hamele to Hoover, 28 February 1923, folder, "Colorado River Project. Settlement of Water Rights. Colorado River Compact" (January and February 1923), box 462, ibid.

116. Memorandum, Hamele to Hoover, 30 January 1922 and Hamele to Morrris Bien, 20 November 1922, box 61, ibid.

117. *Congressional Record*, 4 December 1922; see also Davis to Emerson, 9 January 1922, RG 115, box 61, National Archives and Records Administration–Rocky Mountain Region..

118. Minutes of the twenty-seventh meeting of the CRCC, 24 November 1922, 8–9, Carpenter Papers, NCWCD.

119. Hoover to Carpenter, 27 November 1922, box 20, folder 8, Carpenter Papers, NCWCD.

120. Carpenter to Hoover, 15 December 1922, courtesy of Doris Carpenter, Greeley, Colorado.

CHAPTER 6: THE STRUGGLE FOR COMPACT RATIFICATION

1. *U.S. Statutes at Large* 42: 171. S.B. 1853 was introduced in the Senate on 20 May 1921, and the same bill was introduced in the House as H.R. 6821. It was signed into law by President Warren G. Harding on 19 August 1921.

2. Although the dam, built in Black Canyon, was most frequently referred to as Boulder Dam or Boulder Canyon Dam during compact and ratification struggles, and was not actually named after Herbert Hoover until construction was begun in 1930, it will be referred to as Hoover Dam in most instances throughout this chapter for the sake of consistency.

3. Dean E. Mann, *Politics of Water in Arizona*, 84.

4. In 1924, on the heels of a drought, William Mulholland requested from Congress a domestic water supply for the City of Los Angeles from the

Colorado River. The Colorado River Aqueduct Association formed in the same year to raise funds for construction of a pipeline that would stretch 268 miles from the river to the city. This use of Colorado River water was never part of negotiations at Santa Fe. Arizona, fearful that California would claim priority of appropriation, felt unprotected and at the mercy of a more powerful and rapidly developing state.

5. L. Ward Bannister to Colorado Governor William H. Adams, 21 January 1928, RCC 26815, Adams Papers, Colorado River Compact file, Colorado State Archives. Bannister expressed frustration that Governor George Dern of Utah and Carpenter were "opposed to the Boulder Canyon Project absolutely unless a seven-state agreement can first be brought about."

6. Dern to Carpenter, 1 April 1929, reel 899, Dern Papers, Utah State Archives; inscription on a portrait sent to Carpenter by Colorado Congressman Ed Taylor, 18 October 1939, Carpenter Papers, NCWCD.

7. *Denver Post*, 11 October 1925.

8. Carpenter to Bannister, 4 January 1928, RCC 26815, Adams Papers, Colorado River Compact file, Colorado State Archives.

9. Ibid.

10. Carpenter, "Disposition of the Waters of the Colorado under the Colorado River Compact," 1 May 1929, RCC 26829, Adams Papers, Colorado River Compact file, Colorado State Archives.

11. Carpenter to Secretary of the Interior Ray Lyman Wilbur, 26 May 1931, State Engineer, RG 0037, Colorado River Compact Commission, box 1, correspondence file, Nevada State Archives.

12. Delph Carpenter to Secretary Ray Lyman Wilbur, 19 July 1930, Wilson Papers, New Mexico State Archives.

13. Carpenter to W. S. Norviel, 16 May 1923, box 5, folder 5, Carpenter Papers, NCWCD.

14. Article III (b): "In addition to the apportionment in paragraph (a), the lower basin is hereby given the right to increase its beneficial consumptive use of such waters by 1,000,000 acre-feet per annum."

Article VIII: "Present perfected rights to the beneficial use of waters of the Colorado River system are unimpaired by this compact. Whenever storage capacity of 5,000,000 acre-feet shall have been provided on the main Colorado River within or for the benefit of the lower basin, then claims of such rights, if any, by appropriators or users of water in the lower basin against appropriators or users of water in the upper basin shall attach to and be satisfied from water that may be stored not in conflict with Article III."

"All other rights to beneficial use of waters of the Colorado River system shall be satisfied solely from the water apportioned to that basin in which they are situate."

15. Telegram, Carpenter to Hoover, 10 February 1923, box 5, folder 5, Carpenter Papers, NCWCD.

16. Article III (f): "Further equitable apportionment of the beneficial uses of the waters of the Colorado River system unapportioned by paragraphs (a), (b) and (c) may be made in the manner provided in paragraph (g) at any time after October 1, 1963, if and when either basin shall have reached its total beneficial consumptive use as set out in paragraphs (a) and (b)."

17. Telegram, Hoover to Carpenter, 12 February 1923, Hoover Papers, Colorado River Commission file, container 12, Hoover Presidential Library.

18. Telegram, R. T. McKissick to Carpenter, 14 February 1923, box 5, folder 5, Carpenter Papers, NCWCD. McKissick was California Commissioner W. F. McClure's legal advisor.

19. *Congressional Record,* 67th Cong., 4th sess., 30 January 1923, 1–18.

20. The question referred to Article III (f), which gave both basins forty years to use Colorado River water before the so-called surplus would be divided between them no earlier than 1963.

21. *Congressional Record,* 67th Cong., 4th sess., 30 January 1923, 2, 3.

22. Telegram, Carpenter to Hoover, 13 February 1923, box 5, folder 5, Carpenter Papers, NCWCD.

23. Colorado River Compact, Letter from the Chairman of the Colorado River Commission, Transmitting Report of the Proceedings of the Colorado River Commission and the Compact or Agreement Entered into Between the States of Arizona, California, Colorado, Nevada, New Mexico, Utah and Wyoming Respecting the Apportionment of the Waters of the Colorado River, 2 March 1923, 67th Cong., 4th sess., House of Representatives, document no. 605, 1–12. The report stated that if either basin used more water than that apportioned in Article III, "any rights to such use [are] subject to further apportionment at a later date." 2, 3.

24. Carpenter, "Supplemental Report of Delph Carpenter, Commissioner for Colorado, Colorado River Commission," 20 March 1923, original report printed in Colorado Senate Journal, 5 January 1923, 75–86.

25. "Report of Delph E. Carpenter, Commissioner for Colorado, Colorado River Commission, in re Colorado River Compact," 15 December 1922, 7. This "Report" and the "Supplemental Report," referred to in the previous note, are bound together. They can be found in box 56, folder 5, Carpenter Papers, NCWCD.

26. Ibid, 7, 8.

27. Russell Fleming to M. E. Bashor, chairman of the Senate Committee on Agriculture and to R. W. Calkins, chairman, House Committee on Agriculture and Irrigation, 16 March 1923, box 7, Carpenter Papers, NCWCD. Fleming's eleven-page letter concluded the compact should be rewritten, because its only benefit to Colorado was the guaranty of future development.

28. "Supplemental Report," 34, 35.

29. Ibid, 36, 37.

30. Ibid, 37, 38.

31. Telegram, Hoover to Carpenter, 3 April 1923, box 7, Carpenter Papers, NCWCD.

32. Sweet to Carpenter, 18 May 1923, RCC 26821, Carpenter file, Adams Papers, Colorado State Archives.

33. McClure to Carpenter, 9 July 1923, box 4, folder 6.2, Carpenter Papers, NCWCD.

34. Norviel to Frank C. Emerson, 23 January 1923, State Engineer, RG 0037, Colorado River Compact Commission, box 1, correspondence, January–October 1923, Nevada State Archives.

35. Carpenter to Dean John D. Fleming, University of Colorado School of Law, 22 June 1923, box 78, folder 4, Carpenter Papers, NCWCD.

36. Bannister to Francis C. Wilson, 5 March 1928, Bannister File, Wilson Papers, New Mexico State Archives.

37. *Rocky Mountain News*, 22 August 1922.

38. Bannister to Oliver H. Shoup, 18 November 1922, RCC 26795, Water Defense File, Shoup Papers, Colorado State Archives.

39. Telegram, Carpenter to E. R. Harper, secretary to Governor Oliver H. Shoup, 25 November 1922, box 1, folder 1, Carpenter Papers, NCWCD.

40. Carpenter and Bannister, "The Distribution of the Water of the Colorado River," speech presented to the State Historical and Natural History Society of Colorado," Senate Chambers, State Capitol Building, 18 December 1922, Carpenter Papers, NCWCD.

41. Telegram, Arnold Kruckman, secretary-treasurer of the League of the Southwest, to Governor William E. Sweet, 9 March 1923, RCC 26803, Colorado River Compact file, Shoup Papers, Colorado State Archives.

42. Sweet to Kruckman, 8 May 1923, ibid.

43. Bannister to Sweet, 9 May 1923, ibid.

44. Bannister to Sweet, 9 June 1923, ibid.

45. Carpenter to Norviel, 15 June 1923, Colorado River Commission, Correspondence 1923, container 1, Carpenter Papers, Hoover Presidential Library.

46. Ibid.

47. Sweet to Bannister, 20 and 22 June 1923, RCC 26803, file 178-C, Sweet Papers, Colorado State Archives.

48. Carpenter to Senator Carl Hayden, 8 August 1923, box 44, folder 6.2, Carpenter Papers, NCWCD. See also Carpenter's 1923 diary, box 78, Carpenter Papers, NCWCD.

49. Memorandum to Secretary Hoover, n.d., Hannett Papers, New Mexico State Archives.

50. Ibid.

51. Ibid.

52. Carpenter to Bannister, 20 November 1924, RCC 26803, Colorado River Commission file, Sweet Papers, Colorado State Archives.

53. Ibid.

54. Report of L. W. Bannister to William E. Sweet and Delph E. Carpenter, 23 pp., 22 December 1924, RCC 26961, Sweet Papers, Colorado State Archives.

55. Carpenter to J. O. Seth, 19 January 1925, Hannett Papers, New Mexico State Archives.

56. Carpenter to R. T. McKissick, 23 December 1924, Hannett Papers, New Mexico State Archives.

57. Carpenter to Hoover, 7 February 1927, State Engineer records, RG0037, Colorado River Compact, correspondence file February to September 1925, Wyoming State Archives.

58. Ibid.

59. Telegram, Hoover to Carpenter, 23 January 1925, box 37, brown folder, Carpenter Papers, NCWCD. Hoover also referred to the six-state plan as Carpenter's original suggestion.

60. Donald J. Pisani discusses this era of the Bureau of Reclamation's history in a manuscript tentatively titled "Water and the American State, 1902–1933," to be published by the University of California Press.

61. United States, Bureau of Reclamation, 23rd Annual Report, transmitted to Congress on 7 October 1924, RG 115, National Archives and Records Administration—Rocky Mountain Region.

62. Carpenter to Charles D. Hayt, 26 June 1911, box 47, file 2, Carpenter Papers, NCWCD. The context for Carpenter's remarks about Mead is a report Carpenter prepared in which he opposed codification of the irrigation laws of Colorado, because codification would "plunge our farmers into greater litigation . . . and above all would be a means of ingress for the Federal Government."

63. Mead to Lloyd Garrison, Salt Lake City, Utah, 19 June 1928, folder labeled "Colorado River. Settlement of Water Rights. Colorado River Compact, Perpetuation of Testimony," box 463, entry 7, RG 115, National Archives and Records Administration—Rocky Mountain Region.

64. Both Carpenter and Mead favored local control of irrigation projects, water appropriations based on consideration of the entire river basin, state control of natural resources, concern for the common man and the use of international experience to determine water policy in the United States.

65. See *Denver Evening News*, 3 February 1927, in which Mead is quoted as recommending abandonment of the Colorado River Compact in favor of congressional protection of the upper basin states; George Malone to Nevada Governor F. B. Belzar [*sic*], 13 February 1928, Balzar Papers, Nevada State Archives; and James R. Kluger, *Turning on Water with a Shovel: The Career of Elwood Mead.*

66. Diary, Delph Carpenter, 1925, box 78, Carpenter Papers, NCWCD.

67. The South Platte Compact was signed by Governor Clarence Morley of Colorado on 26 February 1925 and by President Coolidge on 8 March 1926. The La Plata Compact was signed by President Coolidge on 29 January 1925.

68. United States Senate, Hearings Before the Committee on Irrigation and Reclamation, 69th Cong., 1st sess., pursuant to S. Res. 320, October 26–December 22, 1925, 313. The four governors signing this resolution were: Nellie Tayloe Ross, Wyoming; George H. Dern, Utah; Clarence J. Morely, Colorado; and A. T. Hannett, New Mexico. Carpenter included Nevada in the resolution, because Governor Scrugham seemed to understand Carpenter's argument.

69. Ibid., 675.

70. Ibid.

71. Ibid., 679.

72. Ibid.

73. Ibid., 681, 682.

74. Hundley, *Water and the West*, 257.

75. United States Senate, Hearings pursuant to S. Res. 320, 707.

76. Delph E. Carpenter, Statement for Upper Colorado River States Regarding Bill for Boulder Canon [*sic*] Dam (Swing-Johnson Bill) before Committee on Irrigation and Reclamation of the House of Representatives, 1926, 8, box 81, folder 1, Carpenter Papers, NCWCD.

77. *Grand Junction Sentinel*, 13 June 1926.

78. Carpenter, Statement for Upper Colorado River States, 1926, 14–18, box 81, folder 1, Carpenter Papers, NCWCD.

79. Memorandum, P. W. Dent to the Secretary of the Interior, 22 June 1926, Records of United States Bureau of Reclamation, General Administration and Project records, 1919–1929, entry 7, Colorado River project, folder labeled "Colorado River Project, Water Appropriations, Rights and Adjudications through 1929," box 461, RG 115, National Archives and Records Administration–Rocky Mountain Region.

80. Ibid., 11.

81. Ibid., 25.

82. Phil D. Swing to Carpenter, 27 December 1926, box 7 Carpenter Papers, NCWCD.

83. Bannister to W. R. Wallace of Utah and S. G. Hopkins of Wyoming, 24 March 1926, box 7, Carpenter Papers, NCWCD. Bannister was quoting remarks by Secretary Hoover with which he agreed.

84. Carpenter to Dern, 13 December 1927 and 2 January 1928, reel 899, Dern Papers, Utah State Archives.

85. Bannister to Hunt, 29 December 1927, RCC Z6815, Adams Papers, Colorado River Commission file, Colorado State Archives.

86. Ibid.

87. Bannister was referring to the fact that the FPC had agreed to suspend temporarily the issuance of licenses to private companies that wanted to build dams on the Colorado River. If the compact in any form was not going to be approved, there was no need for the FPC to continue the suspension.

88. Bannister was referring to the Federal Power Commission's willingness to freeze activity on the Colorado River, pending the seven states' decision to ratify or reject the Colorado River Compact. The FPC had agreed to a moratorium until March 1929, but because Bannister believed that very little was accomplished during the "short session" of Congress in the late fall, the ratification decision would have to be made in the spring of 1928. RCCZ6815, Adams Papers, Colorado River Commission file, Colorado State Archives.

89. Francis C. Wilson to Bannister, 12 December 1927, Bannister File, Wilson Papers, New Mexico State Archives.

90. Ibid., 23 February 1928.

91. Bannister to Emerson, 1 March 1928, Bannister file, Wilson Papers, New Mexico State Archives.

92. Medical Report for Mr. D. E. Carpenter, 28 February 1928, signed by G. M. Eckel, Hot Springs, Arkansas, box 78, folder 4, Carpenter Papers, NCWCD.

93. Ibid.

94. Telegram, Carpenter to Dern, 18 January 1927, reel 898, Dern Papers, Utah State Archives.

95. Hundley, *Water and the West,* 261–64; Carpenter to Hoover, 13 January 1927, box 83, Carpenter Papers, NCWCD. Hoover replied to Carpenter on 18 January 1927, stating that if Utah were to withdraw, "it will be a blow to the Colorado River Compact and will set back a solution of the Colorado River for many years to come because California will refuse to cooperate at all." See Hoover to Carpenter, 18 January 1927, box 79, Hoover letters, Carpenter Papers, NCWCD.

96. Hundley, *Water and the West,* 263.

97. Ibid., 264. In note 111, Hundley cites Frank Emerson to George H. Dern, 13 April 1927, box 77, Dern Papers; Dern to Carpenter, 21 July 1928, Carpenter Papers, Hoover Library; Carpenter to Dern, 17 January 1927, box 76, Dern Papers, Utah State Archives.

98. Carpenter telegraphed Governor Dern on 14 February 1927, stating that the first paragraph of Article IV "does not affect Utah title to bed Colorado River. Compact does not destroy navigation but merely makes navigation subservient to other more important uses of water . . . this provision necessary to protect upper states against claims by lower states and Mexico that diversions in upper states impair navigability of lower river . . . that title to bed of navigable river passes to state on admission and remains in state until conveyed." See reel 898, Dern Papers, Utah State Archives.

99. Carpenter to Colorado Congressman Charles B. Timberlake, 16 February 1927, Colorado River Commission Correspondence (January–March 1927), Carpenter Papers, Hoover Presidential Library.

100. George H. Dern, Memorandum, n.d., RCC 26815, Colorado River Compact file, Adams Papers, Colorado State Archives. This memorandum is most probably a draft of a letter Dern sent to Governor Billie Adams.

101. Telegram, Dern to Governor William H. Adams, 14 January 1928, RCC 26815, Colorado River Compact file, Adams Papers, Colorado State Archives.

102. Telegram, Carpenter to Adams, 14 January 1928, ibid.

103. Telegram, Adams to Dern, 16 January 1928, ibid.

104. Bannister to Adams, 21 January 1928, ibid.

105. Bannister to Emerson, 22 February 1928, Bannister folder, Wilson Papers, New Mexico State Archives.

106. Bannister to George Akerson, assistant to Hoover, Stanford University, 7 November 1928, container 7, Hoover Dam Documents, 1921–1947 (Campaign and Transition, General Correspondence), folder on L. Ward Bannister, Hoover Presidential Library. Bannister wrote as follows: "We want to hold Mr. Bonfils in line for the next eight years, for without a doubt he is the most potent single influence in the mountain region . . . . I know that he has backed up our Colorado River position always. Between you and me, he has allowed me to write articles for his paper upon it, as if they were the paper's own views and has done this many times."

107. Bannister to Carpenter, 20 May 1930, container 6, folder on River Negotiations–Miscellaneous, Carpenter Papers, Hoover Presidential Library. Carpenter replied that he was "opposed to the League of Nations and to any institution which is so identified with the League as to be its court and legal advisor." See Carpenter to Bannister, 21 May 1930, ibid.

108. Bannister to Carpenter, 1 February 1929, box 26, Carpenter Papers, NCWCD.

109. Carpenter to Stetson, 14 July 1928, box 84, folder 11, Carpenter Papers, NCWCD.

110. George W. Malone to Nevada Governor F. B. Balzar, 29 September 1928, box 0055, folder 010, Colorado River Compact, 1928, Balzar Papers, Nevada State Archives.

111. Carpenter to Lawrence Phipps, 27 March 1928, Wilson Papers, New Mexico State Archives.

112. Malone to F. B. Balzar, 13 February 1928, Balzar Papers, Nevada State Archives.

113. Confidential Information from the Department of Interior, 4 February 1928, based on notes taken by Dwight Heard of Arizona as Elwood Mead spoke. See Balzar Papers, Nevada State Archives.

114. Carpenter to Charles Springer, Santa Fe, New Mexico, 20 January 1927, box 52, folder 10, Carpenter Papers, NCWCD. Carpenter wrote that when Utah voted in favor of a six-state compact, it was "secretly known that Secretaries [John W.] Weeks and [Henry C.] Wallace, constituting two out of three members of the Federal Power Commission, intended to start granting

permits for construction of large power works along the lower Colorado without awaiting ratification of the compact, upon the theory that Arizona's delay indicated that the compact would never be ratified and, therefore, the Federal Power Commission would be at liberty to proceed without awaiting further action by the states. . . . Weeks and Wallace stated that unless something was done in 1925, they would proceed."

115. Pisani, *Water and the American State, 1902–1933*. See the chapter titled "Hydroelectric Power and the New West."

116. William Hard, "Giant Negotiations for Giant Power: An Interview with Herbert Hoover": 577–80. This article was provided by Dwight Miller, senior archivist of the Hoover Presidential Library.

117. Carpenter to John A. Whiting, 9 May 1930, RG 0037, Colorado River Compact Commission, box 1, 1930, correspondence file, State Engineer, Wyoming State Archives.

118. Carpenter to Ray Lyman Wilbur, 9 April 1930, box 85, folder 4, Carpenter Papers, NCWCD.

119. Their fears were well founded. Arizona filed suit in the Supreme Court on 6 October 1930, claiming that the federal government had no right to build a dam on land, half of which belonged to Arizona. The court was asked to find both the Boulder Canyon Project Act and the Colorado River Compact unconstitutional. See *Arizona v. California*, 283 US, 1931.

120. Bannister to Carpenter, 30 September 1930, box 84, folder 16, Carpenter Papers, NCWCD.

121. This was precisely the issue raised by Colorado appropriators in *Hinderlider v. La Plata River and Cherry Creek Ditch Company*, 304 US 92 (1937) when a Colorado corporation sued to regain 1898 water rights lost to New Mexico under the La Plata River Compact. The Supreme Court's recognition of the compact's legitimacy served to validate the principle that senior vested rights are subject to the terms of interstate compacts.

122. Carpenter, "Interstate River Compacts and Their Place in Water Utilization," presented before the San Francisco Convention of the American Water Works Association, 15 June 1928, by Ralph I. Meeker, who assisted in the preparation of this talk. It was published in the *Journal of the American Water Works Association* in December 1928.

123. Telegram, George Ackerson, secretary to Hoover, to Bannister, 18 August 1928, Hoover Presidential Papers, Campaign and Transition, General Correspondence, container 7, Hoover Dam, 1921–1948, Hoover Presidential Library.

124. Bannister to Ackerson, 2 October 1928, in which he attaches a copy of the fourteen-minute speech he delivered on KOA Radio in Denver, 28 September 1928, Hoover Presidential Papers, Campaign and Transition, General Correspondence, container 7, Bannister folder, Hoover Presidential Library.

125. Carpenter to Dern, 26 November 1928, reel 899, Dern Papers, Utah State Archives.

126. Carpenter to Hoover, 31 December 1927, container 78, Commerce Papers, Hoover Presidential Library.

127. Carpenter to Lawrence Richie, n.d., container 11, President's Personal File, Hoover Presidential Library.

128. Hoover to Carpenter, 29 June 1929, box 220, folder 8, Carpenter Papers, NCWCD.

129. Eugene Lyons, *Herbert Hoover: A Biography* (Garden City, N.Y., 1964), 330. The author is grateful to Dale Meyer of the Hoover Presidential Library for locating this reference as well as a letter from Charles A. Dobbel, Stanford University Professor, in which Dobbel explains how and when Hoover Dam was named. See Dobbel, *Time, Inc,* 24 October 1935, Ray Lyman Wilbur Papers, Hoover Dam, Dobbel Material, Name Controversy, Herbert Hoover Presidential Library.

CHAPTER 7: LAST YEARS AS INTERSTATE STREAMS COMMISSIONER

Epigraph: Carpenter to Charles W. Waterman, 19 June 1924, box 86, folder 5, Carpenter Papers, NCWCD.

1. Carpenter to Walter H. Eckert, Chicago, 8 May 1931, box 86, folder 15, Carpenter Papers, NCWCD.

2. Dr. George M. Eckel to Carpenter, 10 January 1933, box 84, folder 3, ibid.

3. Carpenter to W. Stuart Booth, 20 July 1929 and 3 August 1929, box 86, folder 13, Carpenter Papers, NCWCD.

4. Booth to Carpenter, 3 September 1929, box 86, folder 16, ibid.

5. Carpenter to Booth, 10 September 1929, ibid.

6. As noted in Chapter 1, Carpenter admired his father's upbeat philosophy on life. The "Never Despair" poem from the 1860 *McGuffey Reader,* which was still recited by Leroy Carpenter from memory at the age of eighty-three, was frequently in Delph's thoughts when waves of self-doubt and depression rolled over him.

7. M. C. Hinderlider to Carpenter, 16 November 1943, box 50, box of letters, ibid.

8. Alva A. Swain to Dot Carpenter, 1 January 1945, box 52, folder 1, ibid.

9. Carpenter to Judge W. S. Norviel, 26 February 1931, Colorado River Commission Correspondence, 1930, June–September, container 1, Carpenter Papers, Hoover Presidential Library.

10. Carpenter to Shoup, 5 January 1923, box 23, brown folder, Carpenter Papers, NCWCD.

11. C. L. Patterson, Conservation of Water in Colorado, a memorandum issued by the Colorado Water Conservation Board, 1 May 1939, box 23, folder

10, ibid. The memorandum notes that Kansas and Colorado have agreed to divide the water from Caddoa Reservoir when constructed and that the Board's "problem is to promote the financing and construction of the reservoir which will not only benefit the irrigation interests below the site in Colorado, but at the same time promises to be a constructive solution of a long-standing interstate controversy."

12. Carpenter to Shoup, 12 August 1921, RC 8801, Colorado Governor Appointments/Applications, Colorado State Archives. Unless otherwise noted, information on this first meeting between Carpenter and the Kansans is taken from this source.

13. Carpenter to attorney A. W. McHendrie, Trinidad, Colorado, 27 November 1923, box 87, folder 20, Carpenter Papers, NCWCD. Carpenter noted that a number of the "radical elements in the vicinity of Garden City, Kansas are very anxious to proceed with the litigation and are off-setting our efforts at friendly settlement."

14. Carpenter to R. W. Faris, commissioner, Department of Reclamation, Boise, Idaho, 25 October 1932, box 84, folder 18, ibid. Carpenter stated: "Commissioner Knapp and I tentatively agreed upon a draft which was never concluded, owing to opposition by Kansas ditches. State Engineer George Knapp at Topeka published that draft in his annual report during the year 1924 or 1926. It was never printed in Colorado."

15. Carpenter to Vena Pointer, secretary of the Arkansas Valley Water Users' Association, 17 July 1922, box 23, brown folder, ibid.

16. Carpenter to E. H. Gereke, Lamar, Colorado, 12 May 1924, box 87, folder 18, ibid. Gereke was a land agent for the American Sugar Beet Company.

17. Knapp to Carpenter, 31 March 1927, ibid.

18. In 1928, Colorado brought suit in the U.S. Supreme Court, seeking an injunction against Kansas for that state's repeated attempts to force the federal courts to adjudicate priorities between the two states. The High Court's decision in 1943 (320 US 383) revealed its unwillingness to make specific appropriations and its desire to have the conflict resolved through compact negotiation. To this end, Kansas and Colorado resumed talks in 1945 and signed a compact in 1948. When Colorado failed to meet the terms of Article IV-D, Kansas filed suit again in December 1985. Ten years later a unanimous Supreme Court found that Colorado had depleted the flow of the Arkansas River, causing injury to Kansas. See *Kansas v. Colorado*, 514 US 673 (1995). Special Master Arthur Littleworth prepared two reports for the High Court in which he recommended Colorado make cash reparations to Kansas. As of May 2001, Colorado attorney David Robbins sees the Arkansas River Compact as both the "best" and "worst" of compacts; "best, because it fails to specify an amount of water delivered to Kansas that would enable Colorado to be in compliance, and "worst," because without exact compliance figures, Colorado is for all practical purposes incapable of defending itself, especially since Article IV-D also allows Colorado to develop undeveloped Arkansas River water.

19. A. P. Davis, director of the Reclamation Service, to the Secretary of the Interior, 15 May 1922, MS. 1038, box 1, folder 401, Corlette Papers, Colorado State Historical Society. Davis stated that the [Elihu] Root–[Joaquin D.] Casasus Treaty with Mexico, proclaimed 16 January 1907, apportioned 60,000 acre-feet annually to Mexico from the Rio Grande, an amount estimated to be one-twelfth of the dependable supply from Elephant Butte Reservoir. A very lucid study of Rio Grande water history can be found in Douglas R. Littlefield, Conflict and Compromise: Water Politics on the Rio Grande, 1880–1938," unpublished MS in the author's possession.

20. Ibid.

21. Russell P. Fleming, Colorado Attorney General, to A. P. Davis, 19 February 1923, MS 1038, box 1, folder 401, Corlett Papers, Colorado State Historical Society.

22. Carpenter to Albert L. Moses of Alamosa, Colorado, 13 October 1924, ibid.

23. Carpenter to Charles Springer, Santa Fe, New Mexico, 1 February 1923, box 7, Carpenter Papers, NCWCD. He told Springer that Texas should be involved in the commission, even though he was aware that New Mexico and Texas were at odds over Pecos River matters. He also stated that the Colorado legislature wanted him to serve on the commission and he was inclined to accept once the legislation passed the Colorado Assembly.

24. Carpenter to Secretary Hubert Work, n.d., box 52, folder 11, Carpenter Papers, NCWCD.

25. Carpenter to Ralph Carr, 10 January 1924, box 52, folder 4, ibid.

26. Diary, Delph Carpenter, 1924, box 78, ibid. The meeting was held on October 26, 1924.

27. First meeting, Rio Grande River Compact Commission, Broadmoor Hotel, Colorado Springs, Colo., 26 October, 1924, box 48, folder 7, ibid. Unless otherwise noted, additional comments on the Broadmoor meeting are taken from this source.

28. Carpenter to Albert L. Moses, Alamosa, Colorado attorney, 13 October 1924, MS 1038, box 1, folder 401, Corlette Papers, Colorado State Historical Society.

29. Richard F. Burges, to Carpenter, 2 December 1924, box 48, folder 7, Carpenter Papers, NCWCD.

30. Telegram, Hannett to Morley, 11 October 1926, attached to a memorandum, Rio Grande Water Controversy, author unknown, box 48, folder 7, ibid.

31. Telegram, 19 October 1926, ibid.

32. Memorandum, Rio Grande Water Controversy, 10 December 1926, RCC 44639, Delph Carpenter file, State Engineer's Papers, Colorado State Archives.

33. Carpenter to Corlett, 17 November 1927, RCC 26828, Rio Grande file, Adams Paper, ibid. Wilson came to believe that Carpenter was too sick to

carry on negotiations on the Rio Grande while simultaneously engaged in Colorado River Compact ratification. In a letter to Ward Bannister, Wilson wrote, "This is strictly between us, but I am very much of the opinion that Delph Carpenter cannot help us. Even if he should go to Washington we could not hope to get any real assistance from him. Considering his experience and ability this will be most unfortunate, but we might as well make up our minds to the fact and prepare accordingly." See Francis C. Wilson to L. Ward Bannister, 13 December 1927, Wilson Papers, Bannister file, New Mexico State Archives.

34. Carpenter to Wilson, 6 July 1928, Wilson Papers, New Mexico State Archives.

35. Colonel William J. Donovan, federal representative to both the upper and lower basins of the Colorado River and first assistant to the United States attorney general was eventually appointed by President Calvin Coolidge.

36. Littlefield, Conflict and Compromise, 288. In New Mexico, this temporary compact is cited in Laws of New Mexico, 1929, Chapter 41. Ratification dates are as follows: New Mexico, 9 March 1929; Colorado, 19 April 1929; Texas, 22 May 1929. Hoover signed the document on 19 June 1930.

37. Ralph I. Meeker to J. C. Wiley, Del Norte, Colorado, 6 February 1929, MS 1038, box 1, folder 401, Colorado State Historical Society.

38. Denver Chamber of Commerce to Carpenter, 23 February 1929, RCC 26828, Rio Grande file, Adams Papers, Colorado State Archives.

39. Carpenter to Governor George H. Dern, 28 October 1929, reel 899, Dern Papers, Utah State Archives. At the time, Delph was working on a compact for the upper basin states. He cautioned Dern that compact making was "deliberate work and must be done by stages."

40. Carpenter, memorandum in reply to the adverse report of the Secretary of the Interior in re S. 1501, Wilson Papers, New Mexico State Archives. S.1501 was Senator Lawrence Phipps's bill to approve the Rio Grande Compact.

41. "An Act Giving the consent and approval of Congress to the Rio Grande compact signed at Santa Fe, New Mexico, on February 12, 1929," Public No. 370, 71st Cong. (S. 3386). Donovan approved the compact on June 17, 1930. See box 87, folder 26, Carpenter Papers, NCWCD.

42. Carpenter to Albert Moses, 15 November 1932, box 84, folder 5, Carpenter Papers, NCWCD.

43. Greeley Tribune, 21 February 1939.

44. Telegram, Carpenter to T. H. McGregor, Thomas M. McClure, M. C. Hinderlider, and S. O. Harper, 11 December 1934, box 22 folder 11, Carpenter Papers, NCWCD.

45. 1939, Colorado Session Laws 500; Colorado Revised Statutes, section 37-66-101 and 102, as cited in Vranesh, Colorado Water Law, vol. 3, 1723, n. 210. Congressional approval of the Rio Grande Compact can be found in 53 Stat. 785, ch. 155 (1939).

46. Daniel Tyler, Last Water Hole in the West (1992).

47. Carpenter to Willis, 5 January 1924, box 1, folder 22, Carpenter Papers, NCWCD.

48. Carpenter to M. C. Hinderlider, 24 December 1932, container 5, Carpenter Papers, Hoover Presidential Library. See also Carpenter to Secretary Hubert Work, 19 July 1927, in RG 0037, Colorado River Compact Commission, general correspondence, State Engineer, Wyoming State Archives.

49. Carpenter to Work, 19 July 1927, ibid.

50. Carpenter to Francis C. Wilson, 20 September 1932, box 84, folder 20, Carpenter Papers, NCWCD.

51. Ralph Carr to Carpenter, n.d., referring to Carpenter's 1929 speech in Salt Lake City, box 22, folder 9, ibid.

52. Minutes, Meeting of the North Platte River Commission, Washington, D. C., 20 March 1924, box 1, folder 22, Carpenter Papers, NCWCD. According to Colorado Supreme Justice Gregory Hobbs, the U.S. Supreme Court in 1935 put the matter to rest in favor of Carpenter's view when it ruled that acts of Congress in 1866 and 1877 made water of the western United States *publici juris*, subject to the plenary control of the states. See *California Oregon Power Co. v. Beaver Portland Cement Co.*, 295 US 142, 163–64 (1935).

53. Carpenter to Work, 19 July 1927, RG 0037, Colorado River Compact Commission, general correspondence, State Engineer, Wyoming State Archives.

54. Carpenter to Colorado Governor William H. Adams, 16 November 1927, box 87, folder 7, Carpenter Papers, NCWCD.

55. Carpenter to John A. Whiting, 26 March 1932, RG 0037, North Platte River Commission, administrative records, general correspondence, box 1, 1930–1936, State Engineer, Wyoming State Archives.

56. Carpenter to Congressman Edward T. Taylor, 5 February 1932, RCC 26849, North Platte Commission file, Adams Papers, Colorado State Archives.

57. Carpenter to Colorado Senator Edward P. Costigan, 4 February 1932, ibid. It should be noted that the request for federal funds to build the Colorado–Big Thompson Project was couched in the same language. Due to agricultural surpluses, any suggestion of placing new lands into productivity would be seen by Congress as adding to the existing glut of farm products on the market.

58. *Rocky Mountain News*, 15 May 1932.

59. Telegram, Carpenter to Senator Edward P. Costigan, 14 December 1932, RCC 26849, North Platte Commission file, Adams Papers, Colorado State Archives.

60. Telegram, Carpenter to Hinderlider, 5 January 1933, box 22, folder 9, Carpenter Papers, NCWCD. This suggestion emulated Section 4 of the Boulder Canyon Project Act.

61. Tyler, *Last Water Hole in the West*, 23, 24.

62. A very solid study of North Platte River compact negotiations and federal projects may be found in Gordon Olaf Hendrickson, "Water Rights on

the North Platte River: A Case Study of the Resolution of an Interstate Water Conflict," Ph.D. diss., University of Wyoming, 1975.

63. Boulder Canyon Project Act, Public No. 642, 70th cong. (H. R. 5773), sec. 19, 10.

64. 63 Stat. 31 (1949), *Colorado Revised Statutes*, secs. 37-62-101 to 106. In this agreement, the 7.5 million acre-feet assigned to the upper basin by the Colorado River Compact was divided as follows: Colorado, 51.75 percent; New Mexico, 11.25 percent; Utah, 23 percent; Wyoming, 14 percent; and Arizona was awarded 50,000 acre-feet per year. These percentages applied only to the 7.5 million acre-feet and not to any "surplus" water as defined by Article III (b) of the Colorado River Compact.

65. The Bureau of Reclamation planned to build the following projects: Echo Park, Flaming Gorge, Glen Canyon, Navajo, Cross Mountain, Curecanti, Gray Mountain, Split Mountain and others. See John Upton Terrell's two-volume *War for the Colorado River*. Volume 2 contains a legislative history of the Colorado River Storage Project, as well as a description of each project.

66. Carpenter to John A. Whiting, 15 July 1929, RG 0037, Wyoming State Engineer, Colorado River Compact Commission, correspondence file, January–December 1929, Wyoming State Archives; and to Francis C. Wilson, 15 July 1929, Wilson Papers, New Mexico State Archives.

67. Memorandum, 28 August 1929, Colorado River Commission Correspondence, July–August, 1929, Carpenter Papers, Hoover Presidential Library.

68. Ibid.

69. Carpenter to Dern, 8 August 1929, reel 899, Dern Papers, Utah State Archives.

70. Carpenter to Dern, 28 October 1929, ibid.

71. Carpenter to M. C. Hinderlider, 20 August 1930, RG 0037, Wyoming State Engineer, Colorado River Compact Commission, box 1, 1930 correspondence file, Wyoming State Archives.

72. William W. Ray, Salt Lake City attorney, to Carpenter, 4 October 1930, box 84, folder 16, Carpenter Papers, NCWCD.

73. Delph Carpenter, memorandum, prepared for Colorado Attorney General John S. Underwood, 18 August 1930, container 6, folder on river negotiations–misc., Carpenter Papers, Hoover Presidential Library. Carpenter was peeved that Utah was relying on the federal government to provide data the states had already researched.

74. Donovan was also United States representative on a tristate commission to secure a supplemental compact from Arizona, California, and Nevada.

75. *Arizona v. California*, 283 US 423 (1931). The section quoted is from Charles Meyers, former dean of the Stanford Law School, whose article "The Colorado River" was published in the *Stanford Law Review* in 1966. See George Vranesh, *Colorado Water Law*, 2: 864.

76. *Denver Post*, 6 October 1930.

77. Ibid., 12 January 1931.

78. Carpenter speech draft, 6 November 1930, box 84, folder 14, Carpenter Papers, NCWCD. Unless otherwise noted, quoted remarks are taken from this speech.

79. Carpenter to Francis C. Wilson, 9 October 1930, box 87, folder 29, ibid.

80. Charles Meyers in "The Colorado River," the *Stanford Law Review.* 9 notes this was a significant case. The Court preserved the fiction that navigation was being served by the Boulder Canyon Project Act, but at the same time it recognized the importance of multipurpose dams that would be generating and selling electrical power. Meyers concludes: "On this foundation rest many mighty dams that dry up the stream below, thus destroying navigability entirely, if indeed any ever existed." See Vranesh, *Colorado Water Law.* 864.

81. Carpenter to Secretary Ray Lyman Wilbur, 26 May 1931, container 1, folder Colorado River Commission, correspondence January–May, 1930, Carpenter Papers, Hoover Presidential Library.

82. B. B. Moeur, Arizona governor, was incensed at California's sworn objective of blocking any Arizona attempt to build a Highline Canal from the Colorado River to Phoenix (an early version of the Central Arizona Project authorized in 1968) until Arizona's rights to Gila and Colorado river water were stipulated. In response, he sent six members of the Arizona National Guard to report on any attempts by California to place any structure on the Arizona side of the Colorado River near Parker, where the Bureau of Reclamation was getting ready to install a regulatory dam to assist in diverting water through the California Aqueduct. When the Bureau began laying a trestle across the river, Moeur declared the Arizona side of the river under martial law and sent a hundred-man militia with machine guns to defend the site. The dispute went to court, where Arizona's position was upheld. The Bureau was told it could not build Parker Dam without congressional approval. But when California pushed a Parker Dam bill through Congress, Arizona was left without recourse, unless it wanted to sue the United States government. See Marc Reisner, *Cadillac Desert,* 267–68.

83. Carpenter to Governor William H. Adams, 23 May 1931, box 85, folder 11, Carpenter Papers.

84. Carpenter to Wilson, 2 August 1930, Wilson Papers, New Mexico State Archives.

85. Carpenter to Clifford H. Stone, Colorado Water Conservation Board, 19 February 1938, box 84, folder 10, Carpenter Papers, NCWCD.

86. Carpenter to Albert L. Moses, 15 November 1932, box 84, folder 5, Carpenter Papers, NCWCD.

87. Carpenter to Herbert C. Clark, 19 November 1932, box 84, folder 3, ibid.

88. Moses to Paul P. Prosser, 1 December 1932, box 84, folder 4, ibid.

89. Prosser to Governor Edwin C. Johnson, 7 December 1932, RCC 26862, NPG file, Johnson Papers, Colorado State Archives.

90. Bannister to Carpenter, 30 January 1933, box 84, folder 3, Carpenter Papers, NCWCD.

91. Carr to Carpenter, 8 February 1933, box 22, folder 12, ibid.

92. Carpenter to Costigan, 27 January 1933, box 87, folder 8, ibid.

93. Carpenter to Bannister, 21 February 1933, container 1, folder, Colorado River Commission, correspondence 1931–33 and undated, Carpenter Papers, Hoover Presidential Library.

94. Carpenter, "Memorandum for Message," 18 December 1938, in which Carpenter, at the request of Ralph Carr, drew up a one-page statement to be introduced by Carr to the state legislature, asking for the retainer Carpenter had been denied in 1933. See box 1, MS 1208, no. 15, Carr Papers, Colorado State Historical Society.

CHAPTER 8: VINDICATION

Epigraph: Carpenter to Hoover, 5 May 1938, Post-Presidential Papers, Hoover Presidential Library.

1. *Greeley Tribune,* 7 and 9 April 1934.

2. Carpenter to Thomas J. Warren, Fort Collins, 5 September 1933, box 84, folder 16, Carpenter Papers, NCWCD. In a letter to Lawrence Phipps, 19 February 1927, Carpenter stated that the project had been kept in the background "for fear of provoking unnecessary opposition." See Carpenter to Lawrence E. Phipps, container 1, folder: Colorado River Commission Correspondence (January–March 1927), Carpenter Papers, Hoover Presidential Library.

3. Carpenter to Lawrence E. Phipps, ibid. Unless otherwise noted, Carpenter's views on the park are taken from this letter.

4. *Statutes at Large* 38, ch. 19, sec. 1: 798. Act of 26 January 1915.

5. The clause Carpenter wanted Colorado and the Congress to accept stated in part: "By reason of the fact that Colorado is an arid state and its general welfare and the present and increasing necessities of its cities, its agriculture and its institutions require the *first use* (author's emphasis) of the waters of the streams having their origin within said Rocky Mountain National Park, the United States are requested to agree with the State of Colorado, by the act of the Congress to grant to the said state and/or all persons or corporations using or proposing to use the waters of the streams within or adjacent to the Park, for domestic or irrigation purposes, rights of way over, through and upon the lands included within said Park for canals, tunnels, flumes, conduits and other structures or works, reservoirs excepted. . . ." See Carpenter to Phipps letter cited in note 3 above.

6. *Colorado Revised Statutes,* 1999, sec. 3-1-130, 1050, 1051.

7. Carpenter to Charles Hansen, president, Northern Colorado Water Users Association, 5 November 1937, box 84, folder 9, Carpenter Papers, NCWCD.

8. Carpenter to O. G. Edwards, president, Greeley, Colorado, Chamber of Commerce, 28 August 1933, box 84, folder 20, ibid.

9. Carpenter's papers do not contain discussion of the federal power to reserve rights in unappropriated water. In none of his correspondence does he mention *United States v. Winters* (207 US 564 [1908]), the landmark case in which a federal right to non-navigable water was upheld on the basis of federal property and preemption powers. The case involved an Indian reservation. Non-Indian defendants argued that they had made an appropriation of water under state law and were entitled to a diversion sufficient to protect their agricultural lands. All appropriations subsequent to the creation of the federal reserved right were junior. Federal reserved water rights have been found to exist for national parks and national monuments. Carpenter's philosophy of state sovereignty was weakest in its non-recognition of federal supremacy under the United States Constitution. In fact, Congress acquiesced to the creation of water rights by the states, and Carpenter needed congressional approval of the compacts he helped to negotiate.

10. Felix Frankfurter and James M. Landis, "The Compact Clause of the Constitution—A Study in Interstate Adjustments": 729.

11. Carpenter to Hoover, 16 October 1933, container 30, folder labeled Carnegie to Carter, Post-Presidential Papers, Hoover Presidential Library.

12. Carpenter to L. Ward Bannister, 17 November 1938, box 84, folder 18, Carpenter Papers, NCWCD.

13. Carpenter to Clarence Stetson, 5 January 1933, box 84, folder 6, ibid.

14. Carpenter to Hoover, 16 October 1933, box 84, folder 2, ibid.

15. Herbert Hoover, message to the Western Governors Conference on Public Lands Questions, 27 August 1929, Salt Lake City, Utah. This item was sent to the author by Dwight M. Miller, senior archivist, Hoover Presidential Library. Reference is to *Public Papers of the Presidents*, Herbert Hoover, 1929, 262–69. An address by Carpenter titled "Conflict of Jurisdiction Respecting Control of Waters in Western States," presented at this same conference, is printed in the *Congressional Record*, 13 September 1929, 3714–17.

16. Statement by Delph E. Carpenter, 11 July 1929, published in the the *Weld County News* and *Denver Post*, n.d., container 1, folder: Colorado River Commission Correspondence, July–August 1929, Carpenter Papers, Hoover Presidential Library.

17. Carpenter to Charles J. Moynihan, Montrose, Colorado, 22 November 1929, box 86, folder 19, Carpenter Papers, NCWCD.

18. Discussion of the Report of the Committee on the Conservation and Administration of the Public Domain, presented to the Association of Western State Engineers, Sacramento, California, 29 October 1931, by George W. Malone, Nevada state engineer, box 84, folder 20, ibid.

19. George Vranesh, *Colorado Water Law*, 3: 1763. Vranesh cites 93 Colo. 128 (1933) for the Colorado Supreme Court decision.

20. Carr to Carpenter, 8 February 1933, box 22, folder 15, Carpenter Papers, NCWCD.

21. Ibid., 4 July 1933. Carr sent Carpenter a sample petition for rehearing the case in the U.S. Supreme Court.

22. Carpenter to Butler, 21 July 1933, container 4, folder: La Plata River, 1923, 1929–33, Carpenter Papers, Hoover Presidential Library.

23. *Hinderlider v. La Plata River and Cherry Creek Ditch Company*, 304 US 92 (1938).

24. As quoted in Vranesh, *Colorado Water Law*, 1: 537.

25. Ibid.1: 538.

26. Ibid., 3: 1737.

27. Hinderlider to Carpenter, 26 April 1938, box 84, folder 7, Carpenter Papers, NCWCD.

28. Meeker to Carpenter, 26 April 1938, ibid.

29. Carr to Carpenter, 11 February 1938, box 84, folder 3, ibid.

30. Wilson to Carpenter, 17 May 1938, box 84, folder 7, ibid.

31. R. I. Meeker to Carpenter, 23 December 1944, box 50, letter box, Ibid.

32. Carpenter to Senator Carl Hayden, 24 February 1937, box 84, folder 13, ibid. Carpenter believed this tactic would help Arizona get around its frustration over not having a tristate compact with California and Nevada.

33. *The Mexican Water Treaty* (59 Stat. 1219). This treaty included agreements on the Colorado, Tijuana, and Rio Grande. Ratifications between both nations were exchanged on 8 November 1945.

34. Carpenter to Hoover, 5 May 1938, container 30, file: Carnegie to Carter, Post-Presidential Papers, Hoover Presidential Library.

CHAPTER 9: CARPENTER AND THE COMPACT LEGACY

Epigraph: Telegram, Sims and Northcutt Ely to Donald A. Carpenter, 28 February 1951, box 48, folder 6, Carpenter Papers, NCWCD.

1. Roscoe Fleming, "Fight Saved State's Water," clipping, n.d., box 48, folder 6, Carpenter Papers, NCWCD.

2. Carpenter to J. E. Bennett, Wilmington, California, 19 March 1929, box 86, folder 13, ibid.

3. Carpenter to O. G. Lewis, Brush, Colorado, 26 July 1932, box 84, folder 4, ibid.

4. Carpenter to the Federal Land Bank of Wichita, 22 March 1932, box 37, folder 5, ibid. In a letter dated 6 February 1932, Carpenter told the Land Bank he had exhausted all sources of funds. The drought and agricultural prices were too low to make a profit, livestock were "almost worthless," and

he wanted to delay his loan payment until crops were harvested in the following fall.

5. In a letter to W. C. Mullendore at Southern California Edison, 25 November 1932, Carpenter explained that Donald was not allowed to take the bar exams in Colorado because he did not have three years of liberal arts at National University. This was a state rule Carpenter viewed as an "outrage," because it prevented Donald from taking over his father's law practice. See box 84, folder 5, ibid.

6. Carpenter to Charles Roach, Colorado deputy attorney general, 21 December 1932, box 84, folder 6, ibid.

7. Carpenter to Chief Justice John T. Adams, 14 March 1934, box 84, folder 3, ibid.

8. Carpenter to Clarence Stetson, 14 July 1928, box 84, folder 11, ibid.

9. Author interview with Sarah Thompson, 11 February 1994, Sacramento, California.

10. Margaret W. Swanson, chief clerk, Department of State, to Carpenter, 26 June 1930, box 50, Carpenter Papers, NCWCD.

11. Carpenter to Charles D. Todd, Greeley, Colorado, 22 December 1932, box 84, folder 6, ibid. The Union Colony continues as a nonprofit corporation. At the time Carpenter's bill was enacted by the state legislature, the City of Greeley had taken over most of the colony's public responsibilities. The Pioneer Society, entirely separate from the Union Colony corporation, was for a long time under the presidency of Martha Bennett Carpenter, Delph's mother. The Carpenters' connection to and respect for the early pioneers was well known.

12. Carpenter to Herbert Hoover, 16 October 1933 (two letters), container 30, Post-Presidential Papers, file: Carnegie to Carter, Hoover Presidential Library. Carpenter was alluding specifically to the history of the lower basin's extra 1 million acre-feet of water in the Colorado River Compact. His suggestion coincided with Hoover's interest in having Professor Charles A. Dobbel of Stanford University write a complete history of the compact.

13. Hoover to Carpenter, 15 December 1933, ibid.

14. Carpenter to Hoover, 5 January 1934, ibid.

15. Carpenter to Hoover 16 and 28 July 1936, box 79, Hoover letters, Carpenter Papers, NCWCD.

16. Hoover to Edgar Rickard, New York City, 14 May 1935, Post Presidential Papers, file: Hoover Association to Hoover Dam, Hoover Presidential Library.

17. Statement of V. T. Boughton, McGraw Hill, 24 May 1935, ibid.

18. Interested readers can access this document in box 12, folder: Hoover Dam—Dobbel Material—Colorado River Compact History—Undated, Ray Lyman Wilbur Papers, Hoover Presidential Library. The author is indebted to Professor Donald Pisani for calling attention to this document.

19. Reuel Leslie Olson, *The Colorado River Compact*, initially completed as a doctoral thesis, Harvard University, published by the author, September 1926.

20. Carpenter to Reuel Leslie Olson, 14 February 1925, box 6, folder 6, Carpenter Papers, NCWCD. Carpenter was explaining to Olson that a six-state compact, approved by Congress, would allow development on the Colorado River and would take the pressure off Arizona.

21. Carpenter to Olson, 30 July 1925, box 7, ibid.

22. Telegram, Carpenter to Hon. A. Lawrence Lowell, 22 August 1926, Colorado River Commission Correspondence, (July–December 1926), Carpenter Papers, Hoover Presidential Library. The original plan for the minutes was that Clarence Stetson, executive secretary of the Colorado River Compact Commission, would send a rough draft to each commissioner for editing. After receiving corrections, Stetson was supposed to mimeograph the approved version for distribution. Because of political concerns associated with the ratification process, the revised minutes were kept in the office of the secretary of commerce and not distributed until a decade after the compact was signed. The Hoover Presidential Library has both the rough draft and final version.

23. George H. Chase to Carpenter, 4 October 1926, ibid.

24. Carpenter to Northcutt Ely, 13 April 1932, box 84, folder 15, Carpenter Papers, NCWCD.

25. Carr's speech was published in *Colorado Magazine*, 21, no. 1 (January 1944): 5–14. The program for the 1943 meeting of the National Reclamation Association can be found in box 51, folder 3, Carpenter Papers, NCWCD.

26. Ibid.

27. Carr asked the radio broadcaster Lowell Thomas if he had ever heard of Carpenter. Thomas replied that he had not, but that he would be very interested in meeting Delph. See Thomas to Carr, 4 November 1943, box 50, letter box, ibid.

28. Hoover to Carpenter, 3 November 1943, ibid.

29. Sims Ely to Carpenter, 18 April 1944, box 37, brown folder, ibid.

30. Judge George H. Bradfield, Memorial to Delph Carpenter, 1 May 1951, box 20, folder 7, ibid.

31. H. S. McCluskey to Governor George W. P. Hunt, 2 February 1926, box 6, folder 6, ibid.

32. Congressman Ed. T. Taylor to Carpenter, 17 May 1926, box 84, folder 10, ibid.

33. Comments taken from letters by Sims and Northcutt Ely, 18 April 1944, box 48, folder 1; William C. Mullendore, 25 May 1938, box 37, brown folder; George W. Malone, 6 February 1950 in the *Congressional Record*, Senate, 1559; Ralph Carr, 21 February 1939, box 48, folder 3; Alva A. Swain, newspaper article dated 31 January 1936, box 20, folder 1; Memorial of Judge George H. Bradfield, May 1, 1951, box 20, folder 7, ibid.

34. The 1956 Colorado River Storage Project included the following dams: Glen Canyon, Flaming Gorge, Navajo, and Curecanti, now referred to as the Aspinall-Gunnison Project. These storage dams help offset the mistake made by the CRCC in regard to the available Colorado River supply. The reservoirs behind the dams provide drought insurance for the 75 million acre-feet guaranteed to the lower basin for a ten-year period.

35. See Sue McClurg, "A Colorado River Compromise," *Western Water* (November–December 2000): 4–13.

36. See, for example, *Board of County Water Commissioners v. Crystal Creek Homeowners' Association*, 14 P.3d 325, 336 (Colo. 2000), called to the author's attention by Colorado Supreme Court Justice Gregory J. Hobbs; and *New Jersey v. New York* 523 US 767, called to the author's attention by Colorado attorney David Robbins.

37. See, for example, an article in the *Rocky Mountain News*, 3 February 1951, three weeks before Carpenter's death, in which the administration of President Harry S. Truman expressed concern that compacts interfered with the best development of the Colorado River basin, because, among other reasons, "some states might wish to use some of the unused share of other states, but [are] unwilling to make the necessary investment for fear that water might be available only for a short period."

38. Zimmerman, *Interstate Relations*, 40, 50.

39. See Jill Elaine Hasday, "Interstate Compacts in a Democratic Society": 30, 34, 35, 36, 38, 47.

40. Interview with Colorado Attorney General Ken Salazar, as printed in the *Fort Collins Coloradoan*, 11 June 2001. On this same date the Supreme Court ruled that Colorado would have to pay Kansas "about $23 million in damages for water that farmers pumped from the Arkansas River basin in eastern Colorado." See *Denver Post*, 12 June 2001.

41. See the dissenting opinion of U.S. Supreme Court Justice Sandra Day O'Connor in the 11 June 2001 *Kansas v. Colorado* decision, No. 105 Original, 533 U.S. 1 (2001), 1. O'Connor states: "A compact is a contract. It represents a bargained-for exchange between its signatories and remains a legal document that must be construed and applied in accordance with its terms."

42. Frankfurter and Landis, "The Compact Clause of the Constitution": 707, 729.

43. Ibid., 701. In note 66, Frankfurter and Landis cite *Kansas v. Colorado* (1907) US 46, 27 Sup. Ct. 655.

44. Jerome C. Muys, *Interstate Water Compacts*. Report NWC-L-71-011, Legal Study 14, Final Report (Arlington, Va: National Water Commission [July 1971]), 3, 4.

45. Joseph F. Zimmerman, *The Neglected Dimension of Federalism*, 42 ff.

46. Ibid., 260.

47. Ibid., 355.

48. Ibid., 360–69.

49. Ridgeway, *Interstate Compacts*, 309.

50. The author is indebted to Colorado Supreme Court Justice Gregory J. Hobbs for this idea.

51. Hasday, "Interstate Compacts in a Democratic Society": 1–47.

52. Advantages of interstate compacts are discussed in Jeff Boyce, "Wrestling with the Bear: A Compact Approach to Water Allocation": 1–20; Susan J. Buck, Gregory W. Gleason and Mitchel S. Jofuku, "'The Institutional Imperative': Resolving Transboundary Water Conflict in Arid Agricultural Regions of the United States and the Commonwealth of Independent States": 595–628; Eric L. Garner and Michelle Ouellette, "Future Shock? The Law of the Colorado River in the Twenty-First Century": 469–506.

53. Marc Reisner, "The Age of Dams and Its Legacy," speech given 3 November 1999 at Colorado State University, published in *Colorado Water* (December 1999): 20.

54. Carpenter to Judge Charles C. Butler, Colorado Supreme Court, 21 July 1933, container no. 4, Carpenter Papers, Hoover Presidential Library.

55. Carpenter, memorandum, attached to letter to Charles J, Moynihan, Montrose, Colorado, 22 November 1929, box 86, folder 19, Carpenter Papers, NCWCD. Unless otherwise noted, citations following this note come from the same source.

56. Charles F. Wilkinson, address to the American Society of Civil Engineers, Fort Collins, Colorado, 21 June 2000, published in *Colorado Water*: 19–20.

57. Aldo Leopold, *A Sand County Almanac*, 1949.

58. It is the author's opinion that the administration of Secretary of the Interior Bruce Babbitt represented much of what Carpenter taught by example. Babbitt acted on his belief that negotiated agreements required participation of all interested parties. His willingness to seat environmentalists at the same table with land developers, ranchers, and public officials, resulted in land use compromises that appear to have the promise of endurance and sustainability.

Bibliography

ARCHIVAL COLLECTIONS

Arizona. Papers of the Arizona governors and Arizona state agencies. Arizona State Archives, Phoenix, Ariz.

Boyle, Emmett D. Papers. Nevada State Historical Society, Reno, Nev., and Nevada State Archives, Carson City, Nev.

California. Papers of the California governors and California state agencies. California State Archives, Sacramento, Calif.

Carpenter, Delph E. Papers. Northern Colorado Water Conservancy District (NCWCD), temporarily located at NCWCD headquarters in Loveland, Colo. This collection contains the balance of papers not sent to the Hoover Library, plus copies of documents sent to the Hoover Library in 1976. Personal and professional papers, pictures, books, maps, and family mementos were partially organized and placed in eighty-seven archival boxes stored in the basement of the NCWCD.

———. Papers. Hoover Presidential Library, West Branch, Iowa. In 1976 some documents pertaining to the Colorado River Compact were copied from the entire Carpenter collection, at that time under the care of Judge Donald A. Carpenter, and deposited in the Hoover Library. In *Water and the West*, Norris Hundley, Jr., states that "most" of Delph Carpenter's papers were deposited by the judge in the Hoover Library. In fact, the Hoover Library received only a fraction of the entire collection.

Colorado River Commission. Department of Natural Resources, Colorado State Archives, Denver, Colo.

Colorado River Project. Bureau of Reclamation. RG 115. National Archives and Records Administration–Rocky Mountain Region, Denver Federal Center, Denver, Colo.

Colorado River Compact Commission. State Engineer. Colorado State Archives, Denver, Colo.

Colorado. Papers of the Colorado governors and Colorado state agencies. Colorado State Archives, Denver, Colo.

Davis, Arthur Powell. Papers. American Heritage Center (formally Western History Research Center), University of Wyoming, Laramie, Wyo.

League of the Southwest. *Minutes of Meetings.* Los Angeles, 1–3 April 1920; Denver, 25–27 August 1920; Riverside, 8–10 December 1921; Santa Barbara, 7–9 June 1923. Some of these minutes are available to researchers in the Imperial Irrigation District Papers, Imperial, Calif.

Nevada. Papers of the Nevada governors and Nevada state agencies. Nevada State Archives, Carson City, Nev.

New Mexico. Papers of the governors and state agencies of New Mexico. New Mexico State Archives and Records Center, Santa Fe, N. Mex.

Utah. Papers of the Utah governors and Utah state agencies. Utah State Archives, Salt Lake City, Utah.

Wyoming. Papers of the Wyoming governors and Wyoming state agencies. Wyoming State Archives, Cheyenne, Wyo.

COURT CASES

Arizona v. California, 292 US 341 (1934).

Arizona v. California, 283 US 423 (1931).

Arizona v. California II, 373 US 546 (1963).

Hinderlider v. La Plata River and Cherry Creek Ditch Co., 101 Colo. 73, 70 P.2d 849 (1937), rev'd, 304 US 92 (1938).

New York v. New Jersey, 65 L.Ed. 544 (1921).

Virginia v. Tennessee, 148 US 503 (1892).

Weiland. v. Pioneer Irrigation Co., 259 US 498 (1922).

Wyoming v. Colorado, 259 US 419 (1922).

GOVERNMENT DOCUMENTS AND STATUTES

Colorado River Compact Commission. *Records of Hearings: Phoenix, Ariz.,* 15–16 March 1922; *Los Angeles, Calif.,* 12 March 1922; *Salt Lake City, Utah,* 27–28 March 1922; *Grand Junction, Colo.,* 29 March 1922; *Denver, Colo.,* 31 March and 1 April 1922; *Cheyenne, Wyo.,* 2 April 1922.

———, *Minutes of the Twenty-seven Meetings: First to Seventh,* Washington, D.C., 26–30 January 1922; *Eighth,* Phoenix, Ariz., 15 March 1922; *Ninth,* Denver, Colo., 1 April 1922; *Tenth to Twenty-Seventh,* Santa Fe, N. Mex., 9–24 November 1922.

Colorado River Commission, State of California. *Colorado River and the Boulder Canyon Project Act.* Sacramento, 1930.

Colorado River Compact. 45 Stat. 1057. See also *Colorado Revised Statutes* 37-61-101 (1997).

Colorado. South Platte River Compact. *Colorado Session Laws,* Chap. 179 (1925), 529, codified at *Colorado Revised Statutes,* 37-65-101 (1997).

Colorado. *Supplemental Report* on the Colorado River Compact, 15 December 1922, by Delphus E. Carpenter. Reprinted in *Senate Journal, in re* Senate Bill 410, "A Bill for an Act to Approve the Colorado River Compact," at 75–86 (1923).

Colorado. *Report of Committee on Irrigation Investigations of the Senate,* by Delphus
E. Carpenter, George E. West, and J. H. Crowley, in S.R. No. 16 (17th Colorado General Assembly), 31 January 1911.

Federal Power Commission. *Annual Reports.* I, Fiscal Year Ended 30 June 1921,
1–235; II, 1922, 1–316; III, 1923, 1–282; IV, 1924, 1–245; V, 1925, 1–209:
Washington, D.C., GPO.

La Plata River Compact. 43 Stat. 796 (1925).

Laws, authorizing states to negotiate the Colorado River Compact: Ariz., Act
of 5 March 1921 (Laws, 1921, 53); Calif., Act of 12 May 1921 (Stats., 1921,
85); Colo., Act of 2 April 1921 (Laws, 1921, 811); Nev., Act of 21 March
1921 (Stats., 1921, 190); N. Mex., Act of 11 March 1921 (Laws, 1921, 217);
Utah, Act of 14 March 1921 (Laws, 1921, 166); Wyo., Act of 22 February
1921 (Laws, 1921, 166).

Laws, ratification of Colorado River Compact as a six-state compact by states:
Calif.: Act of 8 April 1925, Ch. 33, 46th sess.; Statutes and Amendments to
the Codes, 1925, 1321–22; *Colo.:* Act of 26 February 1925; Ch. 177, 25th
sess.; Session Laws of Colorado, 1925, 525–26. *Nev.:* Act of 18 March 1925;
Ch. 96, 32d sess.; Statutes of Nevada, 1925, 134–35. *N. Mex.:* Act of 17
March 1925; Ch. 78, 7th sess.; Laws of New Mexico, 1925, 116–17. *Utah:*
Act of 13 March 1925; Ch. 64, 16th sess.; Laws of Utah, 1925, 127. *Wyo.:*
Act of 25 February 1925; Ch. 82, 18th sess.; State Legislature; Session Laws
of Wyoming, 1925, 85–86.

Rio Grande Compact. 53 Stat. 785 (1939).

South Platte River Compact. 44 Stat. 195 (1926).

U.S. House of Representatives. "Brief of Law of Interstate Compacts" by Delphus
E. Carpenter, Judiciary Committee. *Hearings on Granting the Consent of Congress
to Certain Compacts and Agreements between the States of Arizona, California, Colorado, Nevada, New Mexico, Utah, and Wyoming,* 67th Cong., 1st sess., 4 June
1921, *re* H.R. 6821.

———. Committee on the Judiciary, "Granting the Consent of Congress to
Certain Compacts." *Hearings* on H.R. 6821, 67th Cong., 1st sess., 1921.

———, H. Doc. 605, 67th Cong., 4th sess., *The Colorado River Compact: Report
of Herbert Hoover, Representative of the United States.*

U.S., Congress, Senate. Testimony by Delphus E. Carpenter to Committee on
Irrigation and Reclamation under S.R. 320, 68th Cong., 2d sess., Colorado
River Basin, pt. 6, *re* Swing-Johnson bill, 15–25 December 1926.

———, *Colorado River Basin: Hearings on S.R. 320 before the Committee on Irrigation and Reclamation,* 69th Cong., 1st sess., (1925), 705–11.

———. "Problems of Imperial Valley and Vicinity," Senate Doc. 142, 67th
Cong., 2d sess., 1922, ser. no. 7977.

———. "Problems of Imperial Valley and Vicinity," Senate Doc. 142 (Fall-Davis
Report), 67th Cong., 2nd sess. (28 February 1922), 1–326.

U.S. Department of the Interior, Bureau of Reclamation. *Boulder Canyon Project Final Reports, Part I: General History and Description of Project.* Washington: Government Printing Office, 1948.

U.S.. *Statutes at Large.* 41: 600. Kinkaid Act, 18 May 1920.

————. 42: 171. The Mondell bill approved by Congress and signed by President Warren G. Harding on 19 August 1921, this act authorized formation of a Colorado River Commission with the objective of negotiating a compact on the Colorado River.

————. *Boulder Canyon Project Act of 1928* 45: 1057. See *Congressional Record,* 70th Cong., 2d sess., 21 December 1928, 837–38, for joint House and Senate approval of the fourth Swing-Johnson bill, which became the *Boulder Canyon Project Act.*

————. 46: 3000. *Boulder Canyon Project Act,* approved by President Calvin Coolidge, 21 December 1928, declared in force by President Herbert Hoover, 25 June 1929.

Wilbur, Ray Lyman and Northcutt Ely. *The Hoover Dam Documents.* 2d ed. of "The Hoover Dam Power and Water Contracts and Related Data," 1933. Washington: GPO, 1948.

NEWSPAPERS

Albuquerque Morning Journal
Denver Daily News
Denver Evening News
Denver Post
Denver Republican
Denver Times
Fort Collins (Colo.) Courier
Grand Junction (Colo.) Sentinel
Greeley (Colo.) Daily Pioneer
Greeley Republican
Greeley Sun
Greeley Tribune
Los Angeles Times
New York Herald Tribune
Pueblo (Colo.) Chieftain
Rocky Mountain News
San Diego Union
The Poudre Valley (Colo.)
Weld County (Colo.) News
Weld County Republican

BOOKS, ARTICLES, THESES, AND UNPUBLISHED WORKS

Alderton, David. *Foxes, Wolves and Wild Dogs of the World.* New York: Facts on File, 1994, 1998.

Anderson, Scott T., Thomas A. Harder, Nancy Yost Laskaris, and Lori M. Mittag. "Equitable Apportionment and the Supreme Court: What's So Equitable About Apportionment?" *Hamline Law Review* 7 (June 1984): 405–29.

Arnold, Peri Ethan. "Herbert Hoover and the Department of Commerce: A Study of Ideology and Policy." Ph.D. diss., University of Chicago, 1972.

Atwood, Albert W. "The Struggle for Future Greatness." *Saturday Evening Post,* 9 October 1926, 22, 23, 80, 82, 84, 86.

———. "Waters of Wrath." *Saturday Evening Post,* 11 September 1926, 6–7, 246, 249, 250, 253, 254.

———. "The River of Life." *Saturday Evening Post,* 11 September 1926, 20, 21, 218, 221, 222, 225.

August, Jack L., Jr. "Carl Hayden, Arizona, and the Politics of Water Development in the Southwest, 1923–1928." *Pacific Historical Review* 58 (May 1989): 195–216.

———. Work Horse: Carl Hayden and the Politics of Water in the American Southwest," unpublished MS in the author's possession.

Bakken, Gordon M. *The Development of Law on the Rocky Mountain Frontier: Civil Law and Society, 1850–1912.* Westport: Greenwood Press, 1983.

Bannister, L. Ward. "Why It Is Hoover Dam!" *Los Angeles Times Sunday Magazine,* 18 February 1934.

———. "Interstate Rights in Interstate Streams in the Arid West." *Harvard Law Review* 36 (1923): 960–986.

Barton, Weldon V. *Interstate Compacts in the Political Process.* Chapel Hill: University of North Carolina Press, 1967.

Bates, J. Leonard. "Fulfilling American Democracy: The Conservation Movement, 1907–1921." Mississippi Valley Historical Review 43 (June 1957): 29–57.

Billington, Ray A. *America's Frontier Heritage.* Albuquerque: University of New Mexico Press, 1974.

Blythe, Stuart O. "Seven States and the Colorado River." *The Country Gentleman* 92 (August 1927): 3–5, 98.

Boyce, Jeff. "Wrestling with the Bear: A Compact Approach to Water Allocation." *BYU Journal of Public Law* 301 (1996): 1–14.

Boyd, David. "Greeley's Irrigation Methods." *Irrigation Age* 2 (1 January 1982): 353.

———. *A History: Greeley and the Union Colony of Colorado.* Greeley: Greeley Tribune Press, 1890.

Briggett, Marlissa S. "State Supremacy in the Federal Realm: The Interstate Compact." *Boston College Environmental Affairs Law Review* 18 (1995): 751–72.

Brigham, Jay Lawrence. "Public Power and Progressivism in the 1920s." Ph.D. diss., University of California at Riverside, 1992.

Bruce, Andrew A. "Compacts and Agreements of States with One Another and with Foreign Powers." *Minnesota Law Review* 2 (1917–18): 500–16.

Buck, Susan J., Gregory W. Gleason, and Mitchel S. Jofuku. "'The Institutional Imperative': Resolving Transboundary Water Conflict in Arid Agricultural Regions of the United States and the Commonwealth of Independent States." *Natural Resources Journal* 33 (1993): 595–628.

Burner, David. *Herbert Hoover, A Public Life*. New York: Alfred A. Knopf, 1979.

Carlson, John, and Alan E. Boles, Jr. "Contrary Views of the Law of the Colorado River: An Examination of Rivalries between the Upper and Lower Basins." *Rocky Mountain Mineral Law Institute* 32 (1987): 21-05 to 21-39.

Carpenter, Delph E. "Application of the Reserve Treaty Powers of the States to Interstate Water Controversies." *Colorado Bar Association* 24 (1921): 45–101.

———. "Conflict of Jurisdiction Respecting Control of Waters in Western States." *Rocky Mountain Law Review* 2 (April 1930): 162–72.

———. "Interstate River Compacts and Their Place in Water Utilization." *Journal of the American Water Works Association* 20 (December 1928): 756–73.

Carr, Ralph. "Delph Carpenter and River Compacts between Western States." *Colorado Magazine* 21 (January 1944): 5–14.

Clark, Ira G. *Water in New Mexico: A History of Its Management and Use*. Albuquerque: University of New Mexico Press, 1987.

Clements, George P. "Parceling Out the Colorado River." *Southern California Business* (January 1923): 13–15.

Cole, Donald B. "Transmountain Water Division in Colorado." *Colorado Magazine* 25 (1948): 49–65, 118–33.

Colorado Water Conservation Board. *Interstate Compacts: Compilation of Articles Appearing in Various Law Journals*. 4 vols. Denver: Colorado Water Conservation Board, 1946.

Conkin, Paul K. "The Vision of Elwood Mead." *Agricultural History* 34 (1960): 88–97.

Dana, Marshall N. "Reclamation, Its Influence and Impact on the History of the West." *Utah Historical Quarterly* 27 (1959): 39–49.

Dern, George H. "Utah's Position on the Colorado." *Community Builder* 1 (March 1928): 41–44.

Dodd, Alice Mary, "Interstate Compacts." *United States Law Review* 70 (1936): 557–78.

Dunar, Andrew J., and Dennis McBride. *Building Hoover Dam: An Oral History of the Great Depression*. New York: Twayne Publishers, 1993.

Dunbar, Leslie. "Interstate Compacts and Congressional Consent." *Virginia Law Review* 36 (1950): 753–63.

Dunbar, Robert G. *Forging New Rights in Western Waters*. Lincoln: University of Nebraska Press, 1983.

————. "History of Agriculture." In *Colorado and Its People*, Edited by Le Roy Hafen, Vol. 2: New York: Lewis Historical Publishing Company, 1948, 121–57.

————. "The Origins of the Colorado System of Water Rights Control." *Colorado Magazine* 27 (Oct. 1950): 241–62.

————. "Water Conflicts and Controls in Colorado." *Agricultural History* 22 (1948): 180–86.

Ely, Northcutt. "Herbert Hoover and the Colorado River." Unpublished MS, General Accession 646, Hoover Presidential Library.

Engelbert, Ernest A. "Federalism and Water Resources Development." *Law and Contemporary Problems* 22 (1957): 325–50.

Fahmy, Peter A. "Delphus E. Carpenter." In "Six of the Greatest: A Tribute to Outstanding Lawyers in Colorado History," *The Colorado Lawyer* 23 (July 1994): 1479–82.

Feldman, Leonard J. "The Interstate Compact: A Cooperative Solution to Complex Litigation in State Courts." *The Review of Litigation* 12 (Fall 1992): 137–67.

Fiege, Mark. *Irrigated Eden: The Making of an Agricultural Landscape in the American West*. Seattle: University of Washington Press, 1999.

Fite, Gilbert C., and Norman A. Graebner. *Recent United States History*. New York: Ronald Press Co., 1972.

Florestano, Patricia S. "Past and Present Utilization of Interstate Compacts in the U.S." *Publius* 24 (Fall 1994): 13–25.

Forester, D. M. "The Imperial Dam, All-American Canal System, Boulder Canyon Project." *Reclamation Era* 29 (February 1939): 28–36.

Frankfurter, Felix, and James M. Landis. "The Compact Clause of the Constitution: A Study in Interstate Adjustments." *Yale Law Journal* 34 (May 1925): 685–758.

Galbraith, W. J. "The Reason for an Interstate Colorado River Pact." *Arizona Mining Journal* 6 (15 January 1923): 17–18.

Garner, Eric L., and Michelle Oullette. "Future Shock? The Law of the Colorado River in the Twenty-First Century." *Arizona State Law Journal* 27 (1995): 469–506.

Getches, David H. *Water and the American West: Essays in Honor of Raphael J. Moses.* Boulder: Natural Resources Law Center, University of Colorado, 1988.

Girardot, Joseph W. "Toward a Rational Scheme of Interstate Water Compact Adjudication." *Journal of Law Reform* 23 (1989): 151–78.

Golzé, Alfred R. *Reclamation in the United States.* Caldwell: Caxton Printers, 1961.

Gressley, Gene M. "Arthur Powell Davis, Reclamation and the West." *Agricultural History* 42 (July 1968) 241–57.

————, ed. *The Twentieth-Century American West: a Potpourri.* Columbia: University of Missouri Press, 1977.

Grunsky, C. E. "International and Interstate Aspects of the Colorado River Problem." *Science* 56 (10 November 1922): 521–27.

Hadley, Howard D. "Progress in Colorado River Project." *Saturday Night* (8 April 1922): 5.

Hamele, Ottamar. "Federal Water Rights in the Colorado River." *Annals of the American Academy of Political Science* 135 (January 1928): 143–49.

———. "The Colorado River Compact." *Reclamation Record* (December 1922): 302–5.

Hard, William. "Giant Negotiations for Giant Power: An Interview with Herbert Hoover." *Survey* (1 March 1924): 577–80.

Hart, Steve. "Western Water Warrior: The Legacy of Delph Carpenter and His River Treaties." *Historical Studies Journal* 14 (Spring 1997): 67–89.

Hasday, Jill Elaine. "Interstate Compacts in a Democratic Society: The Problems of Permanency." *Florida Law Review* 49 (January 1997): 1–47.

Hawley, Ellis W., ed. *Herbert Hoover as Secretary of Commerce: Studies in New Era Thought and Practice.* Iowa City: University of Iowa Press, 1981.

Hays, Samuel P. *Conservation and the Gospel of Efficiency: The Progressive Conservation Movement, 1890–1920.* Cambridge: Harvard University Press, 1959.

———. *The Response to Industrialism: 1885–1914.* Chicago: University of Chicago Press, 1957.

Heard, Dwight B. "The Colorado River Controversy." *Review of Reviews* 76 (December 1927): 624–28.

Heron, Kevin J. "The Interstate Compact in Transition: From Cooperative State Action to Congressionally Coerced Agreements." *St. John's Law Review* 60 (1985): 1–25.

Hill, Raymond A. "Development of the Rio Grande Compact of 1938." *Natural Resources Journal* 14 (1974): 163–99.

Hobbs, Gregory J., Jr. "Colorado Water Law: An Historical Overview." University of Denver *Water Law Review* 1 (Fall 1997), 1–74.

———. "Colorado's 1969 Adjudication and Administrative Act, Settling In." University of Denver *Water Law Review* 3 (1999): 1–19.

Hofstadter, Richard. *The Age of Reform: From Bryan to FDR.* New York: Knopf, 1955.

Hollon, Eugene. *The Great American Desert: Then and Now.* New York: Oxford University Press, 1966.

Holsinger, M. Paul. "*Wyoming* v. *Colorado* Revisited: The United States Supreme Court and the Laramie River Controversy, 1911–1922." *Annals of Wyoming* 42 (1970): 47–56.

Hoover, Herbert. "Colorado River Development." *Industrial Management* 63 (May 1922): 291.

———. "The Colorado River Problem." *Community Boulder* 1 (March 1928): 9–12.

———. "Harness the Colorado." *Southern California Business* (October 1926): 45.

———. *The Memoirs of Herbert Hoover.* 3 vols. New York: Macmillan Company, 1952.

Hundley, Norris Jr. "Clio Nods: *Arizona* v. *California* and the Boulder Canyon Act: A Reassessment." *Western Historical Quarterly* 3 (January 1972): 17–51.

———. "The Colorado Water Dispute." *Foreign Affairs* 42 (1963–64): 495–500.

———. *The Great Thirst: Californians and Water, 1770s–1990s.* Berkeley: University of California Press, 1992.

———. "The Politics of Reclamation: California, the Federal Government, and the Origins of the Boulder Canyon Act: A Second Look." *California Historical Quarterly* 52 (Winter 1973): 292–325.

———. *Water and the West: The Colorado River Compact and the Politics of Water in the American West.* Berkeley: University of California Press, 1975.

Jessup, Philip C. *Elihu Root.* 2 vols. Hamden: Archon Books, 1938.

Johnson, Ben W. "Uniform Laws of Interstate Compacts." Address to the Ohio State Bar Association 29 (1908), as cited in *Interstate Compacts*, 1: 78–87.

Kelly, William. "The Colorado River Problem." *American Society of Civil Engineers: Transactions* 88 (1925): 306–437.

———. "Rationing the Rivers: A Decade of Interstate Waters and Interstate Commerce in the Supreme Court." *Rocky Mountain Law Review* 14 (1941): 12–20.

Kinney, Clesson S. *A Treatise on the Law of Irrigation and Water Rights and the Arid Region Doctine of Appropriation of Waters.* 4 vols. San Francisco: Bender-Moss Co., 1912.

Kleinsorge, Paul L. *The Boulder Canyon Project: Historical and Economic Aspects.* Palo Alto: Stanford University Press, 1940.

Kluger, James R. *Turning on Water with a Shovel: The Career of Elwood Mead.* Albuquerque: University of New Mexico Press, 1992.

Kruckman, Arnold. "Inside Story of River Conference." *Saturday Night* 3 (18 November 1922): 5.

Leach, Richard H., and Redding S. Sugg, Jr. *The Administration of Interstate Compacts.* Baton Rouge: Louisiana State University Press, 1959.

———. "The Interstate Compact, Water, and the Southwest: A Case Study in Compact Utility." *Southwestern Social Science Quarterly* 38 (1957): 236–47.

Lee, Lawrence B. *Reclaiming the Arid West: An Historiography and Guide.* Santa Barbara: ABC-Clio, 1980.

Leman, Kevin. *The Birth Order Book: Why You Are the Way You Are.* New York: Dell Publishing Co., 1985.

Leopold, Aldo. *A Sand County Almanac and Sketches Here and There.* New York: Oxford University Press, 1949.

Leopold, Richard William. *Elihu Root and the Conservative Tradition.* Boston: Little, Brown, 1954.

Limerick, Patricia Nelson. *Desert Passages: Encounters with the American Deserts.* Albuquerque: University of New Mexico Press, 1985.

Lindegren, David E. "The Colorado River: Are New Approaches Possible Now that the Possibility of Over Allocation Is Here?" *Rocky Mountain Mineral Law Institute* 38 (1992), 25-1 to 25-36.

Littlefield, Douglas R. "Conflict and Compromise: Water Politics on the Rio Grande, 1880–1938." Unpublished MS in the author's possession.

Lochhead, James S. "The Perspective of the State of Colorado in 1922: Did We Get What We Bargained For?" *Seventy-fifth Anniversary Colorado River Compact Symposium Proceedings*. Sacramento: Water Education Foundation, 1997, 184–94.

Lowitt, Richard. *The New Deal and the West*. Bloomington: University of Indiana Press, 1984.

Lyons, Eugene. *Herbert Hoover: A Biography*. Garden City: Doubleday, 1964.

Maas, Arthur, and Raymond Anderson. . . . *and the Desert Shall Rejoice: Conflict, Growth, and Justice in Arid Environments*. Cambridge: Harvard University Press, 1978.

Mann, Dean E. *The Politics of Water in Arizona*. Tucson: University of Arizona Press, 1963.

Maxwell, George H. "The Truth about the Colorado River." *The Signal* (4 May 1923): 3.

———. "Shall America Be Developed? The Truth about the Compact." *Arizona Mining Journal* 6 (15 January 1923): 33.

McCarthy, Michael G. *Hour of Trial: The Conservation Conflict in Colorado and the West, 1891–1907*. Norman: University of Oklahoma Press, 1977.

———, and Richard D. Lamm. *The Angry West: A Vulnerable Land and Its Future*. Boston: Houghton Mifflin Co., 1982.

McClurg, Sue. "A Colorado River Compromise." *Western Water* (November-December 2000): 4–13.

Mead, Elwood. *Irrigation Institutions*. New York: Macmillan Co., 1903.

———. "The Utilization of the Colorado River." *New Reclamation Era* 17 (March 1926): 38–42.

Merrill, Karen R. "In Search of the 'Federal Presence' in the American West." *Western Historical Quarterly* 30 (Winter 1999): 449–73.

Meyer, Michael C. *Water in the Hispanic Southwest: A Social and Legal History, 1550–1850*. Tucson: University of Arizona Press, 1984.

Meyers, Charles. "The Colorado River." *Stanford Law Review* 19 (1966): 1, 9.

Moeller, Beverly. *Phil Swing and Boulder Dam*. Berkeley: University of California Press, 1971.

Murphy, Ralph. "Arizona's Side of the Question." *Sunset Magazine* (April 1926): 34–37.

Muys, Jerome C. "Beyond Allocation: Equitable Apportionment and Interstate Watershed Protection and Management." Presentation to the Nineteenth Annual Water Law Conference, San Diego, Calif., 15–16 Feb. 2001.

———. *Interstate Water Compacts: The Interstate Compact and Federal–Interstate Compact*. Legal Study 14, Final Report to the National Water Commission, NWC-L-71-011. Distributed by the National Technical Information Service, July 1971.

Myers, William Starr, comp. and ed. *The State Papers and Other Public Writings of Herbert Hoover.* 2 vols. New York: Doubleday, Doran & Co., 1934.

Nash, George H. *The Life of Herbert Hoover.* New York: W. W. Norton, 1983.

Nash, Gerald D. *The American West in the Twentieth Century: A Short History of an Urban Oasis.* Englewood Cliffs, N.J.: Prentice-Hall, 1973.

———. *The Federal Landscape: An Economic History of the Twentieth-Century West.* Tucson: University of Arizona Press, 1999.

Niles, Russell D. "The Swing-Johnson Bill and the Supreme Court." *Rocky Mountain Law Review* 3 (1930): 1–24.

———. "Legal Background of the Colorado River Controversy." *Rocky Mountain Law Review* 1 (1929): 73–101.

Norviel, W. S. "The Colorado River Compact Means Much to the Southwest." *Arizona Mining Journal* 6 (15 January 1923): 34.

Olcott, William D. "Equitable Apportionment: A Judicial Bridge over Troubled Waters." *Nebraska Law Review* 66 (1987): 734–61.

Olson, Reuel Leslie. *The Colorado River Compact.* Ph.D. thesis, Harvard University. Published by the author, 1926.

———. "Legal Problems in Colorado River Development." *American Academy of Political and Social Science Annals* 135 (1928): 108–14.

———. "Relationship of *Wyoming v. Colorado* to Colorado River." *Los Angeles Bar Association Bulletin* 2 (4 and 18 November 1926).

Pisani, Donald J. "Deep and Troubled Waters: A New Field of Western History?" *New Mexico Historical Review* 63 (Oct. 1988): 311–31.

———. "Enterprise and Equity: A Critique of Western Water Law in the Nineteenth Century." *Western Historical Quarterly* 18 (January 1987): 15–37.

———. *From the Family Farm to Agribusiness: The Irrigation Crusade in California and the West, 1850–1931.* Berkeley: University of California Press, 1984.

———. "The Irrigation District and the Federal Relationship: Neglected Aspects of Water History." In *The Twentieth-Century West: Historical Interpretations.* Edited by Gerald D. Nash and Richard W. Etulain. Albuquerque: University of New Mexico Press, 1989, 257–92.

———. "The Many Faces of Conservation: Natural Resources and the American State, 1900–1940." In Morton Keller and R. Shep Melnick, *Taking Stock: American Government in the Twentieth Century.* Woodrow Wilson Center Series. Cambridge: Cambridge University Press, 2000.

———. "State vs. Nation: Federal Reclamation and Water Rights in the Progressive Era." *Pacific Historical Review* 51 (August 1982): 265–82.

———. *To Reclaim a Divided West: Water, Law, and Public Policy, 1848–1902.* Albuquerque: University of New Mexico Press, 1992.

———. *Water and American Government: The Reclamation Bureau and the American West, 1902–1935.* Berkeley: University of California Press, 2002.

Powell, John Wesley. *Report on the Lands of the Arid Region of the United States: With a More Detailed Account of the Lands of Utah.* 1879. Reprint, edited by

Wallace Stegner, Cambridge: Belknap Press of Harvard University Press, 1962.

"The Quiet Fellow." *Time*, 16 November 1925, 6.

Radosevich, George E., and Donald E. Hamburg. *Colorado Water Laws, Compacts, Treaties and Selected Cases*. Denver: Colorado Department of Natural Resources, 1971.

Reisner, Marc. "The Age of Dams and Its Legacy." *Colorado Water* 16 (December 1999): 16–23.

———. *Cadillac Desert: The American West and Its Disappearing Water*. New York: Viking Penguin, 1986.

Richardson, Elmo R. *The Politics of Conservation: Crusades and Controversies, 1897–1913*. Berkeley: University of California Press, 1962.

Ridgeway, Marion E. *Interstate Compacts: A Question of Federalism*. Carbondale: Southern Illinois University Press, 1971.

Robbins, David W. "Interstate Compact Obligations: Impacts on Colorado Water Supply." *Colorado Water* 16 (October 1999): 25–29.

Robinson, Michael C. *Water for the West: The Bureau of Reclamation, 1902–1977*. Chicago: Public Works Historical Society, 1979.

Rogers, James Grafton. "Some Problems of the Interstate Water War." *Colorado Bar Association* 26 (1923), 107–24.

Rusinek, Walter. "Against the Compact: The Critical Opposition of George P. Hunt." *Journal of Arizona History* 25 (Spring 1984): 155–70.

Sax, Joseph L., Robert H. Abrams, and Barton H. Thompson, Jr. *Legal Control of Water Resources*. American Casebook Series. St. Paul: West Publishing Co., 1991.

———. "Problems of Federalism in Reclamation Law." *University of Colorado Law Review* 37 (1964–65): 49–84.

Scheiber, Harry N. "The Condition of American Federalism: An Historian's View." *American Intergovernmental Relations*, edited by Laurence J. O'Toole, Jr. Washington: CQ Press, 2000.

Scott, Robert D. "*Kansas v. Colorado* Revisited." *American Journal of International Law* 52 (1958): 432–54.

"Sharing Colorado River Water: History, Public Policy and the Colorado River Compact." *Arroyo* 10 (August 1997): 1–12.

Sherk, George William. *Dividing the Waters: The Resolution of Interstate Water Conflicts in the United States*. Boston: Kluwer Law International, 2000.

Sherow, James E. *Watering the Valley: Development along the High Plains Arkansas River, 1870–1950*. Lawrence: University Press of Kansas, 1990.

Simms, Richard A., Leland E. Rolfs, and Brent E. Spronk. "Interstate Compacts and Equitable Apportionment." *Rocky Mountain Mineral Law Institute* (1988): 23-1 to 23-34.

Simms, Richard A., and Jennifer Davis. "Water Transfers across State Systems." *Rocky Mountain Mineral Law Institute* (July 1985): 22-1 to 22-30.

Simsarian, James. "The Diversion of Interstate Waters in the United States," *American Political Science Review* 23 (1938): 907–21.

Sloan, Richard A. "Pact Criticism Is Largely on What It Does Not Say." *Arizona Mining Journal* 6 (15 January 1923): 29.

Smith, Henry Nash. *Virgin Land: The American West as Symbol and Myth.* Cambridge, Mass. Harvard University Press, 1950.

Smythe, William Ellsworth. *The Conquest of Arid America.* New York: Macmillan Company, 1905.

Stegner, Wallace. *Beyond the Hundredth Meridian: John Wesley Powell and the Second Opening of the West.* Boston: Houghton Mifflin, 1954.

Steinel, Alvin T. *History of Agriculture in Colorado.* Fort Collins, Colo.: State Agricultural College, 1926.

Stephenson, W. A. "Appropriation of Water in Arid Regions." *Southwestern Social Science Quarterly* 18 (1937): 215–26.

Stetson, Clarence. "Making an Empire to Order." *World's Work* (November 1922–April 1922, 1923), 922–102.

Stinson, Howard R. "Western Interstate Water Compacts." *California Law Review* 45 (1957): 655–64.

Stone, Clifford H. "Federal versus State Control of Water." *Rocky Mountain Law Review* 12 (1940): 69–76.

———. "Interstate Water Compacts." *Interstate Compacts,* 2: 65–71.

Sundeen, Matthew, and L. Cheryl Runyon. "Interstate Compacts and Administrative Agreements." National Conference of State Legislators, *State Legislative Report* 23 (March 1998): 1–12.

Tarlock, A. Dan. "The Law of Equitable Apportionment Revisited, Updated, and Restated." *University of Colorado Law Review* 56 (Spring 1985): 381–411.

Teele, Ray Palmer. *The Economics of Land Reclamation in the United States.* Chicago: A. W. Shaw Co., 1927.

Terrell, John Upton. *War for the Colorado River: The California-Arizona Controversy.* Vol. 1. Glendale, Calif.: Arthur H. Clark Co., 1965.

Thursby, Vincent V. *Interstate Cooperation: A Study of the Interstate Compact.* Washington, D.C.: Public Affairs Press, 1953.

Trelease, Frank J. *Cases and Materials on Water Law.* American Casebook Series. St. Paul: West Publishing Company, 1967.

Tuttle, Edward D. "The River Colorado." *Arizona Historical Review* 1 (1928): 50–68.

Tyler, Daniel. "Delph E. Carpenter and the Principle of Equitable Apportionment." *Western Legal History* 9 (Winter-Spring 1996): 34–53.

———. "Delph E. Carpenter: Father of Interstate Water Compacts." *Colorado History* 1 (1997): 87–105.

———. "Delphus Emory Carpenter and the Colorado River Compact of 1922." University of Denver *Water Law Review* 1 (Summer 1998): 228–74.

———. *The Last Water Hole in the West: The Colorado–Big Thompson Project and the Northern Colorado Water Conservancy District.* Niwot: University Press of Colorado, 1992.

———. "The Silver Fox of the Rockies: Delphus Emory Carpenter and the Colorado River Compact." *New Mexico Historical Review* 73 (Jan. 1998), 25–43.

Ubbelohde, Carl, Maxine Benson, and Duane A. Smith. *A Colorado History.* 6th ed. Boulder: Pruett Publishing Company, 1988.

Van Petten, Donald R. "Arizona's Stand on the Santa Fe Compact and the Boulder Dam Project Act." *New Mexico Historical Review* 17 (1942): 1–20.

Voit, William K., and Gary Nitting. *Interstate Compacts and Agencies.* Lexington: The Council of State Governments, 1998.

Vranesh, George. *Colorado Water Law.* 3 vols. Boulder: Vranesh Publications, 1987. A revised edition prepared by James N. Corbridge, Jr., and Teresa A. Rice, is titled, *Vranesh's Colorado Water Law* (Niwot: University of Colorado Press, 1999).

Warne, William E. *The Bureau of Reclamation.* New York: Praeger, 1973.

Water Education Foundation. *Seventy-fifth Anniversary Colorado River Compact Symposium Proceedings.* Sacramento: Water Education Foundation, 1997.

Water Resource Committee. *Interstate Water Compacts, 1785–1941.* Technical Paper number 5. Transcripts and Analytical Table. Washington: National Resources Planning Board, 1942.

Weatherford, Gary D., and F. Lee Brown, eds. *New Courses for the Colorado River: Major Issues for the Next Century.* Albuquerque: University of New Mexico Press, 1986.

Weil, Samuel C. "Fifty Years of Water Law." *Harvard Law Review* 50 (1936–37): 252–304.

———. "One Aspect of the Colorado River Interstate Agreement." *California Law Review* 11 (1922–23): 145–55.

———. *Water Rights in the Western States.* San Francisco: Bancroft-Whitney Company 1905.

Wilbur, Ray Lyman, and Arthur Mastick Hyde. *The Hoover Policies.* New York: Charles Scribner's Sons, 1937.

Wilcox, E. V. "The Water Oracle of Greeley." *Country Gentleman* 85 (9 October 1920): 6, 7, 26.

Wilkinson, Charles F. "Achieving Sustainability in an Era of On-Rushing Development: Realistic Goal or Image?" *Colorado Water* 17 (August 2000), 19–23.

———. *Crossing the Next Meridian: Land, Water, and the Future of the West.* Washington: Island Press, 1992.

———. *The Eagle Bird: Mapping a New West.* New York: Pantheon Books, 1992.

———. "Western Water Law in Transition." *University of Colorado Law Review* 56 (Spring 1985): 317–46.

Williams, Wayne. "The Colorado River and the Constitution." *American Bar Association Journal* 12 (June 1922): 619–22.

Worster, Donald. *Rivers of Empire: Water, Aridity and the Growth of the American West.* New York: Pantheon Books, 1985.

————. *A River Running West: The Life of John Wesley Powell.* New York: Oxford University Press, 2001.

————. *Under Western Skies: Nature and History in the American West.* New York: Oxford University Press, 1992.

Zimmerman, Frederick L., and Mitchell Wendell. *The Interstate Compact Since 1925.* Chicago: Council of State Governments, 1951.

Zimmerman, Joseph F. *Interstate Relations: The Neglected Dimensions of Federalism.* Westport, Conn.: Praeger, 1996.

Index

Page references in **bold type** indicate photographs, maps, and other illustrative materials.

Adams, John T., 280
Adams, William H., 230–32
Agriculture: Colorado River basin development of, 113–14; economic development and, 6, 19; environmental impacts of reservoirs on, 291–92; interstate water compacts and, 127–28; irrigated, 36–37, 305n33; Kinkaid Act and, 147; Non-Partisan League and, 128; prior appropriation and, 51–53
Alamo Canal, 111
All-American Canal: Arizona challenges to, 263–65; Bureau of Reclamation support of, 235, 321n71; California and, 221; Colorado River basin development and, 117; Imperial Valley and, 113–14
American Shorthorn Breeders' Association, 110. *See also* Livestock
Ammons, Elias, 93, 317n4
Anthony, Susan B., 42–43
Apportionment, equitable. *See* Equitable apportionment

Appropriation, priority of. *See* Priority doctrine
Arentz, Samuel S., 181
Arizona: Central Arizona Project, 351n82; challenges of Colorado River Compact, 263–65; Compact ratification, 204–7, 276–77; diversions and, 167–68; map of, **168**; resistance to compact agreement, 192–95, 344n114; resistance to two-basin plan, 189–91, 334n84; Salt River and, 17; six-state compact and, 205–6, 223–24; three-state compact and, 204
Arizona Republican, 212
Arkansas River: basin map, **7, 92**; compact negotiations, 202, 244–46; compact violations, 293, 346n18; *Kansas v. Colorado* and, 75–76
Army Corps of Engineers, 17
Aspinall-Gunnison Project, 357n34

Babbitt, Bruce, 358n58
Ballinger, Richard A., 96, 318n21
Bamberger, Simon, 116
Bannister, L. Ward: conflict with Delph, 213–18, 226–29; relationship with Delph, 172, 234, 267; Rio Grande Compact and, 252;

support of Swing-Johnson bill, 205, 231–34

Bennett, Martha Allen. *See* Carpenter, Martha Bennett

Bien, Morris, 198, 221

Big Thompson River, 52–53. *See also* Colorado-Big Thompson Project

Black Canyon, 150, 221, 336n2

BLM. *See* Bureau of Land Management (BLM)

Bonfils, Frederick, 233–34, 343n106

Boulder Canyon: Fall-Davis Report and, 150; League of the Southwest and, 116–17; Reclamation Service interest in, 113, 140

Boulder Canyon Dam. *See* Hoover Dam

Boulder Canyon Project Act. *See* Hoover Dam

Boulder Dam. *See* Hoover Dam

Boulder River, 52–53

Boyd, David, 50–51

Boyle, Emmett D., **129**, 166, 170–71

Bradfield, George H., 288

Breitenstein, Jean, 276

Brewer, David, 17–18, 75, 78

Brown, Charles Wayland, 255

Bull, George M., 169, 173

Bureau of Indian Affairs, 197–98

Bureau of Land Management (BLM), 273–74

Bureau of Reclamation: Central Arizona Project and, 351n82; Colorado-Big Thompson Project, 268–71; Colorado River Storage Project, 350n65; criticism of, 224–25; Elwood Mead and, 219–20; North Platte River Compact and, 255–56; Rio Grande Compact and, 252; state

sovereignty and the, 75, 225–26; Swing-Johnson legislation and, 235. *See also* Newlands Act of 1902; Reclamation Service

Burges, Richard F., 248–50

Bursum, H. O., 133, 135–36

Cache la Poudre River: diversions, 15–16, 77–78; prior appropriation and, 51–52; transbasin diversions and, 258–60; Union Colony and, 4, 32; water district establishment and, 52–53. *See also* Laramie River; *Wyoming v. Colorado*

Caddoa Reservoir, 346n11

Caldwell, Fred S., 216

Caldwell, R. E., **129**, 183, 188

California: Boulder Canyon Dam and, 140–42, 221; Central Arizona Project and, 351n82; challenge to Compact, 215–16; diversions and, 167–68; economic development, 111–12; equitable apportionment and, 290–91; League of the Southwest and, 116–18; six-state compact and, 217–19, 223–24, 231, 235; three-state compact and, 204. *See also* Imperial Valley; Los Angeles, Calif.; San Diego, Calif.

Cameron, Robert, 16

Camfield, Daniel A., 77, 121

Campbell, A. C., 139

Campbell, Thomas E., 131–33, 139, 167, 187

Canal No. 2. *See* Ditch No. 2

Carnegie Endowment for International Peace, 138–39

Carpenter, Alfred Bennett, **56**; geneaology of, 27–28; parental guidance of, 47–48

Carpenter, Alfred G., 88

Carpenter, Daniel, **30**; death of, 55; geneaology of, 27–29; military service, 27, 41; on reclamation and irrigated agriculture, 121; temperance and, 27; Union Colony and, 32

Carpenter, Delphus (Delph) Emory: accomplishments, 22–23, 84, 101, 122, 162–63; character traits of, 26–27, 48–49, 64, 86–87, 165; death of, 278; education and early law practice, 57–64; "Father of the Colorado River Compact," 108, 206, 287, 289, 323n3; Hoover's praise of, 201; loss of position as commissioner, 23, 266–67, 307n64; marriage of, 64, 68, 160–62; Modern Woodmen of America (MWA) and, 68; parental guidance of, 23, 47–48, 55; philosophy of, 294–98; political candidacy of, 68, 74–75; politics and, 14–15, 48–49, 60, 64, 84–86, 88–89; recognition and awards, 212, 241, 276, 279, 286–89, 323n3; relationship with his family, 159–62; as the "Silver Fox of the Rockies," 21–22, 125, 298–99; State Senate responsibilities, 16, 76–84; as the "Water Oracle of Greeley," 49, 322n93. *See also* (financial problems of); (health problems of); (photographs of)

Carpenter, Delphus (Delph) Emory (financial problems of): Colorado government and, 178–79; Crow Creek Ranch and, 126–27, 159, 354n4; family and legal practice, 72–73; Greeley-Poudre Irrigation District and, 84, 96–97; health concerns and, 234; land purchases and, 68–70; loss of position as commissioner, 279–80

Carpenter, Delphus (Delph) Emory (health problems of): declining abilities and Christian Science healing, 243–44; declining abilities and work, 21–23, 228–30, 253–54, 347n33; health and financial concerns, 234; influenza and, 111, 329n4; Parkinson's Disease and, 49, 111, 133, 158–59, 203; work and financial concerns, 79, 100–101, 158–59

Carpenter, Delphus (Delph) Emory (photographs of): as an attorney, **69**, **145**; Colorado River Compact Commission (CRCC), **129**; in the Colorado Senate, **81**; on a coyote hunt, **71**; irrigating the family farm, **61**; as a law student, **62**; in the Rawah Wilderness Area, **164**; as a young boy, **56**, **58**

Carpenter, Donald A.: education and law practice, 280, 355n5; geneaology of, **28**; photographs of, **281**; relationship with father, 101, 159–60, 230; Union Colony House and, 40n

Carpenter, Doris A., 310n43

Carpenter, Farrington R., 273–74

Carpenter, Fred George: Carpenter family history by, 310n43; geneaology of, 27–28; parental guidance of, 47–48

Carpenter, Leroy S.: courtship and marriage, 33–35, 37–40, 44–47, 308n16; death of, 230, 310n43; geneaology of, 27–28; move to Colorado, 33; on reclamation and irrigated agriculture, 16, 121; relationship with Delph, 23,

55–57; religious beliefs of, 44; Union Colony and, 36–37; water rights and, 48; women's rights and, 42–43

Carpenter, Louis G., 94, 114

Carpenter, Martha Bennett: courtship and marriage, 33–35, 37–40, 44–47; geneaology of, 27–28; Methodist Missionary Society and, 44; religious beliefs of, 44; temperance and, 43–44; Union Colony and, 355n11; women's rights and, 42–43

Carpenter, Martha (Mattie), 32

Carpenter, Martha Patricia, 28, 159, 280

Carpenter, Mary P., 29

Carpenter, Michaela (Dot) Hogarty: death of, 279; education of, 66–68; geneaology of, 28; health problems of, 230; marriage of, 64, 68; photographs of, **65, 161**; relationship with Delph, 22, 160–62, 203, 243–44, 278–79

Carpenter, Michaela H., 159, 280

Carpenter, Nancy Scott, 27–28, **31**

Carpenter, Peter, 29–33

Carpenter, Sarah, 159, 280

Carpenter, Silas, 310n43

Carpenter family: geneaology, **28**, 310n43; land purchases in Union Colony, 36, 40

Carpenter Peaks, 163–64

Carpenter Reservoir Bill of 1911, 15, 82–84

Carr, Ralph, 243, 253–54, 267, 275, 286–87

Carr, Sarah Ann. See Hogarty, Sarah Carr

Casper-Alcova Project, **91**, 258–60

Central Arizona Project, 351n82. See also Highline Canal

Chandler, Harry, 117, 326n49

Chase, Lucius, 167

Cheeseman, Lake, 100

Christian Science healing, 243–44, 286

Clayton, William L., 74–75

Clinton, William Jefferson, 290

Closed Basin. See San Luis Valley

Coachella Valley. See All-American Canal

Colorado: Compact ratification, 211; Constitution amendments, 80–82, 305n35, 316n77; Constitution and water rights, 52, 76–77, 315n69, 316n77; cost of violations and litigation, 292–93, 346n18, 357n40; criticism of water compacts, 291; interpretation of Colorado River Compact and, 209–11; litigation against Arizona, 216; map of, **91**; priority doctrine and, 13–14; six-state compact and, 205, 217–19; state engineer, 53; transbasin diversions and, 167; water defense fund, 76–77, 99–100, 245, 259, 267, 280, 317n4; water district establishment, 52–53; West Slope, 208

Colorado, Kansas v. See Kansas v. Colorado

Colorado, Wyoming v. See Wyoming v. Colorado

Colorado Agricultural College, 94, 97

Colorado Bar Association, 63, 214

Colorado-Big Thompson Project, 24, 211, 254, 268–71, 335n101

Colorado Doctrine: adoption of, 112–13; defense of, 76–78, 121–22; establishment of, 51–54; flaw in the application of, 79. See also Priority doctrine

Colorado River: basin map, **151**; Colorado-Big Thompson Project,

211, 254; estimates of water flow, 150–52, 290; hydroelectric power v. reclamation, 166–67; *Mexican Water Treaty, The* and, 354n33; navigation, 195, 197; protecting Colorado rights to, 126, 144–46; return flows, 135; two-basin plan, 166, 173–75; upper v. lower basin water rights, 115–22. *See also* Lower basin; Upper basin
Colorado River Aqueduct, 204–5
Colorado River Compact: adoption of, **199**, 201, 306n37; agreement memorandum, 193–97; Arizona challenges to, 263–65; Arizona ratification of, 276–77; Bannister and Carpenter relationship, 226–29, 234, 239; Carpenter-Hoover teamwork on, 141–44, 241; Congressional approval of, 226–27; dam construction and the, 196; environmental impacts of, 291–92; Grand Lake Project, 269; history of, 282–87, 325n37; hydroelectric power permits and, 237; impact of *Wyoming v. Colorado* on, 173–75; interpretation of, 208–12; map of, **7**; as model for interstate agreements, 293–94; political threat to, 238–39; precedents for, 108–9, 320n57; problems of, 290–93; ratification, 203, 324n18, 356n22; Reclamation Service and the, 96; six-state compact and, 205–6, 217–19, 223–24, 227, 235; three-state compact and, 235; transbasin diversions and, 155, 178; two-basin plan, 170, 174–75, 188–95, 193; Utah withdrawal from, 231; Washington hearings on, 133–36; water division between basins, 179–81,

182, 191–95, 289, 332n49, 334n74, 334n84. *See also* Interstate river compacts
Colorado River Compact, The, 283–85
Colorado River Compact Commission (CRCC): 1921 meetings of, 127–42; 1922 meeting at Bishop's Lodge, 183–201, **184**, **185**; 1922 meetings of, 143–47, 143–56, 171–83; 1922 public hearings of, 166–70; agreement memorandum, 193–97; commissioner appointments, 130; compact legislation draft and, 130–32; Congressional approval of, 134–35; Delph's perceived inflexibility on, 157–58; history of, 282–87; interpretation of Colorado River Compact and, 208–12; leadership in, 171–72, 180, 186, 195; membership of, **129**, 130, 138–39, **185**, 334n81; organizing, 120, 122, 124–26; role in resolving water issues, 134–35; state disunity and, 153–56, 167; *Wyoming v. Colorado* impact on, 171
Colorado River Storage Project, 260–65, 290, 292, 350n65, 357n34
Colorado State Water Users Protective Association. *See* Colorado Water User's Association
Colorado Water User's Association, 97–98, 267
Commerce Department. *See* United States Commerce Department; United States Commerce Department
Compacts, river. *See* Interstate river compacts
Comstock, Charles W., 83
Congressional Record, 198

Coolidge, Calvin, 222, 234, 341n67
Corthell, Nellis, 171
Cory, H. T., 181
Cosmopolitan, 72, 314n45
Costigan, Edward P., 258–60
Country Gentleman, 121, 322n93
Craven, Al, 95
CRCC. *See* Colorado River Compact
    Commission (CRCC)
Crow Creek Ranch, **38**, 68–72;
    coyote hunts and, 70–72; finan-
    cial problems and, 126–27, 159,
    279–80; livestock ranching and,
    97; as respite from work, 101
Curecanti Dam, 357n34
Currier, Warren, 63–64, 313n33

Dams. *See* Reservoirs
Daughters of the American
    Revolution, 68, 160
Davis, Arthur, P.: Colorado River
    basin development and, 113,
    117–18; Fall-Davis Report and,
    147–50; interpretation of
    Colorado River Compact and,
    208–9; relationship with Carpen-
    ter, 96; removal from Reclama-
    tion Service, 219, 255; support of
    Compact, 198; transbasin diver-
    sions and, 167–69; two-basin
    plan, 166; water division between
    basins, 180
Davis, David W., 219
Davis, Steven B., Jr.: CRCC draft
    legislation and, 132–33; CRCC
    history and, 188, 284; La Plata
    River negotiations and, 136–38;
    North Platte River Compact and,
    255; photograph of, **129**; six-state
    compact and, 217–19
Dent, P. W., 225
Denver, City of: Chamber of
    Commerce, 172, 205, 234, 252;

population of, 331n22; Swing-
    Johnson legislation and, 233;
    Union Water Company, 100;
    Water Board, 227; water rights
    and, 227–28
Denver Post, 120, **129**, 179, 233, 279
Denver Republican, 60
Department of Interior. *See* United
    States Department of Interior
Dern, George H., 230–33
Desert Land Act of 1877, 3–4,
    301n2
Devils River, 248
Diamond Creek, 166–67, 187
Direct Election League of Denver,
    82
Ditch No. 1, 308n17
Ditch No. 2, 27, 36–37, 50, 308n17,
    309n22
Ditch No. 3, 27, 36, 309n17
Ditch No. 4, 309n17
Diversions. *See* Transbasin diversions
Dobbel, Charles A., 282–83,
    325n37
Donovan, William J., 252–54, 263

East Slope: Colorado-Big
    Thompson Project, 24, 254,
    331n22; limitations to develop-
    ment, 214; map of, **91**; transbasin
    diversions and, 211; water needs,
    169
Eaton, Benjamin H., 52, 54, 121,
    308n17
Eckel, George, 243
Edwards, Arthur M., 60
Elephant Butte Dam: map of, **7**;
    Reclamation Service and, 6, 154;
    Rio Grande Compact and,
    247–50; Root-Casasus Treaty of
    1906 and, 347n19; water devel-
    opment and, 119, 169, 314n58
Ely, Sims, 128, 140, 278, 287

Emerson, Frank C.: CRCC negotiations and, 146, 188; photograph of, **129**; six-state compact and, 217–19; upper basin leadership and, 233; water development and, 169
Environmental protection, 291–92, 295–98
Episcopal Church, 64, 68, 160
Equitable apportionment: Congressional approval of, 136; Greeley-Poudre Irrigation Project, 90; international precedents in, 181–82, 304n25; *Kansas v. Colorado* and, 10–12, 301n5, 303n15, 325n39; Rio Grande Compact negotiations and, 246–54; state sovereignty and, 95, 124, 131; Supreme Court and, 75–76, 268, 274–77; upper v. lower basin needs and, 167–70; water division between basins, 179–81, **182**; *Wyoming v. Colorado* and, 102–4. *See also* Equitable utilization; Priority doctrine
Equitable utilization, 304n25. *See also* Equitable apportionment
Evans, Colo., 50, 73–74, 165

Fall, Albert E., 132, 140–41
Fall-Davis Report, 147–48, 328n80
Farrar, Fred, 102
Federal Land Bank, 279
Federal Power Commission (FPC): CRCC hearings and, 166–67; CRCC history and, 284; hydroelectric power permits, 196–97, 236–37, 342n87–88, 343n114
Field, John H., 119
Finney County Water Users Association, 245
First-in-time first in right. *See* Priority doctrine

Fleming, John, 212
Fleming, Roscoe, 279
Fleming, Russell, 110, 210
Flood control: California pressure for, 140–41; Colorado Doctrine and, 52; CRCC hearings on, 166–67; dam failure and, 165n; Fall-Davis Report and, 149–50; final compact and, 196; Kinkaid Act and, 147; League of the Southwest calls for, 112–20; Reclamation Service and, 16–17, 113–14
Fort Collins Agricultural Colony, 51–52
Foxes, Silver, 21–22, 125, 298–99
FPC. *See* Federal Power Commission (FPC)
Frankfurter, Felix, 271, 293
Front Range. *See* East Slope

Garden City, Kans., 245
Garfield, James R., 273
Geneaology, Carpenter family, 27–28
George, Henry, 149
Gila River: Imperial Valley development and, 174, 204; water division between basins and, 181, 190, 194–95, 334n74, 334n84
Gillett, L. A., 120
Girand, James P., 166–67, 196–97
Glen Canyon Reservoir, **168**, 170, 178, 357n34
Glendevy, Colo., 163
Grand Coulee Dam, 315n60
Grand Junction Daily Sentinel, 224–25
Grand Lake Project. *See* Colorado-Big Thompson Project
Grand River, 116, 174, 322n80, 332n51
Gray, D. E., 86
Great Depression, 19, 271

Greeley, Colo.: Colorado Doctrine and, 53–54; county seat in, 50; map of, **38**; prior appropriation and, 51–52; Union Colony and, 4–5, 4n, 32, 355n11; Union Colony House, 40–41
Greeley, Horace, 4–5, 16
Greeley, Water Oracle of, 49, 322n93
Greeley Investment Company, 279
Greeley National Bank, 279
Greeley Normal School, 160. *See also* State Normal School
Greeley Oracle, The, 49, 121
Greeley-Poudre Irrigation District. *See* Greeley-Poudre Irrigation Project
Greeley-Poudre Irrigation Project: Carpenter as attorney for, 77–78, 84, 87; creation of, 316n3; financial problems of, 109–10; map of, **91**, **92**; water division between basins and, 318n16; *Wyoming v. Colorado* and, 15–16, 89–95, 317n6
Greeley Tribune: Colorado-Big Thompson Project and, 268; promoting Colorado settlement, 32, 36; women's rights and, 42–43
Green Mountain, 89
Green River, 116, 174, 230–31, 322n80, 332n51
Guggenheim, Simon, 313n37
Gunter, Julius C., 100

Hamele, Ottamar, 197–98, 208–9
Hannett, A. T., 250
Hansen, Charles, 268
Harding, F. W., 110
Harding, Warren G., 132–33, 135, 139, 140–41
Harmon, Judson, 135, 304n26, 326n40

Harrison, Frank A., 98–99
Hayden, Carl T., 208–9, 212
Haythorne, R. M., 86
Heard, Dwight, 212, 221
Highline Canal, 167, **168**, 187, 204. *See also* Central Arizona Project
Hinderlider, M. C.: assumes duties of water commissioner, 267; equitable apportionment and, 268, 274–77; North Platte River Compact and, 259–60; praise of Dot, 244; water division between basins and, 251
Hinderlider v. La Plata River and Cherry Creek Ditch Company, 268, 274–77, 286
Hogarty, Ann Michaela (Dot). *See* Carpenter, Michaela (Dot) Hogarty
Hogarty, Michael Joseph: career of, 64–66, 313n37; death of, 230; geneaology of, **28**; photograph of, **67**
Hogarty, Sarah Carr, **28**, 66
Hoover, Hubert: appointment to CRCC, 140–44, 327n56; Colorado River Compact and, 123–25, 193–201, 208–12; Delph's praise of, 201; Hoover Dam dedication and, 239–41; photographs of, **129**, **200**; recognition of Delph's contributions, 287; Rio Grande Compact Commission and, 247–54; support of dam construction, 236; western land policy of, 271–74
Hoover Dam, **7**, **240**; Arizona challenges to, 187, 263–65; authorization and Compact ratification, 203–4; Boulder Canyon Project Act and, 205–6, 233–34; dedication of, 239–41;

history of, 282–83; hydroelectric power and, 188; Los Angeles proposals for, 140; proposals for, 116–19, 191, 336n2; Reclamation Service and, 148, 315n60

Hopkins, Seldon G., 217–19

Hubbard, Leslie E., 102

Hughes, Charles E., 252

Hunt, George W. P., 167, 187, 204, 221

Hyde, Arthur M., 273

Hydroelectric power: California pressure for, 140; Casper-Alcova Project and, 260; Colorado River basin and, 116–17, **151**; Colorado River Compact and, 196; CRCC hearings on, 166–67; equitable distribution and, 174–75, 235–37; Fall-Davis Report and, 150; Guernsey Dam, 257; Nevada and, 187–88, 204; public v. private ownership of, 167; Reclamation Service and, 16–17, 142, 306n41

Ickes, Harold, 239, 241, 260

Immigration, western: Asians and, 187, 286; Carpenter family, 27–28, 35–36

Imperial Irrigation District, 18

Imperial Valley: All-American Canal and, 113–14, 176–77, 235, 328n80; Arizona challenges to, 263–65; Colorado River Compact and, 210–12; economic development and, 18–19, 111–12, 116; Gila River and the, 204–5; Kinkaid Act ande, 147; six-state compact and, 218; two-basin plan and, 174–75. *See also* California; Los Angeles, Calif.

Influenza, Spanish, 105, 111, 229, 243, 319n48

Initiative and referendum act: creation of, 14n, 80; Delph and the, 14–15; first application of, 82–83, 305n35

Interior Department. *See* United States Department of Interior

International Boundary Commission, 252

International law, 303n14

International water law: Colorado River and, 113; equitable apportionment and, 12–13, 304n25; Harmon Doctrine and, 304n26; *Mexican Water Treaty, The,* and, 354n33; Mexico and, 209, 276, 304n26, 326n40; Nile River Treaty and, 181; priority doctrine and, 320n56; Rio Grande and, 135, 157–58, 252; *Wyoming v. Colorado* and, 93–94

Interstate compacts, 19–20, 293–94, 305n28

Interstate river compacts: Arkansas River Compact, 244–46, 346n18; benefits of, 8–10, 137–38, 358n52; Colorado River Compact and, 209–10, 290–93; cost of violations and litigation, 292–93, 346n18, 357n40; criticism of, 221, 291; environmental impacts of, 291–92; equitable apportionment and, 10–11, 136; La Plata River Compact, 136–38, 222; League of the Southwest and, 120; litigation and, 48, 89, 109–10, 277, 288, 357n41; map of, **7**; negotiating for, 124, 128, 237–38, 260; Nile River Treaty and, 181; North Platte River Compact, 254–60; Republican River Compact, 108; Rio Grande Compact, 246–54; Sabine River Compact, **7**; South Platte River Compact, 109, 222,

255; state sovereignty and, 19–20, 131; state treaty-making powers for, 118–20, 134–35, 287–88; Supreme Court support of, 20–21, 275–76; Upper Basin Compact, 242, 291. *See also* specific River by name
Iowa, 29, 33
Irrigation: Colorado River basin, 113–14, **151**; CRCC hearings on, 166–67; Desert Land Act of 1877 and, 3–4; economic development and, 6, 305n33; environmental impacts of, 291–92; prior appropriation and, 51–53; Reclamation Service and, 16–17; return flows, 108–9; state acreage estimates, 152–53; two-basin plan and, 174–75; Union Colony and, 4–5, 4n, 36–37; water rights and, 223, 288; versus water storage rights, 80–82
Irrigation Age, 114

Johnson, Edwin C., 23, 259, 266–67
Johnson, Hiram, 176, 203–4

Kansas v. Colorado: equitable apportionment and, 16, 75–76, 78, 325n39, 346n18; federal water rights and, 148–49; priority doctrine and, 90, 113; state sovereignty and, 12–13. *See also* La Plata River Compact
Kendrick, John B., 258–60
Kersey, Colo., 73–74, 165
Keyes, Victor, 116, 178
Kinkaid Act of 1920, 117, 147, 322n82
Knapp, George S., 245
Kruckman, Arnold, 112, 116, 139, 215
Kuner, Colo., 165

LaGrange District, 66
Landis, James M., 293
Lane, Franklin K., 113
La Plata River and Cherry Creek Ditch Company, Hinderlider v., 268, 274–77
La Plata River Compact, 136–38, 188, 202, 222; approval of, 341n67; equitable apportionment and, 268, 274–77; Ralph Carr and, 286; Supreme Court decision on, 20–21, 357n41. *See also Kansas v. Colorado*
Laramie-Poudre Reservoirs and Irrigation Company, 89–93, 97, 316n3
Laramie-Poudre Tunnel, **7**, 15–16, 89–93, 109. *See also* Greeley-Poudre Irrigation District
Laramie River: diversions, 15–16, 77–78; Laramie-Poudre Tunnel and, 89, 317n6, 318n16; litigation, 146; research for *Wyoming v. Colorado*, 163–64. *See also* Cache la Poudre River; *Wyoming v. Colorado*
LaSalle, Colo., 165
League of the Southwest, 112–20, 123–24; California dominance in, 140–41; challenge to Colorado River Compact, 215; CRCC and, 139; interstate river compacts and, 131–32
Leatherwood, Elmer O., 176–77
Lee's Ferry, Ariz., 174, 180–81, **182**
Leopold, Aldo, 298
Lewis, Charles R., 73–74
Litigation: Arizona Compact ratification and, 216–18; Colorado River Compact, 263–65; compact negotiation v., 13, 124, 277, 293–94; compact violations and cost of, 292–93; Constitution compact clause and, 78, 119–20;

interstate water conflicts and, 75–76, 89; leadership needs in the face of, 295–98; Leroy Carpenter on, 48; state sovereignty and, 20

Little Colorado River, 181, 194, 334n74

Livestock: Bates milking shorthorns, 97, 127, 279; cowboy lifestyle and, 70–72; Delph's interest in, 68, 126–27, 314n43–44; federal land acquisition and, 271–73; Taylor Grazing Act of 1934, 273–74

Lory, Charles, 97

Los Angeles, CA: Boulder Canyon Dam and, 140; Chamber of Commerce, 117, 167; Colorado River Aqueduct and, 204–5, 336n4; economic development, 18–19, 111–12; hydroelectric power v. reclamation, 166–67. See also California; Imperial Valley

Los Angeles Times, 117, 326n49

Lowell, Lawrence, 284

Lower basin: Colorado River Compact and, 208–12; dam construction in the, 196; hydroelectric power permits and, 237; six-state compact and, 217–19; three-state compact and, 204, 290–91; two-basin plan and, 174–75; v. upper basin concerns, 169–72, 175, 186, 235–36; water division between basins, 180–81, 182, 191–95, 289. See also Colorado River; Upper basin

Malone, George W., 234

Malone, Mark, 323n3

Maxwell, George H., 167, 187, 204

McClure, W. F.: CRCC negotiations and, 146, 167, 172, 187; photo-graph of, 129; praise of Delph, 211–12; six-state compact and, 218; water division between basins and, 180

McCluskey, H. S., 288

McCreery, James W., 64, 84

McCune, A. J., 118

McGregor, T. H., 254

McHugh, J. R., 64

McIntyre Creek, 163

McKissick, R. T., 208, 218

Mead, Elwood: CRCC and, 139–42; North Platte River Compact and, 255–56; Reclamation Service and, 77; as Reclamation Service Commissioner, 225, 315n60; Reclamation Service Fact Finders' Commission, 219–20; Rio Grande negotiations and, 249–50; Swing-Johnson bill and, 235

Mecham, Merritt C., 129, 172–73

Medicine Bow Range, 163–64

Meeker, Nathaniel C.: death of, 50–51; prior appropriation and, 51–52; on reclamation and irrigated agriculture, 36–37, 121; Union Colony and, 4–5, 4n, 16, 32; western settlement and, 312n6

Meeker, Ralph I.: CRCC negotiations and, 143; Rio Grande negotiations and, 251–52; "Silver Fox of the Rockies" and, 21–22, 125; water division between basins, 169, 173

Merrill, Oliver C., 284

Methodist Church, 29, 33, 40, 44, 60

Mexican Water Treaty, The, 354n33

Mexico: Alamo Canal and, 113–14; Colorado River basin development and, 117; Colorado River Compact and, 174–75, 178, 193,

198, 209; Colorado River treaty
with, 276; equitable apportion-
ment and, 12, 157–58; Fall-Davis
Report and, 150; *Mexican Water
Treaty, The* and, 354n33; Rio
Grande and, 248, 326n40,
347n19; water rights and, 112,
134–35, 246, 303n16
Moan, Robert E., 163
Mondell, Franklin, 133, 135–36,
148
Monfort, Ken, 40n
Morley, Clarence J., 217, 250,
341n67
Muir, John, 24
Mulholland, William, 166, 336n4

National Irrigation Congress, 76,
114, 314n59
National Reclamation Act of 1902,
224
National Soldier and Settlement
Act, 113
Navigation: Colorado River and,
195, 197, 231, 233, 342n98,
351n80; Department of Interior
and, 206; Green River, 230–31;
Reclamation Service and, 16
Nebraska: litigation over South
Platte River, 78, 97–100, 108;
litigation over the Republican
River, 105–8; North Platte
River Compact negotiations,
254–60
Negotiation: achieving CRCC goals
by, 157–58; compacts and the
philosophy of, 237–38, 260, 277,
294–95; compacts v. litigation by,
13, 107–8, 124; leadership needs
in the face of, 295–98, 358n58;
Leroy Carpenter on, 48; psychology of, 207; state sovereignty and,
20; v. prior appropriation, 84; on

water division between basins,
191–95; water rights through,
104–5
Nevada: compact problems for, 291;
six-state compact and, 205; three-
state compact and, 204
Newell, Frederick, 17–18
Newlands Act of 1902: hydroelec-
tric power and, 17–18;
Progressivism and, 11n;
Reclamation Service and, 5, 256;
water rights and, 148. *See also*
Bureau of Reclamation; Reclama-
tion Service
New Mexico: Elephant Butte Dam
and, 6; La Plata River Compact,
20–21, 136–38; Rio Grande
Compact and, 250–54; six-state
compact and, 205, 217–19
New York, 27
New York Herald Tribune, 4 & n, 32
Non-Partisan League, 128
Norlin, George, 212
North Platte River: basin map, **92**;
Casper-Alcova Project and,
257–60; embargo v. compacts,
222–23; Nebraska litigation over,
97–100; Pathfinder Dam and, 6;
Reclamation Service restrictions
on, 131, 154, 169
North Platte River Compact, 202,
254–60, 349n62
Norviel, W. S.: CRCC negotiations
and, 146, 167, 186–87; photo-
graph of, **129**; relationship with
Delph, 171, 192–93; water divi-
sion between basins, 183
Nunn, CO, 77

O'Connor, Sandra Day, 357n41
Ohio, 27
Olson, Reuel Leslie, 283–85
Owyhee Dam, 315n60

Pariah River, 193
Parker Dam, 351n82
Parkinson's Disease. *See* Carpenter,
 Delphus (Delph) Emory (health
 problems of)
Parrish Amendment. *See* Colorado
 Constitution amendments
Pathfinder Dam, 6, **7**, 154, 169,
 254. *See also* North Platte River
Pecos River, **7**, 248
Peterson, Donald, 280
Phipps, Lawrence E., 233–34, 269
Phrenology, 64, 313n35
Pinchot, Gifford, 10–11, 24, 79, 96,
 318n21
Pioneer Irrigation Company, 105,
 108
Politics: Delph's aspirations to, 60,
 64, 68; Delph's election to State
 Senate, 14, 74–75, **81**; Delph's
 involvement in, 48–49, 88–89,
 128; Delph's reelection loss, 86;
 leadership needs in the face of,
 295–98
Powell, John Wesley: irrigation and,
 6, 51–52; United States Geo-
 logical Survey, 147; western
 settlement and, 298, 312n6
Prior appropriation doctrine. *See*
 Priority doctrine
Priority doctrine: Carpenter
 Reservoir Bill of 1911, 15, 82–84;
 Colorado River and, 113;
 Compact problems and, 291;
 Desert Land Act of 1877 and, 4;
 international precedents in,
 94–95; irrigation and, 288;
 Kansas v. Colorado and, 325n39;
 litigation over South Platte River,
 78; litigation over the Republican
 River, 105–8; livestock grazing
 rights and, 273–74; Mexico and,
 326n40; Rio Grande Compact

negotiations and, 246–54; state
 recognition of, 8–10, 51–53;
 United States v. Winters and,
 353n9; v. negotiated compacts,
 83–84; water rights and, 302n9,
 305n31, 312n9; *Wyoming v.
 Colorado* and, 102–4, 107, 173,
 301n5, 303n15
Progressivism: as political reform,
 10–12, 10n, 14, 79–80; Steven B.
 Davis, Jr., and, 149; western settlement, 16–17
Prosser, Paul, 266
Public Works Administration, 260
Purgatory River, 245

Rawah Creek, 163
Rawah Peak, **164**
Reclamation Service: Boulder
 Canyon Dam and, 140, 142, 148;
 Colorado River basin reclamation
 and, 113–14; Greeley-Poudre
 Irrigation Project, 96; Kinkaid
 Act and, 147–48; project failures,
 149; resistance to compact agreement, 197; Rio Grande negotiations and, 249–54; San Luis
 Valley and, 76; state water rights
 and, 5–6, 75–76, 121–22; Swing-
 Johnson legislation and, 176–78;
 two-basin plan, 166; upper basins
 fears of, 118–19; western water
 development and, 16–18,
 306n41; *Wyoming v. Colorado and,*
 104. *See also* Bureau of
 Reclamation; Newlands Act of
 1902
Regulation, federal: interstate
 compacts and, 293–94; leadership needs in the face of,
 295–98; Progressivism and,
 10–11, 10n, 79–80; state water
 rights and, 16

Republican River: basin map, 7, 106; Nebraska litigation over, 105–8; prior appropriation and, 246
Republican River Compact, 108
Reservoirs: Arkansas River, 245; Aspinall-Gunnison Project, 357n34; Boulder Canyon Dam, 113, 116–17, 140, 150; Caddoa Reservoir, 346n11; Casper-Alcova Project, 91, 258–60; Colorado River Compact and, 196; Colorado River sites, 115–22, 151; Curecanti Dam, 357n34; Elephant Butte Dam, 6, 7, 119, 154, 169, 247–50, 314n58, 347n19; environmental impacts of, 292; evaporation losses, 178; failure of, 165; Fall-Davis Report and, 149–50; Flaming Gorge Dam, 357n34; Glen Canyon Reservoir, 168, 357n34; Grand Coulee Dam, 315n60; Guernsey Dam, 257; interstate river compacts and, 7; Milton Reservoir, 165; Navajo Dam, 357n34; Owyhee Dam, 315n60; Parker Dam, 351n82; Pathfinder Dam, 6, 7, 154, 169, 254; Reclamation Service and, 5, 148, 350n65; Roosevelt Dam, 17, 221; Seminoe Reservoir, 259; Spencer Canyon Reservoir, 168; Vega Silvestre Reservoir, 250. See also Hoover Dam; Water storage
Reynolds, Hubert, 86
Richardson, Friend, 218
Rio Grande: compact negotiations, 202, 246–54; Elephant Butte Dam and, 6, 7, 314n58; embargo v. compacts, 222–23; Mexican Water Treaty, The and, 354n33; Mexico and, 135, 157–58; Reclamation Service and, 119, 131, 154, 169; Root-Casasus Treaty of 1906 and, 347n19
Rio Grande Compact Commission (RGCC), 247–54
Riparian rights, 112–13, 292, 302n9. See also Water rights
River compacts. See Interstate river compacts
Rivers. See specific River by name.
Rocky Mountain National Park, 92, 268–71, 322n80, 332n51
Rocky Mountain News, 75, 120–21
Rogers, James Platt, 104, 139
Roosevelt, Franklin D., 24, 239, 260, 271–72
Roosevelt, Theodore, 11, 79, 85
Roosevelt Dam, 17, 221. See also Salt River
Root, Elihu, 138–39
Root-Casasus Treaty of 1906, 326n40, 347n19
Rose, Mark, 167
Ross, William B, 254

Salton Sea, 111, 178
Salt River, 17, 194–95, 221. See also Roosevelt Dam
San Diego, Calif., 111–12. See also California
San Juan River, 7, 166
San Luis Valley, 119, 246–47, 250, 314n58
Sargeny, Wesley, 40n
Schneider, C. A., 245
Scott, James Brown, 139
Scott, Nancy. See Carpenter, Nancy Scott
Scrugham, James G., 129, 148, 187–88, 219
Seth, J. O., 247–50
Shafroth, John F., 14, 79, 86
Shoup, Oliver, 118–19, 128, 129, 178, 214

Silver foxes, 21–22, 125, 298–99
Simonsen, Charles, 73–74
Slade, Ewell, 280
Smith, Al, 238
Smith, G. E. P., 167
Smith, Phillip S., 209
Snake River Valley, 305n33
Southard, Charles, 74
South Platte River: basin map, **7**, **92**;
    compact negotiations, 202, 255;
    Nebraska litigation over, 78,
    108–9; Union Colony and, 4–5,
    4n, 32; water district establish-
    ment and, 52–53
South Platte River Compact,
    109–10, 222, 320n57, 341n67
Spanish influenza. See Influenza,
    Spanish
Spencer Canyon Reservoir, **168**
Stanton, Elizabeth Cady, 42–43
Stapleton, Ben, 232
State Normal School, 66, 75. See
    also Greeley Normal School
State sovereignty: Bureau of Recla-
    mation challenge of, 225–26;
    Colorado-Big Thompson Project
    and, 270–71; Desert Land Act of
    1877 and, 4; federal land acquisi-
    tion and, 271–74; interstate river
    compacts and, 137–38, 175–76;
    Kansas v. Colorado and, 12–13,
    17–18; preservation of, 131;
    treaty-making powers and, 124,
    176–77; water rights and, 94–95,
    206, 220–21. See also States' rights
States' rights: Colorado River basin
    development and, 115–16;
    Constitution compact clause and,
    20; Department of Interior and,
    206; Desert Land Act of 1877
    and, 4, 301n2; federal abuse of
    power and, 131; Frankfurter
    opinion on, 271; Hoover support

of, 271–74; interstate river com-
    pacts and, 238; Reclamation
    Service violations of, 154; threats
    to, 17–18, 79, 119, 288; treaty-
    making powers and, 118–19. See
    also State sovereignty
Stetson, Clarence, 158
Stimson, L. L., 270
St. Vrain River, 52–53
Supreme Court. See United States
    Supreme Court
Surplus water. See Unappropriated
    water
Swain, Alva A., 244
Sweet, William E., 211, 215, 254–55
Swing, Phillip D., 141, 176, 180,
    191, 203–4
Swing-Johnson bill: Bannister and,
    231; Bureau of Reclamation and,
    235; Congressional approval of,
    239; Reclamation Service and,
    176–78; upper basin and, 222,
    226, 232–34

Taft, William H., 79, 85, 332n44
Taylor, Edward T., 136, 258, 288,
    313n37, 322n80
Teapot Dome scandal, 132
Temperance: clash between Evans,
    Colo., and Greeley, Colo., 73–74;
    Daniel Carpenter and, 27; Martha
    B. Carpenter and, 43–44; Union
    Colony and, 4–5, 4n, 32–33. See
    also Women's Christian
    Temperance Union
Thomas, Charles S., 95
Thomson, O. B., 280
Tijuana River, 354n33
Tipton, Royce, 119, 252
Townsend, Charles, 68
Transbasin diversions: Colorado-Big
    Thompson Project, 24, 214, 254,
    268–71; CRCC hearings and,

167; Fall-Davis Report and, 150; impact of Supreme Court decision on, 173–75; international precedents in, 94–95; *Kansas v. Colorado* and, 113; Laramie-Poudre Tunnel, 7, 77–78, 89–93; limiting, 167–69; two-basin plan and, 174–75, 288; *Wyoming v. Colorado*, 15–16

Transmountain diversions. *See* Transbasin diversions

Truman, Harry, 241

Two-basin plan. *See* Colorado River Compact

Unappropriated water: Bureau of Reclamation and, 225–26; Colorado Constitution and, 52, 305n31; Colorado River Compact and, 209–10; federal ownership of, 5, 197–98, 256–57, 256n, 353n9; water rights and, 312n9

Union Colony: creation and settlement of, 4–5, 4n, 16, 32, 36; Ditch No. 1, 308n17; Ditch No. 2, 36–37, 50, 308n17, 309n22; Ditch No. 3, 36, 309n17; Ditch No. 4, 309n17; legal status, 84, 282, 355n11

Union Colony House, 40–41

United States Commerce Department, 142

United States Constitution: compact clause, 9–11, 20, 78, 302n12, 303n14, 323n13; role of compacts and the, 119–20, 294; state sovereignty and, 19–20, 271–74, 302n11; state treaty-making powers and, 118–19, 131, 303n13; western development and, 3

United States Department of Interior: All-American Canal and,

321n71; Colorado River basin reclamation and, 113–14; embargoes on water development, 169–70; Federal Power Commission (FPC) ande, 236; Kinkaid Act and, 117–18; navigation, 206; Rio Grande Compact and, 252–54; San Luis Valley and, 119; states' rights and, 206; state water rights and, 75–76

United States Department of Labor, 236

United States Department of State, 252

United States Department of War, 236

United States Forest Service, 79

United States Geological Survey, 147, 163–64, 180–81

United States Supreme Court: cost of violations and litigation, 293; Delph's appearances before, 48; *Hinderlider v. La Plata River and Cherry Creek Ditch Company*, 20, 268, 274–77, 286; interstate water conflicts and, 75, 275–76; *Kansas v. Colorado* and, 17–18, 113, 301n5, 303n15; litigation over the Republican River, 105–8; state sovereignty and, 131; transbasin diversions and, 173; *Wyoming v. Colorado* and, 15–16, 89–95, 102–4, 172, 301n5, 303n15

United States v. Winters, 353n9

University of Colorado, 212

University of Denver, 60

University of Northern Colorado. *See* Greeley Normal School

Upper basin: Colorado River Compact and, 208–12; compact negotiations in, 242, 260–65, 350n64; dam construction in,

196; hydroelectric power permits and, 237; protecting water rights of, 126, 170–72, 290–91; six-state compact and, 217–19, 227; Swing-Johnson legislation and, 222, 226, 232–34; transbasin diversions and, 263–65; two-basin plan and, 174–75; v. lower basin concerns, 152–56, 166, 186; water division between basins, 180–81, **182**, 191–95, 289. *See also* Colorado River; Lower basin

Upper Colorado River Basin Compact, 260–65

Upper Colorado River Commission, 263

Utah: ratification repeal, 205, 231, 342n95; six-state compact and, 219, 343n114; upper basin compact negotiations and, 263

Utilization, equitable. *See* Equitable utilization

Van Devanter, Willis, 104, 107, 173, 332n44

Vermont, 26–27

Virgin River, 188

Volstead, Andrew J., 135–36

Vranesh, George, 276, 306n58

Wallace, Henry C., 343n114

Wallace, William R., 231

War of 1812, 27, 41

Water commissioners, Colorado, 53

Water defense fund, Colorado, 99–100, 245, 259, 267, 280, 317n4

Water districts, Colorado, 52–53, 77–78

Water marketing, 291

Water rights: Colorado River upper v. lower basin, 115–22; Constitution compact clause and, 9–11;

defending Colorado, 51–53, 76–78, 90–95, 121–22; Denver, City of, 227–28; Desert Land Act of 1877 and, 4; equitable apportionment and, 303n16; federal threats to, 79, 148–49, 197–98, 220–21, 256–57, 256n, 260; international precedents in, 93–94; interstate river compacts and, 238; irrigation and, 223; Leroy Carpenter on, 48; Mexico and Colorado River, 209; Reclamation Service and state, 5–6; state sovereignty and, 94–95, 328n76; Supreme Court support of state, 275–76; water marketing and, 291–92. *See also* Riparian rights

Water storage: California pressure for, 140–41; Colorado River Compact and, 337n14; CRCC hearings on, 166–67; Fall-Davis Report and, 149–50; Kinkaid Act and, 147; League of the Southwest calls for, 112–20; Reclamation Service and, 16–18, 113–14, 350n65; rights of reservoirs and, 80–83. *See also* Reservoirs

Weeks, John W., 343n114

Weld County, **38**, 50, 64

Weld County Republican, 73

West Slope, **91**, 227–28, 269

White, Edward D., 95

Whiting John A., 257–58

Wilbur, Ray Lyman, 207, 236–37, 241, 273

Wilcox, E. V., 121, 322n93

Willis, Robert H., 108, 255

Wilson, Francis C., 228, 233, 251, 276

Wilson, Woodrow, 86

Winters, United States v., 353n9

Women's Christian Temperance
  Union, 68. *See also* Temperance
Women's Relief Corps, 160
Women's rights, 42–43, 80,
  310n49
Work, Hubert, 136, 219, 225,
  247–49, 255
World War I, 101, 105, 112–13,
  271
World War II, 286
Wyoming: Casper-Alcova Project,
  257; Pathfinder Dam and, 6; six-

state compact and, 205, 217–19;
  support of compacts, 146–47
Wyoming v. Colorado: federal government and, 99; impact of Supreme
  Court decision on, 107, 109–10,
  172–74; priority doctrine and,
  15–16, 78, 102–4, 326n39;
  research on, 163–64; Supreme
  Court and, 88–95, **103**

Yampa River, 174
Yuma, Ariz., 174, 180–81, **182**